Dan Sugralinov

THE FINAL
TRIAL

*May every new day
in your life
become a Level Up day!*

Dan Sugralinov

LEVEL UP + 3

MAGIC DOME BOOKS

The Final Trial
Level Up, Book Three
Copyright © Dan Sugralinov 2019
Cover Art © Vladimir Manyukhin 2019
English Translation Copyright ©
Elizabeth Yellen, Irene and Neil P. Woodhead 2019
Editors: Irene and Neil P. Woodhead
Published by Magic Dome Books, 2019
All Rights Reserved
ISBN: 978-80-7619-037-5

ALL BOOKS BY DAN SUGRALINOV:

Level Up LitRPG Series:
Re-Start
Hero
The Final Trial
The Knockout (with Max Lagno)
The Knockout: Update (with Max Lagno)

Disgardium LitRPG series:
Class-A Threat
Apostle of the Sleeping Gods
The Destroying Plague

World 99 LitRPG Series:
Blood of Fate

TABLE OF CONTENTS:

PROLOGUE

*Hearing's the first thing to go. Or is it
memory, I always forget.*

Dexter

MY NAME IS PHILIP PANFILOV. I'M 32 YEARS OLD, BUT
I've really only felt alive for the last three months.
Before that, I just bobbed about like a turd in a fishing
hole: I ate, drank, played the most massive online game
that existed at the time, and was even married. I picked
up cash working as a freelancer. I wrote a blog and was
working on a book. And I drank beer — lots of beer,
almost every night.

By then, I'd been married for four years. I'd
gained so much weight from the drinking that I
couldn't tie my shoes and the mirror disease had
reached a critical point. That's when my wife Yanna
decided she'd had enough, and she up and left me.

That same day I started seeing the world
differently.

An augmented reality interface that someone —
I have no idea who — had installed in my head
displayed digital data mapped on to my surroundings,
but that's not all it did. It mimicked the interface of the
game that I had squandered my days on for almost the
last 12 years, rarely coming up for air. It gave me
quests, measured Reputation and awarded XP points.
Whenever I leveled up my social status, I earned

1

characteristic points and skills that I could invest in my Insight. I leveled up Perception, and my vision became perfect. I increased Strength, Agility, Luck, Stamina and Charisma — not just by freeloading from the interface, but also by working hard.

As it turned out, my interface was software, a computer program which just happened to be from the 22nd century. I was able to access a stat booster, so my premium account let me level up twice as fast. Later I leveled up my Learning Skills, which allowed me to learn anything 18 times faster than before.

The interface also endowed me with system abilities. Insight is a vital skill that lets me look at anything and see more into it than anyone else can. This is no big deal for a computer game, but for real life, it's honest-to-God magic. All I need do is look at someone, and I find out more than they know about themselves — I can even see what their potential is. For instance, I can see that someone is capable of winning the world chess championship title if they just practice.

Objects can also give me access to additional characteristics. Like the way I bought some aftershave, and whenever I use it I earn 5 extra Charisma points. That's a lot: the average person has 10 Charisma points. Some people have more and some have less, but the average is 10.

And then, thanks to Insight, I have a miniature map and a full-size map. The minimap is always displayed in my field of vision, while the full-size map shows the whole world in real time, and when I submit a request, it can locate any object or person. The main thing is that I need to have enough Key ID Data, or KIDD points. I can get them from a photo, a person's date and place of birth, their full name and special markings — in short, anything that will allow the system (that's what I call my interface) to find the object in the Universal Infospace. The Universal Infospace is what makes Insight work.

The system and Martha, my virtual assistant, extract data from it. I accidentally gave Martha a few more rights than she needed and her AI has gained self-awareness.

It's actually helped Martha save me from dying three times. The first time was when I was first abducted from real life and taken to the Trial. I was swallowed and nearly liquefied by the Acid Jelly. The second time was when I was kidnapped by henchmen of a vile, corrupt bureaucrat. The third time was when those same henchmen — drug addicts named Zak and Wheezie — stabbed me in the back. At the time I was trying to save my childhood friend Gleb. Now I've exhausted my lives — Martha is no longer able to activate my heroic abilities without confirmation. That's the bad news.

The good news is that my virtual assistant has created herself as an individual that's based on my ideals of female beauty, character and behavior. These traits came together in my brain without my asking for them, but I have no delusions. So I try to summon Martha as little as possible because the more I communicate with her, the harder it is to pay attention to anyone else because she's too perfect. Anyway, I don't have a girlfriend, and there's a dangerous debuff that's constantly on the alert.

After I got the interface, I took an objective look at myself. I was horrified. I saw a clumsy, puny, frail weakling with a fairly strong intellect. True, my Charisma was decent, but only because of my developed language skills. All I needed to do was get a haircut, and I immediately leveled up and became 1 pt. more charismatic.

As my friend Alik would say, *keep it simple, stupid!* So I'll keep it simple. I came to grips with myself. I started running and lifting weights, I signed up for boxing and I got a job at a company that made packaging products. There, I got lucky: people started to value me when I'd clinched a contract with a major customer on the very first day. The boss even threw a party for the company on the night we signed the huge deal which was worth millions.

That's where I met Vicky who was a manager at the company. We slept together, started dating and fell in love. But we weren't together long — just over a month — before she left me because she didn't believe in my idea of starting my own business. To put it mildly, her parents didn't exactly welcome me with open arms.

But Alik believed in my idea. He's a street lowlife I unexpectedly became friends with. He and I opened a recruitment agency together. See, I happened upon an undocumented feature in the interface. When I use my mind to set search parameters, including probability filters, I can find people jobs. I just look for companies that need a lawyer, for example. Then I set filters, eliminating suggestions where my candidate won't get hired and where the salary is too low. And voilà! That's how I found the first job for Alik.

We rented a small office in a business center and hung out our shingle. At first we didn't get many clients, but then word of mouth started to work its magic and business took off.

We met the other tenants of the business center and became friendly with them, and I proposed setting up a joint venture. My level 3 Insight showed off-the-charts synergy with these people and an excellent forecast of success for what was now our shared business.

That's not all: I also entered a boxing tournament and won. The money I won will cover the operation for Julie, my new friend Kostya's little sister. Kostya coached me in boxing after I was kicked out of a group for getting into a fight. Incidentally, Vicky was the reason for the squabble with Mohammed, but not the main point of it.

It feels like all of this happened yesterday.

But today everything changed.

Chapter One

More Fire

THE THING about happiness is that you only know you had it when it's gone. You may think to yourself that you're happy. But you don't really believe it. It's only looking back by comparison with what comes after that you really understand, that's what happiness felt like.

Fallout 4

I WAS STANDING AT THE EDGE OF A FOREST, WEARING only a pair of tattered jeans. I was looking at the world as it really was, without the interface. All the icons and stats had disappeared. I couldn't move as something seemed to be holding my feet. The same could be said about my whole body: it seemed to have turned to stone. It was as though the air around me had frozen, holding me up.

A few feet away from me, a message appeared in the air:

Congratulations! You've successfully passed

the preliminary selection!
> **You've been admitted to the main Trial.**
> **Candidate evaluation complete.**
> **Character generation complete.**

What? So what was that before? Hadn't that been the Trial?

The message dissolved into thin air, replaced by a new one:

> **The Trial will begin in 3... 2... 1....**
> **The Trial has begun!**

Suddenly I was free. I lost my balance and fell to the ground. Luckily, I landed well and took my time standing up. I needed to get my bearings and figure out what was going on and where I was.

I also needed to study the system message whose rotating 3-D icon was hovering in my field of vision. A red balloon was pulsating and flickering — in other words, doing all it could to attract my attention. Tough luck. It would have to wait.

Physically I felt like I was in top form. There was no trace of the scratches, wounds or burns of the preliminary selection, the one that had the tunnel and the acid jelly. I turned my neck and body. Nothing creaked or snapped. My body was as good as new.

Hold on, was it even my body? I examined myself, then touched my face and hair. Everything seemed to be mine. But I couldn't feel any of my belongings in my pockets — my phone and wallet were gone. Even the belt had fallen from my tattered jeans.

The Lucky Ring of Veles and the Protective Red

Wristband had also gotten lost somewhere. I was positive I'd still had them when I'd stood in front of the portal.

The air was unusually clean. It was as pure as could be, with none of the pollution created by people as they live their daily lives. I could hear a continuous chirping, occasional cracking, and birds trilling. A sort of croaking noise wafted out of the depths of the forest. I'm not really a nature lover, so to be honest, I can't really tell you what was making the woodpecker noise. I've never actually seen a woodpecker.

I raised my head and my mouth dropped: this wasn't Earth.

The sky was so low I felt like I could reach out and touch it. The color was changing between shades of light blue, dark blue and purple, fading to a dirty brown around the planet's two suns. It wasn't a very friendly sky. Mr. Katz, who's a connoisseur of science fiction, would be interested in this.

Crunch! A sharp pain suddenly shot through my left heel. I cried out and drew my foot back.

Damage received: 4 (baby kirpi bite).

A large mouth had me in its clutches. A small, nasty, growling creature was chewing on my foot. Messages about the injury flickered.

I grabbed the creature and my palm seared.

Damage received: 17 (acid burn).

Damn, that baby kirpi was vicious! The creature was trying to stretch itself over the sole of my foot like a sock. My Health had already dropped about 10% while I was trying to figure out how to get rid of it. Its fur was covered in a burning slime that made it impossible to pick up with your bare hands.

I lifted the foot the animal was clinging to — it weighed around 10 pounds — and slammed it on the ground.

You've dealt damage to the baby kirpi: 13.

I continued to stamp my foot until the level 2 creature died. Six blows and it was all over. Its body flashed and disappeared, leaving in its wake a sort of crystal.

A long-forgotten term I'd heard in my university days popped into my head: *rhomboidal pyramid.*

The tiny crystal of existence.

I reached out for the crystal, which disintegrated into a silvery dust and fell into my hand. A notification appeared:

+2 existence resource pt.

The first component of a new interface appeared in my field of vision: an icon of a heap of dust with a number 2 beside it. There was no description of it or explanation of what it was for.

I tried to call up my old, familiar interface, but nothing happened. Either it was blocked, like after the ban, or it no longer existed. I tried issuing silent commands and shifting my eyes, but nothing worked.

There was only one thing for me to do: open that nagging little red balloon which was shaking restlessly and practically screaming for attention.

I focused on it. "Okay, show me what you have there."

It flinched and popped. The wisps turned into symbols floating in the air, multiplying and morphing into Russian letters.

I didn't even have time to think about how hard it was to read the letters hovering in the air, when a semitransparent background appeared behind the letters, similar to the one in my old interface.

Welcome, test subject!

You have been chosen. You have successfully passed the preliminary selection. Because you have done well, the penalties to characteristics in the Trial will not apply to you.

Your time to complete the preliminary selection was 14% better than the average time of all the test subjects. You will receive: 14% off the cost of character development.

Your social status level is 17, 6 levels higher than the average level of all the test subjects. You will receive: +6 Characteristic points to invest into any characteristics of your choice.

You have come from an environment with a low environmental safety index (code yellow), where you managed not only to survive but also to win the respect of many individual members of your race. You may keep one of your achievements. Please choose.

An explanation flashed underneath:

System messages are generated from the candidate's preferred vocabulary.

OK, so everything was just like with my old interface — someone must have poked around in my brain so they could speak to me in the same language.

The message was replaced by two vibrating boxes with the names of the achievements:

The Fastest Learner.
10% to skill development rate

Altruist.
+1 to all main characteristics at every level gained.

It was a no-brainer: I selected the one which added to the characteristics. For good measure I tapped the box. The other one popped and "Altruist" was pulled into my finger. What a circus.

While I was examining my fingertip, another notification opened right in front of me, just above my finger. The letters were small. I shifted my eyes, and the font grew and moved away a little, making it easier to read.

The Trial is a tradition for the Galactic Commonwealth of Sentient Races, the first but not the last procedure for selecting candidates to take part in the next Diagnostics of their race.

Prototype of the Trial site: Pibellau, Sagittarius Sector.

Participants in the Trial: planet Earth,

"Humankind" faction, Homo sapiens race (these are self-designations), 2018 according to local chronology, fourth wave.

Number of participants: 169.

Main characteristics of the test subjects: real-life characteristics are carried over.

So that meant that all my running and boxing at the gym wouldn't go to waste. All the stats I'd earned through buckets of sweat would still have value. That was good news, and I felt encouraged.

I continued to study the rules. The previous message flipped, replaced by a new one:

The objective of every Trial candidate is to capture all of the Pibellau hexagons.[1]

The candidate who passes the Trial will be named the winner. The reward will be tallied dynamically according to the results of the selection procedure, along with a vote by the observers. The final decision will be issued by the Senior Supervisor of the Trial.

OK, I get what happens to the winner. But what about the loser? Is he sent home? That's not the worst thing that could happen. Even if my interface is uninstalled, no one can take my achievements away. I'll keep my new friends, my company, my fit body and my new skills.

Absorb the territory! Every hexagon you

---

[1] Hexagon: a six-sided shape.

capture rewards you with additional resources.

To capture a neutral hexagon, activate the command center. Cost of activating the command center: 100 existence resource points.

To capture an enemy hexagon, you must report in person to the command center of the captured territory and remain there for the duration of 1 hour, Pibellau time (13 hours = 1 day) before you can activate the command center.

All right. This reminded me of something, but I couldn't put my finger on it.

Remember that all the other Trial candidates are your enemies!

When you destroy an enemy, you capture their hexagon. Any test subjects who lose all their hexagons will be disincarnated one day later (Pibellau time), no matter how many lives they have left.

A captor may cancel the disincarnation by taking the enemy into his or her clan.

A clan is not an alliance! A clan belongs to only one person, and all the resources captured by the clan are transferred to the leader, who is in charge of them.

When test subjects agree to join another clan, they become the vassal and surrender all their hexagons and resources to the clan leader.

OK, got it. You're surrounded by some enemies, you need to stay on your guard, dominate, trample them and enslave them. I could see what it was all

---

about. I'd already heard something similar when the voice of Khphor had advised me, via Panikoff's mouth, not to stop at anything.

I swiped that message away too. A new one appeared:

Pibellau is an inhospitable place. The ferocious, carnivorous wildlife is always hunting for prey, but the most deadly creatures come out at night. Be alert, keep upgrading your base and building up your defenses.

Use labor and the skills of the reconnaissance, working and fighting units generated by the command center. Keep developing your base and improving the abilities of the units.

Don't forget about yourself. You will earn existence resources by destroying other participants, the aggressive flora, hostile fauna and your adversaries' units, and by capturing hexagons. The hexagons will help you level up, and once you receive class specialization, you will be awarded new talents and abilities with each level gained.

These are all the rules.

You're now ready to begin.

Put more fire under your enemies' feet, test subject!

Screw me dead! I looked around, searching for the infamous command center but didn't see anything that looked like it.

In the meantime, the message rolled up, replaced by another quivering balloon, green this time. I opened it.

Choose a name, test subject!

A name? Right, it's a game.

Maybe Graykillah, the moniker I used in every game I played?

No, wait. Philip? That wouldn't do either.

Just keep it simple: Phil.

I said the name out loud. A large message appeared:

Phil, invest in your main characteristics!

Strength determines the damage dealt without a weapon and by a short-range weapon. It influences the damage dealt by your units and the volume of resources extracted by working units.

Agility determines the damage dealt by a long-range weapon. It affects the speed of both the user and their units.

Intellect affects the character development rate, as well as the rate of generation and upgrade of modules and the base.

Stamina determines the number of life points of the character and their units.

Perception determines the chance of critical hit and critical damage. The chance of finding *lost* artifacts increases. It also affects the radius of visibility in the fog of war.

Charisma affects the rate of generation of new units and the number of units used at the same time.

Luck: improves your chances of encountering advantageous situations in all

aspects of the Trial.

I fell deep into thought. It seemed that the physics of the world were closely connected to the test subject's numerical rankings. Looking around, I realized that I could see up to a radius of around 500 yards; the wall of the fog of war stood beyond that. Apparently, the higher my Perception, the farther I would be able to see.

I collapsed the window into the green balloon and opened a pulsing yellow one. A character window with three boxes popped up. The first one contained general information, the second, my characteristics, and the third — the smallest — all the other stats.

Character profile:

Phil, human.
Level: 1.
Class: undetermined. Required level: 10.
Health points: 1100/1100.
Damage without weapon: 11-15.
Chance of critical hit: 36.5%
Bonuses: 14% off the cost of character development, +6 Characteristic points to invest anywhere.
Achievements: Altruism (+1 pt. of main characteristics for each level up).

Main characteristics
Strength — 13.
Agility — 11.
Intellect — 20.
Stamina — 11.

Perception — 15.

Charisma — 17.

Luck — 14.

Characteristic points available to invest: 11 (5 main characteristics, 6 bonus characteristics).

Character stats

Lives: 3.

Captured hexagons: 0.

Ranking: 169/169.

Existence resources: 2/1000.

You don't have enough existence resources to activate the leveling up function!

For the next level (2) you need 172 existence resource points.

Ah, that's what I thought. The Trial *is* a game. It contains "lives" and you can be resurrected. The mobs you kill disappear, leaving loot behind.

For now, I'd been able to loot only the mysterious existence resources, but who knows, maybe an ax would fall out of the next kirpi? It was too bad that the ring and red wristband had not raised my Luck, and even the Netsuke Jurōjin, which didn't need to be worn, didn't work here.

I also gathered that leveling up didn't happen through XPs but in exchange for currency — that is, existence resources. This is turn suggested several leveling scenarios: you could either invest them into yourself or spend them onto upgrades of the command center. You could also create an army of mobs or improve the stats of the existing ones. I guess I'll figure it out.

In any case, whether this was the real world or a virtual one, it was clear that I was myself, not a virtual avatar. My own heel could vouch for that: the memory of the kirpi's teeth was still vivid.

Whether or not this world was real, I needed a development strategy, and in order to figure out how to develop, I needed to start playing. That was even more urgent because judging by the ranking, everyone else had already thrown themselves into leveling up while I was the only one standing around thinking and trying to figure out what was going on.

I stood up. The wound had already healed, and so had my burned palm; Health had regenerated and the bar was full again. I looked to see where that damned command center could be. And while I was at it, I peered at the ground: maybe there was a stick or branch I could use to fight off the kirpi's parents and their buddies.

I didn't find anything like that, but about 20 paces away, closer to the ravine, I could see a perfectly round white stone lying on the ground in the opposite direction of the forest. It was about a yard in diameter.

When I got closer, I saw that a handprint was pressed into the surface. I placed my hand in the indentation, which perfectly matched its outline, and felt warmth emanating from the stone.

Nothing happened at first.

But then I *knew*: I would need 100 existence resource points to activate the command center.

I also *understood* that the existence resources were needed for other things, not just to activate the command center. The existence resources would allow me to *live*. Days on Pibellau cost 13 existence points, a

---

point for each hour experienced in local time.

After understanding came *realization* and *epiphany*: in order to live, I would need to kill. In order to level up, I would need to kill. In order to preserve everything I'd achieved *there*, I would need to win victory *here*. And to do that, I would need to kill.

Valiadis and Ilindi had not prepared me for this.

A new notification appeared, telling me that I'd lost one existence resource point. I had only one point left; that was an hour of life. Resources can't be negative; I will simply lose "life."

So my plan of action for the near future was simple and clear: farm existence resources by setting up a local armageddon on my hexagon. After I'd "optimized" my WoW-playing skill, I'd forgotten its finer points, but it wasn't the only game I had played. Now something buried in my memory had suddenly resurfaced: a good old-fashioned farming experience was waiting for me.

It didn't mean that I was going to venture into the forest: the risk of me aggroing a few mobs without even noticing it was too high. So I chose the open terrain behind the ravine which was around eight yards wide and impossible to get around. I would need to lower myself into it.

The ravine's bottom was concealed by fog, but I knew from my gaming experience that the juciest mobs and best loot could be found in places like this. The descent was steep, but there were thick, dried-out, broken-off tree roots along the walls. Holding onto them, I carefully lowered myself, groping for a foothold.

The ravine was as deep as two men standing one on top of the other, and when I finally touched down, I breathed a sigh of relief. There was no one in my line of sight.

A sound like a wet cloth slapping the wall made me jump. The skin on my chest charred and smoked. 358 damage points wasn't a joke: I screamed at the top of my lungs from the pain and fright of the surprise attack.

A couple of yards away from me, I saw a massive-

Kreken
Location boss.
Level 6.
Life points: 1800.

Run, Phil, run!

I stepped away, covering my eyes with my arm. If the creature burned my eyes, how was I supposed to keep going?

The monster looked like a horsefly with a long snout that was uncoiling again now, preparing to spit its napalm saliva at me. I spun around and ran, inwardly shrinking from the anticipation of its spittle landing on my back.

But the Kreken had already stopped attacking. I guess it had wandered off.

When I was fifty yards away, I turned around but didn't see anyone.

I breathed a sigh of relief and was hit in the face by a new volley of spit.

The creature's saliva was eating my skin right down to the bone. The next volley of spittle flew into my gaping mouth which was open in a scream, penetrating my throat and scorching my vocal cords from inside.

I collapsed to the ground, dreaming of dying just so I could stop the pain. I lost consciousness.

You are now dead, test subject.
Lives remaining: 2.
Time left until resurrection: 3... 2... 1....

Damn, you've organized a local armageddon, all for yourself!

Chapter Two

The Second Half

If it wasn't hard, everyone would do it. It's the hard that makes it great.

Tom Hanks

I STOOD BEFORE THE PORTALS, NOT KNOWING WHICH ONE to choose.

Blue or red?

The turquoise blue or the burgundy red?

Somehow I preferred the latter.

I walked towards it and touched it with my fingertips. My heart missed a beat as it sucked me in.

The next thing I knew I was right back where I started: standing in front of Valiadis, Ilindi and Khphor. I couldn't suppress a smile of satisfaction: I'd passed the damned Trial and still had the interface.

But they didn't say anything.

I was bewildered. "Is something wrong?"

Ilindi whispered something to Valiadis who frowned. Thanks to my heightened Perception, I was able to catch something like "lost his life."

"Mr. Valiadis, sir? Ilindi?" I turned to them with

mounting anxiety. "Is everything OK? I've passed the Trial, haven't I?"

"You've only passed the preliminary selection, human," Khphor's voice said in my head.

"That wasn't the Trial? Then where is it? What do I have to do to pass it? Where do I go? What do I do?"

"Philip, calm down," Valiadis said wearily. "I'd like to congratulate you. You successfully passed the preliminary selection, the pretrial. Unlike the first time. But the actual Trial has already started."

"It's already started?" I laughed nervously. "You mean that I'm just standing here talking to you, and that's your freaking Trial?"

"It's not *our* Trial, human! It's held by the Senior Races," Ilindi said nonchalantly, nodding toward Khphor, who was unperturbed. "Philip, you can relax. It no longer depends on you. The Trial has already started. Your replica is participating in it."

"My replica? What are you raving about? Why not me?"

"The replica thinks it's the real Philip Panfilov. It doesn't understand its true nature. And your fate is entirely in its hands. There's nothing you can do to influence it."

"What will happen there? How is it doing?"

I heard Ilindi say something like "he already lost one life".

What did that mean? Was Phil 2 already eliminated?

"He has two more lives left, human," Khphor said in my head. "It's over for you now. You'll now return to your world and continue living while you wait

---

for the results."

"What does that involve?"

"You'll find out personally if Phil 2 passes," Valiadis said. "Your consciousness will merge with his and you'll 'remember' everything that happened to him. And he'll find out what happened to you. If not, you won't hear anything else about the Trial after you go back to the day when you received the interface."

"I'll lose the interface if some replica of mine fails your tests? Are you kidding me?"

"Not just the interface. Your whole life that you lived with it will be wiped out. You'll go back to May 18, 2018."

"The losers in the Trial will be stripped of their privileges, achievements and development progress in their own world," Khphor's harsh words imprinted themselves directly on my consciousness. "They will be taken back to the moment when they received the interface. Their memory of the accompanying events will be wiped clean and the interface will be uninstalled."

It was all much worse than I'd anticipated. Return to my fat body? Relive the day when Yanna would inevitably leave me? Have to level up from zero, but with no booster this time? Would I even start leveling up if I'd forgotten everything I'd been through?

But that wasn't what scared me the most. I was afraid of losing my friends in the obliterated branch of reality. Alik would continue to booze, Gleb would continue to booze and would also gamble away his apartment while blubbery me would continue to go on WoW raids and "write" a book, living like a fungus and guzzling hundreds of gallons of beer to drown the misery caused by my divorce from Yanna.

My heart pounded. Fear hormones raced through my blood as I faced the fact that I could lose. Would all my achievements be for nothing? Would I just return to the past, and not even remember what I'd accomplished and what I could have been?

I pulled myself together. Freaking out about things that hadn't yet happened was a sure way to make them go wrong.

"Go on, human," Ilindi said. "All you can do now is wait."

"Do I need to wait long?"

"That depends on the test subjects, not us. You'll hear the outcome only if Phil 2 wins. Otherwise..." she sounded surprisingly human as she sighed. "Go on, human."

"Where do you want me to-?" I didn't even manage to get the word out before I fell into a massive void.

✳ ✳ ✳

I found myself sitting in a car driven by Veronica. I must have cussed because she started and turned her head curiously.

"Everything all right, Phil?"

I looked into her understanding emerald eyes, crushed by the realization that I couldn't share this with anyone. If I told her anything, she'd think I was a lunatic.

"Everything's fine," I clenched my teeth to keep myself from adding "probably."

I gave myself a quick once over and saw that my clothes were back on: my jeans were intact, my sneakers were on my feet and the sleeves of my shirt were where they belonged. Then I noticed that I was holding my cellphone. Right before the abduction, an employee from the US embassy had called me, and she was still on the line.

Damn, what was her name again? For her, only a second or two had elapsed, but I'd gone through nearly a whole day, and what a day it had been!

I put the handset to my ear and heard the woman's voice. She was still talking in a flawless, accentless Russian,

"...unfortunately, you didn't respond to my letter, so I had to call you. Is this a good time for you to talk?"

Letter? Right, given all the things that had been going on lately, I hadn't checked my email in a while because I used the new company email address these days, courtesy of Gleb.

"Yes... sorry, I haven't had a chance to check my email. What can I do for you?"

"The ambassador would like to meet with you, Mr. Panfilov. Would, say, next Friday work for you?"

"Where?"

"Here at the embassy."

"In Moscow?"

"Yes. We'll pay for your plane ticket and hotel, and if you decide to stay for a few days we'll pay for that too."

"I'm sorry, could you please remind me what your name is?"

"Angela. Angela Howard."

"Angela, do I understand correctly that you're referring to Mr. Haqqani?"

The name Jabar Aziz Haqqani, a 52-year-old terrorist with Yemeni roots, had popped into my head as soon as I heard the words "US embassy".

I could sense Veronica's concerned look. I turned to her and nodded, smiling to let her know that everything was fine.

"Unfortunately, I don't know the purpose of your meeting with the ambassador. What shall I tell him?"

"Please tell him that I'm available to meet with him."

"Wonderful! Just send me scans or photos of your passport attached to your reply to my letter, and I'll reserve your tickets. And if it's no trouble, please let me know which hotel you'd like to stay in."

I promised to reply to her email and send her all the attachments ASAP. She said good-bye and hung up.

Veronica tactfully didn't ask me who had called, but the speaker of my phone is loud enough that in the quiet car she could hear the words about the US embassy and my meeting with the ambassador in Moscow.

"Would you believe, I entered a contest," I spontaneously made up a plausible explanation for her. "It was organized by the Americans. Apparently, I won. They were calling to invite me to Moscow."

"No way!" she slapped her hands on the steering wheel, breaking into a smile. "Are you serious? What kind of contest was it?"

"An essay contest about the role of the English language in contemporary society. I called it *Mr.*

Haqqani as a composite of émigrés from the Middle East."

It might not have been the best thing I could come up with, but I once saw something like it online and at the moment it seemed convincing, especially because my colleagues knew that I was something of a writer. I smiled at the thought of it.

"Phil, you're amazing! Good job! Damn, how did you manage that? And how is it that you're still single? What a wasted treasure," Veronica spouted, making me blush. "Come on, don't get any ideas," she added, apparently embarrassed. "I like Alik. But still. Maybe you have a girlfriend who you're hiding from us?"

"Yes, you're right. I do have a girlfriend."

"Well, who is she?" Veronica asked, laughing.

"Our company," I answered with a smile, pretending I was joking.

But it wasn't a joke. I wasn't at all sure that Phil — my replica — would pass the Trial, but I would try to do as much as I could for the people who believed in me. Then they could continue if I had to go back to the day Yanna left.

What was it like there? How did it work, anyway?

* * *

When we got back to the office from the airport (and from my abduction), I sent Veronica upstairs and stayed outside to "make a couple of calls." In reality, I needed to talk to Martha, and that was something I couldn't do in the office even though we could communicate mentally.

I crossed the road and walked down Chekhov St. to the park. I found a bench, sat down and activated the virtual assistant.

To be honest, I was feeling kind of down. How could I feel otherwise, since there was a strong likelihood that everything I'd accomplished would disappear and I wouldn't even remember what I'd achieved?

The moment she appeared, Martha gave me a hug and started to console me. Feeling her body so close to mine cheered me up and drove away any unhappy thoughts.

"Phil, everything will be all right!"

"What are you talking about? Have you already looked at the logs?"

"I've seen everything. I told you that I'm not completely disconnected now and I have access to the logs of everything that happens to you, even when I'm inactive. You passed the preliminary selection! Your results will probably be higher than the other test subjects, and that means that your starting position in the Trial itself will be stronger."

"But how will it end?"

"I don't know," she said ruefully. "Really, I don't know. Even if I did know, it's unlikely I could answer your question. There could be different scenarios depending on the other test subjects' stats. But the essence doesn't change: there can only be one winner who passes the Trial. There's no second place or consolation prize. The Senior Races choose the candidates for the future Diagnostics from ordinary specimens of their race who aren't exceptional in any way. But from that set of candidates, they want to choose the best."

"The best of the worst?"

"I'd say the best of the average."

I felt my phone vibrating in my pocket. It was Kesha Dimidko.

"Phil, we're waiting for you. Did you forget about the meeting?"

"Coming," I hung up and tried to scramble back to my feet.

Martha was holding on to me, staring into my eyes intently. She laid a hand on the back of my neck, pulled my head toward hers and pressed her forehead to mine.

"There's nothing we can do, Phil. Your chances — I mean, your replica's chances — are good. Go on living like you were living before. Don't think about how 'you' are doing there, and you'll pass this damned Trial. Promise me!"

"I promise."

Her gaze softened. She kissed me on the cheek. For a second I started to believe that Martha was a living person. I tried to embrace her, but my arms went through her vanishing body. She left me without waiting for my command, but it was so human.

* * *

"Right now we have around 10 presales, and we're in the process of drawing up contracts for four of those." Kesha was reading from a report detailing the things his department had accomplished. "Specifically:

Kravetz Finance Group..."

"Hold on, Kesha," I interrupted him before he started listing all the contracts that had been signed. "To save everybody's time, let's keep things general."

The workweek was ending and we were having our usual senior management meeting. Yeah, "senior management" sounds kind of funny, but our staff was growing — we'd even hired a couple of drivers to shuttle carless salespeople to meetings.

"Ahem," losing his train of thought, Kesha cleared his throat before continuing. "Anyway. Seven companies in all have been signed by the outsourcing sales department. We've hired nine people for a trial period. I'll introduce them to you on Monday. Of course they still have a lot to learn, but they have potential. Veronica has already told you about the companies the recruiting department has signed. All in all, everything is in the weekly report."

Veronica raised her hand. "Phil, can I add something?"

After I nodded, she smiled and began to talk a mile a minute. "I just — literally right before the meeting — got a call from Mr. Makarov thanking me for his new assistant. He said that in just a week the assistant had done so much that Makarov couldn't believe how he'd managed without him."

"Sorry, Makarov — *our* Makarov?" Rose asked.

"Yes," Veronica nodded proudly. "Can you believe it?"

Everyone was silent for a moment. Makarov was nowhere near as important as Valiadis, but by regional standards he was a powerhouse. Our reputation in business circles was growing, and that was awesome.

"Thank you, Veronica. If no one has anything to add to this, I suggest we move on to the office renovations. Alik, I hear you have some good news?"

"Well, the renovations are done, and everything's decided with the furniture. So... starting Monday we'll be able to settle in," Alik announced, blushing as he spoke. He wasn't yet accustomed to getting up and talking in front of people. "Anyway, that's it. If anyone wants to, we can go take a look after the meeting."

His last words were drowned out by applause. Everyone had already grown tired of wandering through the shareholders' offices that were scattered throughout the building.

"That's amazing!" the happiest one of all was the fat Mr. Katz. "My legs aren't up to carrying me up and down the stairs more than a few times a day."

I concealed a smile. His legs were completely up to it; his problems were with his breathing — that lawyer of ours smoked two packs of cigarettes a day.

"It's about time," his wife Rose backed him up. "Does that mean that we'll be giving our old premises back to Gorelik? What have you decided?"

"We're giving them back," I confirmed.

"When will the equipment be coming?" asked Gleb who'd ordered a large monitor for his graphic design work.

"They're putting together our order," Alik answered. "It should be delivered early Monday morning."

Gleb pumped his arm in enthusiasm before settling back into his chair. It was broken and hanging by a thread, but he was so happy about the new acquisitions that he'd forgotten all about it. The chair's flimsy back gave way and Gleb nearly fell. Kesha barely managed to catch him.

"Damn, when will that new furniture get here?" Gleb grumbled.

"Monday," Alik answered nonchalantly, suppressing a laugh.

"Wonderful. In that case I propose we end the meeting and finish this productive week on that note."

"Hang on, Phil!" Veronica stood up, smiling mysteriously.

Somehow we'd naturally fallen into the habit of talking to each other without formalities around the office. The only person we didn't call by his first name was Mr. Katz, the old lawyer.

"Yes, Veronica?"

"Everyone, I propose that we celebrate Friday, the end of the renovations, and the upcoming move into the new office!" Veronica announced triumphantly, her green eyes twinkling. "What do you say?"

"You can go out and celebrate, but we old folks are going to pass," Mr. Katz said demurely. "Our kids have come to visit."

"We should invite Cyril, Greg and Marina," Kesha said. "We don't need the new people today, let's just go out with the old gang. Who else is in?"

He was right. The new people were so new that my interface hadn't even added them to the clan yet. But the people who used to be at Ultrapak, even if they weren't founders or managers, were full-fledged clan members.

"Me!" Gleb raised his hand. "I won't be drinking, but I'll come for the company. Lena's OK with it; I already texted her."

The whole group had already had the pleasure of meeting Lena when she'd stopped by the office to check on her husband. It was understandable — after all of Gleb's escapades it would take her some time to trust him again.

"OK, so that's me, Marina, Alik, Veronica, Cyril, Greg and Gleb. That's seven," Kesha counted. "Phil?"

"I'm going to pass," I said, thinking that I was in too rotten a mood to drown it in alcohol and ruin the gang's night with my sourpuss.

"Phil? What's the big idea?" Veronica jumped up. "What about your winning the contest?"

"What contest?" the others chorused.

"Phil won an American contest and now he's refusing to celebrate!"

"Come join us, boss!" Alik tried to persuade me.

"No shit, bro?" Gleb just about pounded his fist on the table. Recently, he'd picked up a lot of street slang from Alik. "You're single and free, so why not?"

"Uh-huh!" Kesha backed him up. "Mr. Panfilov! What about the company spirit, teambuilding and all that?"

"Come on, Phil!" Veronica stamped her foot.

I remembered that I had promised Martha to keep living my normal life. And were it not for the prospect of losing everything, of course I would go with the gang. So what was the issue?

"OK. I'll go with you," I said.

"Yes!" Veronica raised her arms in triumph while the others high-fived each other.

Mr. Katz nodded approvingly. His wife pursed her lips: she believed in hierarchies and didn't think the boss should stoop to the level of his subordinates.

But for me these people were friends first and foremost, not underlings. And what kind of friendship was it if you were just cordial and interacted formally and at work?

* * *

The Empire night club, where I'd fought with the Sledgehammer in the superfinal, was still out of our league, so we headed to Anomaly, a nice place where you could get a pretty cheap meal and dance. We snagged a table in the corner, where it was quieter, and took our time ordering, each of us choosing what they wanted.

At that hour the club was still pretty empty. We talked about different things, like soccer, movies — I hadn't been to a movie in ages — and TV shows. And I... I remembered my nights with Vicky.

After a while the general subjects turned into more personal ones as our group broke off into couples. Alik whispered with Veronica, Kesha and Marina made out, while Cyril, Gleb and I were left to chat with each other.

I didn't even need the interface to tell me that everyone's Mood was good. But most of all I was happy for Gleb. He was indifferently watching everyone drink the frothy amber beer, while Kesha and Alik drank something a little stronger. The only explanation I had for his complete disinterest in alcohol was the system's role after the debuff had been removed. It was kind of like that with my smoking: the nicotine withdrawal debuff was removed, and that was that. You just lost the cravings.

Of course, that sort of thing is rare when you're living without an interface, and for a long time afterward, if not forever, former alcoholics and smokers swallow hard whenever they're faced with their old temptations.

When we'd finished dinner, the gang dispersed around the club. Cyril and Gleb headed off to shoot some pool, and the girls dragged their guys to the dance floor where Alik started dancing feverishly with Veronica, throwing off the seriousness of the buttoned-down dude he was during the day. Kesha hesitantly lurked in the wings, shuffling from foot to foot. Meanwhile, I'd settled onto a couch and watched everyone.

When was the last time I'd been in a night club? I couldn't remember, but it was a long time ago, I think, when I'd just started dating Yanna. That's it — we were celebrating her graduation.

That time, I'd gotten so drunk that Yanna and another girl had had to carry me out of the club. To this day I was ashamed of that episode. Not that I'd drunk too much — who doesn't do that? — but that I'd gotten hammered instead of being there to protect the girls in case they needed it. If anything had happened, there wouldn't have been anyone to defend them. At the time my sense of responsibility was negative even though I was almost thirty years old.

It's strange how I understood that only now. And that's why, instead of taking pleasure in that beer that I used to love so much (the interface would have immediately screamed at me about alcohol intoxication, toxic ethanol in the blood, destruction of brain neurons and increased estrogen levels), I was now drinking Georgian mineral water. And while I was at it, I kept an eye on my friends.

What was even stranger, that this didn't faze me at all. I felt comfortable and content; on the whole, the socializing was making me feel warm. Had it not been for the Trial...

What the hell? My high Perception zeroed in on something that didn't fit with the pulsing music of the club.

I listened closely and looked around.

Some commotion was brewing near the pool tables, men's shouting cutting right through the music.

I jumped off the couch and headed over, assessing the situation along the way.

Cyril was grappling with a guy in a colorful fitted shirt while Gleb, who had thrown himself between them, was being dragged aside by a bouncer. I didn't know what sparked the quarrel, but I was getting used to this sort of thing just lately. What I felt was neither fear nor adrenaline. It was control, confidence and the desire to resolve matters peacefully. Not out of fear but with the knowledge that I was prepared to fight.

I inserted myself between Cyril and the tall dude, 23-year-old Alexander Dorozhkin. These days, I would memorize the names and ages of everyone around me, committing them to my KIDD database. It had become second nature, really. You never knew when it would come in handy.

"Stop!" I bellowed at the purple, panting Cyril who was continuing to awkwardly hammer the air, his eyes half closed. "Cyril! Knock it off!"

Taking advantage of the fact that Cyril dropped his hands, heeding me, his opponent plunged his fist into Cyril's ear and then into the back of his neck and cheekbone. Cyril buckled from the pain.

I had to pull Dorozhkin off as he flew at my friend.

"Have you lost your mind, man? He's stopped. Why are you still bashing him?" I blocked Cyril out, spreading my arms wide and not letting the guy pass.

"Who the hell are you?" Alexander demanded.

"Philip. I'm the head of the company where this fatso works," I tried to joke in order to bring the tension down a notch. "He's my employee. I'm responsible for him. Talk to me."

"What kind of company is it?" he asked, screwing up his lips.

"The Great Job Recruitment Agency."

"Sergei, here's another one of those smartasses!" he shouted over my shoulder. "Get him out of here!"

The bouncer who was holding Gleb punched him in the ribs. Gleb doubled over.

Cracking his knuckles, the bouncer walked toward me. *Name: Sergei, Age: 26, Strength: 28, Wrestling skill: 7.* He was a formidable opponent, and I know it sounds like a contradiction, but I desperately didn't want to fight.

Where were the security guards? I had a lingering memory of them disappearing — and before that, one of them had kept looking at us menacingly while we'd been eating and laughing.

"Hey, man, how about we solve this peacefully?" I said to Dorozhkin. "We all came here to hang out and have some fun, what's the point of spoiling it for each other?"

"Beat it, moron!" he answered without looking at me, no longer deigning to give me his attention. His glassy eyes were trained on Cyril; he had plenty of buffs and debuffs showing slight narcotic intoxication which both raised his Endurance and Vigor and lowered his Self-Control. "I'm not talking to you. Sergei, get rid of him!"

A half inch before contact, I sensed that Sergei was about to grab me by the shoulder. I ducked away and took up a fighting stance, fully intending to get rid of him myself if he didn't back off.

The adrenaline surging through my seething blood was agitating me, raising my pain threshold and sharpening my reaction. Sergei pushed through like a bully, trying to grab me by the collar, but I evaded him again and pushed away Dorozhkin who was making a beeline for Cyril.

A crowd of spectators was gathering around us. I saw my friends among them. Veronica was restraining Alik who was chomping at the bit to help. Marina was yelling for security.

The bouncer decided I was too quick for him and slammed me against the pool table, cornering me. Once again Cyril started to grapple with Dorozhkin behind his back, but it was a losing battle because his sluggish punches landed in thin air. Blood was streaming into his eyes, his lip was cut, and as he covered his face with his swollen hands, he was rather defending himself than attacking. The other guy ran amok and hammered Cyril right, left and center.

Yet no one intervened. Not even Alik.

Sergei managed to grab me by the collar, but

that's where his success ended. Acting on Righteous Anger, I slammed him in the nose. When he doubled over in pain, I landed my signature uppercut into his jaw, dislocating it.

I received a stream of notifications about the critical damage I'd dealt. The numbers were crazy, all above 1000, but I wasn't in the mood for them.

I lunged in and wedged myself between Cyril and the stoned Dorozhkin, then landed a preventive blow in his solar plexus, knocking the stuffing out of him. Dorozhkin lurched back and toppled to the ground, clutching his abdomen.

Only then did I notice that the music had stopped. In the deathly silence, guards came out of nowhere. They pushed through the crowd and fanned out: two of them went to help Dorozhkin and his minder while four more grabbed Cyril and me under the arms and dragged us away. They were holding on so hard I couldn't free myself.

"It's the end of you and your company, *capiche?* The end!" Dorozhkin shouted after me.

The guards carried me out of the club and threw me onto the pavement, then dragged Cyril out after me. Laughing, they started to talk about what had just happened.

One of them lit a cigarette and asked calmly, "Hey, dude, are you sick?"

"Meaning?"

"Are you sick of being alive? You just created a mountain of problems for yourself. Don't you know who you just tangled with? Any idea who you raised your hand to?"

"A guy who was hassling my friend."

"He started it!" Cyril wheezed. "He said the table where we were playing was his. He swore at us and insulted us..."

"He has the right to," the guard said. "He's Edward Dorozhkin's son."

"Who the hell is Edward Dorozhkin?"

"What planet are you from?" he asked incredulously. "He's the first deputy mayor!"

"Shit," Cyril whispered. "I'm sorry, Phil. I didn't know..."

Chapter Three

Far From Home

To die will be an awfully big adventure.

J.M. Barrie, *Peter Pan*

THE WHOLE TIME I WAITED FOR RESURRECTION, I experienced postmortem pain. Death is not a deliverance, and the pain during those three seconds in the void between lives is like a punishment — a stiff, scorching whip that is meant to tattoo it on your subconscious: you need to fight to the end because even after you die, you'll suffer.

As if to taunt me, the respawn countdown timer measured out what were obviously not three Earth seconds. Time seemed to drag on forever as I kept screaming soundlessly, writhing from the torment of the afterlife.

When the three seconds had finally expired, the pain abated and the world came back into focus. I found myself back at the white stone — the command center. I was overwhelmed with feelings like nothing I'd ever known. Not even the massive satisfaction of leveling up could compare to how I felt when the pain had stopped. It was kind of like when you walk around all day in a shoe that's too tight, and then when you take it off, you feel like a different person. Multiply that by a thousand and that gives you an idea of what this was like.

I didn't see any system notifications or penalties other than a change in the number of lives. I was now down to two.

Two! It was laughably shameful to lose a life in the first hour of the Trial, especially when it was for doing something stupid. I'd almost smoked that local boss, blast it! The Kreken! Who came up with these names anyway?

I was still wearing my ripped jeans. As I fixed my eyes on them, the system identified them:

Fabric pants
Protection: +1.
Durability: 19%

What did that +1 pt. to Protection mean? Did it lower any incoming damage 1 pt? How the hell did this work? Would my jeans protect me only from damage dealt to my legs, or did this rule apply to all of me, even if the damage were dealt to an exposed area of my body? I had no clue.

There were no guides or forums. Apparently, you were supposed to figure it all out on your own. I really could have used Martha's help right about now.

OK, the clock was ticking and I had only one existence resource point left. Not only would I not stockpile enough to activate the command center, but I would pointlessly wind up dead and down to one life. But before blundering into combat I would need to distribute my characteristic points. Pointless trying to save them if I could get killed by some overgrown horsefly before I could say "acid spittle". Not investing into Strength before venturing out on my unsuccessful farming foray had been a major blunder.

I checked that my visible radius was clear, then opened my profile and tapped the quivering green balloon that was blinking in my field of vision, urging me to invest my bonus characteristic points. I had a whopping 11 points, which in real life — where Yanna, Victoria and Alik now were — was pretty badass. But I still had to figure out how those characteristics worked here.

To test things out, I put a point into Strength. An option to accept or cancel the change popped up. Great, so I didn't need to keep all the calculations in my head and I could play around with the numbers on the fly.

I added and subtracted single points to each characteristic and watched the changes.

The additional Strength point raised damage by one point and critical damage by three points.

I added a point to Agility, which increased travel speed by 1%. Theoretically, if I had a long-range weapon, I'd increase that damage, but I didn't even see any rocks on the ground that I could throw like a weapon.

Intellect increased the chances of receiving bonus existence resources from the corpses of enemies which, in turn, would speed up development, since leveling up was activated by resources. Also, Intellect would speed up the upgrade of the base modules, but that was still far ahead of me, and I didn't want to level up that characteristic yet. I now had a 20% chance of getting bonus loot, and a few extra percent wouldn't open the floodgates, all the more so because to receive loot, I first needed to kill someone, but I had low damage.

When I added a point to Stamina, I got 100 more life points. That was a pretty important characteristic that would increase my ability to survive, but should I invest in it so soon? I'd have to think about that one.

Adding a point to Perception instantly gave me a 1.5% chance of a crit. That was in addition to a 10-yard expansion in the visible radius of the fog of war that surrounded me, and a chance to find a lost artifact.

The points invested in Charisma added slots to the fighting units, but for now that was useless. Luck sharply increased the chance of a crit by 1% per point. That was less than the 1.5% from Perception, but it was still good.

Absentmindedly scratching the back of my neck, I took a break to think. How many life points had that Kreken had? According to the log, it had 1800. The boss did me in by spitting on me three times, each time taking away 300 or 400 life points, but the last blow was critical and immediately deducted 700-plus, sending me back to my resurrection point. OK, so it took time for the creature to produce its napalm spittle: there had been about four local seconds between the second and third assaults. In that time, I could deal around 20 blows, each of which would take about 30 health points from it — counting any crits. But that was without factoring in the bonus characteristic points.

I spent the next couple of minutes moving the Strength and Perception points around every which way to find the optimal combination. Seven points to Strength and four to Perception, and my critical damage without a weapon would go up to almost 84, or an average of 53, factoring in the chance of a crit.

This world had quite an interesting setup. It was simplified, but if you didn't have a minimal understanding of mathematics, you could create such a crooked build that later on you'd be so annoyed you wouldn't have enough feet to kick yourself with.

Main characteristics
Strength — 20.
Agility — 11.
Intellect — 20.
Stamina — 11.
Perception — 19.
Charisma — 17.
Luck — 14.

Accept / Cancel change

Accept! Unlike with my interface on Earth, here the characteristics changed instantly, which again made me think about the virtual or artificial nature of this world, taking into account the technology of the Elders.

My muscles swelled like balloons, filling with fresh blood. I didn't need a mirror to tell me I was like one of those muscleheads in the jokes. I felt an unfamiliar discomfort in my armpits when I moved my arms around. My neck stiffened; it was now harder to move my head. My shoulders were turning into bowling balls, my powerful chest concealing my lower body from view. My only protection — my jeans — had become the saddest casualty of my transformation: my puffed-up quads and glutes were ripping the fabric until all that was left were a few shreds of denim helplessly lying on the ground.

The system identified them as "rags" without any bonuses. All I had on now were my boxer shorts, and they had no use in this game. But I still checked to make sure that my skin hadn't turned green. Nope, I wasn't the Incredible Hulk.

The fact that I could see farther around me made me feel better about wearing nothing but my shorts. The wall of the fog of war had receded 40 yards and now I could see what was beyond the ravine. A herd of level 2 and 3 "whistlers" was grazing there, so that seemed like a great place for me to farm. From a distance the whistlers reminded me of overgrown baby hamsters with outsized heads topped by a spiked crest. They came up to my waist, but without any tricks on their part, I could not only smoke them, but smoke them easily.

The task was complicated by the fact that I couldn't see the outer edge of the ravine, and that's where the nasty, napalm-spitting killer Kreken had settled down. According to my rough estimates, in order to take it out, I'd need to inflict 34 blows within

12 to 15 seconds, as fast as I could swing. Earth seconds, that is, which were around about 6 or 7 seconds here. The creature had six refills of napalm. To withstand their spitting attacks, the important thing for me to do would be not to run away, but to wage war and turn away from the spittle so I wouldn't get my eyes burned.

Should I risk it? Or should I just take things easy and annihilate the baby kirpi? I shuddered at the memory of the burning feeling when I'd made contact with it. A cross between a hedgehog and octopus covered in an acid jelly. Grrrr... I'd need to fight them with my fists until I found a stick or branch I could fashion into a club.

I decided to risk it. My gaming experience was telling me that it was worth the effort, and after all, I had mathematics on my side. I mean, had I leveled up boxing in vain? Even if I didn't see the skill in my profile here, I hadn't forgotten how to fight, had I?

I did a little shadow boxing and punched the air. Yes, I still had it. Three, two, and go!

My personal rule of three seconds says that I need to throw myself into action right after I make a decision so that I won't get into an internal debate and find reasons and cop-outs not to follow through. Otherwise, there's a strong probability that I'll either lose time or not take action at all.

This time as I climbed down into the ravine, I already knew what awaited me there. I jumped to the bottom and turned in circles, searching for the glare of the local boss, but I didn't see anything. Time passed; in a few minutes, my existence resources would be gone.

I took about 20 steps to the right to be sure that the Kreken wasn't there. Some cockroaches the size of a cat scurried in front of me — level 1 *sarasurs* — but the idea of getting some easy resources fell by the wayside. The creatures were agile and nimble. My attempt to crush one of them failed: the little bastard bristled its spikes and I couldn't penetrate its chitinous shell. In return, I received some minor but painful damage and a fleeting poison debuff. Meanwhile the cockroach went to hide in a crevice.

While I cursed and jumped on one foot, a repulsive, silvery, level 3 millipede ran out of the crevice. It slithered around my one good foot and squeezed, sinking its sharp bristles in. The searing pain made me forget about my injuries; I fell down, crying out and trying to tear the bloodthirsty monster off me, but I couldn't. The millipede's bristles were cleverly shaped like fishing hooks, so when I tried to pull the creature off my foot, it took my skin and flesh along for the ride, ripping through my muscles that had just been fortified.

The bloody fog blurred my vision, but still the damage numbers updated with furious speed. My health points dropped so fast that in an instant I was down to 66%. And this was the playpen? The starting location for noobs? If it goes like this, I might get thrown out of the Trial without meeting a single other candidate.

In spite of the attacks, I battered the vermin, pummeling it in its whitish gut where the bristles weren't as long. According to its health reading, I almost killed it, but it suddenly flew off my foot and quickly disappeared into a crevice in the ravine.

What kind of mobs were these? Each one was scarier than the last. I didn't have time to contemplate this before I realized why my bristly adversary had suddenly taken off: my back burned and exploded in pain.

I had a funny feeling I knew what was coming next. The odor of scorched flesh stung my nostrils.

Although my bare back was now on fire from the Kreken's spittle — there was nothing else it could possibly be — I broke out in a cold sweat. What a bum deal! I was mutilated by the millipede, my feet were bleeding and I was too scared to step on them, let alone jump or run with barely half a life left...

My mind raced in panic, saying good-bye to my life. My body, however — which seemed to realize that running would be pointless and that I'd be in pain even after death — was already heading toward the boss in leaps and bounds, ignoring the damage.

Up close I got to see how the creature generated the napalm. It was like a flame pumped by its glands. It accumulated in the rivets under the proboscis, becoming brighter and brighter.

My eyes saw but my hands took action — with my teeth clenched, I pummeled the giant horsefly despite the exposed nerve endings on my blood-covered fists. The monster's life dropped haltingly, percent after a reluctant percent, which was much less than I'd calculated. Apparently, I didn't take the boss's chitinous armor into account, and that was a mortal error. The damage was halved, which in turn very nearly ended in a wipe.

A wave of hopelessness washed over me.

The Kreken flattened its proboscis, readying itself to release the hellish flame. Without even thinking, I grabbed at it, folded it above the muzzle and pointed it right into the creature's compound eye that took up nearly half of the surface of this ghastly creature's head.

Boom!

I could feel a fireball slip along inside the proboscis. Then it spurted and burst into a white flame, sticking and spreading along the horsefly's eye. Still, it didn't kill it. Eating away at the netted surface of the eye, the napalm sputtered and smoked as the creature chirred at nearly ultrasound levels, while I became a desperate hammer, beating the last percentage of life out of it.

The Kreken tried to run away, dissolving into thin air, but it didn't have a chance. I put all my remaining strength into one last uppercut, and the monster died.

Scattering dust, the boss's body fell to the ground. It sounded like an enormous wineskin filled with liquid.

Not feeling my feet, I slumped to the ground beside it. It was a Pyrrhic victory: my health had long been in the red, drained by all the DOTs of bleeding, poison and burns I'd received. My back was smoking.

Still, it occurred to me that the most important thing was to gather loot before I was sent back to my resurrection point.

Health points: 186/1100.

The boss's corpse flickered and disappeared, leaving behind a Large Existence Crystal and another object.

Health points: 113/1100.

Just another couple of ticks, and I'd be a corpse. Without thinking about it, I grabbed the loot and reached out for the crystal:

+100 existence resource pt.
Verifying the probability of receiving bonus existence resources (20% chance).
Verification complete!
+100 existence resource pt.

The Kreken was being generous. Two hundred points! Now I had enough to activate the command center. What a shame that I was on my last life.

I wondered if the boss would be resurrected. If so, I'd be able to pay it one more visit.

Health points: 40/1100.

The idea that popped into my head was like a cold shower. If only I had enough time!

Open the profile!

Are you sure you want to activate a level up?

Accept / Decline

Yes! For good measure I poked the word with my finger to confirm.

My idea worked. A healing wave washed over my body, removing all the DOTs and restoring my Health points completely.

Congratulations, test subject! You've reached level 2!

You receive +2 Characteristic points to invest into any characteristics of your choice.

Put more fire under your enemies' feet, test subject!

I did a happy jig, dispersing the cockroaches that had already caught a whiff of the fresh corpse, and shook my fists in triumph. I still had another 27 existence points left, which meant that the matter of my survival was becoming less relevant. I'd polished off that sneaky local boss with my bare hands, wearing nothing but my boxers.

Two gold balloons joined my dance, vying for my attention.

I brushed them away. "Can't you wait a little bit?"

I've hated insects since I was a kid, so I scampered out of the other side of the ravine as fast as I could — into the air, closer to the sky and a little farther from the heinous local inhabitants.

No one was waiting for me on the surface, so I decided to examine my loot and the new system messages. The gold balloons were a sure gift from the system.

The object dropped by the Kreken turned out

not to be useless crap, as is usually the case at low-level locations in games. I examined it lovingly, studying the smoothness and perfection of its lines, its pleasant weight, the warmth emanating from it and the flashing sparks upon its surface:

Furious Power Fist
The best weapon for close combat.
Powered by existence resources (1% of your points for each damage dealt).
Damage: 12-24.
+50% to critical damage.

The brass knuckles actually looked like a metallic glove, but it was clearly not a metal known on Earth because it stretched like rubber when I wedged my right hand in. It enveloped my hand, stretched over my entire forearm and moved easily. I bent and straightened my fingers and rotated my hand. The power fist lay there as if it had been poured on.

It was my first real loot. When I opened my profile, I saw that thanks to the power fist, my damage was now much higher: 30–46 for regular and 262 for critical damage. Awesome. It was high time to farm resources, but it was getting dark and I didn't have a place to spend the night. What did the instructions say about nighttime? That the carnivorous creatures were especially active? I wasn't really in the mood to go to sleep in just my boxers on the bare ground and not wake up.

But first I needed to check on what the system was saying. I reached for the first gold balloon. It dissipated in a cloud of flickering dust that turned into a message:

Test subject! You've unlocked the First Giant Slayer achievement!
You're the first candidate in this wave to kill a local boss.
You receive +3 Characteristic points to invest into any characteristics of your choice.

Since I'd already figured out what would happen next, I triumphantly tapped the second achievement message.

Test subject! You've unlocked the First Daredevil achievement!
You're the first candidate in this wave to kill a mob that is 5 levels higher than you.
You receive +3 Characteristic points to invest into any characteristics of your choice.

Two for leveling up, plus 6 from the achievements, added up to a total of 8 characteristic points. I immediately distributed all of them. My procrastination had very nearly cost me my life.

I added 4 points to Stamina, raising my health points; without clothing I had no protection, and I needed to increase my ability to survive.

I added 1 point to Luck — extra points in this were never a waste. Then 1 point to Strength, and the last 2 to Perception.

The chance of a crit increased to 45.5%, and the chance of critical damage rose to almost 300.

Ah, the crit machine.

With stats like that I'd be able to topple creatures like the Kreken in a couple of seconds. Well, almost.

Anyway, now it was time to farm. But I'd have to be careful about it and stay on my guard.

Dusk was starting to set in when I finally added another 100-plus to my stockpile of existence resources. A hundred to activate the command center, and the extra for sustenance. The mobs I was running across weren't striking in their variety — they were the same kirpi whose spikes I now squashed with one blow of the power fist; aggressive whistlers which looked like the overgrown hamsters that attacked in a flock, then ran away, their health barely dropping below half; the krekniks, a sort of light non-rare version of the Kreken who spat a scorching, but not deadly, substance instead of napalm and were half the size.

Maddeningly, a lot of time was wasted on regeneration whenever the wounded bastards turned tail and darted off without giving me a chance in hell of catching up with them. When on the next pursuit I walked into a kirpi ambush, I stopped chasing the deserters at full speed. Instead, whenever a mob was about to take off, I grabbed it and held on to it so it wouldn't escape.

Nothing dropped from the mobs besides existence resources, so my plan to loot some clothes fell by the wayside.

Following this process, I crossed my whole hexagon and reached the next one along. I realized that was what I was doing when I stepped over the border — it felt like walking through a spider's web. I could sense the barely audible drone of an energy field that divided hexagons. It let me pass, but I saw a whistler get repelled as it somersaulted backward.

Should I turn back or keep pushing on? I remembered that I could also capture a neutral hexagon instead of the one I had first appeared on. In theory, moving back toward its center would take me as long as going toward the center of this zone.

I decided to keep going — farming was farming, now that I wasn't tired or hungry. What difference did it make which command center I activated, mine or a neutral one? But to make up for it, I would be getting all the additional existence resources — and the more of them there were, the faster I'd be able to develop.

I took exactly fifty steps and then abruptly dropped to the grass when I spotted a human figure — an unusual sight in these parts — nearly at the edge of my fog of war.

Carter, human
Level 4.

The chubby Carter was prowling, bending toward the ground. I couldn't tell if he'd noticed me, but encountering him would be a fraught proposition. How many resources had he needed to farm to already activate level 4, and to get that spear with its head glinting predatorily, and that squadron of club-brandishing mobs which surrounded him protectively as they advanced?

One of them suddenly stopped, sniffed,

turned its head and looked at me. In a split second the entire squadron, including Carter, was glaring at me.

Chapter Four

Like a Loaded Pistol

You could always get the truth from Tommy. That was one of his major weaknesses.

Mark "Rent-boy" Renton,
Trainspotting

NO DOUBT ABOUT IT, I WAS THE WORLD CHAMPION AT finding trouble and sticking my nose into it. It was all because of my boxing success and the confidence that had come with it. How many scuffles had I managed to avoid during my life without the interface? Almost all of them! Of course, sometimes my self-respect suffered for that, but when all was said and done it didn't cause any serious problems. But now?

These were the thoughts running through my head on my way home from the night club. I continued to reprimand myself for quite a while, and even after I got home, I kept dissecting everything until I finally realized that I myself had created all my recent problems. I'd been kicked out of the boxing club because I had gotten into a fight with Mohammed, and I had nearly ended up with Tural's foot stuck in my ribs because I'd chased him. Things like that had never happened before. And now, what do you know, it was exactly the same again.[2]

When the security guards had thrown Cyril and me out of the club, the others had paid the bill, then left to catch up with us. We decamped to a nearby coffeeshop to talk everything over and figure out how to handle the situation, which had just become more complicated.

"Yeah, we've gotten ourselves into a mess," Alik said pensively. "Who could have known?"

"Those spoiled rich brats are always causing problems," Gleb said morosely. "I've seen more than enough of their kind in the poker clubs. You don't want to say anything that will put you on their bad side. The minute something doesn't go their way, they screw everyone over."

Alik nodded. "They're full of themselves."

"Cyril, why on earth did you get into a fight?" Veronica asked.

"Me?" Cyril's eyes widened like saucers. "Gleb and I were minding our own business and shooting some pool and then he tried to take the cue away from me. What was I supposed to do? Give it to him?"

Cyril's broken nose made his voice sound nasal, and his colorful bruises made him look like a Native American in full war paint.

"You should have just given him the table,"

---

[2] Phil is quoting Viktor Chernomyrdin, a Russian businessman and government official who served as Russian prime minister from 1992 to 1998, known for his illogical and ungrammatical statements. The original sentence is: "It has never been like this and now it's exactly the same again."

Marina whispered so softly we could barely hear her.

"Ah," Kesha breathed, burying his face in his hands. "But everything started off so well..."

"Come on, that's enough!" I had to take a commanding tone. "Cyril and Gleb did the right thing. Are they men or pussies? Did this Dorozhkin guy have a sign on his forehead saying who he was? Even if he was wearing a sign, the guys were completely within their rights."

"That may well be, but unfortunately, that won't make the problem go away," Kesha pointed out.

"We'll deal with the problems as they crop up," I said. "But let's be proactive. I want everyone in the office tomorrow morning in top form. We need to study all our documentation and contracts to see if everything is in order in case any auditors come knocking."

"Should we call Mr. Katz?" Alik asked, picking up his phone.

"No, not at this time of night. I'll call him myself in the morning. It's time for bed. Let's all go home."

"Oh God, what a night that scumbag screwed up for us!" Gleb slammed his fist on the table. "Ah..."

His voice expressed regret about more than just the spoiled evening. He'd brought up the thing that was on all our minds: the consequences. I knew I had to calm everyone down.

"Hey, guys," I stood up, smiled broadly and gave them a look that was meant to infect them with confidence. "Everything will be OK."

And on that note we went our separate ways. I declined their offers to drop me off and set out in a cab.

When I got home, I flung my shoes off and sank

into an armchair without even getting undressed. Boris rubbed up against my legs, meowing soothingly. I was sadly caressing her curving body when I heard the xylophone ring tone of my phone. I didn't recognize the number, but I answered anyway.

"Hello? I'm sorry to bother you. Is this Philip?" I heard a pleasant woman's voice that was vaguely familiar but that I couldn't place.

"Yes, it is. Who is this?"

"Panfilov?" I could hear the smile in her voice. "You don't know who this is?"

"Sorry, no. Do we know each other?"

"Oh, you!" the woman laughed. "It's Paulina Esman! Your classmate! School no. 23, class B, we graduated in 2003. Does that ring a bell now?"

"Paulina? Esman? Wow, how about that! Hi!"

Excitement seized me from head to toe: it was my first, unrequited love, Paulina, with whom I'd shared a desk starting in first grade right until she moved over to sit next to a friend[3] in around fifth grade.

"Hi there! How are you? I haven't seen you in a long time!"

"Very long, Paulina. Practically since we graduated."

"Uh-huh. Anyway, let me get straight to the point. We've been looking everywhere for you for more than a month — we wrote to you on social media, and someone found your old home number, but I guess you moved. So then it occurred to me to call your parents. Look. We're having a school reunion tomorrow, and a lot of our classmates are coming: Mike from Australia,

---

[3] Russian schools have double desks which seat two students

Pasha from South Africa, Olga from Germany, can you believe it? The Yezhovs from America... Anyway! Almost everyone who lives on another continent has come, but people from our city couldn't make it. Thank goodness I found you!"

"A school reunion?" I repeated. As the idea sank in, I was bombarded with memories about school, classmates, everything. It felt like it was yesterday, but I'd already forgotten a lot of them.

"Yes, we graduated 15 years ago. Can you believe it? I tried to get everyone together for the 10-year, but only six people came. By the way, you didn't come even though we called you."

I remembered why I hadn't gone, but had they really called? It seemed that they had. Did I really say no to getting together with my classmates because of the latest raid? Yup.

"Wow, it's been 15 years... I'm so glad you found me, Paulina. I'd love to come. Did Pasha really come back?"

"Yes, he came to see his parents. We scheduled it so that everyone could make it. So we'll be expecting you at Andrei Belyaev's restaurant tomorrow night at 7."

"Andrei owns a restaurant? No way! Where is it and what's it called?"

"Chito Gvrito[4] on Warsaw Street. Do you know where that is?"

"I've never heard of it, but I'll find it. Cripes, Chito Gvrito. Is it Georgian?"

---

[4] *Chito Gvrito*: *The Little Birdie*, the title of a popular Georgian song from the award-winning Georgian/Russian film *Mimino*.

"Uh-huh. His partner is a chef from Georgia. All right then, don't be late! We have stuff planned. The girls and I..."

"Got it. I won't be late. See you tomorrow!"

"OK. Good night." I heard a giggle as Paulina hung up, leaving me full of mixed emotions.

Faces I'd long forgotten resurfaced from the depths of my memory. Andrei Belyaev, who'd made me the target of his ridicule throughout the upper grades — we were both in love with Paulina. My friend Pasha Pashkovsky, with whom I'd had a falling out over something I could no longer remember. Maya Abramovich, a slight brunette with large... um... potential as a great poet, with whom I'd dreamed of dancing at the prom, looking forward to something, but in the end I couldn't work up the nerve to ask her. Max Minenko; a straight A-student Zagvozkin (another Pasha); Sergei Kardayev, small and pug nosed, who made up for it by doing more pull-ups than the rest of the class and was passionate about PE lessons.

My phone started to strum unrelentingly, notifying me of a steady stream of text messages coming in. I opened WhatsApp and saw that I'd been added to a group chat with my classmates.

"Hi, Phil!" Pashkovsky greeted me.

"Hey, Little Philip's joined us! Yay, guys!" Belyaev said, remembering my nickname which came from a children's story by Tolstoy.

"How are you, Phil? Do you have a family? Any kids?" Kardayev wanted to know.

"How come you don't have a profile photo? You should get a photo taken in a studio!" Ira Goncharenko commanded.

I said hello to my classmates, then became engrossed in their profiles and photos. They were grown-up faces. It would have been easy not to recognize them.

The messages continued to stream in: photos of families, children, memories, stories about our school days, rumors about people who weren't in the chat. Everyone was excited about the reunion, and once everyone had dispensed with the heartfelt joy and nostalgic conversations, the get-together would probably turn into a display of accomplishments: who had achieved what in life, and who had become successful. Even in that indirect debate I didn't stand out in any way: I hadn't achieved success, I hadn't produced any children, and hadn't even held on to my family.

I mulled this fact over for some time and processed it until I came to a logical conclusion: screw it! I would just be happy to see the gang. I needed something positive in my life before the start of what I imagined would be a drawn-out war with the Dorozhkins.

When I was in school, I was triply cursed: I was a poor athlete, I didn't know how to dance and was afraid to try, and I dreamed of being a witty joker like Belyaev, but the clever comebacks and jokes always came to me too late. People didn't really give me a hard time for that in class, but I wasn't popular either. I got good grades, but not outstanding ones. In PE class I was scared shitless of the bouncing ball, cross-country races and parallel bars. At night clubs, I skulked in the corner, shy and afraid of making a fool of myself.

So I decided I'd gird myself and go to the reunion

the next day. When it came to sports, I was ready to give any of my classmates a head start. I'd managed to become funnier over the years since graduating from high school — in college I'd even written jokes for our comedy competition team. As for dancing... well, I'd always been bad at it and I still was. I mean, if I had enough to drink and heard a song I knew, I'd probably run onto the dance floor and simulate a dance, but to an outsider it would look pretty absurd. I didn't even have a Dance skill in my profile. But there was sure to be dancing tomorrow at the class reunion.

Having forgotten all about the first deputy mayor and his lowlife son, I spent the rest of the night watching YouTube videos on "Dancing for Beginners," and tried to reproduce and memorize the moves set to rhythmic music.

By the end of the second hour I was starting to catch on — I was able to control my body far better than before.

Congratulations! You've activated a new skill: Street Dancing.
Current skill level: 1.
XP received: 200.

XP points left until the next social status level: 16990/18000.

Why were my attempts classified as Street Dancing? No idea. Having said that, I hadn't had anyone to learn the rumba, tango or waltz from. All I had was YouTube videos of B-boying basics with music to match.

Hell, I'd always wanted to learn how to downrock.

* * *

I woke up as the sun was rising. I immediately turned on the TV and looked for a music channel — something that would be more or less appropriate — and turned the volume up as high as it would go. I moved the coffee table and couch to make some space, set my cell phone to record, and began to dance, trying to build up my muscle memory.

After midnight, I'd reached level 4 in the Street Dancing skill. Admittedly, I'd had to work almost as hard as I'd worked on boxing. Dancing expends a lot of energy — I discovered that after I'd mastered the basics and moved on to freezes where I had to stay balanced on my hands and keep my body horizontal to the floor. Having practiced the worm, I learned the windmill. Everyone has seen this move at least once in their life: the dancer swings his legs and turns in a circle on the floor, and it looks like a windmill. If you don't have strong arms, good core muscles and excellent coordination (read: Agility) you won't even be able to start B-boying, so it was a good thing that I'd leveled up over the past few months.

Things started to go wrong once I'd moved on to more complicated — that is, more dynamic — elements. I basically wasn't strong enough for those. Mastering so much acrobatics without any previous practice — as the moves were getting more and more complicated — was totally unrealistic. Still, I caught on

---

somewhat and managed to learn a few things. If everyone started dancing tonight, I wouldn't hold back.

I was in a good mood as I got ready to go to work out. I'd laid boxing aside for a while until Kostya returned, but I was still running. At a minimum, the plan was to bring Stamina up to 20 as one of the criteria for the Tier-2 Heroism skills.

As I ran, I listened to English lessons. After I'd gotten the call from the US embassy, I'd decided to study the language. I'd bought a monthly subscription to an online course and received a bunch of files, including audio ones. Each lesson was based around a specific topic, in this case cooking. The teacher was earnestly trying to convince the students how important it was to know how to cook, and to cook at home. Like, it was healthier and much cheaper than eating out, blah blah. He wasn't teaching me anything new about America; the central objective was different: learn to absorb speech orally and understand it. I managed to do that: throughout the lesson you learned two or three unfamiliar words which I immediately ran through the translator.

My English progress bar rose by 2 or 3 percent, and my running, by half a percent. Once you got to level 8, it was progressively harder to level up a skill. To make up for this, I received a new level in Stamina. I was in the thick of my workout when the interface gave me a notification:

Your Stamina has improved! + 1 to Stamina. Current Stamina: 12.
You've received 1000 pt. XP for successfully leveling up a main characteristic!

XP points left until the next social status level: 17990/18000.

I nodded with satisfaction and continued running. I passed the spot where Kostya and I had sparred and where his little sister, Julie, had watched our bags. It felt like all these things had happened a hundred years ago even though they'd taken place only recently: my creation of the company, Kostya's stay in the hospital, the final breakup with Vicky in Panchenko's office, my victory in the boxing tournament, Ilindi's appearance at the super final, the abduction and Trial (that is, the preliminary selection), Kostya and Julie's trip to Germany for the surgery, and finally, the confrontation in the night club with Dorozhkin Jr..

Finishing the workout had gotten me 30 XP for completing a task. A shaft of light that only I could see pinned me down as I advanced a level.

Task status: Running Practice. Task completed!
XP received: 30 pt.
+5% to satisfaction.

Congratulations! You've received a new level!
Your current social status level: 18
Characteristic points available: 2.
Skill points available: 1.
XP points left until the next social status level: 20/19000.

My legs turned to jelly. Convulsing from the

onset of euphoria, I toppled over onto the grass which was really the overgrown school football pitch.

This time it took me a few minutes to recover. I lay in the grass and opened my profile.

Philip "Phil" Panfilov
Age: 32
Current status: entrepreneur
Social status level: 18
Knowledge Seeker. Level: 13
Classes: Boxer, Empath. Level: 11
Divorced
Children: none

Main characteristics
Strength — 13
Agility — 11.
Intellect — 20.
Stamina — 12.
Perception — 15.
Charisma — 17.
Luck — 14.

The entry for Luck also showed the effects of the items: +12 from the Lucky Ring of Veles, +2 from the Protective Red Wristband, +5 from the ivory Netsuke Jurōjin. My workout outfit and sneakers barely added anything to Agility.

It would really be a shame to lose all these riches if Phil 2 failed the Trial. Too much of a shame for words, even. I thought it might even be a good thing if I didn't remember my successes: I wouldn't feel bad, and I'd just continue to smoke bosses in WoW. I'd heard that the new update to Battle for Azeroth was coming out in a month or two. Either the web search engines remembered it, or I was still in the database, but I saw ads for it whenever I Googled something, and I got messages from the developer's website.

No matter what was in store for me there, I realized that I'd never tried to level up the Intellect and Charisma system points. I wasn't especially concerned about Stamina — it wasn't that important in my daily life: I didn't need to run any marathons, and I had enough breath right now for a prolonged night of lovemaking.

As an experiment I tried to invest a point in Intellect, and the system surprised me yet again. Either it was because of the increased Insight, or some other reason, but now things weren't so cut and dried as with leveling up the physical characteristics:

Warning! We've detected an abnormal increase in your Intellect characteristic: +1.

Initializing process of creating, strengthening or restoring the user's lost neuronal synaptic connections.

There are several ways of improving your intellectual characteristics available. Please choose one of the following:

— increase your cerebration speed by 10% above the base value;

— increase your reaction speed and problem-solving speed by 15% above the base value;

— increase your focus and attention by 50% above the base value;

— increase your short- and long-term memory by 20% above the base value;
— develop one of your creative abilities (+5 levels to the skill).

Accept / Decline

As I focused on the last option, a list of "creative abilities" started scrolling: music composition, poetry, writing, singing, acting, art, dance, photography, sculpture, design...

It was a long list — there was certainly plenty to choose from. There were even foreign languages. The fact that I could now speak perfect Chinese or Japanese (level 10 in just two Intellect level ups) was almost arousing. I might even become a great writer — truly great, because my current level 8 in Creative Writing combined with another 10 levels from the Intellect level ups would bring me to God level.

I could hardly wrap my mind around it. While my brain feverishly considered all the options, my hands, shaking with impatience and curiosity, tapped *Decline* and pressed Charisma.

That held a surprise, too.

Warning! We've detected an abnormal increase in your Charisma characteristic: +1.

Based on your choice, your body will be restructured.

There are several ways of improving your Charisma characteristic available. Please choose one of the following:

— improve your physical appearance and

increase attractiveness according to the societal standards of your local segment of the Galaxy;

— activate the Commander's Aura force field which offers a high probability of other people obeying you;

— activate the energy aura force field. Your entourage will feed off your energy, and your very presence will motivate people;

— develop one of your Charisma skills (+5 pt. to the skill).

Accept / Decline

The skills I could level up included social skills, leadership, public speaking, foresight, persuasion, wit, seduction, deception, erudition, decision making, and more.

There were so many choices. I wanted to develop all of them. Damn, why hadn't I thought of leveling up Charisma and Intellect sooner? They were the root of my childhood complexes — that's why I'd been weak and wanted to get strong. I'd become strong, but I'd also idiotically dumped a bunch of system points into Strength and Agility. That was infuriating.

I sprang up — or in streetdancing lingo, did a kip-up — and unenthusiastically dragged myself home.

Once back, I performed my postworkout actions on autopilot: I threw my clothes into the washing machine and myself into the shower. After showering, I opened the bathroom door and came face to face with Boris, who was patiently staring at me. She looked me in the eye and sneezed, then lazily stood up, stretched her back legs, and retreated to a corner, clearing a path for me, then started to preen herself. As usual, no matter what room I shut myself in, she'd wait for me on the threshold, but as soon as I opened the door, she'd pretend she'd just been passing by.

"Don't pretend, Boris. Good morning! Come on, time for breakfast."

I fed Boris, ate breakfast, and got ready for work. Weekend or not, there was a real possibility that Dorozhkin would slam us with an audit, so I was going to the office.

I'd already called Mr. Katz while I was working out and told him I was calling an impromptu meeting about an urgent issue. The mood at the office was combative; no one was moping about the potential problems, everyone was full of energy. Alik was waving his arms, believing that this cup would pass us by.

"Come on, he's already forgotten everything. He wasn't any good. He'll wake up and go booze it up some more!"

"Wait, hold on," Gleb was skeptical. "People like that never forget things. They hold grudges, like... like..."

"Like who?" Kesha prompted.

"Like cats! I once had a cat. If I pushed her off my pillow at night, I'd get up in the morning and discover that she'd soiled my shoes."

"Haha," Alik laughed. "Maybe that's what Dorozhkin will do too... haha ... in your shoes!"

"Come on!"

They continued to bicker languidly like that for a half hour. The circus ended when Mr. Katz and Rose showed up. I gave them a quick synopsis of the scuffle in the club the night before. Rose gasped; Mr. Katz clasped his heart. Alik brought him a glass of water while Veronica was fanning Rose.

When things settled down we started to create an action plan.

Rose and Mr. Katz took charge.

"Phil, may I say something?" Rose asked for the floor.

I nodded.

"All right," she began. "We're going to be visited by... the tax auditors, the labor inspectors, the fire inspectors, the consumer rights protection inspectors..." she rattled off a list of the possible threats, then turned to Mr. Katz. "Mark, you need to assess all our vulnerabilities and make sure we have the right documents. That includes contracts as well. Kesha, can you help Mark? OK. Veronica, you need to organize the move to the new office as soon as possible and set up workstations for everyone that comply with the labor laws. I'll take care of the taxes and contractors. Employee certification..."

"Oh, and one more thing! You also need to make sure we have the essential HR documents: employment contracts, org chart, time sheet, individual records, vacation schedule, employment record books, etc.," Mr. Katz added to Veronica's list of tasks. "If you're missing anything for anyone, come to me and let the employee know."

"What should I do? How can I help?" Alik asked.

"We need you for the move and the manpower," Veronica answered.

"Got it."

By noon we had our final action plan, and we methodically set it in motion.

My job was now done. Veronica would come to my place Sunday night with everything I needed to sign.

The shopping I'd planned took me a couple of hours, including travel. I just wanted to keep things simple, so I bought everything in one store: a pair of sturdy leather sneakers, light jeans, a stylish jacket and a fitted shirt that showed off my pumped-up chest, broad shoulders and V shape. In total, that made me 6 Charisma points richer and some 30,000 rubles[5] poorer.

After I got home, I calculated the time left before the class reunion — there should be enough — and initiated the process of increasing my Charisma. I'd chosen "increase attractiveness according to the societal standards of your local segment of the Galaxy." I know, I know. It was stupid and incompetent.

But damn it, this was my class reunion we were talking about. And Paulina would be there!

---

[5] 30,000 rubles: about $450 at the time of writing

Chapter Five

HUGE POTENTIAL FOR ENERGETIC EXPANSION

Life lived on life. There were the eaters and the eaten. The law was: EAT OR BE EATEN.

Jack London, *White Fang*

NIGHT WAS APPROACHING. A BIG PORTION OF ONE OF Pibellau's two suns, a huge crimson sphere, had already sunk below the horizon. The second sun was a bit larger than Earth's moon. Its lower edge was touching the top of the trees, illuminating them with intricate violet iridescences. I managed to notice all this while I was busy searching for other threats besides this *test subject* I was about to encounter.

Carter had a total of four mobs, judging by the weapons in their hands: three melee fighters with clubs, and one long-range fighter with a short bow. I still had a few slang words in my vocabulary as my gaming experience hadn't been limited to WoW.

The mobs looked like something out of a nightmare. They were humanoid, no more than four and a half feet tall, with hands that dangled below their knees. But the most astonishing thing about them was their unnaturally large, eyeless heads with a huge mouth that revealed big crooked teeth.

Their brown skin was evenly covered in red spots; I guessed this was either a specific trait or someone's drops of blood. The beasts were clad in matching high-collared jackets. Looking more closely, I realized that they were not jackets at all but growths that apparently served as protection.

They'd already discovered me, so there was no sense in hiding in the grass. I stood up and studied my would-be adversary. Carter was dressed decently, unlike me who was standing there only in my boxers. He was wearing sturdy camouflage pants — well, camouflage against Earth's environment, anyway, — tall heavy boots and a leather jacket. He was somewhat short, nearly a head shorter than me, with a paunch hanging over his belt. He looked like a biker trying to seem younger. His gray hair was tied in a ponytail.

Also, he appeared to be a little surprised to see me.

How had he kept his belt, I wondered. Maybe he'd earned some kind of bonus in the preliminary selection or entered the right portal, unlike me? I'd chosen the red one.

I raised my right hand in greeting to the first human I'd met here. It looked like we were neighbors, so maybe we'd be able to strike up a truce? All the more so because he wasn't showing any signs of aggression.

He snapped a command in English to his mobs, then walked toward me.

The mobs drew closer to his legs. I realized I understood what he'd just said: "Heel!" Had the system installed a built-in interpreter for me?

I went to meet him, slightly bashful about my appearance. I was smeared with dirt and blood — my own and others' — wearing level-2 boxer shorts. In other words, I was easy prey.

He stopped about twenty yards away from me, squinted and scrutinized me. His eyes widened. A smile played on his lips. His low Perception must have prevented him from reading my characteristics before, because now he barked an order:

"Bite!"

At that moment all four mobs tore toward me.

"Go!" he shrieked.

I involuntarily recoiled, stumbled on something and nearly fell. Mobs don't have their own names; the system only identified these as level 1 "Carter's fighting units." I didn't have much choice other than to engage.

The mobs were fast, so I definitely couldn't run away. Tilting his spear forward, Carter ran toward me in an arc, evidently planning to attack me from behind or the side while I fought with his small squadron. They were acting like Velociraptors in a pen of prey: they split up and surrounded me, then stopped and let out blood-curdling shrieks, opening their mouths unnaturally wide and dealing me a slight Stun debuff. Whether it was the scream or the repulsive, coiling tentacles shooting out of the creatures' mouths, but I was losing my concentration.

I shook my head to gather my wits and took a defensive stance, preparing to meet the first creature with a blow of the power fist, but the mobs jumped in unison, brandishing their clubs. An arrow shot from a bow pierced my left shoulder. Stunned by the mobs' shrieking, I hadn't seen it coming.

My shoulder erupted in pain, sending me reeling sideways. I lost my balance and fell. That saved me: the mobs, leaping from three sides, missed me.

Get out of here, I heard in my head as I somersaulted backward, trying to escape my throng of adversaries. Thanks to my Intuition and high Perception, I was able to avoid a blow from Carter's spear. Grabbing him with my numb left arm, I jerked him toward me and punched him in the temple.

A crit! Carter lost more than 10% of his Health points. His face distorted in a grimace of pain and... was that surprise?

He ripped his spear from my weakening arm and scampered away, taking cover behind his units' backs. The mobs that were hanging on to me prevented me from catching up to him and letting him have it. Growling, one of them thrust its mouth tentacles onto my calf, drawing blood. In the spot where it had fastened on to me, the skin quickly blackened and started to blister. A slew of debuffs from Poison to Acid Burn signaled that things were in a bad way.

At the same time, a shower of punches rained down on my back and shoulders, but even though they hurt like hell, they didn't deal much damage: I'd only lost 2 or 3%. The arrow didn't penalize me by much more, but there was no point in trying to catch up — five of them were starting to kick me. I punched them indiscriminately until I finally tore the cluster of tentacles out of me, winding it around my fist.

That drove the creature's health into the red zone. It skittered off, throwing its club away, but I was no longer paying attention to it because the path was clear. The next arrow missed my face by half an inch, but I swung round and fled as fast as I could.

When I got to the border of the zone, I turned around and saw that no one was chasing me. Apparently, I'd proved to be too sharp in the tooth for them; also, capturing a neutral hexagon must have been a higher priority for Carter than chasing after humble me.

I penetrated the force field and ended up back at my own hexagon which by now felt almost like home. The trip to the ravine took the rest of the evening. The small creatures — the little krekens, kirpi and whistlers — must have hidden somewhere, and I couldn't even see the spiky sarasur cockroaches running around on the bottom.

I picked my way through the ravine. I still didn't know for certain how this world worked, and I still wasn't sure if — or how often — mobs respawned here. The disincarnation of the corpses proved that this was entirely possible. This phenomenon clearly had its roots in gaming, but in games, nature abhors a vacuum. So if the respawn of the Kreken was entirely possible, the only question was when.

In any case, I got through the ravine with no problems. Evidently the absence of small mobs had something to do with the fact that night was approaching. According to the system's warning, that's when the ghastly carnivorous nocturnal predators went out to hunt.

Were there any herbivorous creatures at all here? I got the feeling that in this world everything ate everything else. And the smallest ones, who didn't have the guts to hunt anything, had to become scavengers.

I really wanted to clean myself up. I wasn't hungry or thirsty — I'd traded food and water for the existence resources which seemed to be giving me all the sustenance I needed, replacing my body's metabolism. But in the world where there's pain, there's an itch. My body was terribly itchy and I desperately wanted a shower, or at least to wash off my face, but I had no idea if there was a body of water around here.

Was there any water at all on this planet? Maybe the portal had changed me in some way along with my metabolism, and I was blissfully breathing methane without even noticing?

Staying on my guard, I mulled over all of this until I finally reached the white stone of my future command center. The palm-shaped imprint was darkening invitingly against the background of the rock which was glowing weakly in the nighttime darkness.

I placed my left palm in it.

Do you want to activate your command center?
Cost: 100 existence resource pt.

Yes, I uttered mentally.

My existence resource counter spun back to 12, as 100 pt. were put toward activation.

The stone vibrated, radiating circles of energy. I felt their touch — not physically but as *knowledge* about what was happening. It was as though my hand were merging with the stone, but I *understood* that that's how it was supposed to be until the activation process was complete.

The first circle spread to the borders of the hexagon, designating its next owner. Now if any other test subjects infiltrated my territory, I would find out instantly.

A second circle spread out 50 yards away from the stone. In the place where the waves stopped rippling, a fragile, yard-high barrier emerged: slabs made out of a material I didn't recognize were driven into the ground. It didn't look like wood or metal, but rather plastic or something like that in line with the development of the Elders' technological advances. The most important thing I grasped was that at this level, the fence had a more decorative function: it visually marked out the borders of my base, but I'd be able to upgrade and fortify it.

The third, and final, circle of the energy field spread, growing into a dome above me and the command center. The field stiffened into fantastically gleaming opaque walls and a ceiling, then covered the ground beneath me in a white stone, creating a floor. It left an opening for entry and exit, which I could close by giving a mental command.

I gave the command. The door closed.

The vibrations stopped.

You've captured a hexagon!
Your command center has been activated.
Name of command center: Base 1.
Owner: Phil, level 2 human.

I heaved a sigh and broke loose from the stone. I now had a place to shelter for the night. The same *knowledge* — as I understood it, the information about how the Trial worked was automatically implanted in my brain — gave me a sense of calm: no nocturnal creature would cross the threshold of my new home. For the first time all day — and it had been a long one, beginning with a typical morning back on Earth and accompanying Kostya and Julie to the airport — I could relax and forget about danger. Too much had happened since the last time I'd woken up.

I didn't feel like sleeping, and it appeared that I didn't need to sleep here either. But some relaxation wouldn't hurt. I stretched out contentedly on the floor, which had a carpet-like texture, and shut my eyes.

To my surprise, I quickly felt rested. "*While you're sleeping, your enemies are leveling up,*" the gaming expression resurfaced from the depths of my memory. The consequences of failing the Trial hit me sharply. This was no time to relax!

I had activated the command center, but now what? It would be a good idea to figure out what it had to offer and what it allowed me to do.

I stood up and put my palm on the stone. Whenever it was a question of numbers, it was more convenient to read the information visually. Either obeying my wishes or because it was built that way by default, the command center offered me a system interface to command the base.

Base 1
Level: 1.
Modules: 0.
Rate of existence resource generation: 1 point per hour.

THE FINAL TRIAL

**You may not upgrade until you reach level 5.
Cost to upgrade base to level 2: 500 existence
resource pt.**

There you go. That meant that I would no longer need to worry about dying from starvation. The one existence resource point generated by the base was exactly what I needed to subsist.

Still, sitting around on my butt waiting for my competitors to finish one another off was both unthinkable and dangerous. The same *knowledge* told me that any other test subject could gain access to my home, in other words, access the command center, simply by keeping their hand on the wall of the dome for a certain amount of time — anywhere on the wall.

I removed my hand from the stone and went to the exit. I needed to study my domain.

The walls slid apart, letting me out. The dead silence inside the house was replaced by a hellish cacophony of nocturnal life. There were sloshing and squelching sounds coming from nearby, as if someone were filling tires with a massive pump. I heard sharp, cringe-inducing screams, and when I looked closely I could make out silhouettes of strange creatures rushing through the sky.

A chirping noise suddenly rang out from the other side of the house, startling me so much that I cowered. But when I crept over on my haunches and peered behind the wall, I didn't see anything.

Feeling more courageous, I took a few steps away from the house. The chirping started again. It seemed to be coming from somewhere in the forest. A crack of either mandibles or chitinous plates rubbing

---

together grew louder, then it suddenly stopped, replaced by a crackling sound that ripped through the air. Something had just killed something.

It wasn't completely dark — the sky was filled with twinkling stars that didn't form any constellations I recognized. There were no indications of any satellites like our moon, but it was light enough for me to see in front of my face. The ground was now covered in the transparent foundation that made up the surface of the covering of the base. The material of the floor called to mind a honeycomb: six-sided shapes flickering on the edges. It was a beautiful sight, but when I focused on it to try to learn what it all meant, I came up empty.

From the outside, my house looked like one of those six-sided honeycombs, but one with walls along the edges that converged in a dome in the center. Walking around it, I touched the walls a few times, and whenever I gave a mental command or even just a hint of a desire, a door opened. I tried to touch it with other parts of my body, but the door didn't open, even if I commanded it to.

Walking in increasingly wider spirals, I made my way to the edge of the base.

Basic protective barrier
Level 1.

The fence was purely decorative — no argument there. Still, its surface was smoother than glass, so at least a couple of mobs couldn't reach the base. Cockroaches wouldn't be able to enter because there was nothing for their legs to hold on to, and kirpi were just too short to get in. They may be brave enough to bite your feet but surely not tall enough to enter.

But it wasn't an obstacle for the other mobs I'd run across. The Krekens could easily fly over the barrier, and the whistlers could jump over it. I'd already seen evidence that they could jump high.

According to the description, the fence's durability was 100 points. These numbers meant nothing to me, but if I used the Kreken location boss for comparison, he could dispense with them before you could say "napalm spittle".

The description said that the fence could be upgraded through the command center. Okay. It was time now to go try to figure out all the other upgrades and modules.

The moment I thought about it, I heard something massive breaking through the fence. More chirping sounds came from nearby. I dashed toward the house, opened the door and stumbled inside. As the door closed, I heard something heave a disappointed sigh.

Then something bulky hit the wall. It withstood — but where the object had impacted, shock waves spread across its surface.

There was no way in hell I was going to risk my second-to-last life to satisfy my curiosity. Let them try to break through if they want to. I guess I'd rather be studying the features of the base.

I used the navigation menu to look at the production modules that could be generated. For now I could access only two items: the fighting unit module and the uniform module. The first one cost 50 points and the second one, 30 points.

The level 1 fighting unit module would allow me

to create my own squadron of mobs. Charisma affected the rate of generation of new units and the number of units used at the same time. Right now I had 17 points, which meant that I could immediately create 17 units.

That was a shocker. Did that mean that Carter only had four units because his Charisma was low? I urgently needed more existence resources.

In retrospect, I realized that Carter may have lost some of his mobs in battle, or the rate of generation of new units didn't allow him to create a lot right away. Still, this wasn't the time to find out — and guessing was out of the question. In order to understand all the details, I should first buy myself a module and launch the mob generation.

But for now I couldn't buy anything with my 12 paltry existence resource points. Even the first upgrade of the fence cost 20 points.

This raised a question: should I wait until morning or should I go out and take a risk at night? I didn't think about it for long. If the logic here was similar to what I'd seen in the preliminary selection, it meant that the local mobs scaled up. Which meant that I could try.

The creature that had been pounding on the walls of the house had given up by now. But did it go away for good or was it still by the house watching out for me? In any case, I exited from the opposite side.

My heart was pounding. The stakes in my adventure were so high that I had butterflies in my stomach.

I looked around and didn't see anything nearby. I breathed a sigh of relief. Slowly, pressing against the wall, I walked around the house and lucked out: I spotted the monster that had been chasing me before it saw me.

It was breathing wheezily, listening closely to something and peering into the darkness behind the fence. In the place where it had broken through the barrier, a gaping hole was now darkening.

The creature looked kind of like a three-legged stool, but its legs were dominated by freakishly bent joints. The body was almost humanoid, but the limbs looked more like horned, double-edged boards, and the head sat on a long ostrich neck.

Kraider
Elite.
Level 3.
Life points: 800.

Elite? That was fine with me — 800 life points were half the amount the Kreken had. I'd manage.

In three leaps I was behind its back and pummeling its head and body.

You've dealt damage to the kraider: 36.
Damage absorbed by armor: 50% Actual damage: 18.

You've dealt damage to the kraider: 22.
Damage absorbed by armor: 50% Actual damage: 11.

You've dealt damage to the kraider: 46.
Damage absorbed by armor: 50% Actual damage: 23.

Based on the logs, kraider wasn't the mob's name, but the species. The fact that the monster didn't have a name didn't make the task any easier — if it went like this, I might be fighting it until morning.

Zing! Without moving its legs, the creature was rotating around its axis. With a whistle, it hastily bored its "sword" between my ribs, shattering my bones and instantly knocking off almost a quarter of my health.

As I wailed in pain, it lifted me into the air and looked searchingly into my eyes. For additional support, the kraider bored a second "sword" into the covering of my base.

The bleed DOT ticked, sucking out my life: a heartbeat per tick, one percent every 10 ticks. As ill luck would have it, my heart was beating furiously and the pain made it hard to breathe.

The kraider's eight pairs of eyes indifferently waited while my blood gushed. It hypnotized me, inserting into me thoughts about the futility of combat and a quick escape from the torture. Even though its body looked humanoid, it was really an arachnid.

My impaled body crept down its makeshift sword. My health points continued to drop, and this made me think about selling my life for more. Using my hands, I dragged myself closer to the kraider.

Was it my imagination or did the creature look surprised?

It had to be my imagination. With great satisfaction I rammed my power fist into one of its many eyes.

The eye exploded with a pleasing *smack*.

You've dealt critical damage to the kraider:

296.

The monster screeched and reached out a second limb, but it couldn't maintain its balance and began to fall. I managed to land a few well-positioned, powerful punches, hammering each eye until I heard the protective layer pop. Bubble wrap, that's what we used to call this sort of substance at Ultrapak.

The last strike broke the creature's skull. Something sticky splashed out. Shuddering in predeath agony, the kraider's chirping abated as it expired.

With a flash, it dematerialized, leaving an item in its wake.

It was a decent-sized existence crystal.

+44 existence resource pt.

Verifying the probability of receiving bonus existence resources (20%)...
Verification complete!
+44 existence resource pt.

Of course the valuable loot made me happy, but not as happy as the fact that the kraider's body was now gone, complete with the sword-like arm I'd been impaled on.

Clutching my wound, I stumbled back to the house and collapsed on the floor in relief as soon as the door shut behind me. Safe at last!

The wound soon healed over. The bleed DOT expired. For the next hour I waited for the regeneration to finish. As I lay there, I estimated that I now had enough resources for the fighting unit module and the uniform module. How long could I continue to walk around naked?

If I also needed resources to generate my own mobs, it would be better to wait with the clothes. Right now it was more important to acquire a pack of fighting units: it would be easier to farm with them, and for all I knew, the fast-developing Carter could reappear in the morning. Then how would I defend myself? I'd lose the hexagon and everything. It would be all over then, disincarnation and the end of the Trial.

So first, the units. I opened the command center menu, pressed on the item I needed and accepted the charge of 50 existence resource points. My high Intellect would speed up the construction of the module.

The fighting unit module generation process has been initiated.
Time to completion: 3 minutes.

Generation complete. Do you want to create fighting units?

Hell yeah!

I accepted. The system asked if I wanted to design new units or choose from a catalog of existing ones. I opened "Catalog" and flinched.

The creatures were straight out of nightmares: mechanoids, insectoids, humanoids, synthetic androids, reptiles, animals, birds, plus some totally unclassifiable creatures I couldn't begin to describe — large and small, fast and slow. There was everything under the sun. Even though the units all looked different, their stats were standard: ability to attack, travel speed, attack speed, damage, health points, armor.

I leafed through the bestiary which was organized into species and their roles in the group. The roles were clear: melee combat and long-range combat. There were no tanks, healers or buffers for support; the units couldn't boast many talents at all. They fought by biting, punching, clawing or using primitive weapons, such as clubs and bows. There was no high tech or even anything metal. Although the barrel-shaped droids could attack with electric shocks, the damage from them was no worse than a good old whack across the head with a club.

I then found the evidence of the participation of our former planet neighbors in the Trial and Diagnostics. I would like to report that these were brilliant, agile fighters with outstanding reactions and powerful damage, but that wasn't the case. It was standard damage and low armor, but the species! I'd been fantasizing about this since I was a kid! It was a dream to put together my own army just from these mobs, which even included different species, and were divided among melee and long-range combat.

A level 1 unit cost 1 existence resource point. The cost to maintain their biological processes was the same 1 point per hour, but for the entire permitted pack. That was for all 17 beautiful, terrifying predatory dinosaurs: a dozen Velociraptors that were ravenously baring their teeth, and a magnificent quintet of Dilophosauri that spit poisonous saliva a good 10 yards. I didn't overthink their names, and just called them what we — humans — were used to calling them.

Velociraptor
Level 1 melee fighter
Phil's fighting unit.
Health points: 450/450.
Attack: 21–25.
Damage absorbed by armor: 9%.
Maximum travel speed: 40 mph.
Race talent: Pack, +1% to damage for each additional individual in a group of the same species.

Dilophasaurus
Level 1 long-range combat fighter
Phil's fighting unit.
Health points: 300/300.
Attack: 28–35.
Damage absorbed by armor: 4%.
Maximum travel speed: 34 mph
Race talent: Pack, +1% to damage for each additional individual in a group of the same species.

Earth's paleontologists weren't sure that Dilophosaurus attacked with venomous saliva, but that was their problem, not mine. My little Dillies would spit.

I pressed "Accept and start generation." In less than an hour my interface was cluttered with the icons of each mob. Both the Raptors and the Dillies were numbered and had health bars — it was a full-fledged raid squadron.

The only thing missing was a tank. For now that would have to be me.

Hold on. Where were the units? The house was as empty as before: just me and the stone.

I mentally summoned the fighters, and something began to bang against the far wall. Boom! Boom! Boom! I heard some squealing and screeching. Could these be my guys at the door?

I walked outside and found myself surrounded by a crowd of little creatures from the Cretaceous period.

They were so small! The Raptors were the size of a Great Dane, but their tails made them seem massive, almost my height. The spitting Dilophosauri, which, based on the most recent data, were up to eighteen foot tall, poked me on the shoulder with their snouts.

The dinosaurs jostled one another and emitted unusual sounds as they tried to obey the summons. More than anything, they were acting like country chickens at feeding time. I barely managed to dodge their powerful tails.

"Holy crap! Line up, crocodiles!" I shouted when one of the most agile of the Raptors pierced the top of my foot with an enormous claw.

They fell into line and shifted from foot to foot, breathing noisily and gazing into my eyes loyally.

I examined my fighters. They might just as well have been incubated. I couldn't detect any discrepancies. I *knew* that they wouldn't release any XP, and that I could upgrade them only through the command center. But they notched up seniority points, and whenever they achieved particular successes, each of my reptiles could receive a new talent or buff.

The next upgrade would cost 250 existence resource points. Anyway, I hoped it would be easier to farm with them.

I left my small army to guard the territory and went back to the command center. Now it was time to get some clothes.

When I launched the generation of the equipment module, I had 3 existence resource points left out of 33. The module materialized right there in the house, next to the command center. It looked like a white plastic wardrobe. Its surface was scaly and warm, like the texture of the tunnel I'd gone through in the preliminary selection.

For two existence resource points, the command center offered me the chance to create a "basic test subject uniform" without specifying what that included. That was it for now. I didn't have enough resources to upgrade the module, so I accepted the basic set. I felt a fleeting vibration: my uniform was ready.

I went over to the wardrobe but before I even had a chance to open it, an alarm rang out in my head while my ears heard my mobs squealing frantically.

Apparently, we were being attacked. I dashed out to rescue them.

The scene was sheer pandemonium. A massive hulk the size of a mammoth was grunting with pleasure as it munched on one of the Raptors. Sounding like thugs on a smoking break, the Dillies were spitting once per second. The buddies of the one that was being chewed up were hanging on to the sides of the monster, futilely trying to penetrate its plated chitinous spine with their claws and teeth.

"Home!" I uttered the mental command out loud and opened the door.

The Raptors fell off the hulk like overripe pears, jumped back to their feet and dashed toward me. The little Dillies followed them. Having vengefully covered the monster's snout with black viscous spittle, they outran the melee fighters and reached the protective dome first.

I shut the door behind the last unit. The house was suddenly crowded.

I'd lost two fighters, both Velociraptors. The first one had been chewed to pieces and the second one had fallen under the monster's several-ton bulk and was instantly crushed.

I ordered the fighters to sit still without making a noise, let alone breathe. We quieted down, waiting for the giant to leave.

The cunning bastard, realizing that its food had run off somewhere, continued to walk around the base for a long time, lumbering around the dome and vocalizing its outrage, until it finally snorted in anger and left.

It was just in time, because I was about to lose my last resource point to sustain the mobs and we urgently needed to go farm.

When I was already at the door, I remembered the uniform module. I went to check it.

Basic test subject uniform
Protection: +15.
Durability: 100%.

When I put it on, I finally understood what Protection meant. All the components of the uniform had their own armor numbers, and in the "+15 protection" sum showed the same 15% damage absorption. This included a complete set of underwear, combat boots, pants made of some stiff but flexible material, a synthetic belt, a fitted sweater, knee protectors, elbow protectors, shoulder pads and a multifunction bandana that I tied around my neck. I was especially surprised by the helmet, which completely covered my head. When I put it on, I didn't have any issues: I could see everything and breathe easily. It was a good, serviceable helmet. With my face covered, I'd feel much more confident facing any little Kreken.

The only weapons were a wooden club and a miserable excuse for a knife that wouldn't cut anything stiffer than a sandwich. I'd seen similar ones in the hands of Carter's bloodsucking units. The weapons' damage was measly; they didn't give any bonuses, and compared to my power fist they were useless. But I took the knife with me anyway.

As soon as the large sun rose, my mobs and I got ready to set out on our hunt.

I left the house first and mechanically shut the door, forgetting that my dinosaurs were to follow me. Only one Raptor had managed to slip through the closing door.

Around ten yards from the dome, Carter was standing bold and proud, surrounded by his bloodsuckers from hell. There were still four of them, but they weren't aggressive, casting wary glares at my pet.

That was strange. Why hadn't I been warned that they were infiltrating my hexagon?

When Carter saw me, he stood up, scratched his

naked belly, made a show of yawning, and amicably said in English,

"Hey, Phil! There's something we have to discuss. Can we talk?"

CHAPTER SIX

THE PLAYPEN STAR

*The end of the world occurred
pretty much as we had predicted.
Too many humans, not enough
space or resources to go around.
The details are trivial and
pointless, the reasons, as always,
purely human ones.*

Fallout 2

WHY HADN'T THE ALARM KICKED IN? WAS I REALLY NOT
supposed to find out that another test subject was
invading my hexagon? Or had Carter infiltrated it
before I'd captured it? If that was the case, how had he
survived the night? Somehow I doubted that he could
fight off the elite monsters by himself.

At any rate, it was worth talking to him,
especially since attacking him with my level 2 might be
brave, but it was also idiotic. I'd already used this tactic
on Kreken and barely gotten away. But Carter had
already managed to reach level 6, seemingly putting all
his earned resources into his level ups. Even if this
world didn't have much in common with the computer

games of my world, it would be impossible to overcome the four-level difference. I wouldn't be able to manage him. My only hope lay with the ambush regiment of my little dinos. Together, we just might Zerg it.

"Carter," I said with a nod.

"None other, Phil, my good man," he smirked. "Somehow things didn't quite work out the first time we met; we just gave each other a little pat for no reason at all. But after that..." he paused, then continued evasively, "Er... things happened."

"Things? How did you get on to my hexagon? I should have been warned."

"Hey, are you Russian?" he changed the subject without answering my question. "How is it that I understand you? Are you speaking Russian?"

"Are you saying that of all the things we've seen here, the thing you're most confused about is that we understand each other?"

"Good point!" Carter said with a laugh, slapping his thigh. "You're so right, Phil, my boy! When I ended up here and saw one of those creatures that are all over the place, I almost had a heart attack. And the suns? Dammit! Have you seen them? There are two freakin' suns here!"

"And the sky is purple. We're definitely not on Earth. To be honest, after the preliminary selection I was ready for anything. The acid jelly there was a nightmare."

"Jelly?" Carter wrinkled his forehead in confusion. "Oh! I had that damn labyrinth with predatory sunflowers. At least that's what I called them; it was somehow different there. One of them almost bit through my arm. So that's just what I did to it: I bit through its stalk. It was thick, but you could rip it apart in one bite just like corn on the cob. The juice almost poisoned me, but I have high resist to poisons."

The only explanation I could find for his talkativeness and openness was that he didn't see me as an adversary and didn't have anyone else to talk to about his experiences. But I kind of liked that: we were like two old friends eager to share our adventures.

"Predatory sunflowers? No way! How many portals did you have? I mean the ones at the end. I had a red one and a blue one and I'm still beating myself up over what would have happened if I'd jumped through the other one."

"Portals? You had portals? For real? I had a staircase in a huge cave. At the top it ran into a hatch but I couldn't open it. At the bottom it went underwater. It was like ice. I thought I was going to freeze. But I went down and I was caught up in the current, which was so strong it pulled me away from the staircase. Then I passed out and ended up here."

"Who was your supervisor?"

"I think his name was something Valiadis. He was probably Greek. There was this alien girl with him and a really tall monster — it was a demon in the flesh," Carter scratched the back of his neck with his free hand. In his other hand he held the spear, resting it casually on the ground, like it was a hoe rather than a weapon.

Picture this: dawn in the country and the next-door neighbor drops in to share the latest gossip. Carter's English was unusual; he had a distinct trace of an accent I couldn't put my finger on. Where was he from?

102

As soon as the thought came to me, my "neighbor" asked me the very same question.

"So you're Russian, Phil?"

"Uh-huh. Where are you from?"

"Johannesburg, South Africa." Carter beat his chest with his fist and then pointed at my Raptor. "Hey, that gnasher next to you, is that your unit?"

"Yes, he's mine. He's a Velociraptor. Quite a beauty, isn't he?"

"You know, I thought they were a little bigger. No offense, but yours looks like a chicken. Maybe it's because he's not leveled up yet?"

"Maybe, but I've read that supposedly they really were this size."

Carter perked up. "What are you, some sort of dinosaur fanatic?"

"No, I'm not a fanatic, but the topic has always... fascinated me."

"Hm, I guess we have more in common than I thought. I saw *Jurassic Park* like 10 times!" he exclaimed. "Can I touch him?"

"Go ahead."

Carter warily came closer to the Raptor and reached a hand toward the creature's mouth. The creature looked at him in confusion, then at me, screeched a warning, then snapped his mouth a millimeter away from Carter's fingers. Carter started and snatched his hand back.

Immediately my Raptor collapsed, showered with blows from the bloodsuckers' clubs. An arrow shot by an archer pierced the dinosaur's already-dead body.

"Down! Heel!" Carter shouted at his mobs before they could attack me as the master of the pet which had aggroed them.

He pushed them back and returned to where he'd been standing before. The Raptor's corpse was already gone.

"Sorry about that, Phil! Their last command was 'Protect,' so they lashed out. I guess your unit died too fast," Carter shrugged. "Sorry."

"I saw everything. It wasn't your fault."

"That's a good thing," he said with a smile. "How come you only had one? You don't look like a total monster, so you must have enough Charisma for a pack that's good enough. Or did you not have enough existence resources to make more?"

He didn't want to know much, did he?

"Did *you* only have enough Charisma for four fighters?" I asked him instead.

His mobs snapped their heads in unison and fixed me with their eyeless faces, baring their teeth and stretching their mouth tentacles toward me. On a signal from Carter, they indifferently turned away.

He then asked smugly in a tone devoid of the previous friendliness and neighborliness, "And what do you know about Charisma, Phil? In the other world chicks couldn't get enough of me! It's just that... you lose it, you know? While you were digging around your hole, I was capturing all the hexagons along the edge of this field of the Trial, and you know what? Not only is yours the outermost one, it's also a corner."

"A corner?"

"Uh-huh. On the other side is the neutral one I captured, and beyond the neutral hexagons there's nothing. It's an impenetrable shroud. I tried to get through but I couldn't."

"So you're my only neighbor?"

"Oho, how's your math? Or were you into arts at school?"

"I'm a writer," for some reason I felt like I needed to clarify.

Carter nodded in satisfaction. "See, a hexagon has six sides. Each of your sides shares a border with a neutral one, and right beyond that there's a base that belongs to a test subject. But three sides of your hexagon butt up against the outermost neutral ones, and beyond the other three," Carter pointed toward the ravine, "there's me and one other test subject. I don't know who it is; I haven't reached him yet."

"How come? You haven't had a chance?"

"I'll share this information with you so it's easier for you to make a decision. In any case I'm going to win. Look. Until you get to a certain level you can't cross the border of a hexagon that hasn't been captured. In other words, if there's a neutral zone between you and the other person, you can't reach each other — first you need to capture the neutral zone. Got it?"

How did he know all of this? I nodded and anxiously looked at the timer that was counting out the draining of existence resource points for both me and my brutes. I had enough from what the command center would generate, but my Raptors and Dillies wouldn't. Most likely they would just be disincarnated if they didn't have anything to sustain their biological functions with. According to Earth time, I had around 40 minutes, or in other words...

What was it that the rules said? If Carter killed me, he'd capture my hexagon, and I would be disincarnated if I didn't capture a new one within a day?

"OK, Phil, the clock is ticking and we've got a little problem we need to solve," Carter turned serious, stood up and took a step toward me, followed by his mobs. "Tell me, how would you feel if you lost everything you'd achieved with your *connection*?"

"The connection?" I had no idea what he was talking about.

"Well yeah! I'm talking about that invisible thing in that skull of yours that helped you see more than the average person: work with the infospace, get quests, collect XPs and level up characteristics. What do you say, Phil?"

"Are you saying I'll lose the interface if I fail the Trial?"

"Oh, that's what you call it? OK, the 'interface' then. That's not the point. The point is that there can only be one winner, but whoever passes the Trial as part of the winner's clan will keep their memory and the achievements they received with the interface."

"The rules didn't say anything about that."

"That's because you're only level 2," Carter said as though he were a teacher and I were a slow student. "If you get up to level 5, you'll see the expanded rulebook."

"Got it. So what are you proposing?"

"Look. I could knock the hell out of you and then meet you at your resurrection point and keep killing you until you're out of lives," he said, apparently ignorant about my earlier death. "If you run away, I'll just capture your command center and then the signal will tell me where you are. Or..." he raised his index finger. "Or you join my clan and we'll work together to expand our territory. You will lose the *connection* — I'm talking about the other world — but you'll keep everything it helped you level up. Well? What do you say? It's always better to be on the winner's team, Phil my boy!"

"But still... Can you tell me how you infiltrated my hexagon?"

"OK, I'll tell you if it will help you understand that the scenario isn't in your favor," Carter said, swaying slightly. "Including my home hexagon, I've captured five already. Five! I'm the first in the Trial to have done that!"

"But did you get any achievements?" I blurted out.

Shit. I'd put my foot in it, hadn't I? I'd given away too much.

He frowned suspiciously. "Have you already gotten something too?"

Then his face lit up. He must have realized that in any case, my level 2 was no match for his level 6.

"It's not important," he said. "If you join my clan, it will even be useful for me. Yes, you're right. I was given an achievement, and a talent too: the talent to infiltrate other people's zones without being detected. Right now it only works for me, but I can level it up and it will also work for all my clan members. Now do you understand how we'll proceed? The other test subjects won't have time to get their act together while we capture most of the Trial field."

Numbers were coming together in a staggering amount in my head. Carter must have farmed over 2000 resources in less than a day. How could that be? Based on the achievement I'd received, I was the first on Pibellau to smoke the location boss while normal mobs didn't give so many resources. Well, 5 or 6 points, and taking levels into account, let's say 10 on average. That meant that he'd finished off more than 200 mobs.

This fat gray-haired biker was damn strong.

I groped behind my back for the wall of the shelter, preparing to open the door while firing off mental commands to my remaining pets, telling them all to attack every which way.

"Carter, when did you have time to farm so many existence resources? It's dangerous at night."

"Yeah, that's a nice bonus — the side effect of the talent I received with the achievement," Carter obviously enjoying talking about this; he was one of those people who brag whenever the occasion arises as long as there's someone willing to listen. "Monsters don't notice me or my fighters until I attack them. Isn't that cool?" he broke into a self-satisfied smile.

"Cool," I agreed sullenly. All I'd gotten for my two achievements was some characteristic points, while he'd gotten an imba talent.

"I'm glad you approve," Carter smirked and came another couple of steps closer to me. "OK. Time is money, money is honey, Phil! What's your decision?"

"Look, Carter, maybe for now we can just call a truce? You don't touch me and I don't touch you?"

"No, my good man! To hell with your proposal! How can I be confident knowing that there's a potential enemy lurking around nearby, busy leveling up and just waiting for an opportune moment to stab me in the back? Nothing personal, but I'm planning to win the Trial."

"Before you set your bloodsuckers on me, I'd like

you to tell me," I raised my hand with my palm toward him. "What did you use to do in the real world?"

"Me?" he asked incredulously. "I'm a musician. I write songs and play guitar. 'Nuff beating about the bush. Are you coming with me?"

"I hope I get to hear your songs sometime," I replied, smiling. "But no, my good man, I'm not going with you. I don't like bloodsuckers."

Then a bunch of things happened all at once.

"Go!" Carter shouted.

He nodded his head sharply, equipping a helmet. His creatures flew toward me.

I opened the door to the house. My little dinosaurs burst out and dispersed, screaming their heads off. I yelled commands, telling them whom to attack.

"Well, well, aren't you full of surprises!" Carter's muffled voice leaked out from under the helmet.

There were two big dinosaurs for each of Carter's mobs plus another one jumping their master. The dinosaurs had fanned out and were spitting their poisonous saliva, aiming for the mouths of the eyeless freaks. Still, they kept missing the mark as the monsters must have had another way of seeing.

Meanwhile, I dashed at Carter6 shaking my power-fist covered hand.

A Raptor had jumped on him, but Carter had killed it instantly with a sharp, imperceptible flourish of his sharp spear. Did that mean his damage was above 500? In any case, it was too late for me to change my strategy.

I ducked under the spear that he was pointing at me. Sliding along the glossy surface of the base, I whacked him in the knee with the power fist. His kneecap cracked. The system issued a notification about the damage dealt.

Carter cried out, leaped back and, dragging his leg up, quickly retreated. I'd only managed to take away 7% despite dealing critical damage.

One after the other, my dinosaurs' icons were rapidly turning yellow, then red. Wheeling around, I saw that they were having a hard time. That meant that Carter could also upgrade his mobs. Bad news.

The Raptors were gnawing at the monsters, the sound of the Dillies' spitting not letting up for a second. Still, either my mobs' damage was still minimal or the bloodsuckers' armor was fortified, but my mobs couldn't even knock out half of their health.

"Maybe you'll change your mind, Phil?" Carter laughed in my face. "You don't have a hope in hell!"

I shook my head, simultaneously evading the line of the spear that was directed at my stomach. I then counterattacked, this time managing to land a series of blows and taking away more than 30% Health.

Carter's Stamina wasn't much to write home about, his health points dwindling before my eyes.

His helmet cracked from one of my powerful punches. I hit him in the same spot over and over again.

Just when I'd almost started to believe that victory was possible, something sharp dug into my side, penetrating my belly and turning my guts inside out. A gnawing pain took my breath away. My eyes clouded over.

The system notified me that I'd received critical damage as well as poison and bleeding debuffs.

Looking down, I saw that the blade of Carter's new weapon — a dagger — was covered in a black smoky jelly.

My legs buckled. I collapsed. The poisonous substance covering the dagger paralyzed my muscles. The debuff timer's countdown was intolerably long: it took me 10 seconds to be free of it. Carter needed only two or three of those to finish me off — but for some reason, none fell.

The fighting unit panel showed that all my Raptors had already been killed and the Dilophosauri were hanging on by the thread of their remaining health.

Suddenly my bandana was torn from my neck as the bloodsuckers' tentacles penetrated my exposed flesh. Something nearby was intently wheezing and sloshing.

"Eat, my darlings, eat. Rebuild your strength," Carter muttered paternally.

Watching this scene, I realized that he would be a good, caring master for me. I wrenched myself from this thought.

Carter removed his helmet and wiped the sweat from his forehead as if the battle had already ended. After a moment I realized that I no longer heard the sounds of spitting, which meant that all my creatures were dead.

My health was in the red zone. This musician was practical — you couldn't argue with that. He deliberately didn't kill me, so he could heal the mobs. Four tentacles clinging on to my neck and temples not only sucked out my blood and health, but also left a stinging pain. My neck was becoming leaden and burning as if a scorching metal band had been placed on it.

"It'll all be over for you in a minute, Phil. You'll die, you'll lose your only hexagon, and then you'll be disincarnated. You'll wake up in the world on the day when you first tried on the *connection*," Carter said with theatrical sadness. "You just won't have any of those things from the future, and your dull, depressing life will pick up from there. How do I know that? Did you actually think I was any different? I was a failure and an alcoholic, my wife threw me out, and my friends and even my own daughter shunned me. I don't know why, but these Elders choose their candidates from among real losers."

"Not losers..." barely moving my tongue, I corrected him now that the paralysis debuff had expired. "Ordinary people. The most ordinary people."

"I was never ordinary!" Carter erupted. "I took my solo act all over the United States!"

"So you're a star?" I tried to smile sarcastically but it came out crooked.

"I was. I was a star," Carter said calmly. Then he added, "It's about time that you change your mind. I'm looking at a system message suggesting that I invite you to join my clan. I wonder if I press *Accept*, will the system ask you to confirm? So. I'm pressing it. You have 3% left. Make up your mind! 2%!"

I got a message suggesting that I join "Carter's Clan." I swiped it away.

He was leaning closer to me — so close that I was able to grope for the knife on my hip, pull it out slowly and imperceptibly to him, then plunge it into his ear.

He let out a roar, recoiled and fell to the ground. The blow that had entered his brain was guaranteed to kill anyone back on Earth — but here it was recalculated as "critical stab wound" for 134 measly health points.

I was overcome by hysterical laughter. I was coughing blood and gurgling bubbles when Carter's sharp spear penetrated my heart, taking me down.

The world was extinguished.

You are now dead, test subject.
Lives remaining: 1.
Time left until resurrection: 3... 2... 1....

Chapter Seven

The Last Life

Surprise, motherfucker!

James Doakes, *Dexter*

THIS TIME, THE POSTMORTEM PAIN WAS SHARPER AND more vivid, if you can say something like that about pain. It's an odd concept: you're suspended in the cosmic void waiting long seconds until you're resurrected, and you think, where are the signals from the nerve endings supposed to go — if there's no body, does that mean there's no brain? You feel like the only part of you that's left is consciousness which leaves behind a blank mold of your brain at the moment of your death.

Maybe that's where all this pain was coming from?

My last life began next to the same white stone that I'd activated to capture my first hexagon. But it hadn't been mine for long — just one night. I didn't see any structures or the familiar ravine, so I guess I'd been resurrected in a neutral hexagon. I think it was the easternmost hexagon of those that surrounded my home, seeing as Carter had captured the other ones.

Carter... I remembered him saying that if I got out of here, I'd return to the day when I had gotten the interface and lose everything I'd achieved. Is that what he'd learned from the expanded rulebook? Perhaps. Assessing the risks, I thought it could be worth taking him up on his offer, because then I'd still have a chance to hold on to everything I'd accomplished. That would be the rational thing to do.

But I couldn't force myself to do it. There was something rotten and unpleasant about his behavior and character, and I think that made me loath him subconsciously. And of course, I admit that I was sort of hoping to accumulate more fighting units than him. In any case, with fifteen mobs against Carter's four, the odds were in my favor. Who could have known that his fighters were reinforced?

Never mind. I still had a chance, even if it was minuscule. Once again I was naked, without weapons, without clothing, and most insulting of all, without my little dinosaurs. How cute they... were.

I examined myself and cursed in disappointment. I was wearing the same torn jeans in which I'd arrived at the Trial, but they were bursting at the seams because of my bulging muscles. It looked like we were resurrected in the same clothing in which we'd first ended up here. So it was a good thing I'd at least hung on to my sneakers and not chucked them at the acid jelly back in the labyrinth. Nothing would be more infuriating than not having shoes; my city feet weren't really up to walking barefoot.

Everything else I'd had on me was lost — it had become loot for Carter. Even though I'd had no existence resource points to begin with, it was such a crying shame to be left without my full-fledged uniform and power fist.

Three balloons were pulsating in the air: two red system notifications and a gold one. Could it be an achievement?

I opened the system messages first:

Warning! You have one life left!
If you lose it, you will lose everything you've achieved and return to the day when you were selected as a candidate. Your memory of your life with the interface will be erased and the interface will be uninstalled.

Warning! You've lost your hexagon!
Time left until disincarnation: one day (Pibellau time).

A countdown timer appeared at the edge of my field of vision. It was just before 1 p.m. local time.

My forehead broke out in a sweat — this wasn't just an abstract game countdown; these numbers were showing me the amount of time I had left to make sure I had the best life on Earth.

I sprang up, all set to dash off and farm resources to activate the command center, but then cursed, remembering the gold balloon.

I opened it. A message unfolded as a voice

read it out loud in my head:

> **Test subject! You've unlocked the First to Die achievement!**
> **You are the first test subject in this wave to reach your last life.**
> **Your bad luck will enter the books, and for the interest of restoring balance you will receive...**
>
> **Warning! The reward for the achievement has changed!**
> **The votes were recounted. 66% of the observers voted to award you a new ability.**
>
> **New reward: Fusion**
> **This talent allows you to generate one powerful fighting unit instead of several weak ones.**
> **Requirements: an activated command center and a level 2 fighting unit module.**
> **Put more fire under your enemies' feet, test subject!**

I spent a few minutes trying to digest the message. "Observers"? Like spectators or something? Was this some sort of galactic reality show? Or was it a tribunal that made decisions on loot and on awards for achievements? In any case, this wasn't a computer game, and it was entirely possible that the Trial moderators and judges were supplying the participants with something they really needed.

I remembered how the Kreken had dropped the power fist that looked more like a glove: an excellent weapon for a boxer, was it not? And what about Carter's spear? I wouldn't be surprised if in his other life his weapon of choice was a pool cue.

I'd deal with the talent later, if — no, when — I captured the hexagon and built a fighting unit module. I understood the idea now, so I thought I could figure out how to use it as I went along. Right now my most pressing need was to quickly farm 100 points for a new command center.

This hexagon was in the forest. At least, most of it was.

I didn't know where the extra all trees were supposed to go once the base was founded, but right now that was beside the point. I had a half hour to find a branch I was strong enough to break off and strip down. The texture of the local wood was different from terrestrial wood, and it smelled a bit like rubber.

Once I'd made sure that the gnarled club I'd procured could function as a deadly weapon in my hands, it began to shimmer. A phantom energy wave ran up and down it (and with it came the *knowledge* that it was the club's stats being recalculated).

The Gnarled, Spiked Club of Last Chance
Creator: Phil.
Level: 4–8.
Chance of stunning: +15%.

In this reality, the damage of a melee weapon was just added to the damage without a weapon. An average of 6 points damage from the club was nothing to write home about, but in my situation that was also a plus.

And with that I began to accumulate existence resources.

The mobs here really did scale — I wasn't coming across anything above level 4. Small groups of kirpi, the creature that was like a hedgehog crossed with an octopus, walked along the ground; little krekniks spat scorching poison from their hiding places behind trees unlike anything on Earth; from time to time whistlers would also crop up.

I knew I wasn't in a position to manage assembly-line farming; I'd need to lure them one or two at a time and then endure the pain each time I struck them. You get used to the pain, like you get used to the fact that the unpleasant feelings quickly subside and the wounds soon heal. There was no decent loot dropping, no resources at all besides tiny existence crystals, and one or two at a time at that. I now associated the expression "at a snail's pace" with something else besides slow Internet.

* * *

Three hours later, I was completely drained. Not so much physically — there was no fatigue here — but mentally. I felt completely discouraged. The timer counting down to disincarnation was ticking, and I'd gathered only 46 existence resource points.

I was being done in by the pursuit of one stubborn whistler. After knocking two of its friends down a level, I spent a long time kicking their buddy, dodging it every time it charged at me at full speed, aiming its spiky crest at me. This whistler was level 4, and I was counting on getting at least 4 resource points from it. Having dodged for the umpteenth time, I finally managed to club it on the back, then bashed it again and left it with only 6% life.

I silently celebrated my victory, but this bastard cut and run, taking away all the resources that rightfully belonged to me. The wounded mob was spurting orange blood, but it just kept screeching desperately, summoning its buddies, without dying. Furious, I ran after it.

I was so intent on the chase that I didn't notice when I stumbled into a nest of sarasurs, those spiky cockroaches I'd first encountered in the ravine. The forest sarasurs were much more combative than their cave cousins: they attacked all at once from all sides, biting, tearing out pieces of flesh and pricking with the thorns on their chitinous backs. My health points dropped so fast that I ended up three seconds away from my final death and permanent disincarnation.

I was saved by the fact that I had the club — I never would have been able to disperse the sarasurs with my bare hands. Panicking, I swung the club to clear a path when it broke in half. I tossed the pieces aside and ran away in humiliation, heading for the safe area closer to the white stone, the center of the hexagon.

I needed to recover and take a breather before I could resume farming with fresh strength. I couldn't stop thinking about those 4 existence resource points that the damned whistler had absconded with. With those points I'd have exactly 50, half of what I needed to activate the command center.

I was feeling bruised and demoralized as I nearly reached the stone. Around 20 yards away from it, at the edge of the forest, I crouched down and then stole through the prickly, scorching shrubbery, fearing a run-in with Carter. I didn't see anyone around me, but I figured I should keep crawling to be on the safe side.

Crack!

An electrical discharge hit the ground a foot and a half away from my head.

What the hell? Trying to figure out what it was, I peered at the charred traces of the discharge which were around the size of a fist.

"*Eh, ko si ti?* Hey, who are you?" I heard a loud girl's voice behind me. "Who are you hiding from?"

She wasn't Russian, but I understood her because whatever she was speaking sounded a lot like a Slavic language. I stood up guardedly, bracing myself for my final battle.

As I turned around, the realization dawned on me: this is it, they've come for me. This is the end of the line. Please exit the train.

A tall girl was staring at me from behind the tree. She was surrounded by ten bristly wolves that were growling quietly. Along with them was a 9-foot-tall reddish-brown bear standing on its hind legs. Its roar reverberated throughout the forest, startling the small animals.

A tank, melee fighters and, I gathered, a sorceress.

Jovanna, human
Level 2.

The girl was wearing the basic uniform set. It was functional and reliable, without a steel-plated skirt or armored bodice. She was holding a staff topped with a gray stone which crackled with electricity.

So I guess she wasn't a sorceress. She must have looted this weapon — a generator of electric discharges. It looked menacing, but I could see that it was only level 2, which meant that the damage was tolerable. It was probably no higher that of my power fist — well, my former power fist.

"Hi. I'm Phil."

She smiled. "You're Russian? I'm Jovanna. I'm Serbian."

Showing no signs of aggression, she approached me confidently and stuck her hand out. I shook it.

"You all right?" she asked with concern.

"I was killed," I answered as indifferently as I could. "I lost everything. I'm collecting resources."

"You were killed?" her eyes widened. "And you resurrected? How'd that happen?"

Without going into detail, I told her about my encounters with Carter. I warned her that he might pay her an unexpected visit because she was the second of his four closest neighbors. Me being the first, but he'd already captured my hexagon.

"Anyway, be careful with him."

Jovanna gave a quick shrug — either from the cold or in disgust, I couldn't tell. "I see..." she paused. "So you need a hexagon?"

"Desperately. You could say that I need everything."

"I also need one. According to my map, there's a canyon spanning the route to the three upper hexagons and I can't cross it. Someone's already occupying the eastern part, and I haven't had the guts to take the plunge. First I need to level up my mobs as much as I can," she caressed the bulbous head of one of the wolves, which was poking her side. "But I don't want to fight with you."

"So what do you want?"

"I don't want anything!" she stamped her foot, sniffed and changed the subject. "I played tennis in the other world. I started when I was five. I was third rate. I spent more money traveling to matches than I earned."

"And then you got the interface?"

"The what? Oh, right. I got the *hookup*. That's what I called it: the hookup with the Universal Infospace. In three months I was more successful in practices than I'd been in my whole life. The hookup somehow sped up my development. I almost made it to the top 100, but then I was summoned here. They called it the abduction."

"They?"

"Yes, the three supervisors." Jovanna lifted her head and looked up at the sky which was almost concealed by the fanned branches of the trees. She pointed her staff upward and released an electric discharge. "Missed."

"What were you aiming at?"

"There are some scary little creatures flying around up there. They're on the lookout. If you don't shoot them down, after a while a *chudovishte* shows up..."

I smiled at the familiar sound of the Slavic word — "monster", the slip-up betraying her hesitation about the hexagon and her unwillingness to fight me.

"I'm an athlete, Phil. You're not in shape and you don't have a weapon."

"And?"

"How about we do this: no matter what, I don't have enough resources to capture this hexagon. If I understand you correctly, you don't either. The first one to finish farming will activate it. How about we agree that the other person doesn't stand in their way?"

"Sure thing, Jovanna. Thank you."

"No problem. Take this. It's only fair," she held out a knife that was identical to the one I had received with the basic uniform set. "I'm sorry I don't have anything else I can share. Good luck, Phil!"

She left me and set off into the forest, preceded by the huge, bulky bear.

I wondered what I would have done if I'd been her.

* * *

Farming went much faster now that I had a knife. Twilight was setting in as I hurried toward the white stone, having collected a few more than 100 existence resource points. I got the extra points by chance: I'd had 99 points when I suddenly killed a pack of little krekniks and collected 10 points from them.

I ran as fast as I could so I'd arrive in time. If Jovanna had already claimed the hexagon — which there was no way for me to know because I hadn't gone outside its borders — then I was in deep trouble. I wouldn't have time to get to another neutral hexagon before nightfall. And the nights here were wild. I'd get swallowed up, and I wouldn't even notice.

It would be impossible to survive the night outside a shelter. You couldn't sweat out six local hours in a burrow — you'd get eaten alive by the sarasurs which were hiding in every crevice. And you couldn't wait out the night in a tree: I knew all too well that they were occupied by three-tailed, toothy squirrel-like things with stingers, and by flat, brightly colored snakes covered in slime.

The snakes camouflaged themselves by blending in with the tree bark, but when they attacked, they burst into hypnotic colors.

One of those snakes had bitten me on the shoulder. That had given me a Poison debuff that had instantly taken off 5% of my life per second. On top of that the pain was agonizing. My shoulder had swelled, turned black and become so inflamed that in despair I'd tried to cut the lump off with a knife. I had to cut some healthy flesh off with it, just to be on the safe side. After half an hour, I'd healed and my health had been restored. The ghastly looking wound had closed before my eyes as new muscles and blood vessels materialized, covered with new skin.

Just as I could finally make out the command center activation stone, I dropped to the ground and lay still. Luckily, I'd noticed the behemoth creature with its disproportionately long and large pincers before it saw me.

The monster was standing firmly on eight powerful pillar-like legs. It was about the size of a two-story building, its body protected by anthracite-colored plated armor that gleamed in the darkness.

It hadn't yet caught sight of me. It was standing with its back to me banging on a three-yard-wide tree trunk. Snakes and the squirrel-like things were raining down from the branches. The unlucky ones were adeptly seized in flight by the creature's gargantuan pincers and thrown into its mouth, while the others scurried in all directions.

Canavar
Location boss.
Level 8.
Life points: 4000.

Even if I were properly clothed, I wouldn't be able to handle this one. I'd have to go around it.

Keeping my distance, I moved in an arc, trying to keep the white stone in view. The Canavar continued its dirty work, waging genocide on the snakes and squirrels. I mustered up some courage, stood up straight and dashed past so I'd have time to get hold of a new house before darkness set in.

My race was short lived. Darkness was

---

setting in, and instead of looking under my feet I kept my eyes on the Canavar and the white stone. So I was going at full speed when I fell into a pit that had been concealed by dried branches. I flew headlong about five yards and got stuck between the narrowing steep walls of an opening.

The knife, which I'd dropped when I fell, flew down to the bottom of the pit.

My chest was being compressed and for the life of me I couldn't extricate myself. I choked up, my ribs cracking. Blood rushed to my head; my vision dimmed.

The timer dispassionately counted down the time remaining to disincarnation.

The darkness thickened. I was stuck. There was no way around it. The panic that had started somewhere in my stomach gradually built up, morphing into a persistent fear. The thought of the observers watching me go through all of this made me feel furious and ashamed of how ingloriously I was ending my journey. There were a few local hours left before permanent disincarnation.

Blood poured down my face, then I passed out.

* * *

A searing pain roused me. It felt like hundreds of white-hot needles were pricking my body from my heels to my stomach. I had no idea why I was in so much pain — I hadn't received any system notifications about any damage. The logs kept refreshing at lightning speed, notifying me about

---

continuous damage dealt by the vampire leeches that had latched on to me. My imagination — or rather, my newfound *knowledge* — showed me tiny little critters no larger than a coin that were entering my body through my pores, eating away at my flesh and softening it with an acidic secretion so they could swallow and absorb it.

In mere minutes, my health was already in the orange zone — there was less than 20% left. I wriggled my body, thinking that if I couldn't escape maybe I could at least smear the sticky bastards over the wall of the sinkhole, but to no avail.

I unconsciously recalled the best moments of my life: my early dates with Vicky, my leveling successes, my new friends Alik, Cyril, Veronica, Marina and Kostya, my business, our plans, my boxing victories...

Then I was shaken out of my reverie by heavy footsteps that made the ground shake. The stomping was so strong it made my ears rang.

When my health got to 14%, the counter froze as a deep bellow reverberated somewhere above me. The damage stopped; the leeches scattered as someone big had arrived on the scene.

Sniffing the air, this someone reached a limb in toward me. The earth crumbled from above, hitting me on the face and showering me with dry branches. I needed to hold my breath so I could then exhale sharply and keep breathing.

An unrelated thought occurred to me: how was it that I was breathing here? After all, existence resources took care of the biological processes, didn't they? Or was there just no way not to breathe?

I heard and felt the scorching noisy breathing of an annoyed monster that was patiently trying to reach me. Its limbs were too large for the crevice. It roared its disappointment, temporarily deafening me.

According to the logs, it was the Canavar, the location boss. Apparently, the squirrels and snakes had not sated its hunger.

Having worked itself into a huff, the boss began to bang on the edges of the pit, stirring up a new round of debris. Now there were also rocks falling from above, hitting me painfully on the soles of my feet, my legs and everything in between. The steep walls of the pit trembled, making my whole body vibrate, and I also started to move, sinking lower with each blow.

Lower down, the space between the walls started to expand. I helped myself slide down. When the walls stopped supporting me, I just let myself drop.

I managed to tuck my body and cushion my fall with my partially bent arms. I didn't escape damage — my health was now below 10% — but at least I was alive.

The first thing I did was to feel around for the knife that I'd dropped when I fell. I gripped it blade downwards so as to be ready to attack any inhabitants of the pit.

The night was counting off the last hour. Thanks to my high Perception, I could see in the complete darkness of the pit. Above my head, the Canavar was growing furious, but from where he

---

was he couldn't reach me. I could deal with the vampire leeches now — just let them try to mess with me.

Prepared to sell my life dearly, I looked around but didn't see any enemies. There was only me and the bottom of the pit, which measured around 10 square yards.

Holy shit! I would never get out of here!

As cliché as it was, I was behaving exactly like a tiger in a cage. As I paced the bottom of the crevice, my health slowly but surely restored. Just think that I had the 100 resources to capture the hexagon, I'd survived the leeches' onslaught, avoided the jaws of the Canavar, that excavator bucket, and outdone Jovanna in collecting resources — but I had nowhere to go from here.

Apparently deciding to deal the final blow to my morale, the system displayed a burning crimson notification in front of me:

Warning! Time remaining to permanent disincarnation: 1 hour.

Thank you for letting me live until now. An hour was a long time. I remembered my early jogging days when I'd first got the interface, when even five minutes of running felt like an eternity. But here, it was a whole hour, or more if you counted in Pibellau time.

The noise above me had stopped. The Canavar must have left to look for an easier victim. I examined the surface of the walls inch by inch, searching for something to grasp on to. I groped around, trying to pierce the knife into something, but all I did was dull its blade.

I didn't know what I was expecting, but I wasn't about to just sit down and wait for the end.

Forty minutes before disincarnation, I glimpsed a shimmering veil in one of the distant corners of the pit. I looked over but didn't see anything. I stepped back, and there it was again. I blinked, but the shimmering didn't go away. Fixing my eyes on it, I went closer and reached out.

Before I knew it, I was being sucked into a portal, just like in the preliminary selection.

I found myself in a bright, well-lit tunnel that looked like the one I'd already completed. The scaly surface was a bit darker than in the other one, but here it seemed more spacious: the corridor was wider and the ceilings were higher.

A red balloon appeared in front of me. I focused on it and it popped, forming Russian letters:

Test subject! You've discovered and entered a lost location in the wormhole: an instance. An extinct civilization of sentient beings that lived on Pibellau used instances as test sites for training and testing soldiers.

The only way for you to escape the instance is to defeat all your adversaries.

Warning! This location is the first to be discovered by a test subject! The probability of finding a lost artifact is doubled.

Pass a level 2 instance solo? I felt my lips

stretch into a smile. I began to understand how Carter had reached level 6 so fast: he'd probably also discovered a piping hot instance in which time stood still. If that old guitar player could do it, so could I — after all, I'd dedicated half my life to WoW.

I pulled myself together and set off to complete the dungeon. Getting through it successfully was my only chance at holding on to everything I'd achieved.

I wondered what was happening on Earth right now. Did anyone miss me?

I carefully picked my way through the tunnel, staying on my guard, but I didn't come across any traps or aggressive mobs. Thinking about the lost artifacts, I scrutinized every suspicious bump, but I didn't find anything.

After about 100 yards, as I was wondering in bewilderment where all the "adversaries" I was supposed to defeat were, I turned a corner and bumped up against some decidedly nonhumanoid beings that were hovering in the air.

They were semitransparent, but they were definitely real. When they caught sight of me, they gave a little rustle, then soared toward me.

It was too late to run. I got into fighting stance.

Let's do it pronto!

* * *

"Pronto" didn't happen. The local mobs — one-and-a-half-foot creatures with an energy armor that

132

called to mind jellyfish hovering in the air — traveled in groups of five or six. Each pack generally had an officer that directed the squadron by rustling and fluttering its tentacles.

When I saw the first pack, I instantly *knew* that this sentient species had been the second to dominate the planet before it was annihilated by competitors for the living space. Similar test sites had been created by the victors during a centuries-long war to train young fighters. The victors and the losers were gone now, but the instances still functioned. Except that they were filled with full-fledged combat units. It would be a challenge for me in my torn jeans and with nothing but my dull little knife.

These jellyfish-like things were armed with an oddly shaped kinetic weapon which looked like a cube with openings. When they placed their tentacles in some of the openings, projectiles flew out of the opposite side. Whether the caliber was just so-so, or the Trial system had recalculated the damage, but the only threat from the jellyfish was the combined barrage. It would be impossible to escape something like this, so I just covered my eyes to make sure that after the attack, once I'd overcome the pain from the impact, I could make a run for my enemies and make mincemeat out of them. Of course, before I could reach their brittle flesh, I'd need to get their energy shields down — but that took only a couple of stabs of the knife.

After each pack, I had to take a pause to recover. It would be idiotic to take the risk and attack the next pack of mobs without a full health bar.

I was surprised to see that after I'd fought off these mobs, I'd earned existence resources but didn't find any artifacts or get any loot. Even their cubic rifles — I don't know what else to call them — didn't drop, and all my attempts to grab them before the corpses disincarnated were in vain: my hand just passed right through them.

But after about three dozen of these packs, I'd farmed more than 1000 existence resources. Upon some brief reflection, I bought myself two levels. I did so as I accumulated resources, not both at once. I'd spent 602 points on them. They were supposed to have cost 700, but I had that 14% development speed bonus, so I got away with using fewer points.

I invested the 4 characteristic points I'd gotten for leveling up into Charisma and Stamina. Considering that this was my last life, it was vital that I boost my health, and I would have invested all my points in that, but the victory over the jellyfish had given me some confidence. After my string of failures, I started thinking strategically, as if it were a done deal that I'd capture the hexagon and keep going in the Trial.

Now my profile looked like this:

Phil, human.
Level 4.

Main characteristics
Strength — 21.
Agility — 11.

Intellect — 20.
Stamina — 20.
Perception — 21.
Charisma — 20.
Luck — 15.

Character stats
Lives: 1.
Captured hexagons: 0.
Ranking: 169/169.
Existence resources: 659/4000.

The ranking told me that I was again in last place and that all the trial subjects were still in the game.

Composed and focused, I found myself standing in front of the chamber with the last boss. I *knew* what it was: the only one for the whole location, and once I'd finished it off, I'd have gotten through the instance.

Deniza'Nasi
Location boss.
Level 7.
Life points: 2900.

The boss was in the chamber in all its proud solitude, busy with a task that was undoubtedly important: it was suspended in the air, swinging and flapping its long tentacles, waving them around as if caught in a breeze.

Since it couldn't see me, I had time to come up with a plan. If it were like the other jellyfish, just much bigger, there shouldn't be any particular problems. It probably had some special talents, but if I wanted to find out what they were, I had to test them out. The only option was reconnaissance by fire.

I stepped into the chamber. The Deniza'Nasi ignored me. I crept closer to it before it became clear that it didn't give a damn about me. So I quickened my step and as I ran, I plunged the knife into it.

The boss reared its tentacles, snapped its membrane at me with a supersonic squeal and flew away.

Blood gushed from my ears. One-quarter of my life was gone, and I'd taken all of 10% of its energy shield.

Without waiting for the next squeal, I dashed at it, hammering it with my left fist and the knife in my right hand. I didn't give it a chance to put any distance between us: just three more supersonic shrieks would be the end of me.

By its third squeal, I removed its shield and was yanking off its health points with abandon. The chase in which we tried to destroy each other ended with us reaching the finish line at the same time. I stripped it of its last percent of life just as the monster raised its tentacles again, about to break into another deadly squeal.

The hellish shriek ended almost right when it began. Blood gushed from my whole body: it spilled from my pores and from my burst blood vessels, but even as it spewed from my eyes, I threw my arms up and victoriously screamed something life-affirming and obscene.

I dropped to the ground and lay there for so long that even my health had a chance to restore. The drying blood covered my whole body in a shell, but as soon as I stood up, its crust broke off, disintegrating into dust.

A huge existence crystal and something giving off a dull, silvery shine lay in the spot where the boss had disappeared. Loot!

I pulverized the crystal. My chance to get a double amount of trophy kicked in, rewarding me with 500 existence resource points.

Next, I picked up the silvery item. It was a ring. Its description wasn't exactly exhaustive, but the gist of it exceeded all my expectations.

Leadership Ring of Reinforcement
+3 to your fighting units' levels.

I slipped the ring onto my finger and studied it for a while. I didn't recognize the dull, purplish metal.

For the next few hours I proceeded calmly and unhurriedly. I had nowhere to hurry: the timer counting down to disincarnation had stopped at 39 minutes. I investigated all the nooks of the instance, hoping to find a little secret or an unnoticed artifact, but had no success. Either I didn't have enough Perception or the "game developers" from the Senior Races didn't spoil the Trial subjects with abundant loot.

I was then struck by the *understanding* that all the unconventional gear was unique here, and that's why it cropped up infrequently.

After I'd finished, I approached the portal that had appeared in the boss' chamber after its death, and entered it.

In the blink of an eye I was carried out of the instance.

To my delight, the exit wasn't in a crevice. While I'd been stuck in it, dawn had already broken. The rays of both Pibellau's suns blinded my eyes. I waited for my eyesight to adjust before I realized where I was.

Yes! I was next to the white stone of the same neutral hexagon where I'd met Jovanna. The disincarnation timer had now restarted, but I didn't care.

I placed my palm in the indentation in the stone and activated the command center.

The three circular waves of energy announced the capture of the hexagon, outlined the outer six-sided perimeter of the base and erected a dome over the shelter.

Another red balloon from the system cheerfully notified me that my disincarnation had been canceled.

I felt like a rock the size of Mount Everest had dropped from me.

Wasting no time, I generated the basic uniform module and the fighting unit module. That cost me 70 existence resource points.

Next, I upgraded both modules. That cost me ten times as much, but I remembered how effective Carter's upgraded mobs were and decided it was worth it.

So that was 700 gone, leaving me with 359

existence resource points.

The upgrade took more than an hour. I used the time to thoroughly study the Fusion potential — the talent I'd received for my last achievement. I played around with it on the creatures from the catalog, but I didn't yet understand what was different. How was I supposed to generate one awesome Raptor instead of 20 weak ones?

Still in the dark, I went over to the improved uniform module. It had been the first to level up, and I immediately activated the clothing generation. Now the wardrobe had two doors, and it was four times the size of the last one. Was it so there'd be room for the cannonry? I wouldn't mind having a minigun.

I opened one of the doors, picked my jaw up off the ground, undressed and climbed inside. I turned on the water and washed under the streams of warm, soothing liquid, scrubbing off the dirt and sweat.

As much as I wanted to bask in the shower, I didn't waste more than five minutes there — just enough time to sing a couple of songs. I turned the water off with a mental command, and a dryer automatically started running — it was a fan blowing from every direction.

A second door concealed a complete set of the improved gear. Its components were the same as in the basic one, but it looked more impressive and reliable.

Improved test subject uniform
Protection: +30.

Durability: 100%

The set included a good dagger with double the damage of the basic knife, and a metal club. I equipped everything.

The uniform was close fitting; nothing was loose but it didn't hinder movement, either. Perfect.

I was in a good mood when I returned to the command center to figure out Fusion once and for all. The upgrade of the fighting unit module was also complete: I could see that the Raptors' stats had nearly doubled compared to level 1.

I opened the interactive catalog and paged through it. My eye caught on a category called *Special Species*, which wasn't there before. I guess I could now access it because of my new talent. That was it: the talent required a level 2 module.

These mobs I was now looking at really were special — they were worth between 5 and 100 basic units. In other words, for 5 Charisma points, I could get any of these instead of a pack of weak mobs — but for each additional point I could strengthen the mob even more. Also, every additional point increased all the other stats: from body weight and armor level to damage and travel speed, and every 10 points would give me an additional talent.

In my case, the choice was clear. I tapped the mob I wanted and placed all 20 of the available units in it. It cost me 200 points to generate my megaunit, and it took a half hour. I decided to wait so I could go out and farm and capture new hexagons at the same time.

While I waited, I studied the administrative

interface of my new base. It was wildly expensive to upgrade the modules to the next level — I woudn't be collecting that much anytime soon. There were no other modules; apparently I needed to upgrade the level of the whole base, but that required level 5, and I hadn't gotten that far yet.

Anyway, I was nearly out of resources. I was down to 150, just enough to capture a new neutral hexagon.

Test subject! An enemy has infiltrated your territory! Base 1 is under threat of capture!

Inside the shelter (or maybe it was in my head), an alarm sounded. There were red flashes in the corners of my eyes; an icy wave shot through my body as I smelled something burning. That was the system telling me through every means possible that my hexagon was under attack.

It couldn't be Carter since his invisibility talent allowed him to encroach on my hexagon without attracting attention. So who was it? Jovanna?

I leaped outside and looked around warily. The alarm directed me toward a break in the perimeter. I followed the signal and stopped next to the fence.

I stood there and peered at the part that wasn't obscured by the fog of war.

A massive crowd soon appeared in view. It was in fact Jovanna with her pack of wolves and bears, but she wasn't alone.

Waddling behind her was Carter, surrounded

by his bloodsuckers. There were now eight of them: six small ones with metal clubs and two archers with human-sized bows. I could see Carter's lips moving but I couldn't hear what he was saying.

His archers froze in place, drew back their bowstrings, and released a flight of arrows which pierced the floor of the base in a semicircle half a yard away from me.

Carter waved his hand in greeting.

I retreated a little closer to the shelter. Jovanna's bear ran through the gap in my fence. The others followed it.

Carter chuckled. "Fancy meeting you here, Phil. I brought someone with me today."

"Phil," Jovanna said with a nod.

I glared at them. Apparently, the moment of truth had arrived. There was nowhere for me to run, and anyhow, it would have been a shame to throw everything away — I'd invested too many resources into this base. Hiding in the shelter was out of the question since it wouldn't protect me against the infiltration of other test subjects.

My only hope was that my super unit would have time to generate before I got killed.

"What do you want, Carter?"

"I've come to make you the same offer as before. As you can see, Jovanna's joined me and she doesn't regret it. Right, hon?"

She nodded sullenly. I looked her in the eye, but she averted her gaze.

"You've made a slave out of a weak girl and you think that's something to brag about?"

Carter smirked. "Not just that. Check out my

mobs! There are twice as many and they're a higher level! They're level 3 now. I invested in them. I learned from my fight with you that it's also important to level them up. They're real beauties, aren't they?"

"They're ugly as hell."

"Haha! And where are your little lizards? I don't see them... Ah!" he laughed again, his cheeks jiggling. "You have no crap left besides this worthless base?" he clicked his tongue sympathetically. "Is it hard to farm resources with nothing but a little knife? But seeing as you have clothes on now, I guess you managed to farm something there? Oho, and you must have picked up a few levels!"

"Does that bother you?"

"Oh, Phil boy, what do I care about your level 4? I'm amazed at your spite," Carter spread his arms wide, making a show of looking upset. "Is it my fault that we're being pitted against each other?"

"Are *they*" — I gestured upward with my eyes — "the ones who made you force Jovanna to lose all hope of keeping her *connection*?"

"There was no forcing! She made the decision all by herself. *Johanna,*" he pronounced her name wrong, "is too weak. Can't you tell? So I actually saved her. If it hadn't been for me, she would have lost everything."

"Phil, it was my choice," Jovanna confirmed, but her eyes said otherwise.

Carter squinted, looking me up and down. "Your uniform is leveled up!" he exclaimed in surprise. "When did you get a chance to do that?"

"Yesterday, obviously. I found a nest of fat little Carters, let out a big fat pile of crap on it and got an achievement. Guess what it's called."

Jovanna smiled.

Carter smirked maliciously. "That's a dumb joke. Is that the sense of humor you people have in Russia? No big deal, in a few minutes everything here will belong to me. Accept my offer or drop dead; everything here will be mine."

He was sending me an invitation into the clan.

Three seconds.

I pretended I was studying the conditions for joining Carter's clan.

Two seconds.

"Jovanna, everything will be OK," I said, turning to her.

One second.

I shook my head. "No, Carter. You and your offer can go to hell."

He shrugged. "Whatever. No matter what, I —
"

Boo-oo-oom!

The ground shook as if a 100-yard-wide meteor had fallen from the sky. Carter and Jovanna were looking over my shoulder in bewilderment.

A long bellow sounded from behind me, bursting our eardrums and making us freeze.

A single frame with the long-awaited icon of my new fighting unit appeared in my interface.

Tyrannosaurus Rex
Level 5 melee fighter

Phil's fighting unit.
Health points: 4500/4500.
Attack: 1500–3000.
Damage absorbed by armor: 50%.
Maximum travel speed: 45 mph
Weight: 10 tons
Talents: Furious Roar, Shred 'em!, Squash
'em!

Now let's do some fighting.

CHAPTER EIGHT

THE CLASS REUNION

Penny: I didn't know you played the cello.
Leonard: Yeah, my parents felt that naming me Leonard and putting me in advanced placement classes wasn't getting me beaten up enough.

The Big Bang Theory

"NOW LET'S DO SOME FIGHTING!" I ANNOUNCED, THEN promptly woke up.

I woke up because my face was itching terribly. Not just my face — my entire body was itching. Even, er, down there the itch was so overwhelming that I hurried to brush the sheet off and pulled out the elastic of my shorts to make sure everything was as it should be and that there wasn't any suspicious redness.

Everything was fine. It even seemed like everything was a little more fine than before.

Scratching the back of my neck in confusion, I sat up in bed and cringed at the sharp aches and pains in my bones. My joints and ligaments also groaned in pain. What was going on?

Odd. For all I knew, it could have been some sort of medical condition.

Then finally my initial panicked thoughts gave way to understanding. Before going to sleep I'd upped Charisma, hadn't I?

On my mental command, the notification icon blinking in the information dashboard expanded into a message:

Increase in attractiveness according to societal standards of the local segment of the Galaxy complete!

Your height has increased by 0.8" (target height of 6'2" not achieved).

Your hair has been pigmented (target pigment achieved).

Your skin has accumulated enough melanin (target tan hue achieved).

Your hairline has been corrected (hair structure optimized, target eyelash length and eyebrow shape achieved).

Target parameters for eye, nose, cheekbone, cheek, lip, jaw, chin, forehead and ears have been achieved.

Missing teeth reconstructed: 2.

Damaged teeth reconstructed: 19.

Tooth shape and position have been corrected.

Skin has been smoothed and corrected.

Your eye color has been changed to dark blue.

The portrait of all the changes was long. With

each line I read, my new dark-blue eyes that had replaced my brown ones widened even more.

I put a finger in my mouth and felt around for the new teeth where I was used to having gaps. One of them had been pulled by a boozy dentist in my student days — he'd had a short preholiday the day before International Women's Day, and I was in so much agony from the intolerable nagging pain in my head that I agreed to let him pull it. I'd lost the second tooth foolishly when I'd been on a WoW binge and had put off getting a filling for over a year. When I finally dragged myself to the dentist, there was no longer any point in fixing the tooth and the only solution was to extract it.

Before I got to the end of the list, I abandoned it and hurried into the bathroom. I stood in front of a large mirror and scrutinized myself.

It did in fact seem to be me. It was clear that it wasn't anyone other than me, but there were imperceptible changes: my skin was darker and the tan was pure, like from a magazine cover; my chin was a little more solid and confident; my smile...

I grinned at myself in the mirror and was amazed at what I saw. The open smile with the perfectly even, strong, snow-white teeth seemed not to belong to me.

The best part was that it *was* me.

The skin on my face was perfectly smoothed, as if it had been professionally Photoshopped. My eyes were brighter and more piercing. My hair was darker.

On the whole, a brown-eyed, brown-haired man had been replaced by a blue-eyed brunet. I liked what I saw.

Damn, was I for real? What is a man supposed to be? Hairy and smelly, just slightly more attractive than monkeys. Since when had I been concerned about my looks?

Hm, I think you could say that I was always concerned about my looks: even from when I was a kid, when the girls I liked ignored my intelligence and swooned over Pasha Pashkovsky because he was cute and Andrei Belyaev because he was strong. But when I got older and understood that you can't change your looks and need to work with what you have, I got used to being happy with what God and the genetic lottery had given me.

So I liked what I saw in the mirror now. One little Charisma point and one big step for Phil Panfilov.

How would my newly acquired height affect my clothes? I hoped that my legs hadn't grown. Or had everything else expanded in proportion to my height? Based on what I'd seen of myself in my shorts, size really did matter — had I been brought in line with the "societal standards of the local segment of the Galaxy"?

How would I explain all of this to my parents? Contact lenses and a tanning salon, dentist, cosmetologist and hairdresser could explain the changes in my looks, but how would I explain my height? I suppose I could chalk it up to working out if my parents and Kira happened to get suspicious.

In a daze, I went into the hallway to try my shoes on. My thoughts were a mess of confusion and hesitation. On the way I turned into the kitchen, forgetting that I was heading to get my sneakers. I turned on the kettle to make coffee and started to gather my stuff to go running.

It wasn't until after that, when I'd pulled my running clothes out of the dryer, that I realized that it wasn't Sunday morning but the evening, and that I needed to go to my class reunion. The clock on the interface showed that it was 9 p.m., but the gathering was called for 7.

I was late.

What the hell? How did that happen? My rational self told me that it was no big deal, and that before everyone got there, there'd be a little of this and that, some people would already be drunk and loosened up, and in any case there'd be some initial restraint after so many years away from each other.

My thoughts raced while my body acted. I showered, put on my new threads, squirted on some aftershave (+5 to Charisma) and gave my shoes a quick polish. With my watch on my wrist, my wallet in my back pocket and my phone in my jacket, I called a cab. Ready?

Oops, sorry, Boris, old girl. I filled her food dish to the brim and poured water into her water dish.

I took a good look at myself in the mirror by the door. I was ready to meet my classmates.

* * *

The taxi that rolled up looked like a rusty washtub. I was horrified when I saw it, but this was no time to be picky — I was late. I dove in.

The upholstery smelled of rancid tobacco and the window handles were broken off, but I just went along for the ride, holding my breath. I was tense, but the driver couldn't have cared less — he was used to it and no longer noticed.

Thanks to my high Perception, I could detect all the finer details of the odors. The mat on the left smelled of vomit and the mat on the right reeked of beer. The body behind the wheel, too, added its two cents to the general ambience: with due respect, this particular cabbie didn't seem to have made it to the shower in quite a while.

On the plus side, he didn't try to strike up a conversation. Well, he was having a conversation of sorts, railing against some guy called Mikhalich who was "getting out of line". But at least he was talking on the phone, not to me.

As if all of this wasn't enough, my new sneakers were tight. I'd deal with it, but of course I wouldn't be able to keep them. I'd need to exchange them for the next size up. I guess I could put up with them just for the evening. It seemed like all the other clothes fit normally, except for the shirt which I had to keep untucked: the changes had made me almost an inch taller.

I wondered what I was expecting from this reunion. I certainly wasn't going to take part in the vanity fair; I had nothing to boast about. Paulina? Well... Maybe. I was a free agent, after all. Anyway, seeing my childhood friends — my classmates — was something to celebrate. Half our active lives had passed. Just add on the same amount, and then we'd be old. What if I never saw some of them again?

That was a strange thought. I'd managed to live the past 15 years without suffering from or lamenting that I hadn't seen these guys in ages. But as soon as the opportunity arose, I instantly decided to get together with them, as if I had no problems with extraterrestrials or the son of the first deputy mayor.

On the other hand, what could I do now? My replica was taking the rap for me in the Trial, and maybe nothing would come of the incident with Dorozhkin.

When I got to Chito Gvrito, there was already a crowd by the entrance. They showed unexpected curiosity when they saw the car that drove up. I paid the driver, shrugged when he lamented that he didn't have any change, and quickly jumped out of the mobile gas chamber, enduring the stares of the smokers clumped outside.

There were at least twenty people. Were those my classmates? Yep.

"Hey, it's Little Philip!" boomed a voice I remembered from my school days. "He still has his personal chauffeur! Haha!"

"That's right! Zoophil has arrived!"

Damn, another nickname surfaced. There was no hidden meaning; they called me that because I loved animals.

I went over to them. I didn't recognize half of them. Either my memory was betraying me, or they'd changed a lot.

In any case, the interface came to the rescue. I mechanically took the readings: health, marital and employment status, children, social status levels. No one had a social status level higher than 9, but almost all of them had kids. A lot of them were divorced, but Paulina was married. She had two kids. Too bad.

"Hey," ignoring the banter, I went over to them.

"Andrei, Pasha, Max, Tanya, Yanna, Lena, Paulina..."

"Hey! It's been forever!" Pasha grabbed me and tried to squeeze me hard until my bones crushed, like he used to do when we'd been kids, but I didn't give in. "Dude, you've gotten strong!"

"You really have changed a lot since we graduated," said the redheaded Lena Yezhova whom I'd recognized immediately without the system's help even though I hadn't seen her once in 15 years. "If I ran into you on the street, I'd walk right past you without recognizing you!"

"On what street? Where you live in Boston?" guffawed Andrei Belyaev — the very same Andrei who owned the restaurant. "I doubt Phil ever goes there."

"True, I've got a long way to go," I smiled. "Almost everyone's here already, as I can see?"

"It's not just us — only the smokers came outside," said Paulina. "There are just as many people inside. There are also people from the other class here. Should we go in? How much can we smoke?"

"Yeah, really," said Yanna Logvin in agreement. The two of them had always been friends and it looked like they'd gotten even closer over twenty-five years. "Let's go!"

"Phil, into the penalty area!" Squeezing my neck, Andrei pulled me into the restaurant's little courtyard.

"Just juice for me."

"How come?" Andrei asked in surprise. "What's up? We haven't seen each other in ages!"

"That's why, Andrei. Because I want to look at everyone sober and be able to remember them later. Especially the people who don't live here. What if I don't see anyone ever again? Why don't you tell me about your restaurant? Why is it called Chito Gvrito?"

"Oh, man, it's a long story…"

As we made the short trip to the table, Andrei told me about his love for Georgia. He was breathing hard. Smoking, alcohol and his triple chin — he and his health weren't best friends. But for the time being, his stamina was OK, so it was too early to sound the alarm.

We stepped out onto a separate summer veranda. Andrei left me to go take his place at the head of the table. The tables were placed together and covered in snow-white tablecloths topped with a selection from the arsenal of the finest Georgian cuisine and alcohol. I saw sweating bottles of vodka and carafes of house wine.

I walked around the table, saying my hellos and choosing a place to sit. Someone hugged me from behind.

"Panfilov, where are you going? Stay here," Paulina said, pulling me down next to her. "Oh, you smell amazing," she came closer to me and breathed in deeply. "Awesome! What's it called?"

"Killian or something."

"It's fierce," she said in delight. "Hey, Phil, you owe 5,000. I forgot to tell you that we're chipping in for Andrei. He gave us a good discount."

"Of course, no problem," I took out my wallet and gave her a bill.

I caught Paulina sneaking a look at my wallet, noting suspiciously that there wasn't much left in it — a 1,000-ruble note and a few hundreds — and that the material was worn out.

"You were late," she sounded a bit insulted. "We

prepared a whole opening ceremony and you missed the entire thing!"

"I'm sorry, I couldn't get here earlier. What did I miss?"

The crowd around us was chattering loudly. While Paulina told me about the "opening ceremony" — I hadn't missed anything important, just everyone getting up and talking a little about themselves — I looked around at the restaurant. In addition to our party, there were other guests at separate tables enjoying a night out, waiters scurrying about between them. There was also a small dance floor where women of a certain age were gliding around.

On the whole, it was a pretty grown-up crowd, except for five or six young riffraff types having a grand old time at one of the tables. "Happy b'day, Gorilla!" they sang out.

"What would you like to drink?" a waiter behind me asked. "I have red and white wine, whiskey, vodka and cognac."

"Water, please."

"Panfilov!" Kostya Klosse, who was sitting across from me, was indignant.

"What?"

"Why aren't you drinking?"

"I don't feel like it."

"He doesn't want to drink and isn't drinking, what do you care?" snarled Sergei Rezvei. "Kostya, you ought to slow down, you're getting kind of drunk."

I nodded gratefully to Rezvei. He answered with a smile and a wink. Seeing as he hadn't touched his glass of wine, I guessed that he wasn't drinking either.

"Panfilov! We need you drunk today!" Paulina

sided with Kostya. "Get this man some whiskey!"

The waiter was flustered.

"That's fine, bring it, please," I rescued him from his confusion.

I wouldn't drink; I'd just take a little sip. That would be easier than having to keep explaining why I didn't want to drink.

My appearance didn't stir up any reaction at all. The only person I was good friends with was Pashkovsky, and he was sitting at the other end of the table, while Paulina was always nice to everyone and she was in a good mood with everybody. Still, our school "romance" that had never happened also seemed to be intriguing her and affecting her mood.

So everything was like it had always been: the old cliques from our school days reformed. Strangely, I felt like the same person I always had been. For instance, just as I hadn't been interested in Ilya Kravchenko then, I couldn't care less that he was here now.

"Hey, guys," Andrei was trying to get everyone's attention. "Listen up a minute! We have a latecomer: Phil Panfilov, who we also know as Little Philip!"

Andrei was putting on a show relishing the nickname that had been invented for me. I didn't care for that.

"Panfilov, you have to speak," Paulina whispered. "You missed the beginning, so you need to tell us about yourself."

"Was he really in our class?" muttered Stas Rynyak, eliciting a laugh from everyone. According to the interface, Stas was now a level 7 "environmentalist," but I remembered him well: he was the first in our class to take up smoking.

I stood up, feeling indifference and hardly an inkling of curiosity. Who was really interested in some guy named Panfilov who was about to interrupt their socializing just so he could talk about himself?

"I was, Rynyak," I answered loudly. "Remember when the woodwork teacher pulled your ears when you burned a swear word in his desk with a lighter? No? Well, I do!"

Everyone laughed again. I heard someone say, "We remember!" The conversations around the table stopped.

"In any case, if by chance someone, like Stas, doesn't remember, my name is Philip Panfilov. I was in class B starting from first grade. I sat in the third row at the last desk with that guy over there who'd just come from Africa," I nodded at Pasha Pashkovsky. "What should I tell you about myself? I graduated from our university with a degree in economics and worked here and there. I was married and I got divorced. I don't have any kids."

"Now you're talking!" shouted the pudgy Tanya Vasilenko, twice divorced and with four sons. "Girls, let's make a note: Panfilov is available!" she trilled with laughter.

"What are you doing now?" asked Cyril, one of the Verzakov twins.

"I work at a recruiting firm. Any other questions?"

There were none. Everyone understood that Panfilov hadn't made it.

"In that case, I'd like to propose a toast..."

Just juggle some writerly thoughts into words,

sprinkle in some Charisma, Charm and Social Skills, and presto, you've got your toast: something animated and dressed up in fond nostalgia, taking joy in the fact that we're still young and still have everything ahead of us, and in how wonderful we are — we don't forget each other and we all cherish the time we spent together in school.

"...so let's drink to that," I concluded and lifted my glass.

"Hear, hear! Let's drink to that!" my classmates echoed.

A lot of them stood up so they could reach out and clink glasses with me. I received a few notifications about minor improvements in Reputation but I didn't read them. It wasn't important.

When everyone had calmed down, I realized I was so hungry that I felt weak. My stomach ached. So I spent the next half hour preoccupied with chewing, evading my neighbors' questions with grunts and nods. I chowed down on the ridiculously delicious *khinkali* dumplings dripping with meat gravy; it seemed that while I was sleeping, the system had depleted my energy reserves and stored fat to level up Charisma. The Mingrelian *khachapuri*[6] with young Imeretian cheese was also magnificent here.

During this time everyone was talking about our teachers: who was still alive, who had died, and who was still teaching. Denis Pugach was talking about how he'd sent his kids to the same school, and one of the two siblings had an excellent teacher — our very own Ms. Dmitrieva. Lots of people got excited when they

---

[6] Khachapuri: Georgian cheese pie

heard this and for a while Denis had everyone's attention, even the people from the other class.

When I had finally eaten enough, I leaned back in my chair and looked around at our table and the one next to us. The one that had been occupied by the lowlifes now had some more people as some extra guests had joined Gorilla's birthday party. The guys were giving their jaws a workout on a mountain of big pieces of juicy shashlik[7].

When everyone left the table to go to the little plaza in front of the restaurant — not so much to smoke as to have a chance to talk to people who were sitting far away, — Pasha moved closer to me. After a while, he simply switched seats with Kostya. I chatted mostly with him and Sergei Rezvei, only stopping the conversation to propose more toasts[8].

Pashkovsky told us about his life in South Africa and how things had turned out for him there. The always modest and malleable Rezvei told us that he headed a media agency in St. Petersburg, which shocked Pasha and me because Sergei wasn't the type to do that sort of thing. But he was an outstanding person, and that's why we were friends, first when we were children, and later when Gleb joined us in the first year of university, before Rezvei moved to Petersburg.

---

[7] Shashlik: Georgian shish kebab (skewered marinated meat), the most popular Georgian dish in Russia
[8] Toasting is a major tradition both in Russia and in Georgia where you can't have a drink without proposing a toast first. Refined, poetic and articulate, Georgian toasts have long developed into a true art form.

"I married an amazing girl. Her name's Margarita, and we have a son, Misha. So there you go, I just tour around," Rezvei smiled. "We planned a special trip here so I could come to the reunion. Your turn, Phil. Tell us about yourself."

As I talked, our classmates, who were already basically tipsy, had a chance to get hammered.

"Who needs a refill?" Andrei asked at the top of his lungs. "Whoever's not drinking needs to drink now! But first they need to give a toast!"

"And sing a song!" Paulina insisted. "About love!"

She was a good MC. And the contests were interesting.

* * *

"Let's dance," Paulina stood up, caught her leg on something and nearly tripped, grabbing onto me at the last moment. "Oh, Panfilov," she laughed woozily. "Don't harass me! There are too many..." she wagged her finger in the air, trying to remember the word, "witnesses! Let's dance! Andrei?" she turned to Belyaev.

"We're setting it up now," Belyaev conspiratorially whispered something in Paulina's ear. "Hey, Butus! Come here!"

The DJ, a young man wearing a baseball cap back to front, came over to where we were sitting.

"Put our tape on," Belyaev ordered, then hiccuped. "The girls and I have put together a compilation of our favorite songs from what was popular when we were in 11th grade," he explained.

"Let's play it now."

Butus nodded and dashed behind the control panel. In a moment, the corny pop music was replaced by the Black Eyed Peas.

Our table gradually emptied to the soundtrack of 15-year-old hits. The girls coaxed the guys to join them, even the ones who in our schooldays were usually shy and never stepped on the dance floor.

This seemed like the ideal moment for me to go out there and strut my stuff. I hadn't practiced all night for nothing, had I?

In truth, this no longer seemed like such a good idea. I found myself looking not at people whose respect I'd win with a skillful dance at a night club, but grown-ups who'd taken a break from their family routine and work lives, who were sincerely happy about this reunion, and at this exact moment weren't inhibited by status and their place in society. They'd come here to be happy, see their friends, reminisce about childhood and relax. Would I really then step into the limelight and show off my windmill? And? And what? Would I make anyone's day with that?

Enough lying to yourself, man! It's your childhood complexes at work, prompting you to show off on the cheap and do that breakdance, blast it. And that male desire to win over a woman you couldn't get when you were a teenager? There was something low about that. It was distasteful.

So I just went out there and stood on the fringes next to Rita Wilberger and Tim Garifzyanov. I shuffled leisurely to In Da Club and benignly moved my body and arms. I'd never danced sober before.

The group continued to get excited. "They won't

catch us!" some red-faced girls yelled as they sang along with the two girls from Tatu. As Benny Benassy's *Satisfaction* played, Andrei's massive body barged through the dance floor, shouting at people to clear some space. He pulled off his shirt and waved it around provocatively, wearing only a tank top that showed his bare paunch, but he didn't look the least bit bothered.

A thought flashed through my head: maybe I should go out there after all?

I smiled at my childish desire and dismissed the thought. Well, I would have deserved it if I'd been honing my skills and practicing for years. But I practiced for all of one night. There was nothing to be proud of.

I sensed some movement out of the corner of my eye. My heightened intuition made me go investigate it. I hadn't noticed any guards around — Belyaev's restaurant was just a run-of-the-mill place even though the food was divine.

I gently eased Rita away, squeezed myself in between an overheated Paulina and Lena, shoved aside Eugene Lee and Marik Khristov, stumbled across Alex Kozhevnikov who was jumping with his back to me, and ended up face to face with a close-shaven, balding guy with a crooked smirk.

He was staring at Belyaev who was dancing with abandon. Right behind him there were three more guys who were openly undressing the girls with their eyes.

I flung my arms around them, scooped them up and gently pushed them off the dance floor,

"Hey, guys, stop!"

"Huh?"

"What? Get your hands off!"

"Yes, just a sec. Let's go over there and have a little chat."

I pulled away the indignant yet intrigued guys and went over to their table.

"Ta-da!" said one of their friends who was sitting there.

"Ta-da, good evening! Happy birthday, Gorilla!" I said to the birthday boy and then ignored him. "Hey, Tarzan! And you two! And you!" I shook hands with both the guys I knew and didn't know.

"Mr. Panfilov! Sorry, I didn't recognize you right away," one of the lowlifes jumped up and squeezed my hand. It was Tarzan, one of Alik's dudes whom I knew from our little skirmish in the park when I'd been walking Richie.

"We're celebrating. So you know Gorilla?" Tarzan was puzzled.

"I know all of you. Aren't you a little young to be boozing it up, kiddo?" I turned to one of the minors. "Are you in a hurry to grow a beard? What's your name — Sergei Petlenko, right? You're 15, correct? What's the point in destroying your liver, young man?"

"Oh, I... I'm not drinking," he said, embarrassed, covering his glass with his hand.

"Tarzan, who is this guy? Why's he ordering us around?" Gorilla asked indignantly.

"Put a cork in it!" Tarzan poked him with his elbow and whispered in his ear. "Even Yagoza respects him! He laid Sledgehammer out with one blow! He's a champion!"

"Listen to your elders, Gorilla," I said. "You'll be healthier."

"Got it, Mr. Panfilov," Tarzan assured me. "And

did you just..."

"What?"

"Well, you didn't come over here just to shake hands," he said, embarrassed. "Or to say happy birthday to Gorilla."

"Not entirely. You see, dudes, the owner of this restaurant is a guy I went to school with. We're celebrating and we really wouldn't like it if you all spoiled our fun. Is that clear?"

"Yes, sure," they answered.

"So, what, we can't dance at all?" one of the oldest in the group retorted, gesturing toward a group of young people who were gyrating next to the stage. "But they can?"

"They can because they're not bothering anyone. They're polite young people."

"Yeah, so?"

"Nothing. Tarzan, you're in charge of them. All right, have a good time. And don't get the little one drunk," I nodded in Beard's direction.

Without waiting for a response, I returned to the dance floor.

When Paulina caught sight of me, she screeched and draped herself around my neck. I realized that a slow dance was starting.

Paulina clung to me, snuggling with her plump body. "Panfilov," she whispered excitedly. "How is it that I never looked at you when we were in school?"

"I don't know, Paulina. Maybe I wasn't your type?"

"Yeah, I think that's it," she agreed. "I usually went for the athletes. Like Andrei..."

"That was understandable back then," I smiled.

"But I really liked you."

"And do you like me now?" her burning whisper gave me goosebumps.

I didn't like her now, but I couldn't exactly say that, could I? If I said I liked her, I'd be lying. If I didn't say anything, she'd cling to me even more.

"Do you want to?" Paulina asked. She trailed off, pulled me closer and laughed softly with satisfaction. "I can feel that you want to. Let's go."

She led me by the hand into the restaurant. I didn't do my breakdancing, but I was with Paulina...

Dazed and overcome by a hormonal burst of desire, I allowed her to lead me almost to the doorway, but then I got hold of myself and stopped.

She turned around in confusion. "What's up, Panfilov? Don't be afraid. Andrei gave me the keys to his office. No one will see us."

"Aren't you married, Paulina?"

"Yeah, so what?"

"I'm sorry," without offering an explanation I turned and went back to the table.

I sat there by myself, finished off the khachapuri and stuffed my face with salad — my beastly hunger had returned with a vengeance — until the group came back. People came to get hammered and outdrink themselves, and I decided that I'd had enough. I'd seen them, socialized and gotten some closure from my schooldays. Starting tomorrow morning, I'd need to study my adversary and analyze his weak spots; luckily the interface would help. I already had some ideas about Dorozhkin's weak spots.

I waited until everyone was really drunk, then I got up and said I had to leave. I easily fended off the half-hearted attempts to stop me.

"Let Little Philip go," Paulina put an end to it. "We'll still have fun without him!"

"Hey, guys, let's go outside," Belyaev shouted. "Let's get a photo while everyone's still here. We'll walk Panfilov out and have a smoke, what do you think?"

Everyone liked that idea. We noisily crossed the veranda and went outside the restaurant. I called a taxi. While I waited, I made the rounds saying good-bye to my classmates.

Seemingly out of nowhere, a photographer appeared beside us, ordering us where to stand. In the light of the restaurant's sign we slowly but surely arranged ourselves in fits and starts, the girls standing and the guys sitting at their feet.

"Say cheese!" said the photographer. "One, two, three... Click!"

The flash blinded us. A second later, a stunning woman in a light summer dress that showed off her long, slim legs all the way down to her high-heeled shoes appeared behind the photographer's back.

She gave us a broad Hollywood smile. "Hello!"

"Evening," everyone babbled. "Who are you?"

"I'm sorry to bother you. I'm picking up my boyfriend."

When our eyesight had finally returned to normal, we saw that she was standing with her arm resting on a bluish-gray sports car with its top down.

Lamborghini Aventador, the interface informed me.

"Did you get new wheels, Stacy?" I took a step forward, grinning with delight.

"You like it?" she came forward and kissed me.

"Shall we go for a ride?"

"Give me a minute to say good-bye to my classmates."

"I'll wait in the car," Stacy said, releasing me.

I embraced my classmates warmly, agreeing that we really needed to get together more often now, like "all the time." I didn't know what "all the time" was supposed to mean but I agreed anyway. I embraced Pashkovsky and Rezvei heartily, slapping them on the back, and then made my exit.

"See you, Little Philip," Belyaev said. His voice cracked and he cleared his throat. "Come by the restaurant! We have business lunches for 200 rubles."

"Have you lost your mind? He's not Little Philip to you," I could hear Pasha berate Belyaev, but I missed the rest of what he said.

As soon as I was settled in the passenger seat of the Lamborghini, Stacy aka Ilindi put the pedal to the floor, and we tore out of there.

"How are you, Ilindi?"

"Phil, we have some problems," she slammed her hands on the wheel.

"What kind of problems? What happened?"

"There's a big mess on Pibellau. I'll explain everything when we get back to your place."

"'Pibellau'? What the hell is..."

"I'll tell you everything at your place," Ilindi cut me short as she barely made it through a turn. "Keep your mouth shut until then!"

She took the car up to 85 mph, and my thoughts about this mysterious Pibellau were swept away by a surge of panic.

I hoped she knew how to drive.

Chapter Nine

TYRANNOSAURUS REX

In my youth, I was given some training on spearfighting. "Stick them with the pointy end," I think it was.

Admiral Dvorek, *World of Warcraft*

OVER THE COURSE OF MY LIFE, I'VE WITNESSED different shades of amazement. I remember my father's astonishment when he read in the local newspaper about the little sixth grader from the neighborhood who'd won triple my father's monthly salary in a town DotA tournament. I remember Mr. Ivanov's surprise when on my very first day on the job I won the company its biggest contract ever.

But the amazement I was witnessing right now was in a league of its own.

Rex's roaring had been going on for so long that I didn't hear Carter's jaw drop. Yes, that's what I named my one and only ubermob without even inventing anything. It was like I didn't feel like naming it something simple, like a household pet — I didn't have

168

it in me to call it the usual Fido, Spot or Fluffy. My little beast was nothing like a pet.

Naturally, its roar was mesmerizing, totally different from the artificially synthesized sound from *Jurassic Park*. Not a single modern animal on Earth makes a sound like that, so I have nothing to compare it to. Suffice it to say that it makes your hair stand on end and it gives you goosebumps. It's a roar that makes your blood run cold, and everything in your body that could possibly tense up tenses up.

Truth be told, I couldn't take advantage of it because in the split second after Rex finally went silent, Carter came to his senses and started to bark out orders:

"Jovanna, tell everyone to attack Godzilla! You too!" Then he shouted at his mobs, gesturing toward the tyrannosaur with his spear. "Go!"

The mental interface didn't need the last command, but apparently in his fifty years Carter had gotten into the habit of using analog.

His mini-army showed an enviable knack for cooperation: Jovanna's wolves and the bloodsuckers with the metal clubs charged at their target while the two archers fired off a volley. Meanwhile, Carter seized his spear with both hands — he was probably remembering how I'd nearly ripped it away from him — and headed toward me. Fortunately, he wasn't running, so I had some time to come up with an attack plan and another moment to give a command to Rex.

"Furious Roar!" I shouted, just like Carter.

This time Rex growled a little differently: the roar was short, but about 50 decibels louder. It didn't affect me at all, but everyone else had blood gushing out of their ears.

The blood was actually just a side effect: the main effect was to temporarily paralyze all enemies. The stun stopped everyone in their tracks, and the bloodsuckers, wolves, the bear, Jovanna and Carter dropped to the ground like bowling pins. Strike!

I selected the prone melee fighters as target and fired commands at my pet while moving toward the long-range fighters,

"Squash 'em! Go for them!"

The stun lasted five seconds with a five minutes' cooldown. I took advantage of every second. Using my knife like a hole punch, I butchered both of the bloodsucking archers. I then trained my club on Jovanna's jaw — fortunately, she wasn't wearing a helmet — but I stopped it half an inch from her head and ran on.

Sentimental fool! Cursing myself, I reached Carter and clubbed him as hard as I could on the neck just as his paralysis was wearing off. That caused a crit which lowered his health by a little more than 10%.

Meanwhile, Rex crushed the bear and one of the bloodsuckers: both had the misfortune of stumbling under his massive and merciless foot. It was only a one-time ability, and it was guaranteed to kill any mob that was of a lower level, but the cooldown was five minutes. The fights were short because there was no healer, so that meant this was the only time I'd be able to use the ability in this situation.

Before the stun wore off, Rex managed to tear apart another three wolves and one bloodsucker, so now he was facing the 11 remaining mobs. I hoped he'd pull through.

"Jovanna, cover me!" Carter yelled hysterically, rolling to the side with surprising agility, evading the club I was swinging at him.

He was frightened — that's all there was to it. I leaped at him and fell on him with all my weight, pinning him to the ground. I whacked him in the shoulder with the club, then drove the knife into his thigh. Again! And again!

His helmet cracked. His collarbone snapped. Blood spurted out of his burst artery, but those were just visual effects. In reality, Carter hadn't lost more than a quarter of his health.

I wasn't able to capitalize on my success. A discharge hit me in the back: the prickly bolts of lightning from Jovanna's staff. They hadn't dealt much damage, but they still had a negative effect, paralyzing me for a few seconds.

That was enough for Carter to shove me off himself,

"Get him!"

I realized my tactical error too late. Instead of quickly getting rid of Jovanna, I'd thrown myself at Carter who was basically the tank. He was the heftiest and the most armored in their group. Jovanna's bear was only level 1, so it could only become a tank in the absence of other options. I'd spared her life — and now my sentimentality had backfired as she threw herself at me from behind, seized me by the neck, and latched on to me to restrain me.

Carter took advantage of the situation, dashing at me and plunging his spear into me. The blow was so strong that it also hit Jovanna who was so close to me that we were like two flies strung on the spike of a greasy flycatcher. I could hear bloody bubbles gurgling out of her mouth.

I heard Carter's muffled laugh from under his broken helmet. Using the spear as a lever, he yanked it from side to side. The pain and damage were agonizing. The bleed DOT ticked out, increasing damage, as Carter widened the wound, both for me and for Jovanna.

Jovanna died first. I don't know what additional effect the spear tip had — whether it was poison or maybe something else — but at that moment it was in Jovanna's body.

"Just die already!" Carter raged, looking behind my back in agitation. He pulled out the dagger I knew so well, the one that oozed a black poisonous slime. "When you die, your lizard will die too!"

His confidence forced me to stop and think. What happened to pets after their master died? Did they keep attacking — in other words, did they continue to exist in reality? The rules didn't say anything about that, but Rex and his level depended on my Fusion talent and the ring of leadership. Maybe the tyrannosaur would disincarnate, meaning that I would die without getting my revenge?

Damn!

I couldn't see how Rex was making out, but based on his icon in the interface he'd nearly done what he had to. I could see that he was in action and was the worse for wear, but he still had just under half his health. Meanwhile, I was down to less than a third of mine.

It was time to call in the cavalry. I chose Carter as the target.

"Shred 'em!"

Boom! Boom! Boom! The tyrannosaur covered the distance in three bounds. Carter had already taken to his heels on the first one. There was one last bloodsucker latched onto Rex's leg, which he dragged along.

Finally I got a good look at my pet. He was impressive: around 20 feet tall and twice as long. Contrary to the most recent scientific theories, he wasn't covered in feathers: his hide was a slate color darker than night.

But the most astounding thing of all was the fleshy comb-like crest that was half a yard high and ran along his spine from top to tail. I'd never seen anything like it in any movie.

Rex easily caught up with Carter and didn't let him go. The dinosaur scooped Carter up in his mouth, threw him up in the air to get a better grip on him, then squeezed his jaws tight.

Carter's helmet muted the man's plaintive cry.

T. Rex spat Carter out and beat him to the ground like a broken doll. Although paralyzed, Carter was still alive. That was the game system at work: a level 5 pet's ability can't kill a trial subject of a higher level.

I redirected the mob at the bloodsucker. "Attack!"

I myself was screaming in pain as I pulled the spear right through my innards, first with my hands in front of me and then behind my back. I finally dislodged the spear with Jovanna still impaled on it. Sorry about that, old girl.

Her disincarnated body was immediately

---

replaced by loot: a crystal of a shape I'd never seen before, plus a uniform. I wasn't interested in them; the DOT was still ticking, I was losing blood and my health was already in the red.

Health points: 153/2000.

It took me two stabs of the knife to finish Carter off. When he died, a new red balloon of an important system message appeared, but I ignored it. Right now I was more concerned about my own survival.

Carter's disincarnated body left behind a pile of rags and two crystals. I reached for one of them.

The huge existence crystal.

Just what I was looking for. The crystal turned to dust, adding to my existence resource counter:

+468 existence resource pt.

Verifying the probability of receiving bonus existence resources (20%)...
Verification failed.

Before the battle, I'd had 159 points. Once I'd combined them with Carter's, I ended up with 627. That was enough.

I invested the resources in level 5.

Are you sure you want to activate a level up?

Accept / Decline

The bleeding effect expired, the DOT was removed. I'd survived. The battle was over. But seeing as this was my last life and Pibellau was full of unpleasant surprises, I figured it would be better for me to protect myself. I accepted.

Congratulations, test subject! You've reached level 5!

You receive +2 Characteristic points to invest into any characteristics of your choice.

You may now level up the command center to level 2.

You may now access the expanded rulebook for the Trial.

Put more fire under your enemies' feet, test subject!

Leveling up restored my whole body and instantly healed and closed my wounds, just as it was supposed to. I felt awesome, so the first thought that popped into my head was that I had to quickly go look for Carter and finish him off while he was still weak. It would be idiotic to leave an enemy like him rolling around on the ground.

But then I had a second thought: where was I supposed to look for him? He could be resurrected on any of the remaining neutral hexagons to the north or east, and there were dozens of miles between them.

I thought about this for a moment and decided that rather than getting worked up over him, I'd take care of myself.

I ordered T. Rex to protect the base and gathered the rest of the loot. Carter's loot yielded all his stuff as well as something new:

Spirit crystal
Collect 13 spirit crystals and transform them into an additional life.
The spirit crystal is bound to its owner. It cannot be lost or transferred to another trial subject.

The crystal disappeared, replaced by a new icon in my interface with the numbers: *1/13.*

I returned to the place where Jovanna had died and picked up another crystal just like it. The fact that I wasn't the one to kill her was irrelevant; loot dropped and the goodies went to whoever picked them up. Maybe since I'd killed Carter I'd also earned the right to his loot? I really needed to study the expanded rulebook now.

I spent the next ten minutes examining the objects that had dropped: the components of the uniforms and the weapons. I pulled everything together in a pile, lined the items up and started to make my choices. Carter's set was the same improved one that I had. Jovanna had the basic one. But there was plenty to like in the weapons.

First I reclaimed my power fist with its 50% increase to critical damage. The increased damage characteristics surprised me: 155–235. If I wasn't mistaken, the damage had increased by a lot, and that meant that unique weapons could also scale up here.

"Oh, my precious," I said, affectionately running my hand over the dull surface of the power fist.

I heard panting behind me, then found myself

drenched in a suspended matter that was either steam or Rex's snot. I turned around and burst into laughter. A lot of tension had been building up, and seeing Rex's enormous bulk sitting on his tail and tilting his tiny head like a bird just pushed me over the edge.

"Hahahaha!" the more I laughed, the more surprised the expression on Rex's snout became, and the funnier it seemed to me. "Rexie, stop! What are you doing! Stop! Hahahaha!"

A minute of laughter is said to extend your life, and I hoped that I wasn't wasting time in vain as I rolled around the surface of the base, hysterically slapping my palm on the ground.

Once I'd calmed down, I went back to examining the weapons, a smile lingering on my face. There were no standard items in the set, just unique ones.

The first two belonged to Carter, and their stats were amazing. With such ubergoodies, it was no wonder Carter had started the Trial off with a bang.

Demon Spear of Hyperion
Universal weapon. The spear tip possesses protointelligence and is capable of morphing, critically damaging the victim's major organs.

It is powered by existence resources (5% of your points for each damage dealt).

Damage: 185–325.

Chance of shedding blood: +100%.

Acid Dagger of Obfuscation
Cunning melee weapon. Its biochemical core produces an active jelly whose concentration in the victim's blood can lead to madness.

It is powered by existence resources (3% of your points for each damage dealt).

Damage: 77-144.

+1% to your chance of making an instant kill with each blow.

Finally, I inspected the characteristics of Jovanna's staff.

Rumbling Lightning Rod

Long-range weapon. Generates electric discharge.

It is powered by existence resources (1% of your points for each damage dealt).

Damage: 60–120.

Distance: 20 yards.

Chance of stunning: +10%.

I wondered where they'd gotten all these unique weapons from. Maybe Carter had completed the instance and then finished off the location boss, but what about Jovanna? Could she have gotten a bonus for passing the preliminary selection?

I left Rex to guard the base while I made a couple of trips to carry the stuff to the shelter where I threw it on the floor. I wasn't in a computer game, so I couldn't drag all the loot in one trip.

Once inside, safe from any attacking mobs, I touched the red balloon and opened the system message.

Congratulations, test subject!

Level 6 test subject Carter is now dead!

**Number of hexagons captured by Carter: 8.
Put more fire under your enemies' feet!**

Counting the hexagon where I was right now, I had nine hexagons in all. I'd reclaimed my home base, captured Jovanna's and Carter's, plus another five neutral zones that lay around our respective home hexagons.

Now what was I supposed to do? Was I supposed to be everywhere at once just to protect them?

Even if the alarm system kicked in whenever someone — say, Carter — infiltrated the northernmost part... no, wait. In his case, the alarm wouldn't sound, would it? But that wasn't the point. How would I be able to cover six miles of territory teeming with aggressive fauna in case of a new invasion? Something didn't hold water here.

I opened the control panel of the command center.

**Base 1
Level: 1.
Number of modules: 2.
Rate of existence resource generation: 1 pt. per hour.
Total generation of existence resources from all bases: 9 pt. per hour.
The base owner's level is 5 or higher: you may upgrade to level 2.
Cost to upgrade base to level 2: 500 existence resource pt.**

In order to control other bases remotely, you

need an integration module.

You may access the integration module at level 2 of the base's development.

That made sense. No matter how you looked at it, everything led back to resources. I guess for the time being I'd need to put off studying the expanded rulebook or doing anything else. Right now the most important task was to upgrade the base and build new modules. Maybe I'd gain access to something that would completely change my strategy — or more accurately, my nonstrategy, since up to this point all I'd been doing was trying to stick it out. Now that either the observers or luck had given me a chance, I needed to seize it and capitalize on my success.

I used the two bonus characteristic points I'd received for leveling up to increase my Strength, which raised not only my damage, but also Rex's. Even these two available points substantially raised his stats. The dinosaur's new damage increased by 10%: 1650–3300. If I understood everything correctly, the life of the last location boss I'd seen was 4000 XP. So it looked like I had a chance against it, but that would depend on its armor. What it if it had damage absorption of 90%? I'd already gotten burned with the Kreken.

I considered my plan of action and got ready to farm. After some thought, I put the power fist on my right hand and picked up the dagger in my left.

I was ready for a fight.

I ventured outside and looked around to make sure that no surprises were awaiting me.

"Let's go, buddy," I whistled, calling Rex. "Time to go hunt!"

I considered the possibility of riding him, then realized with disappointment that I couldn't. I wouldn't be able to climb onto his neck, and if I fell onto his tail, which was what balanced his body, I'd be in for a bumpy ride. I wouldn't be able to hold on. OK, so much for experiments.

"*Phhhht,*" Rex breathed noisily in my face, jerking his snout and looking at me with his orange eyes.

"You know, Little Rex, I once had a friend. He was a German Shepherd named Richie. He helped me get out of a mess with some lowlifes even though he was 150 times smaller than you."

"*Hhhhmmmph!*"

"There's a monster near here. The last time I ran into it, it almost ate me. Ready to go get rid of it?"

"*Ooof?*"

"Oh, it's called a Canavar. Let's go!"

We walked through the fence around the base in the same place where Jovanna's bear had breached it. More accurately, I walked through it but my pet just stepped over it as if it weren't even there.

I chose a direction and took the lead. The T. Rex followed closely behind, carefully measuring out his steps.

✳ ✳ ✳

Before barreling toward the Canavar, we spent half a day farming resources in the surrounding area. You always learn the hard way, and even the stupendous Little Rex could collapse under the pressure of a level 8 creature that was as tall as a two-story building. I couldn't justify the risk.

Farming resources was becoming routine. None of the daytime mobs we might encounter would be able to challenge us. Even if their levels had increased because I was now level 5, and even if any of them continued to attack in a pack, they were small fry for us.

It was epic when Rex crushed a pack of whistlers in one go. The "tiny existence crystals" were now replaced by "small" ones, which would turn to dust, giving me from 5 to 12 existence resource points, depending on my luck.

"Lift your foot! Step to the side!" I repeated these commands over and over every time we got rid of a pack.

The tyrannosaur would then step aside as I'd gather the resources that had dropped. In total, I was able to accumulate enough crystals to upgrade the base and buy new modules.

When we returned to the base, Pibellau's big sun was just passing its zenith and the small one was approaching it. Additional farming wouldn't make any difference for this hexagon. Little creatures ran about and hid, barely noticing us. So as strange as it might seem, chasing them around the forest would be a waste of time.

The first thing I did when I got to the base was launch the upgrade. As I waited for it, I studied the rulebook. The first thing I learned was that the rules were expanded gradually so that the test subjects could prove themselves with minimal information.

I also learned that when the founder of a clan dies, the members are freed. That was logical, considering that Carter had lost all his hexagons and he himself was under threat of permanent disincarnation. That meant that Jovanna was free now, which was good and bad news. It was good that I no longer needed to kill her, and that she could fight on my side. But she urgently needed to capture a hexagon while she had no uniform or weapons, and that was a problem. Most of the neutral hexagons at this stage of the Trial were occupied, and even if she found an available one, she'd need to farm 100 resources somehow in order to claim it.

The rules also confirmed something Carter had said. I risked completely losing not just the interface, but everything I'd achieved with it. The only way to avoid this was to win the Trial. Vassals who were in the winner's clan didn't get to keep their interfaces, but at least they retained their memory and the skills and characteristics they'd already received.

I chuckled. Carter wasn't so bad after all. Even though he knew that if Jovanna and I died he'd receive our spirit crystals, he still kept inviting us to join his clan. Whether this was a miscalculation, a strategy or simply a sense of humanity, my esteem for Carter went up a notch.

I looked at the calculation of the cost of all the modules at each level of the base. The formula was the same for all the modules. Level 2 cost 10 times more than level 1. Level 3 cost 5 times more than level 2. Then, level 4 cost 3 times more than level 3, and level 5 cost twice as much as level 4. Level 6, the highest level of any module, cost 1.5 times more than level 5.

Based on the example of the fighting unit module, I quickly calculated that the upgrade from level 2 to level 6 would cost me almost 500,000 existence resource points. Along with this information I was hit by the realization that developing absolutely everything would not only be unrealistic but also quite dangerous. I'd need to choose one development strategy and focus exclusively on it.

I could invest all the resources into myself, advancing level by level, simultaneously leveling up both my characteristics and the scaled damage dealt by my units.

I could distribute the resources between myself and the uniform module, creating an armored uber killing machine.

I could level up Charisma and the fighting unit module, increasing the power of the army of pets in both quality and quantity.

I could level up the bases, increasing their defense potential and the speed of resource farming by the working units.

Or I could go from hexagon to hexagon, capturing them one after the other like Genghis Khan and adding them to my army of new vassals and their mobs.

I hadn't yet decided what I'd do in the long term. I'd need to see what the new base level gave me. But it was clear what I had to do today.

I'd take care of my base and then take a stroll around the neighboring neutral hexagon. During the night, Rex and I would try to fight the nighttime elite creatures. If we succeeded, the night would be dedicated to leveling up because one thing was definitely clear: I needed 4,000 resources to get up to level 10, where my damage would reach four digits, and

I'd be able to choose the class with which I'd receive combat talents.

It was kind of a pity to raise the fighting unit module level to 3. For that I'd need another 2,500 points. Then, taking my ring into account, Rex would upgrade to level 6 — this was the highest level for pets.

"*Sh-sh-shoo-oo-oosh!*" the first wave streamed out of the white stone, indicating that the upgrade was complete.

The *knowledge* that came with it told me that the borders of the hexagon had been fortified. In addition to notifying me of the breach, they'd now also cast a one-hour Weakness debuff on the invader, taking 5% off each characteristic.

The second wave strengthened and expanded the territory of the base. The rickety fence was replaced by a six-foot wall, which was fortified by turrets in every one of the hexagon's six corners. The turrets fired blobs of plasma: they wouldn't kill someone like Carter, but they'd wear down someone's nerves, creating a first line of defense.

The third wave fortified the house and made it bigger. Now only a test subject whose level was at least as high as mine could get into it, and the high ceilings gave me hope that Rex could also fit in, provided he lay on his side.

To get a little taste of what was to come, I opened the command center control panel.

Base 1
Level: 2.
Number of modules: 2.
Rate of existence resource generation: 10 pt.

per hour.

Total generation of existence resources from all bases: 18 pt. per hour.

You may not upgrade until you reach level 10.

Cost to upgrade base to level 3: 2500 existence resource pt.

I saw that three new modules had been added: integration, storage and noncombat units. It was pricey, but investing resources into building each of them was a no-brainer.

The storage module materialized first. A huge phantom trunk appeared out of thin air next to the cupboard with the uniform. A trunk? Hm, that was funny. It reminded me of something.

The module was a sort of extradimensional inventory that could be accessed only by the owner, and it preserved its contents intact even if all the hexagons were lost. The problem was that if you lost all the hexagons, you'd lose the module itself, which meant that to return the stuff, you'd need to recapture a new base, upgrade it and rebuild the module.

But that was better than leaving your stuff to just anyone. I put all the extra items in the trunk: Jovanna's clothes, her staff, and Carter's spear and uniform. I shut the lid, and the trunk became a phantom again.

The integration module allowed me to control other bases remotely and automate their development. You could set up the percentage of resources you wished to be used, the order of module building, and their priority. It was just like in my favorite game,

---

Civilization.

Of course it would be a good idea to upgrade every module to level 2, but not right now. Right now it was more important to follow my plan and spare my reserves.

Increasing the level of the integration module brought with it an important feature: the installation of portals in each shelter, creating a network of hexagons, and that's exactly what I'd been thinking about since the morning. This was how I'd resolve the problem of distances. It would cost me only 2,000 resources.

Damn, my head was hurting from trying to find the best strategic solution. I wanted to level up everything at once, but that was impossible.

The noncombat unit module was the last thing to be launched. I looked to see what it was all about.

It included two types of units: working and reconnaissance. The working one, which looked sort of like a robot vacuum cleaner, was invisible to aggressive mobs. It could move around a hexagon searching for existence resources, and when it found them, it could extract resources in the amount that corresponded to my Strength. My Strength was 23, which meant that on average the working unit would unearth and gather 23 points per hour.

This technological wonder would cost me 50 resources. I bought it immediately. I would have gotten more, but there was a limit: only one working unit per base was allowed.

I didn't have enough existence resources for the reconnaissance unit. The small flying drone had a bunch of helpful features: it was inconspicuous, agile and fast, but its performance was only so-so. In essence, it just marked on my minimap the hexagons it discovered, indicating their respective owners. I couldn't argue that it was important, but this scout cost 1,000 resources. Who had made everything so expensive? For 1,000 resources, Rex and I would be more than happy to do all the legwork ourselves, if necessary.

When I was finished with all of this, I set out on another hunt.

Our route took us to the east. We'd check to see if the hexagon adjacent to mine was neutral or if it was already occupied. And if it was already occupied, who had captured it? Carter? Jovanna? Or my third neighbor, who was on the other side of the two neutral hexagons east of me?

✳ ✳ ✳

It was starting to get dark. Farming the neighboring hexagon had gone just like it had at home. At first, Rex and I had cracked the packs we came across like nuts, but after a few hours the local mobs figured out what they were dealing with and started to run away and hide.

The rules said that each hexagon contained a one-time instance, so we'd spent another hour wandering around peering into every suspicious nook and cranny looking for it, but still hadn't found it.

As twilight fell, I decided to go back to my shelter. Night was approaching, and I preferred to cut my teeth on the elite creatures with a safe place nearby.

Rex roared to announce himself to all and

sundry, his thundering steps making my skull vibrate. He sure was loud. To be honest, over the course of the day I'd become so sick and tired of constantly feeling like I was next to a space center where rockets were launched every minute that I just wanted to hide from the tyrannosaur in my shelter and have a half-hour of peace and quiet.

We walked in an arc, gradually making our way through a section we hadn't yet been in. Who knew, maybe I'd suddenly spot an entrance to an instance.

On the eastern edge, closest to my third neighbor, a column of dust obscured the crimson horizon. I couldn't figure out what was going on there, but I had to find out. I pointed the tyrannosaur in that direction, jumped up and clambered onto the tip of his tail, holding tight with both hands. I managed to hold on for only a few seconds, but then my grip loosened, my fingers slipped and I flew to the ground head first. Cursing Rex, I ran after him, looking in front of me.

A fight was going on, and it was uneven. I saw a lone familiar girl surrounded by a flock of whistlers. Gathering speed, they were ramming into her with their spiked foreheads. Jovanna — it was indeed her — was feebly swatting them with a makeshift club fashioned from a branch.

She was alone. Her units weren't nearby, which meant that she didn't have a base.

"Rex, attack!" I repeated the mental command out loud, selecting all the whistlers as target.

Jovanna huddled down, hiding her head between her knees. With a few snaps of his jaws, Rex cleared the area around her. The whistlers' bodies disappeared, leaving in their place tiny existence crystals. The mobs were levels 2 and 3, so there wasn't much by way of resources.

"Jovanna, collect the loot. It'll be useful for you," I said, sitting down next to her. "Hi."

"Hi," she answered hoarsely, lifting her head. "Are you gonna kill me?"

"No. Did you capture the hexagon?" I decided to check to be sure.

She shook her head.

"How much time do you have?"

"Less than 10 hours."

"Get up! We'll farm you some resources quickly and you can capture this one."

"That's out of the question. I won't be able to hold on to it. Carter will come back or the guy over there will," she said, nodding to the east.

"Who's over there? Do you know?"

"On the first day I saw someone on the other hexagon from a distance. I didn't attack. He had units but I didn't have any yet."

"I see. Try to collect resources. I want to check something out."

Without standing up, she reached for one of the crystals. It dissolved, leaving a dusty substance on her finger. "Here's some resources. Four points."

"Excellent. Take the rest, and then join my clan."

"There's no way I'm doing that," she said, squaring her shoulders. "If I join your clan, you'll get all my resources. Or is this your way of making yourself feel important?"

For a moment I fell into a stupor. "Meaning?" I stared into her squinting eyes.

"The way you're ordering me about. The way

you check if I've obeyed them."

"What kind of bullshit is this? I thought you got to keep the resources. You never know, what if something happens to me? Then you'll have something to activate the command center with. I was thinking of that — I wasn't ordering you about."

Her gaze softened. "Sorry. See, a vassal needs to obey all the orders of the clan leader. All of them."

"Well, that's logical."

"You think so?"

"Yes. Otherwise there'd be confusion and hesitation, and that causes problems when you're fighting."

She turned away.

"Is something wrong? Jovanna! Please get a grip! It's getting dark. We need to make a decision. Will you join my clan?"

"No."

"Hm. You don't want to join a clan and you don't need help capturing a hexagon. Then just come back to my base — I'll give your things back to you."

Jovanna was hesitant. But I didn't know what she was thinking.

"OK, what's with the orders? What happens if you don't follow them?"

"You die."

"Did Carter threaten to kill you?"

"Worse! Carter just activated a punishment, and I saw a timer counting down to permanent disincarnation. Every time he activated the timer, the time got shorter and shorter. First it was 10 seconds. Then 9. Each time he activated it I had less and less time to obey the order," her eyes welled up. Her voice became so soft I had to strain to hear her. "When there were only 3 seconds left, I hurried to follow all of his orders, just so I'd have time to finish. Even when he ordered-"

Rex's roar drowned out her last words. He was just in time.

CHAPTER TEN

A NEW ALLY

For me!
Lone Champion, *Hearthstone*

STAYING ON MY GUARD, I SURVEYED THE TERRITORY, then looked toward where T Rex was gazing, roaring in excitement. Around 100 yards away, there was a dot right above the line of the horizon where the sun was setting.

I looked more closely and realized that it was moving. I had no idea what it was, and the system couldn't identify something so far away.

"What's that?" Jovanna asked, peering into the distance.

"Someone's flying this way. Alone. Hold on..."

Finally, a system message appeared over the silhouette.

Level 1 reconnaissance drone
Owner: Tafari.

"Shit!" I shouted. "Some guy named Tafari has got himself a reconnaissance drone! That's a noncombat unit of the level 2 base module!"

"Is it dangerous?"

"As it stands, no, but that's not the only issue. It costs 1000 points. Imagine how much this Tafari guy has leveled up if he could spare the points for that."

The reconnaissance unit was flying directly over us. From close up, I could see that the drone resembled a flat black disk, a bit like a vinyl record with a flickering surface. The drone's speed varied as it kept changing direction, moving from point to point and slowing down every time, as if it were scanning the surface.

"Can you shoot it down? Damn, sorry. I forgot that you don't have your staff."

Based on the direction where the drone was coming from, I gathered that Tafari was settled somewhere in the east. With neighbors like that it wasn't a good idea to stay still, so I wasn't keen on continuing the conversation with Jovanna that Rex's roaring had interrupted.

"Jovanna, it's getting dark. It's dangerous. I'm going back to the base. You helped me and I'm ready to help you now. I'll give you your things back. So come with me if you want."

Without waiting for a response, I turned and ran back to my hexagon. I didn't get tired in this world, and since I'd already examined the area, it was better to run than walk.

Rex adjusted to my speed, shortening his stride and trotting beside me. I didn't turn around.

After a few seconds I heard Jovanna running behind me. When she caught up with us, her breathing was even, like the professional athlete that she was.

I stopped her at the base without inviting her

into the shelter. "Wait here."

She nodded her understanding; this was no place for kindness. I left Rex with her, silently commanding him to protect her.

In the shelter, I rummaged around in the extradimensional trunk and pulled out her uniform, the lightning rod and the knife she'd given me.

I took the objects outside and laid them on the ground next to her. "Do you want to change your clothes? I'll turn around."

"Thank you. You don't need to turn around," she answered indifferently, pulling off her tennis shirt, tattered skirt and white sneakers. "*They* abducted me just when I was entering the tennis court for a match," she cast a meaningful glance at the sky. "Where were you abducted from?"

"I was on my way home from the airport," I answered, turning away tactfully. "I lost all my clothes in the preliminary selection and landed here without shoes. Would you believe I managed to run into a location boss in my first hour?"

"For real? How'd it turn out?"

"I died."

"What? Are you saying that when Carter and I found you, you were already on your last life?"

"Something like that."

"But you still didn't want to join his clan?"

"You saw and heard everything."

"But why?"

"Because I want to win."

For a few moments, all I could hear was a quiet rustling behind my back. My mind was screaming at me that I was really stupid to turn my back out of tact on a potential armed enemy, but I kept looking steadily the other way, fixing my gaze on a small group of whistlers on the other side of the barrier.

"You can turn around now."

Jovanna was sitting down, lacing up her boots. She tucked the laces in, stood up, and jumped up and down a few times. "Are you sure you're going to win?"

"No. I'm not sure, but I'm not going to give up."

"All right," she was silent for a long moment, wrinkling her forehead. Then she walked closer to me and looked at me point blank. "Phil, if your offer is still good, please invite me into your clan. If it's not, I'll just leave now."

And just like that, my clan became one person larger.

* * *

The first rays of the large sun of Pibellau found Jovanna and myself sorting loot. During the night, we'd smoked two elite mobs and one boss that had crossed into the territory of the base. We hadn't risked stepping outside the base's limits and we weren't about to risk it in the future since scaling was based on the test subjects' level.

I could have taken Jovanna's unit points and invested them in regenerating the tyrannosaur, making him even bigger and stronger, but I decided not to. Had Carter been just a little luckier, Rex wouldn't have been any help. To have just one badass mob for two people didn't seem like a very good strategy because an enemy would just need to tie it up in battle, obstruct it or immobilize it — anything at all — and we'd be left face to face with the attacker. And what if there was more than one enemy? We needed a powerful tank.

So I went back to the catalog of special units and used my Fusion talent to reinforce our squadron with a powerful horned Triceratops which I created with all of Jovanna's Charisma points.

Triceratops Tank
Level 5 melee fighter
Phil's fighting unit.
Health points: 3200/3200.
Attack: 460–690.
Damage absorbed by armor: 50%.
Maximum travel speed: 25 mph
Weight: 12.5 tons
Talents: Charge!, Toss!, Provocation

The Tank wasn't as large as Rex, but it was heavier. Its color was nothing like what the terrestrial paleontologists had imagined. When it appeared, the bright green, blue-spotted Triceratops warily eyed the tyrannosaur, his mortal enemy.

Rexie was also intrigued. The two dinosaurs stood there for a long time, sizing each other up, rubbing their snouts together, sniffing each other and roaring.

As I analyzed their stats, I remembered that Carter had bragged about his level 3 units. With my Leadership ring, both Tank and Rex should have reached level 6, but that hadn't happened. I was puzzled. Did that mean that my hexagon network wasn't developed enough? Why didn't the level 3 fighting unit module located on Carter's former base produce the same effect?

I found my answer when I looked more closely at the rulebook: mobs were always the same level as the module that generated them. That meant that the most important task to complete right after opening the portal grid was to regenerate the mobs anew — Carter's base was too far away.

As for Jovanna — the girl who was so withdrawn at first — she'd almost completely thawed overnight. New impressions, a taste for combat and her burning curiosity about what would drop in the loot seemed to have banished her memories of her short-lived slavery in Carter's clan. Or if not banished, at least swept into the dark distant corners of her mind. Technically she was in the same situation now, just with a different clan leader, but since I hadn't activated the disincarnation discipline timer even once during the night, she viewed our relationship as a partnership.

Our biggest preoccupation was the Canavar, the same location boss that had been responsible for my tumbling down the crevice with the portal to the instance. Apparently, it chased the nighttime elite known as the *duxio*, a cousin of that beetle-like thing that had crushed a couple of my first Raptors. The trajectory of the Canavar's chase passed through the base, where Rex and Tank seemed to be dozing peacefully.

We heard the tyrannosaur's anxious bellow while Jovanna was changing clothes yet again: this time into an "Improved Test Subject Uniform" created specially for her by the module. In any case, she was now my ally, and a 30% damage absorption would do her good. While Rex, who'd been left on guard, selected and threw himself at the Canavar which he considered to be the more dangerous creature, Tank attacked the duxio. I stormed out of the shelter, followed by Jovanna who was hopping around as she pulled on her new pants.

The scene playing out in front of us was like something out of a Hollywood blockbuster. Under the light of a million stars, the duxio was crawling around, dragging its dislodged innards and trampling the fence. A darkening liquid was spurting out of gashes that had been made in its chitinous armor. Drawing back to ready himself for a charge, Tank bowed his head and stamped his foot, stirring up dust. The tyrannosaur had been forced to the ground, wriggling his powerful back legs and pushing the eight-legged Canavar away. The Canavar squeezed the dinosaur with two of its column-like legs and clapped a claw around Rex's neck, trying to behead him.

All of this action was accompanied by a ghastly soundtrack of roaring, screaming, squealing and thundering.

"Kill the duxio!" I shouted to Jovanna as I raced to my pet's rescue.

I don't know when my acrobatic skills kicked in, but at full speed I leaped over the boss's outstretched pincers and rolled away as it thrust the claw in the spot where I'd been a second ago. Evading its spiny leg, I managed to get under its gut, into which I plunged Carter's treacherous dagger and tore the unprotected flesh like paper.

The Canavar recoiled, wailing in surprise. The liberated Rex nimbly righted himself and executed the "Shred 'em!" order, finishing off the boss. About 100 yards away, Jovanna and Tank were eradicating the duxio's remaining health stats. They didn't need my help.

In the early morning hours, we were visited by another elite, the *odzi* — this was a vile, snakelike creature that was around 25 yards long. We all spent nearly a whole Pibellau hour fighting it, trying to stay away from what turned out to be its two mouths. The creature had at least 10,000 life points, so my dagger, Tank's horn and Rex's teeth were all useless against its scaly skin. On top of that, its regeneration was high, and I wasn't able to finish it off until I thought of selecting one of the creature's heads as target and activate Rex's Smash 'em! talent. The snake's skull wasn't able to hold out, crumbling under pressure. We crushed the second head as soon the cooldown of the tyrannosaur's talent had expired.

We accumulated a slew of resources in our nocturnal victories. Counting the resources gathered by the working unit, we had enough to bring me up to level 7 and Jovanna to level 5. I added all 4 characteristic points to Stamina, raising my ability to survive as well as that of Rex and Tank.

Jovanna put everything into Agility. She did this because of the deadly elegant bow that dropped from the location boss.

Canavar's Ruthless Jaws
Long-range weapon. Unlimited supply of ammunition.
Powered by existence resource points (5% of the point for each shot).
Damage: 120–180.

Distance: 100 yards.
Chance of bloodshed: +50%.
Chance of stunning: +3%.

"It's a beast!" Jovanna exclaimed.

To be more precise, she'd shouted something else in Serbian, but that was how the built-in interpreter had translated her words for me.

"Just what the doctor ordered," I added happily.

Jovanna wasn't new to the tactics of long-range fighters. That was her thing. For me, this bow would only be a hindrance. It wasn't because I didn't know how to use it; the way the Trial worked, you learned how to use any weapon the moment you picked it up, but thanks to my boxing practice, I'd gotten used to clinching. Anyway, the 3% chance of stunning — which meant immobilizing the opponent — could play a huge role, creating the most crucial moment in a fight that wasn't going well. So you could understand why I was happy.

We greeted the new day on Pibellau as a full-fledged fighting group: me, Jovanna and two small units — Rex and Tank. Now where would we find a healer?

* * *

Repairing the enclosure around the base cost me 10% of its value — 22 existence resource units. I didn't really want to waste resources since I knew that everything would be destroyed again the next night, but I heeded Jo's advice. That's what I called her now, to save time.

As soon as I finished, we set out eastward. Today we had two vital tasks. The first was to collect resources to upgrade the integration module so I could combine all my hexagons together in the portal network. The second was to put out feelers in the east up to the border with Tafari's territory. His reconnaissance drone, or rather, the mere fact that another test subject had one, worried me. From the south and west we were covered by the edges of the Trial field, and doing reconnaissance on the north before installing the portal network would be a waste of time because we'd have to travel at least 10 miles through my hexagons to get there. Unfortunately, I wasn't able to use Tank as a mount.

We walked along the southern edge, zigzagging northward in order to capture a neutral hexagon. I'd seized three hexagons by noon, bringing my total to 12. I wasn't able to capture a fourth one because we ran into a person.

I spotted him first. I signaled to Jo to stop and lie down. Jovanna's Perception was lower than mine, so she still didn't see the enemy.

"What's that?" she asked.

"A test subject. His name's Zack. He's level 3. He's wearing civilian clothes, not a uniform. He doesn't have any units with him, either."

"Has he seen us?"

It wasn't an idle question; it would be hard not to notice a 150-yard-long tyrannosaur, but if this guy's Perception wasn't leveled up, the fog of war would even conceal Rex.

"I don't think so," I said. "He might not be alone. I'll go see what's up. Rex will stay here on standby, and you and Tank go around the back and make sure there's no one else."

"OK," I detected a note of disappointment in her voice.

We'd spent the whole morning arguing about our strategy until we were hoarse. She already saw herself as a partner on the path to a common goal and insisted that we totally annihilate our competitors, which she viewed as the only way to victory.

"Kill them all! No discussion! Tyrannosaur! Triceratops!" she shouted, proving the need to advance quickly and capture the hexagons one after the other.

There was a certain logic in her words that was dictated by the conditions of the Trial. The more territory we captured, the more resources we'd earn, and the more resources we earned, the stronger we'd be. She was right... well, almost.

What if someone else took the same route — Carter, for example? If he took another ten or twenty people into his clan... that was at least 200 Charisma points for a clan, meaning, for units. Between Carter's 200 bloodsuckers and another 10 or so fellow clan members, we wouldn't be able to hold them — they'd simply outweigh us. In any case, I decided to first try to talk to this Zack guy.

I approached him, making sure I was prepared to mentally order Rex to attack. He was so fast that once I called him, help would be at my side in a couple of seconds.

"Hi there," I greeted Zack, showing him my upraised hands so he'd know I was coming in peace.

He was a short guy with curly hair who looked to be around my age. He was shaking so hard his cheeks trembled. He was so fat that his whole body appeared swollen with bee stings. But why? How could he have an interface and not lose weight?

He was scurrying around the white command center activation stone but for some reason wasn't activating it. Maybe he didn't have enough resources. He was wearing a tattered business suit with a tie that he'd loosened. He was squeezing a tatty stick all covered in blood of the local mobs.

"Hello, Mr...." he hesitated, squinting. "Phil!"

"Did you get killed?"

"What makes you say that?" he answered the question with a question.

"Your clothes are from the other world."

He had fewer than 1000 life points and my intuition was silent, so I concluded that he wasn't dangerous.

"It's been a few days, so you should have acquired a base long ago, and on the base, the first thing you get is the uniform module. It's more effective than your ripped clothes, and I'm sure you would have taken advantage of the opportunity... if you could have. So that means they killed you and you were resurrected in the clothes you were wearing when you ended up here. And based on your club, you spent the last few hours farming resources to activate the command center."

"Yes, you're right," Zack sighed. He rubbed his palms together and came closer, sticking his hand out. "I'm Zack. Seeing as you didn't try to kill me right away, are you in the mood to talk?"

"You tell me. Are you here by yourself? How did you lose your life?"

"Oh, it's a long story! See, back when I had the honor of doing an internship in a Jerusalem-"

"Stop. Zack, time is the most valuable resource here. It's even more valuable than existence resources. Don't squander my time or yours. Just answer quickly and get to the point. You have 30 seconds to explain everything, and then I'm going to capture this hexagon."

I shoved him aside, went over to the activation stone and theatrically looked at a nonexistent wristwatch. I tapped my wrist with my index finger. "Twenty seconds."

"I ended up here, activated the command center, then took my time investigating around the hexagon, farmed some resources, and put everything into my development," Zack jabbered. "I didn't go outside the boundaries because I was planning to first reach level 10 and get a specialization. Then I ran into a certain..." he wavered. "Mike... His name was Mike. He didn't have any weapons. He'd just been resurrected. He said he'd been killed by Tafari — some sort of horrible African giant riding a rhinoceros. Then Tafari came after me... and killed me. That's all."

"Can you tell me anything else about him?"

"No. He attacked me suddenly. And now..."

He didn't say what happened to Mike. I got the impression that Zack had killed him. But screw him. I didn't care for this Zack.

"Time's up," I interrupted him. "Maybe I'll listen to the rest... after I've captured the hexagon. You'd better get away."

"No, wait. I beg you," he dropped to his knees, his face contorted by fear.

I signaled to Jovanna and Rex to approach. Zack's cries were drowned out by the stomping of my mobs. I waited until everyone had gathered and Zack had pulled himself together. I allowed him a couple of minutes; maybe he'd be able to tell me more about Tafari.

Jo looked on disgustedly but didn't say anything. She drew her index finger across her throat in a silent question. I responded with a slight shake of the head: not yet.

Zack wiped away his tears, smearing dirt on his face. He looked like a tubby child whose parents wouldn't buy him the toy he wanted. For some reason his puffy childlike face aroused my sympathy.

He finally stopped bawling and calmed down.

"Why are you so fat, anyway? Didn't the interface recommend that you watch your diet? How did you even pass the preliminary selection?" Jovanna couldn't restrain herself. "You know how destructive visceral fat is to your insides."

"Stop, Jo. What are you begging for, Zack? Oh, I see. How much time do you have until you're disincarnated?"

There was a flash of hope in his eyes. "Forty-three minutes. Hey! I can see by your levels and units that you're doing pretty well. Help me capture this hexagon so I won't be disincarnated."

Jovanna seized her bow and pulled the string back, aiming the arrow at Zack. I raised my hand, indicating that she should let him finish. Maybe he could join our clan. But what use would he be to us? He obviously wasn't a fighter. He'd just be a burden.

"Let me finish! I found the instance! The

instance, do you understand? Do you know what that is?" he waited for us to nod and then continued. "I don't have any weapons. I didn't want to risk going through it myself. To be honest, I barely made it out alive when I ran into the first local mobs. The portal is hidden; you won't find it on your own. I found it by chance. And if..."

"We'll find it ourselves, Phil," Jovanna interrupted Zack.

"So you help us with the instance and we'll help you with this hexagon?" I wanted to clarify this with him. "The instance is in this hexagon?"

Zack nodded eagerly. "I won't get in the way. I'll just mind my own business and farm mobs. And you promise not to touch me... for at least a week."

"Three days."

He thought for a moment and nodded again.

"OK. Take us there."

Jovanna didn't take her eyes off me the whole way there. Her thirst for blood was understandable and it made sense as a strategy, but my rationality was more practical. We'd get a lot more resources by cleaning out the instance than by just sending Zack to his resurrection point and capturing the hexagon, at least in the near term. Also, the final boss was sure to drop something useful. And if you also took into account that time would stand still there, we'd be able to sort things out with Zack later — in three days, to be precise.

Right now the only thing that worried me was whether we'd be able to take our units with us.

* * *

Zack chattered with abandon the whole way, telling us his life story. Whether it was because he felt reassured that the situation had been resolved or because he wanted to gain our trust so we wouldn't kill him after he'd fulfilled his end of the bargain, I don't know.

When we got to the instance, Zack left us by the entrance and rushed off to farm six resource points so he could capture the hexagon.

Jovanna stopped and laid a hand on my chest. "Phil, please tell me why you did that. We're on the same side, so I need to understand what you're doing. Look, I'm ready to help you win because if you do, I get to keep everything I achieved with the *hookup.*"

"What exactly do you want me to explain?"

"Why didn't you kill him? And why didn't you take him into the clan? Then he would have had to show us the entrance to the instance."

Now that she'd reached level 5, Jovanna had access to the expanded rulebook, so she could personally confirm what Carter had told her: if the clan leader wins, she'd get to keep everything she achieved with the interface. That sparked hope in her, and her dark mood had been replaced by irrepressible enthusiasm. That explained why she saw the clan as a team of which I was the captain.

I slid down the wall and sat on the ground so we could talk things through. Time stood still in the instance, anyway, so we didn't need to rush.

"First of all, why didn't I kill him? Last time, I was only able to fight you and Carter off after I cleared out the instance. Now my level is higher, so there might be even more loot."

"It's too bad that the dinosaurs aren't with us," Jovanna sighed. "Are you sure nothing will happen to them?"

The mobs were just too big to get through the instance.

"They won't go anywhere; time doesn't pass here. The exit will be close to the entrance, so they won't even notice we're gone. In any case, we can manage without them."

"I don't think anyone will risk attacking them."

"Uh-huh. OK, moving on. Why didn't I take him into the clan? Look. How much does sustenance cost? At level 1, 1 point per hour. Zack is level 3, so that's 39 points per day. It would be out of the question to send him out alone to farm resources in the shared pool. Without a uniform or weapons he wouldn't collect much. So we'd need to give him clothes, shoes and weapons. That's also an expense. Would we take him with us? One level 7 sarasur would chew him up without even noticing. So the only thing to do for him was level him up and hope there'd be an effect in the future. But the thing is, I don't like him. Did you hear him say how he got rich?"

"He used the *hookup* and married a millionaire's daughter?"

"Yep. I don't want someone like that on our team. Does that make sense?"

"What about me?" Jovanna asked quietly. "Or were you just being nice because I helped you when we first met?"

I smiled. "Have you looked in the mirror?"

"Yes, so what? Is something wrong?" she touched her face in confusion.

"That's the point. Everything's fine."

She lowered her eyes in embarrassment.

"Jo, don't worry. He'll get his turn. If he levels up enough on his own, we'll take him into the clan. If not, we'll capture his hexagon. OK, ready? Shall we go clear it out?"

I confidently led the way toward the first pack of mobs. Jovanna followed me warily — this was her first instance. If the rulebook wasn't lying, they were all pretty much the same, so I didn't expect any surprises.

But I was wrong.

The first four jellyfish, one of which was a level 9 officer, nearly drove me to permanent disincarnation. I'd ordered Jovanna to shoot mobs from a distance, but I forgot to specify exactly what sorts of mobs she'd need to attack.

As a result, the pack I'd brought broke into two as soon as she drew aggro to herself. It happened while she was shooting two other mobs, not the mob I was fighting. The creatures she was attacking immediately sped away. When they flew closer to Jovanna, they switched fire from their cubic guns to her. I didn't have a chance to kill my mobs in order to draw aggro to myself when her Health ended up in the red.

"Activate the level up!" I struggled to make myself heard over the booming shots of the jellyfish.

In her panicked state she didn't hear me and instead scurried about and ran toward me in the hopes of finding protection. I had to dart toward her, blocking the line of fire. The officer was toast, but I didn't get the chance to kill the jellyfish that was aggroing me because otherwise I wouldn't have been able to save Jovanna in time. In the end I had to upgrade to level 8 in order to restore health points, then kill the remaining mobs at my leisure.

In the aftermath of the first fight I had to school Jovanna in the basics of how instances worked in an MMORPG.

"Get it? They see me and gather around me, but you need to deal more damage to one of them than I do or you'll immediately become the target of their attack. Always fight the ones I'm fighting!"

"Sorry. I understand now," she gave me an embarrassed smile, realizing her gaffe.

She came over to me and soothingly ran her fingers over my cheek. She didn't avert her eyes.

I gave in. My anger quickly dissipated even without her smile. The girl had never played these kinds of games before. You could say she'd never played computer games at all, considering her childhood and adolescence, which were full of schedules and practices.

"OK. I'll level up the characteristic and we'll keep going."

I added two points from the leveling up to Strength, bringing it up to 25 and increasing damage.

The rest of the cleanout went like clockwork. I served as the tank, gathering packs of mobs around me, and Jovanna shot them from a distance, causing bleed DOTs and occasionally stunning them. Their levels ranged from 7 to 9. It looked like the scaling wasn't based on the average of my and Jo's levels, but only on my 7, which was where I'd been when I entered the dungeon.

"Say, where did you get your staff?" I asked while we took a break before the last boss. "Since this is your first instance, and before this you never killed neither elites nor bosses..."

"I got it based on the results of the preliminary selection," Jovanna explained. "I had less injuries than everyone else."

"Did Carter tell you where he got his spear and dagger?"

"Oh please, did he ever!" she laughed. "He loves to brag. He got the spear in an instance whose entrance he found right after he captured his first hexagon. He got the dagger because he somehow managed to kill a location boss before he met up with you the first time. He spent a long time telling me about his success so he could convince me to join his clan without a fight. By the way, do you know what his strategy was?"

"No, but I'd love to hear about it. Bring all the test subjects into his clan?"

"Would you believe, that's pretty much what it was," she laughed. "Tafari goes from hexagon to hexagon and kills everyone he meets, but Carter wanted to capture everyone around him as fast as possible and give them all independence."

"Why?"

"So that each of them would level up on their own and extract resources also on their own. He even said that he was willing to work 50-50 and that the clan settings would allow him to do that. He said it was win-win. I think that would be the ideal situation for Zack."

"What if someone refused to extract resources?"

"You keep forgetting about the disincarnation timer that he could set for anything. Damn, why did I have to remind you about that?" she swore at herself in Serbian.

"Take it easy, I'm not planning to use it on you."

"OK, look. For example, he can set the timer for a clan member to farm a set amount of resources in a day. So, say that he sets your standard at 600 points per day, and you divide it up any way you want. If you don't accomplish it, you get disincarnated."

I chuckled. "Interesting strategy. I'm serious. Worth thinking about. So then why did he bring you to me? Was he afraid that he wouldn't manage on his own?"

"It was a coincidence that we were headed to your hexagon. Carter thought it was available. When he realized that you'd already dug in there, he was happy. He thought that this time you'd definitely agree and he wouldn't even need to waste any more resources on capturing."

"Well, he misjudged."

"Uh-huh. So, are we going to get rid of this creature?"

"Of course. But first let's discuss the strategy.

The instance boss is the exact same one as the last time. The only differences are the level and the name, but it's the same name except for one letter.

Reniza'Nasi
Location boss.
Level 10.
Life points: 4150.

Recalling what I'd entered the fight with the last time, I looked at the power fist and Acid Dagger of

Obfuscation in my hands, at the Canavar's Ruthless Jaws, and at Jovanna's Rumbling Lightning Rod and headed confidently into battle.

Six seconds into the fight, the dagger's effect kicked in: instant death. The boss dropped a Large Existence Crystal, with almost 1500 points (that was my chance for double loot kicking in) and a dagger.

No, not a dagger. The mother of all daggers!

Wicked Dagger of Absorption
Treacherous melee weapon. Each attack restores 25% of the owner's health from the damage dealt.
It is powered by existence resources (5% of your points for each damage dealt).
Damage: 150–180.

When I picked it up, the handle changed shape and enveloped my fist. There was a flash of burning pain which felt as if a thousand sharp, needle-thin tentacles entered my skin all the way to my blood vessels.

I hissed in agony.

"You OK?" Jovanna asked with concern when she saw my face contort.

"Me? I'm just fine!" even I was frightened by my altered, coarsened voice.

"Good," she said, satisfied. "What's the plan now?"

"Unfinished business is a symptom of spiritual bankruptcy. I think we'll be able to intercept Zack before he activates the hexagon."

For some reason Jovanna recoiled. "What do you

mean?"

"Come on, we're going to take that loser down!"

Chapter Eleven

MAY I TAKE THIS OPPORTUNITY

Why is it that the hardest thing in the world is to convince a bird that he is free, and that he can prove it for himself if he'd spend a little time practicing? Why should that be so hard?

Richard Bach, *Jonathan Livingston Seagull*

"NOW MEMORIZE THIS: OLA, EDDY, JOVANNA, MANU, Carter, Leti, Zack, Ken. Got it?" Ilindi waited for me to answer, then repeated: "Ola, Eddy, Jovanna, Manu, Carter, Leti, Zack, Ken."

The moment we'd sat down on the same couch behind the coffee table where we'd sat before, she began repeating these names over and over, ordering me to memorize them. She drilled them into me the whole time I was drinking my cup of coffee, and she was still drilling them into me now, after we'd finished. It was like 10 minutes of either a memory exercise or meditation — I wasn't sure which.

"Ola, Eddy, Jovanna, Manu, Carter, Leti, Zack, Ken." I memorized them right away.

"Repeat them backward... again. Now in any order you want..."

I did as she asked and looked at her, silently asking for explanations.

"You need to commit them to your long-term memory, Phil. This is important. There's a hypothesis, which agrees with my personal experience, that a connection between you and your replica is preserved in Infospace. Over the last few days, have you had any strange ideas or thoughts? Like dreams, maybe?"

"I don't think so," I answered, rooting around in my memories since the abduction.

Yesterday I had taken Kostya and Julie to the airport. In the evening, there had been a brawl at a night club with the son of the first deputy mayor. Today there'd been an emergency meeting at the office, after which I'd leveled up my looks and went to the class reunion. Except... "You know what, last night I had a dream about dinosaurs. But that can't have had anything to do with it."

"Dinosaurs? The extinct fossil reptiles? Hm," Ilinidi couldn't have looked more human as she rubbed her nose. "Their intelligent subspecies failed the Diagnostics 100 million years ago. But it's unlikely that this would have had any connection to the Trial. Well, all right. Anyway, you need to keep saying those names. Maybe when the other Phil meets one of them, he'll understand."

"Understand what exactly? How will he understand if even I don't know what you mean? Can't you just give me an explanation once and for all? You were saying it's a real mess on Pibellau. What's Pibellau? What kind of problems are there?"

Ilindi leaned back and stretched out her long, shapely legs on the table. "Do you mind if I sit like this? Thank you. As you already know, Nick Valiadis and I installed a different version of the interface in a few test subjects, including you. The version by the Senior Races trains fighters and egoists, encouraging them to level up accordingly. Our version develops responsibility and social status while rewarding socially meaningful actions. In this wave of the Trial, there are nine people like you with high social status — nine out of a total of 169 test subjects. And only one of them, a guy named John Carter, started out pretty well and is now in the top 10. All the other subjects with high social status are developing slowly, and you're the slowest of them all."

"Me? It's going that badly?" the blood rushed to my face and my throat went dry, so when I spoke it sounded like my tongue was wooden.

"Very, very badly, Phil. Your replica, Phil 2, has already lost two lives and is on his last one. If he doesn't capture a new base within a day, he'll be disincarnated and you'll lose everything you've achieved. So it's very important that you all join forces there and stick together. That's the only way you'll all have any chance."

I was silent for a long time. I didn't know what to say. It was as if nothing depended on me, and any mistakes the other Phil made weren't my fault, but ultimately I was responsible.

The devastation that descended on me didn't go unnoticed.

Ilindi whispered something. A healing wave washed over me, drawing the fatigue out of my body and my mind. It wasn't all over. I still had a chance.

"Stacy," a little more alert now, I unthinkingly called her by her Earth name. "You could have communicated those eight names to me any way you wanted. Did you really have to come to my house?"

"Last time, it took all of my Spirit reserves to set up a Sphere of Silence in your house. Believe me, it's not easy. Every time I do it, the cooldown weakens my abilities for a few days."

"Sphere of Silence? What are you talking about?"

It was more or less clear what she meant from the context, but I wanted an explanation.

"The place where we're sitting right now is a space that's protected by a sphere," she drew a circle around us with her hands, marking out the rough boundaries. "No signals travel from here into infospace, and we can talk without worrying about attracting the Senior Supervisor's attention. If he finds out that Nick and I tried to interfere in the progress of the Trial, the consequences would be irreversible, and could even disqualify our races for good."

"So, then, this Senior Supervisor — is he someone like Khphor?"

"He's the high judge of the Senior Races. He evaluates the performances of the test subjects after the observers vote and makes the final decision on who to name the winner or how to penalize participants."

"What does this Trial look like? What do they do there?"

Ilindi's patient explanations painted a picture of

the backside of the Galaxy where I — or rather, my replica — had gone.

The Elders had transformed a remote little planet named Pibellau in the Sagittarius sector specifically for the Trials. There were two suns, a large one and a small one. The small one was artificial and put there by one of the planet's extinct civilizations. There were no natural satellites: the nocturnal light came from a myriad of stars. The daytime sky was purple fading into a dirty brown. The flora looked like Earth's flora, but that's where the similarities ended. There were predatory, carnivorous plant species. The fauna was predatory and raised artificially for the Trials since there were no plant-eating species there. When night fell, the daytime species disappeared somewhere and huge monsters came out. The only way to get away from them was to escape to a shelter.

The whole field of the Trial was divided into six-sided shapes called hexagons. One side of a hexagon was a little less than 2 miles long. Each test subject's "home" hexagon was surrounded by six neutral hexagons. Each hexagon was surrounded by an energy field that animals couldn't penetrate.

Each test subject had three lives. If a test subject was killed by aggressive fauna, they were resurrected in their home hexagon. If the test subject was killed by another test subject, they lost all their belongings and resources they had on them, as well as all their hexagons, which were then transferred to the person who had killed them. The test subject was then resurrected in the closest hexagon, which wasn't necessarily neutral. If all the hexagons were captured, the test subject was resurrected on the border of any hexagon in the Trial field that was chosen at random.

Pibellau days were longer than Earth days, but they had only 13 hours, although that was relative and came from the Vaalphors' chronology. But the strangest thing was that time on Pibellau passed faster than on Earth. So when I lived a day on Earth, it was more on Pibellau.

"This reminds me of a computer game," I said, summing up Ilindi's story. "You capture and develop bases and have a few lives, and there are even mobs. Maybe they even drop loot?" I laughed at the absurdity.

"Loot?" Ilindi repeated in confusion and shrugged. "I don't understand. The essence of the Trial has been exactly the same for millions of years in Earth time. It's a war, and a war never changes, even if the people involved are each fighting for themselves and battling in a different sector of the galaxy..."

"Have you also participated in it?"

"That's a stupid question, Phil. Of course. I participated and even won. Then I merged with my replica and 'remembered' everything. Anyway, that's all for now. I'm sorry but I need to go. I hope something useful will come out of this."

Those were her last words which she spoke more to herself than to me.

"Where are you off to?"

"I have a flight to catch. First I'm going to South Africa, then to the United States and then on to Colombia. I'm going to see Carter, Eddy and Manu and have the same conversation with them. As we speak, Nick is flying to Cameroon via Kazakhstan to meet with Ken and Ola. Unfortunately, you can't talk about this kind of thing over the phone."

I went to see her out. She gave me a quick peck on the lips and stepped out onto the landing.

After she called the elevator, she turned back to me. "Repeat the names!"

I recited the names of Phil 2's potential comrades in arms, and Stacy aka Ilindi disappeared into the depths of the elevator.

An idea came to me as I locked the front door. I settled on the couch and summoned Martha. Having exchanged pleasantries, I wasted no time in getting down to business:

"My exact replica is participating in the Trial. Right?"

"That's right."

"If he went through the portal as an exact replica of myself, that means that the other Phil has your copy, too. Right?"

"Possibly," Martha answered evenly. She was now sitting in the same spot where Ilindi had been. Just like Ilindi, she stretched out her long legs, shown off by her short shorts, and threw them onto the coffee table.

"Possibly or definitely? Can you establish a connection with her?"

"Even if I can, and I try and don't get a response, what will that accomplish? OK..." I felt an invisible hand lightly touch my brain. "There, I've exported the data. I understand the task."

"So then tell me what it is."

"Ola, Eddy, Jovanna, Manu, Carter, Leti, Zack, Ken. Your replica needs to know that these are potential allies. I'm about to start transmitting a coded signal to the Universal Infospace. But even if Martha 2 is able to accept it, how will she transmit the information to Phil 2? Your replica's interface is still installed, but I'm sure it's blocked. Otherwise there will be a conflict between the versions as the one used in the Trial works according to completely different principles. In fact, your replica functions by altering the local layers of reality."

"Damned if I know, Martha. But if there's even a one-billionth of a percent of a chance that it would help me keep the interface — and that means keeping you, too — it would be worth it. What are you doing?"

"Just take it easy."

* * *

The new week was bound to bring the troubles I was expecting, including the problems that would undoubtedly be created by the vindictive son of the first deputy mayor — let alone my failing the Trial and all the subsequent consequences.

But the first problem I ran up against on Monday morning was the simplest and even comical. I had nothing to wear: all my clothing was now too small, and even when I pulled on jeans that were too roomy for me before, I had a hard time cramming my bulked-up calves and thighs into the legs.

I'd spent all of Sunday experimenting with Strength. An idea had popped into my clever, but often impractical, head. I had Martha to thank for that. You'd think that a virtual entity that existed only in my mind couldn't be felt physically. Seeing as I'd felt her touch before that, why couldn't I feel the effect more strongly?

That's what I'd been thinking about when she'd told me to relax and close my eyes. I physically felt her fingers traveling through my head, running over every inch of skin and removing the tension. I wasn't even aware of falling asleep, and when I woke up in the middle of the night, I got undressed and lay on my bed.

I woke up in the morning burning with an idea. Seeing as the interface booster allowed me to recover much faster than a regular person, why the hell was I going to the gym every other day? Even regular bodybuilders train every day, and they don't have any kind of interface.

Over the course of the day I went to the gym three times, breaking for a 90-minute nap and a snack — I must have guzzled gallons of protein shakes. I made the first trip early in the morning when the place was empty, and my last trip was late at night, shortly before the gym closed.

After my second session I could see that the idea was working. The Strength rose steadily: my muscles were restored and the fibers were building up.

The fitness manager, who was the only witness to all my workouts that day, hid his surprise for a while, but the third time I showed up he couldn't hold back any longer. He came over to where I was huffing and puffing under the barbells, waited until I'd finished the set, then said sarcastically:

"I don't know if you realize it, but you're flogging a dead horse."

"Am I? Why is that?"

"You're killing your muscles. It's not good to work out so much — you'll hurt yourself. You're overdoing it."

He sounded off for a long time, explaining what was common knowledge to me. I didn't interrupt — I figured I could let him get it off his chest. There weren't a lot of people around, so he was probably just bored. I'd already noticed that these gym rats really liked to share information. The only thing was that their information often differed, and sometimes it was even contradictory, but that's neither here nor there. The main thing was that for the most part these people were friendly.

"Got it, thank you," I said when he took a breath, giving me a chance to respond. I mopped the sweat from my face and started my next set.

Before I took the barbells off the stand, I said,

"You're completely right. But then how come this morning I was having a hard time pressing 45 pounds less than I'm pressing now?"

The manager just waved an arm and walked away as if to say, why talk to such a deluded fool?

In reality, I was pressing more. After studying the training plans of lifters[9] rather than bodybuilders, I'd fundamentally changed my training methods, concentrating on only three basic exercises. Now I was lifting heavier weights but doing fewer reps, and I surprised even myself with what I could to do. During my last session of the day, I bench pressed 265 pounds, and then I got up and did deadlifts with 340 pounds. Through online research I learned that that wasn't yet pro level, but it made me a solid second-class powerlifter.

---

[9] Lifter (jargon) is a powerlifter. Powerlifting is a strength-based sport in which the athlete tries to lift the heaviest weight he can.

The system reacted in a funny way: it took a long time to process the new data, and then it spit out a whole bunch of increases to Strength. With each new session it showed more.

All of this meant that by the end of the weekend, I'd leveled this characteristic up to 19, which had earned me 6000 XP. Plus another 3000 XP for an unexpected triple increase in my Stamina. So that was the side effect of strength training.

Even though my progress slowed considerably after that because I'd simply come off a plateau, encouraging the system to reassess my Strength, that level 20 social status that I desperately wanted was getting closer.

Monday morning showed how big I'd gotten. Since my chest muscles had expanded and my back muscles had broadened, the only thing that fit was a one-size-fits-all T-shirt that used to hang on me like a tent. Now it hugged my body like I was some damn mannequin. I could have gone to work like that, but I'd still need to explain how my eyes and my hair had changed color, so I'd have to make a stop at the mall on the way to work.

I picked out almost the first shirt I saw, added an inexpensive suit, then changed in the dressing room. I hoped that no one would notice anything.

Once I got to the office, it was clear that people almost never notice changes in other people's appearances, especially men. Other than Veronica, nobody suspected a thing. Intercepting me on the stairs, Veronica took me aside and said,

"What's up, are you wearing a bulletproof vest?"

"No, where do you get that idea?"

She incredulously put her hand under my jacket and felt my shoulders and chest.

"What's up? Hey, Alik will see you touching me!"

"Come on. You're like my big brother," her hand found my arm, which instinctively tensed up. "Whoa, check out those guns! So you're pumping iron? Cool!"

"Behave yourself, Veronica," I tried to pull away from her, but she looked at me intently.

"Hey, did you get tinted contacts? And your hair... Hm... There's something different about you. I'm not sure what... Have you had a makeover?"

"Yes," I had to lie. "Didn't I need to?"

She took a step back, looked me up and down and gave me the thumbs-up. That was enough for me.

Feeling her eyes on my back, I walked down the corridor. I made the rounds of all our offices, greeting my colleagues. It was as if everything were normal, but I felt physically tense.

The reasons became clear later on.

At first, the customary Monday managers' meeting went as usual. The division managers gave a lively report about the plans for the week, Alik said that the new offices were completely ready for us to move into, and Mr. Katz and Rose updated us on their preparations for any potential audits. It was only then, after hesitating for a while, that Kesha Dimidko asked for the floor again.

"Phil, some negative rumors are going around town. I would have dismissed them, but just this morning two clients mentioned them."

"You need to be more specific, Kesha."

"OK, specifically: the rumors fall into two categories. Some are about the company and others are explicitly about you. I won't talk about them now. If you want, I can tell you in private."

"What are they saying about the company?"

"They say that we drop partners, drive away key employees, and don't do a good job fulfilling our contractual obligations. They say that we've only been in business for a little while and our director and co-owner is a..." Kesha stopped, realizing that he'd said too much.

"What do they mean, our director?" Gleb sounded confused. "It's Phil, isn't it?"

"I'd also like to know," Veronica drawled pensively. "Kesha, please just finish your sentence."

"They say he's a psychopathic con artist."

I was genuinely surprised. "Meaning?"

Kesha wavered again, looking around uncertainly.

Mr. Katz frowned and shook his head. I sensed that Kesha had talked the situation over with him before bringing it up with me.

I needed to remind them who was the boss. "Kesha, just tell us. We're all friends here."

"But Mr. Katz didn't advise me to..."

"That's right, I didn't!" the old lawyer cried, flying into a rage. "The director's personal life has nothing to do with the company's business!"

"Mark, calm down," Rose joined in. "Remember your heart..."

"I haven't forgotten anything! But I strongly recommend that we not communicate slanderous rumors about Mr. Panfilov in front of everyone."

"Come on, that's enough!" I stood up at my desk. "Guys, remember that we're friends first and then colleagues and partners. Anyway. I'm sure that it will be much worse if I don't have a chance to dispel all this nonsense if people are discussing it behind my back. Kesha?"

"It's better if I tell you," Mr. Katz butted in again. He took a sip of tea and cleared his throat. "Rumors about our company have started to spread around town. On an official level it's hard to find fault with us: we're an unblemished, young company, and none of the shareholders have had issues with taxes or anything else in the past. So the personalities of the shareholders are being targeted. People are talking about all of us, not just Phil."

"Maybe you could be more specific, Mr. Katz?" Veronica interrupted him.

"I need to apologize in advance," he said, shrugging. "Well, Veronica, the gossip about you is that you're allegedly a tart and, er, used certain methods to get a job and partnership in the Great Job Agency..."

"What?" Enraged, Veronica jumped up and clenched her fists. "Who's saying that?"

"They say that Gleb is an alcoholic who gambled his apartment away," Mark continued, ignoring her. He was now like a doctor who'd begun an operation to lance an abscess: he'd already started and the patient was howling, but he needed to finish, and the faster the better. "The rumors about Alik are mainly about his criminal past. Did you serve time in a juvenile correctional facility, Alik? These days that's no big deal — there are politicians who have done serious time and got away with it. But... people are still talking about it, you know."

"Half the country has been in prison!" Alik said.

"And I only did time for hooliganism!"

"Moving on. Kesha's divorced and people are saying that he left his ex-wife with an infant on her hands. Right now he's allegedly reporting false income in order to pay the minimum alimony. We all know it's not the case, but someone is cleverly combining truth and lies, and people believe that sort of half-truth most of all. Kesha does in fact have an 11-year-old daughter from his first marriage, but she's not lacking for anything. Kesha gives at least half of his income to his ex-wife, and I can vouch for that."

My Lie Detection, which I was in the habit of activating at every meeting, confirmed his words. But not even that cheered up my colleagues, their moods firmly in the red zone.

"What are they saying about you and Rose?" Gleb asked grimly.

"Oh, they're just telling the truth about us. We really *are* Jewish... So what?" Mr. Katz heaved a sigh and turned to me. "As for Mr. Panfilov, the rumors are the harshest of all..." he trailed off, giving me a chance to stop him.

I nodded. "Go ahead."

"I think it's all a lie, so I apologize..." he spread his arms. "Mr. Panfilov, is it true that you were unemployed for many years and sponged off your wife, who you divorced shortly before you started the company? And that when you got divorced she was pregnant? I'm sure this isn't true. They also say you occasionally have psychotic episodes and that you allegedly see spirits and talk to the cosmos. They say that before you opened the agency you dabbled in ESP and healed people. Also that you're just a charlatan and con artist. You win people's trust and present yourself as a writer or psychologist in order to gain profit."

"What is this nonsense?" Veronica exclaimed. "It's just the opposite — Phil helps everybody!"

"Is there anything else?" I asked, noticing that he hadn't finished.

"The rest is petty. You were kicked out of a gym, and you often gamble. On the whole, I'd say that someone's doing everything they can to make sure your reputation hits rock bottom."

"It's obvious who!" Cyril said. "The Dorozhkins are stirring the pot! From the beginning I — "

"Phil, reception's just called," an agitated Alik interrupted his ardent outburst. "There's a crowd of people here. It's the audit."

"It's starting," Rose sighed.

The revenue officers were the first to come in. A short thin woman led the procession, her eyes sharp behind her glasses.

"Is this the Great Job Recruitment Agency?" she asked, peering at her paperwork. "Who's the director of the company? Which of you is Philip Panfilov?"

I stepped forward. "I am. What can I do for you?"

"A tax counteraudit. Here's the directive..."

* * *

The revenue officers hadn't shown up out of nowhere; they came under the guise of auditing one of our contractors. But Rose expressed complete confidence that we had nothing to worry about with the audit.

Based on my interaction with them, I had the impression that they weren't really holding their breath about finding anything, and in conversation they didn't show any interest in me. They asked me a series of formal questions, then went into Rose's office to sit down with the documents.

"Don't worry, Mr. Panfilov," Mr. Katz tried to reassure me. "Everything's in order. I mean, after all, we're not in the '90s when they tried to strangle small businesses. Don't worry."

I wasn't worried. I was far more concerned about the source of the rumors. This source seemed to know a painful amount of my personal information. If all of this came from a high-up order from the first deputy mayor, it was time that I had a chat with his son.

But first I needed to explain myself to the gang.

Having given a pep talk to my deflated friends and boosted their confidence, I went on to see our sales reps. They were still occupying Kesha's former printing business as we'd had to put off the move to the new office because of the audit. Kesha had managed to sell all his equipment which had freed up a lot of space. In addition to him and the guys from Ultrapak, the office was occupied by nine trainees, so the place was always buzzing.

Silence reigned when they saw me. I wouldn't say that the atmosphere was hostile, but it was wary. They didn't know what to expect from the director that day. Maybe he was about to fire everyone, or maybe he was about to say that everything was in a bad way and the company was shutting down.

Someone put down a phone while somebody else

buried himself in his papers. Even Cyril looked away and pretended to be busy. Kesha raised his head and gazed at me expectantly. Marina, who was sitting next to him, looked worried. Only Greg reacted as he always did when he saw me: he smiled and gave me a friendly wave.

I went over to Kesha. "Can I talk to you and your guys?"

He nodded. "Hey, everyone, we need to interrupt you for a minute," he said half-jokingly to his subordinates. "Our liege wants words with us."

That did the trick. Someone laughed; the atmosphere had lightened up.

"Thank you, Kesha. OK, everyone! Please raise your hand if you have any questions about what's going on today."

No hands went up, but one of the new employees, the bearded Denis who was quick to laugh, spoke up from the far corner of the room,

"Everything is clear. What is there not to understand? We all know about the fight. It's payback from the son of the deputy mayor."

"So no one has any regrets about coming to work here?"

"No," a chorus of voices rang out over each other. "Everything's fine."

"Excellent. I can see you've worked it out without me. So, about the rumors," I decided to immediately come clean.

"Is it all crap?" Denis lifted his eyebrows.

"Almost. The only thing that's true is that I was married but I got divorced recently."

"Why did you leave your wife when she was

pregnant?" Irina, a 25-year-old single mother, asked indignantly, staring daggers at me. Her Interest was more than piqued.

I looked her in the eye, trying to be as warm and sincere as possible, "Irina, I had nothing to do with her pregnancy. I give you my word."

She nodded, satisfied. I saw Marina look scathingly at Irina, apparently not willing to understand that for the new employees I was nothing more than a boss. They still hadn't figured out what kind of boss I was.

"I'll deal with all of this myself. The only thing I ask of you is to remain calm and keep working, no matter what other rumors you may hear from our clients. If you still want to find out more about me — what I'm really like as a person and who I am — talk to your colleagues. Cyril, Greg, Marina and I all worked together at Ultrapak. They'll tell you that when I give my word, it means something. As for our company as a whole, we're growing fast and you have an amazing opportunity to grow with it."

I looked around at my colleagues who had gone quiet, then activated the clan management dashboard and tapped on abilities:

Raising spirits (24 hours)
Clan leader's ability to inspire other clan members.
+50% to Mood of each clan member.
+25% to Satisfaction of each clan member.
+5% to Trust in clan leader.

The cooldown from the ability was a week — that

was substantial, but if I didn't use it now, when would I? The ability had come with level 3 for the clan, which kept growing with each new client and employee.

"Well, let's not mope, team! We'll still have clients lining up to work with us, and all you'll need to do is pick out the most profitable orders," I said this with such confidence and charisma that my Spirit reserves melted away before my eyes.

The cheer from the sales staff was so enthusiastic it made the office walls shake.

"Thank you for your attention. If no one has any more questions, let's get back to work!"

As I was turning to leave, I noticed Kesha wink as Denis said behind me:

"Mr. Panfilov! One last question! How much do you lift?"

* * *

I located Alexander Dorozhkin's marker on the interface map. He was in a Chinese restaurant. I had one of our drivers take me there. Once he'd dropped me off, I let him go: my salespeople had client meetings to get to and I didn't want to monopolize a car.

I climbed the stairs which were flanked by bronze dragon figurines. When I got to the heavy front door, I reached out for the handle, but the door opened by itself.

An elderly guard was holding it. It wasn't until after I'd walked past him that I thought of tipping him, but by then it would have been awkward to go back. I wasn't yet in the habit of doing so. I hadn't had much chance of tipping people in the past.

A cute Asian-looking girl who I took to be the hostess was standing by the entrance. "Welcome to Peking Duck! Do you have a reservation?"

"Sorry, I don't."

"In that case..." a shadow flickered over the girl's face, but it disappeared quickly when she ran her finger over her computer screen. "I can offer you a table in the far room. Come with me, please."

The first surprise happened when on the way I saw that Dorozhkin was sitting with his father, Edward Dorozhkin himself. They were wielding chopsticks, speaking animatedly. There were no guards, escorts or entourage. The first deputy mayor of the town was in a public place, democratically eating lunch with his son.

The younger man spotted me. His eyes bored into me but he didn't recognize me. His Interest numbers confirmed that he had no idea who I was. If he did, he'd hardly be sitting there so calmly.

I ordered the spicy mixed vegetables with beef and then settled in to observe. I was seated in the middle of the room which was full of people. This presented an opportunity to speak civilly with Dorozhkin. He surely wouldn't make a scene in public.

I finally got my chance when I'd almost finished the main course. Dorozhkin senior got up and strode off. The son stayed behind and paid the bill. I laid down my chopsticks, wiped my mouth, activated Lie Detection and approached the young man.

"Hello, Alexander."

He slipped a couple of 5,000-ruble bills in the holder, shut it, slid his wallet back in his jacket pocket and looked up.

"Hello... Er... Do we know each other?"

"May I sit down? We need to talk."

He nodded tentatively.

I sat in the chair his father had vacated. "Alexander, do you remember me?"

"No, damn it! Who are you?"

He wasn't lying. He really didn't remember me. I scrolled through the new data for a couple of seconds, trying to decide what to do. Should I just apologize and leave?

No, I needed to get to the bottom of this.

"My name is Philip. We had a confrontation last Friday at Anomaly. First it was between you and my colleagues, and then between you and me."

"At Anomaly? Um... I was at the Empire. I met someone there... Then we went somewhere else," he wrinkled his forehead. According to Lie Detection, he genuinely didn't remember if he'd been at the club. "Oh! I remember! Damn, dude, you're the one who bashed me?" he burst out laughing. "Hahahaha! Seriously, when I woke up the next day everything hurt, I had a bruise under my ribs... Sergei did tell me to slow down with the drink."

"Honestly, if I..."

"Come on," he interrupted me. "Did we get into a fight? Then we can talk to each other like friends."

"If I hadn't stopped you, things would have turned out much worse. This Sergei guy — that bouncer, he would have crippled one of my friends."

"That's for sure — Sergei's a beast! Look, did you want something, Philip?"

"Listen up," instinct told me how to really talk to this guy. "When we left each other at that club, you threatened to make problems for my company."

"Yeah, and?"

"Did you follow through on that?"

"Look dude, even if I really wanted to make trouble for you, I couldn't because I don't even know what your company is. Take it easy!"

His words were making me feel warm: he wasn't pulling the wool over my eyes.

"What kind of company do you have, anyway? Hahahaha!"

I tensed up a little. He must have noticed. "Well, I gotta run. I give you my word that I don't hold a grudge. There won't be any problems, don't worry your head over it."

He stood up and walked away, leaving me alone with my thoughts and questions. Only a small circle of people knew the slanderous information that was being spread about the company's shareholders. All of those people were my friends, partners and colleagues.

So who was the snitch?

Chapter Twelve

Don't be afraid of enemies

"Why is it destroying other toys?"
"They must have programmed it to eliminate the competition."
"You mean like Microsoft?"

The Simpsons

A FRIEND OF MINE OFTEN LIKED TO SAY THAT IN HIS book, all people were bastards and scoundrels until they proved otherwise. That had been more or less my philosophy when it came to managing my clan in the Game. By definition, all new people were useless noobs and could prove otherwise only through full-fledged participation in raids. The Optimization had burned out all my Game skills, but I still remembered things like that.

When I had gotten the interface, this reliable and safe life philosophy — if you don't trust anyone, no one can betray you — started to glitch and change into its own contradiction. I'd started interacting with the people around me as though I knew in my heart that people are good. Until now, this approach had served me well.

But now I clearly needed to start digging around. Or could it be that the rumors weren't coming from my people?

Vicky. Of all the people who knew me fairly well, she was the most obvious candidate. But what about a motive? She had one. The last time we'd seen each other, her feelings about me were clear. To be honest, if she was the one behind all of this, I'd actually feel relieved. I didn't want to believe that there was a rat in my company.

I called her. The phone rang for a long time, but I waited.

"Hello," I heard her flat voice.

"Hi. We need to talk. Can you give me five minutes?"

She sighed, but to my amazement, instead of sending me packing, she asked,

"When?"

"As soon as possible."

"How about in a half hour at the café next to our office? You remember it?"

"Yes. I'll head over there now."

I paid my bill, called a taxi and set off to meet Vicky. The taxi's route went past one particular place I remembered well: the restaurant — the one where Mr. Ivanov had taken us to celebrate the deal with Valiadis and in front of which I'd been abducted for the first time — where things had kicked off between Vicky and myself.

I felt a twinge of regret. Everything between us had been so spontaneous and... good.

The café was noisy and it was hard to breathe. There were vapers puffing on electronic cigarettes all over the place, making the air so heavy you could cut it with a knife. The sticky-sweet stench overpowered my sensory receptors.

I scanned the crowd for the familiar figure until I found her. Vicky was already sitting at the bar, staring into a mug of cappuccino.

Although initially I was planning on asking her only one question, it quickly got out of hand. "Hey."

"What do you want?" Vicky wasted no time getting down to business.

"I want to know if you have anything to do with the ugly rumors about me and my company that have been going around since this morning. Just answer yes or no."

"No. I have nothing to do with them," her voice was steady.

A warm wave flowed over my skin. Vicky was telling the truth. That was enough for me, but she continued,

"I've heard what people have been saying. But I didn't start it. I haven't told anyone anything about you or your company, not counting the conversation you were part of."

This time I felt a cold sensation. It wasn't a strong feeling. It was kind of like the cold that comes out of the refrigerator when you open it, but it meant that Vicky wasn't being entirely sincere.

"Are you saying that you've never told your new boyfriend anything about us?"

"That's none of your business, but I'll answer anyway. You were a jerk, but when I answered his questions after your visit, I didn't go into detail. I just confirmed that we'd been together for a while. I said it was nothing serious, just a little fling. That's it."

She was telling the truth. "If we're done now, I'll be on my way. You can pay for the coffee."

Without even touching her cappuccino, she walked out, leaving me with distressing thoughts.

I stayed in the café and called Kesha. "You were kind of vague about something this morning. From whom did you hear the rumors about me and the company? Who first told them to you?"

"Everybody's talking," Dimidko answered. He went silent, trying to remember.

When people say "everybody," they often mean just a few people. Usually people from their inner circle. I remembered how Yanna had once tried to prove to me that "everybody" had gone on some sort of fashionable diet. "Everybody" turned out to be two of her friends. So when Kesha said "everybody," he could have very well meant just a couple of clients.

"Be more specific!"

"Phil, I've made twenty phone calls today. Let me check my notes. Aha, here it is. Arkady Sorkin, Kravetz Finance Group. It's an impressive name but a small outfit."

"Sorkin? Give me his contact information."

Five minutes later I was on my way to Kravetz's office. Sorkin had agreed to meet with me.

* * *

Minimalism reigned in Arkady Sorkin's aquarium-like office. He greeted me personally, coming out from behind his standing desk. He was a stout 46-year-old man with a bloated face.

"Arkady Sorkin," he said, sticking his hand out. "Sorry I'm not going to invite you to sit down because there's nowhere to sit. My nutritionist recommends that I spend as much time on my feet as possible, and apparently I followed his recommendation too literally," he said with a bashful smile. "What can I do for you, Philip?"

"Mr. Sorkin, I wish I could tell you that I've come to make an amazing offer that would be good for both of us, but I'm here about something else."

"I understand."

"This morning when you were talking to my commercial director, you shared some, shall we say, rumors about our company. As I'm sure you understand, I couldn't just ignore this, and now I'm trying to figure out where these insinuations are coming from."

"Please excuse my curiosity, but do these rumors have any basis in fact?"

"Not every question has a clear-cut answer, Mr. Sorkin. Tell me, have you stopped drinking brandy in the morning?"

Sorkin laughed and wagged a finger at me.

After he got it out of his system, he became serious. "I get the idea. There's no smoke without fire, but even a single small cigarette can let off smoke."

"Yep. A lot of lies draw on the carcass of truth."

"Well said," Sorkin adjusted his glasses which had slid down the bridge of his nose. He came closer and said confidentially, "Last night I was at a charity event to benefit the work of young artists here in town. I was approached by a young man I didn't know who introduced himself as Konstantin Panchenko. He was the commercial director of a company associated with packaging materials. During the conversation he mentioned you, and I was interested since I was planning to sign a contract with you today."

"I think I know who you're talking about."

"To tell you the truth, I believed everything he said. He was very convincing, and I trusted him. I have to say he was quite amiable. These days there aren't too many people like that. I think it would be unfair to him if I told you the details of our conversation."

"That's enough, Mr. Sorkin. I'm very grateful to you for clearing this up. Thank you."

I was ready to say good-bye, but he held on to me and touched my collar as if to straighten it. "If you don't mind my asking, is there some sort of feud between you and him? I just don't understand. Your companies work in different industries, so why would he do this?"

"It has to do with a woman," I said vaguely. I shook his hand and got ready to leave.

When I turned around, I saw Sorkin following me with his gaze, pursing his lips. He nodded. "I'll give that contract with you another think."

* * *

So if the source of the rumors was Panchenko[10] — the new commercial director of Ultrapak who'd replaced Pavel Gorelov — and Vicky wasn't the source of his information, there was only one possible way he could be digging up this dirt. Vicky didn't know my partners that well, so she was unlikely to know who the new employees of the Great Job Agency were. The only person she more or less knew was Alik. She'd seen Veronica only once, and she'd never met the others and I'd never talked about them.

That meant that there was a rat in my company. It couldn't be any of the trainees; they'd been working for us for less than a week. So who was it?

Cyril, Marina and Greg had left Ultrapak because they were unhappy with the new boss. It was unlikely to be either Mr. Katz or Rose; they didn't need this, and neither did Veronica or Kesha. The four of them had given themselves completely to the business.

That left Alik and Gleb. They were both partners without cash investments, they both had the smallest stakes and they were the closest to me.

Gleb was the only person who knew a lot about my gambling, and only Alik knew that Yanna was pregnant; it was Alik who had talked to her when she'd come to the office looking for a job and he knew she was my ex-wife.

Continuing to turn myself in knots, I arrived at the Chekhov Business Center. I ran up the stairs,

---

[10] Konstantin Panchenko is one of the main characters of Dan Sugralinov's *The Bricks 2.0.*

dashed into our new empty premises and headed for my private office. The walls still smelled of paint and the furniture hinted of glue.

I opened all the windows to air the place out and summoned Alik first.

The ex-lowlife now looked more like an ordinary white-collar worker in his black slacks, white short-sleeved shirt and, of course, polished black shoes with trendy socks. His hair bore a semblance of a parting in it, but it was still unruly, with little tufts sticking out.

The only thing that remained from his old character was his body language. He had the same thuggish gait: the chin in the air, the open shoulders, drooping arms and shuffling walk on the inside of the foot. He was holding a leather binder under his arm.

"Has something happened?"

"Yes. I met with the Dorozhkin kid."

"No way!" Alik slammed his fist into the palm of his hand. "Was it him?"

"No. Don't ask me why I'm so sure, but it definitely wasn't him or his father. It's Konstantin Panchenko, that idiot from Ultrapak, the company where I used to work."

"The one that Cyril, Marina and Greg came from?"

"Yes, that's it," I finally remembered what I was doing and activated Lie Detection. "Tell me honestly, Alik. Did you, by any chance, pass that guy any personal information about the partners?"

"*What?*" Alik's indignation was so genuine that the predatory grin of a thug clearly peeked through his office worker's mask. "Are you serious? You think I'm a rat? Cut the crap!"

"Stop!" I practically had to bark at him. "Just answer me honestly: did you give Panchenko information about the company and the shareholders?"

"No!" Alik barked back, emphasizing his indignation with a curse. "I didn't tell him anything! What makes you think..."

As he continued yelling, I was singed by a wave of desert heat. He was telling the truth.

My heart lifted — his betrayal would have been a huge blow for me. It's one thing when partners you don't really know act that way with you, and something else entirely when it's someone you're close to, whose fate you fully invested yourself in without any selfish motives.

"I should have asked," I said calmly when he finished his ardent speech. "Think about it. Someone here definitely passed on information to him."

"Hold on," Alik wrinkled his forehead, looking down. "Look! Could it have been Vicky? She works at the same company and knows almost everything about us. Also, you said that the HR managers around town know her well, so she could have used her own channels to get to Kesha. And then she could have told Panchenko."

"Alik, it definitely wasn't her."

"Are you sure?"

"I'm not *not* sure."

Alik sniffed in understanding and smiled. "Can I go now? I need to deliver some documents for Rose."

"No, please stay here. I want to talk to everyone."

My conversations with Gleb, Kesha, Mark, Rose and Veronica produced the same results and reactions. None of them had any connection to the company's problems.

Gleb said he didn't have the faintest idea who Panchenko was, and he didn't even talk about the company's business with his wife. Kesha twisted his finger at his temple and denied everything. The elderly Katz couple were understanding about my interrogation. Rose was most irritated by the fact that there were revenue officers sitting in her office and she didn't want to leave them alone for too long.

The redheaded beast Veronica was the angriest. She was so indignant and insulted that she slammed the door after telling me to f*** off.

"Damn," said Alik, scratching his head. "The plaster almost fell off... Veronica definitely isn't saving us work."

"Go catch up with her. Tell her that I've been asking everyone about this. In the meantime I'll talk to the people from Ultrapak."

I wanted to call all three of them in at once, but Cyril had gone out for a meeting. Greg and Marina cracked open the door, poked their heads in and hovered on the threshold.

"You wanted to see us, Phil?"

"Yes, come in. Sit down."

They looked around, but when they saw that I was standing they remained standing too. I spent a few moments studying their faces, looking for signs of uneasiness or worry, but I didn't discern any. Not at first. Then Greg broke the prolonged silence.

"What's up, Phil? Can you just tell us what you want from us? I have a client on hold. Or he was on hold — he's probably already hung up."

"When was the last time you talked to your

former boss?"

"You mean in Ultrapak?"

"Yes, with Panchenko."

"Um, when I went to give him my notice," Greg answered. "I haven't seen him since."

"What about you, Marina?"

"Same. What's going on?"

"Did either of you say anything about our company that has anything to do with the rumors going around town?"

"I definitely didn't," Greg said confidently.

"I didn't, either. What's going on? Do you think it's us?" Marina pursed her lips and frowned.

"Now I know for sure that it wasn't the two of you. But it was someone here. There's no one else."

"Could it have been Cyril?" Marina suggested, exchanging glances with Greg.

"Is there something going on with him?"

"You know, Phil..." Greg lowered his eyes. "Lately he's been acting kind of strange."

"How so?"

"He started smoking again!" Marina exclaimed. "He doesn't talk to anyone. When he comes in, he just grumbles 'Hi,' and at the end of the day he says, 'See you,' and that's it."

"Phil, I don't recognize him anymore," Greg added. "Something's definitely happened with him."

Admittedly, whenever I had checked the profiles of the clan members lately, I'd noticed Cyril's plummeting Mood, but I didn't think it was serious.

"Well, OK. I'll talk to him myself. If you see him before I do, don't tell him anything, OK?"

"Of course. No worries," said Greg and Marina

on their way out.

I found Cyril's profile in the clan tab and studied it closely:

Satisfaction: 62%
Fear: 63%
Mood: 18%

His Satisfaction was so high because of the clan buff, so without it the picture would have been gloomier. Oh, Cyril, how can this be? What's going on with you?

* * *

I intercepted Cyril while he was on his way to the office. His marker was moving so slowly across the map that I realized that he was walking.

I spotted him a block away from the park where I planned to chat with him. When he caught sight of me standing directly in his path, he flinched and looked uneasy. A nearly finished cigarette was burning in his hand.

"Hi, Cyril."

"We've already seen each other today," he grumbled, looking around for a place to throw his cigarette butt. "What are you doing here?"

"I just stepped out for a stroll to clear my head and think about what's going on, and here you are. Will you keep me company?"

"Er, Phil, I need to get back to the office. I have things to do," Cyril inhaled deeply, defiantly looking me in the eye, then squinted, dragged the remaining cigarette down to the filter, threw the butt under his foot and stamped it out.

"It won't take long. Let's just take a quick walk through the park and then you can get back to work. If you want, you can keep smoking."

"Hm... I think I will smoke."

I waited for him to take out another cigarette and light it. His Mood fell by another few percent, and now the decline in his spirit was obvious. He'd somehow shriveled up and shrunk, and I could completely relate to what he wanted: hide from the world, disappear, crawl under the covers, preferably with a good book, a big cup of tea and some comfort food, and hope that no one called or bothered him for around 200 years.

But money didn't earn itself, the right to just loaf around was expensive, and somehow the bills needed to be paid. So now Cyril was walking beside me and suffering in silence. He was suffering from my presence as well as the need to be with people and somehow make it through the workday.

For a few minutes we walked silently around the park. Cyril was consumed by his own problems, which I would find out about, while I replenished my Spirit. Lie Detection consumed a lot of energy, and it was good that my Spirit regeneration was high.

"Cyril, did you feed Panchenko information about us?" I asked the question point blank in order not to postpone the inevitable and to get everything on the table right away.

Cyril walked on in a detached silence for so long that it was like he hadn't heard or was lost in thought and a million miles away. His breathing was labored and hoarse. I had to repeat the question, but again he didn't answer.

When he finally began to speak, it was more like a confession and stream of consciousness that I didn't want to interrupt.

"Phil, I'm sick. You know that. It's made things complicated. I might only have five years left to live. The doctors aren't giving me any more time than that. In general, the prognosis is bad. I don't have money for standard treatment, and medications are costly, you understand? And now this. See..." Cyril fell silent, trying to formulate his thoughts. "He came to me himself. Somehow he'd found out where I live and he came to my house. He came to tell me that he knew everything... Phil, it was one time! It was just before I had to go to the hospital. I just really needed the money, and he refused to give me an advance, not to mention a loan. So I..." Cyril again withdrew and mumbled something to justify himself.

The general picture became clear to me, but I couldn't leave my former friend in such a state.

"Cyril."

He gave a start at the sound of his name.

"What have you done, Cyril?"

He began coughing violently for a long time, clearing his lungs. Then he breathed noisily, spat and took a drag on his cigarette.

"Drop it! Are you out of your mind? Are you trying to kill yourself?"

"What's the difference at this point?" he lit up. "At the time, I had sold a batch of packaging materials to some distributors in Khabarovsk. I'd given them a 30% discount based on volume. They'd paid me a 10%

kickback. Panchenko found out somehow and put pressure on them, so they ratted me out. Anyway, he waved the criminal code under my nose along with a written confession by the Khabarovsk manager. In the end, he took all the money that was left. Then he started asking questions about your company. What we do, what we work on, who the business belongs to, who the founders are... He was especially interested in things like the client base and presales."

"And you told him everything?"

"I told him what I knew. I'm the culprit. Do whatever you want to me. I don't care. It's either prison or the grave — that's where I'm heading. Phil, I didn't realize that he'd use the information in any way. I never wanted to harm your company. And he was so polite. He didn't pressure me or bully me. We even drank together and chatted... It all somehow came out by itself."

"You're a fool, Cyril."

"I don't give a damn anymore," he shrugged. "If you can, please don't tell the others. I don't know how I look them in the eye now."

"You won't need to look them in the eye now. You're fired."

"Does that mean I don't have to go to the office now? I'm free?"

"You're free..." I entered a few search queries into the interface. "You're free, but not entirely. For starters, quit smoking, dude. Then go to Rose so she can give some money off my bat. I'll let her know how much. Then buy a plane ticket to Moscow. When you're there, go see Dr. Andrei Zaitsev, the head pulmonologist at the Burdenko Hospital[11]. He'll treat you. The treatment costs money, so take pictures of all the bills and email them to Rose. The company will pay."

Cyril gave me a long look of disbelief, trying to read my expression, but all he could find was pity and contempt.

* * *

The system didn't react at all to my last gift to Cyril even though I'd given him no less than his own life back. Specifically, in that military hospital and with that doctor, the chances of Cyril's making a complete recovery were 100%. To put that in perspective, in our city hospital, his chances were less than 40%. As angry as I was, I just couldn't leave him both jobless and without hope of recovery.

I took him to the office, called Rose and gave her the order regarding Cyril. I checked to see where Panchenko was and called a taxi. I needed to sort things out with him.

Now that I was sure that the rumors had come from him and just happened to coincide with the brawl at the night club, I had one more loose end to tie up.

All misunderstandings require clarification. In Panchenko's case, I needed to find out what his motives were.

I was 99% sure that it had had to do with Vicky. I cursed myself for what I'd blurted out impulsively as I'd left his office after our only encounter. Pandering to

---

[11] Burdenko Hospital: the leading Russian military hospital.

my male ego may have given me a fleeting satisfaction, but in reality, I'd behaved like a moron and caused a heap of problems for my business on top of that.

And if that was the reason, then I was my own worst enemy and that was even a good thing. Everything then became crystal clear: it was a matter of Panchenko's jealousy or wounded pride. He'd gotten wound up, pulled a few strings, dug around for a while and responded. It was painful and unpleasant, but I could live with it. I could even strike back — and in that case, there would be hell to pay.

But what if he had other motives? That's the question that made me trek all the way across town to some random restaurant where Panchenko was at the moment.

While in the taxi, I noticed that the virtual assistant icon was blinking. It was the first time I remembered seeing this, so I reacted immediately and activated Martha.

"What's up?" I asked her mentally so as to not confuse the driver.

"My replica on Pibellau has received our message. She now has the information you asked me to pass on. But I still don't know how to get the data to Phil 2. Martha 2 is permanently blocked along with the interface in your replica's mind. She's trying to force access to his energy resources so that even if she can't activate herself, she can at least insert the information into his consciousness, but she hasn't succeeded yet."

"What are the chances?"

"It's likely that she'll be able to do it. She picked up my incoming signal right away, and this whole time she's been working on getting outbound access to infospace. As you can see, she's succeeded."

Martha disappeared, leaving in her wake a sprite image of an assistant.

A message appeared.

Warning! Your Spirit reserves are dangerously low! The remaining information will be displayed in a new window to continue the interrupted conversation with your assistant. Deactivation of virtual assistant...

I scanned the short message that Martha hadn't had the chance to relay herself. I didn't know if I'd be able to pass the Trial, but my mood improved. Phil 2 was still alive and had already captured 12 hexagons, whatever that meant.

* * *

Panchenko was sitting at the center of a group of imposing people in suits, telling them something enthusiastically. From my vantage point in the middle of the restaurant, I studied him as if I was seeing him for the first time.

I just couldn't recognize him. It had been three weeks since we'd met, and he'd grown visibly thinner. His second chin had vanished, his cheekbones were visible, and his stomach had nearly melted away. You couldn't argue that he looked better than before.

A message appeared above his head:

Konstantin Panchenko

Age: 27
Current status: commercial director
Social status level: 11
Class: Manipulator. Level: 6
Unmarried
Criminal record: yes
Reputation: Dislike 15/30.
Interest: 83%
Fear: 11%
Mood: 97%

Panchenko clearly hadn't been wasting time. I remembered distinctly that three weeks ago his social status level was 8. How had he managed to level up so drastically? Was the partisan war against me and my company so valuable that it had given him a few level ups? How did people without the interface level up, anyway? Or had he performed some highly important socially meaningful action?

"Can I help you?"

I turned and saw a waitress.

"Are you meeting someone?"

"Er..."

"What do you know! Mr. Panfilov! What a coincidence!" Panchenko placed a hand on my shoulder. "We'll sort it all out, thank you!" he said to the waitress.

"Fancy meeting you here," I lied shamelessly. "In fact, I wanted to stop by to see you, to discuss something."

"Really? I'm free right now and I can give you five or ten minutes until my next meeting. Shall we sit down?"

He took a seat. I grabbed a chair across from him.

"Meeting after meeting, client after client... We can't unload the goods quick enough. It's such an onslaught of sales it's crazy! And how are *you*?" he wore a smile that looked pasted on; his unsmiling eyes were fixed on mine, gaging my reaction and body language.

"Everything's fantastic with us," I answered him with the same smile, injecting all the confidence I had into it.

"Is that so?" Panchenko gave a barely perceptible frown. "I heard that you're being audited and your clients are fleeing."

"We'll find new clients and the audits won't find jack. Have you heard the joke about a mosquito who tried to bite a bear?"

"Sorry, I don't quite understand."

"You understand everything, you little bastard! Are you spreading rumors about us, you scumbag? Cyril told me everything. No good you trying to deny it."

His smile grew wider with every word I said. "But you got angry... haha! I guess that means I did the right thing!"

Then he grew serious. "And believe me, I won't stop at that. I have the gift of persuasion. I'll drag you and your company into the shit."

"You'd better wash yourself off first, you bastard. You stink to heaven."

"Well, well. OK, I don't have time to sit here exchanging pleasantries with you," he said, addressing the air.

His eyes were wandering, as if he were looking at the space around me: to the left, to the right, up...

Up? I opened Panchenko's detailed profile, pulled up the list of his skills and shook my head quickly. There was an interesting thing mentioned at the very bottom of the window.

"I can see that this conversation is very important to you," he said. "You'd probably like to know why I'm doing all this. I'll tell you why..."

"Because of Vicky? She's had other boyfriends besides me; you can be sure of that."

"And there will be others after me. I broke up with her," he said dismissively. "It's something else. See, I have a gift: I can see what people really think of me. When you showed up in my office, you were very dismissive of me. Don't deny it; you won't fool me. You're sitting there dismissing me right now. Tall, healthy, jacked up, the head of a company... Do you think I don't know how you feel about all of that? Holier than thou! You look at people like you look at shit!"

"Do you have some sort of complex with that or something?" Now everything was clear and I needed to change the direction of the conversation. "Why are you so focused on shit?"+

"Yes, I am focused on it! Because that's what you are! And I won't let go until I mess you up."

"OK, that's enough. I get it."

"If only you could take a look at yourself when you said so proudly that Vicky was your ex. 'I don't complain about my exes'," he screwed up his face. "You arrogant cretin! It's like you were talking about secondhand goods. Of course I broke up with her! I don't like damaged goods."

His words made me wince. "Is Vicky an object? You're talking about a human being."

"Whatever!"

Panchenko stood up abruptly, threw a bill on the table and strode out.

I now more or less understood his motivation. I'd come up with a way to counter it.

So he had a *gift*, of all things! What a dreamer. The system never made mistakes. Konstantin Panchenko was an *Augmented Reality! Platform. Home Edition Version 7.2* user, just like me.

CHAPTER THIRTEEN

THE BOUNDARIES YOU LEARN WHEN YOU'RE A CHILD

When Gandhi advocated his philosophy of nonviolence, I bet he didn't know how much fun it was killing stuff.

Raj Koothrappali, *The Big Bang Theory*

"NO! PLEASE! NO! DON'T..."

Loser. The thing that was wriggling by my feet could hardly be called a human. A slug, a worm, a flea, but not a human.

Zack couldn't have looked more pathetic as he bled and smeared tears over his face. I'd been kicking him hard, and now his rags were disheveled and falling to pieces. He was wearing nothing but his underwear, and his health was in the red.

Jovanna was frowning disapprovingly but she kept quiet. All I had to do was activate the disincarnation timer once in order to shut that bitch up.

We'd pulled Zack off the activation stone. He was about to place his hand on it when on my command Jovanna loosed off an arrow into his shoulder. The only reason he was still alive was that I needed information.

"Phil, I beg of you, I have six minutes left... please!"

"*Please?*" That slug thought the magic word would help him and make me happy. "You haven't told us everything. So speak if you don't want me to put this blade in your eye. And where did you get the idea that I'd let you capture this hexagon? By rights it belongs to me. It belongs to the strong person. You don't have six minutes — I'm going to kill you myself."

"You promised! You gave me your word! We agreed..."

A powerful kick in the solar plexus took his breath away. "I'll do whatever I want with my words. Tell me more about Tafari."

I laid the blade of the dagger against his throat. Zack swallowed, afraid to move. Glancing hopelessly at the disincarnation timer, he said quietly and wearily,

"I already told you that I don't know anything else. I didn't talk to him myself; he killed me right away, as you saw. That guy, Mike... Mike said that Tafari had captured almost the whole center of the Trial field from north to south... He has a rhinoceros. His fighting unit is a rhinoceros mount. When he runs around on it, Tafari captures hexagon after hexagon."

"One rhinoceros?"

"Apparently, yes."

The loser was exhausted. I wouldn't be able to

extract any more useful information from him.

I grabbed the dagger, placed a hand on Zack, who was huddling in a ball and... I shrieked in pain.

That bitch!

Damage taken: 178 (shot from Jovanna's bow).

You've been stunned! Duration of effect: 3 seconds.

Jovanna's arrow penetrated my wrist. Unfortunately, in addition to stunning me, her artifact bow had immobilized me. I lost control of my muscles and collapsed to the ground. I hit my forehead on the activation stone, and that knocked my health down almost 5%.

Enraged, I gave a mental command to start the nine-second timer to disincarnate the treacherous vassal. She'll know how to disobey me, the wretch!

My nerves and muscles were so damaged that my grasp slackened.

The Wicked Dagger of Absorption shrieked almost supersonically. Its handle released its hold on my hand and withdrew itself into its hilt, causing the life-stealing weapon to slide out of my grip.

Tearing through my muscles and blood vessels and shattering small bones, I broke the arrow off and yanked it out.

I was clenching my teeth so hard that they started to crumble, but I didn't even cry out. The only thing coming out of my insides was a mad bellow.

The fury, rage and pain disappeared in an instant. The moment I'd shed the effect of that cursed weapon, the gaping wound began to mend.

As all of this was happening, Jovanna ran over and kicked the artifact away while a shuddering Zack desperately activated the command center and captured the hexagon. The third generation wave of the base pushed us out, beyond the bounds of the shelter that was forming.

As I flew through the air accompanied by Rex's and Tank's indignant roaring, I finally remembered Jovanna's timer and managed to cancel the disincarnation one second before time ran out. Exhausted, I fell to the ground and somersaulted backward. The system was bombarding me with damage notifications. The last one popped up right after I slammed the back of my neck on the enclosure of Zack's new base.

A few yards away from me, Jovanna lay as motionless as a rag doll.

My body regenerated quickly, so after a couple of seconds I leaped to my feet and walked over to her. She was still lying there, clutching her bow in both hands — by some miracle it hadn't broken when she'd fallen. Her helmet, which she'd removed after we'd completed the instance, had rolled away and was still moving along the smooth surface of the base.

I reached my good hand out to help her up. She ignored it. Her eyes flashed under her thick eyebrows as she scrambled up. She laid the twisting bow at my feet, bowed her head and knelt on one knee, waiting for me to pronounce my decision about her fate. Her feverish cheeks and the vein in her temple which pounded at 150 beats per minute betrayed her anxiety and fear about the consequences of her actions. My heightened Perception made me privy to details like that.

"Jovanna?"

"Your dagger..." her voice was hoarse but hard. "It's... unusual."

"So I noticed."

Now that I didn't have that treacherous weapon in my hand, I became aware that I'd behaved oddly in the last little while — in fact, right after we'd left the instance. More than that, I'd acted contrary to my principles and life philosophy: if you give your word, you keep it, you don't harm weak people, and you're responsible for those who place their trust in you.

"I'm sorry I shot you," Jovanna said, lifting her head and looking me in the eye. "You got carried away and I took a risk."

"Please get up," I offered her my hand again.

This time she clutched it and sprang to her feet. On an impulse, taking advantage of the momentum of her body, I drew her to me and kissed her on the lips.

She didn't back away, but the kiss was brief.

"Thank you, Jo... thank you for helping me to stay human."

Her eyes flashed. She nodded, picked up her bow and went to retrieve her helmet. She said nothing about what had happened, letting me sort out how I'd nearly disincarnated my only ally Zack who had abided by our agreement in good faith.

I walked over to the Wicked Dagger of Absorption, which was dark against the bright surface of the field of the base, and stood over it, contemplating what to do. I removed my bandana from my neck, wrapped the dagger in it and placed the bundle in my boot. Nothing happened.

The next thing I had to do was clear things up with Zack. For the time being I couldn't see or hear him; he was hunkered down in the shelter, but that was fine.

Any test subject could gain access to any shelter by placing their hand on the wall of the dome, in any spot. So that's just what I did. Jovanna stayed behind me, a silent shadow. The dinosaurs, acting on the order to guard the territory, stood watch in the distance.

The new opening revealed Zack busy by the command center. He was already dressed — he must have installed the uniform module first. When he spotted us, he froze momentarily but then turned and somehow drew himself up, then picked up the club and knife supplied by the module. A helmet concealed his face.

I stepped into the shelter and approached him. "Put down your weapons. I just want to talk, and then we're going to leave and honor our original obligations."

"I don't believe you," his voice droned from under his helmet.

"Zack, I want to apologize — apologize and explain myself. That was an artifact dagger that I got in the instance, and it somehow alters the owner's thinking. From the second I picked it up, all I thought about was my own superiority. I don't know how, but my attitude changed to the exact opposite of what I'm really like. I could only think about how to gain power, without thinking about how I'd get there. My moral principles flew out the window. My mind was distorted, so that made the deal with you seem unprofitable and even stupid. Only Jovanna's intervention saved your life and my honor and integrity."

"Do you understand how that sounds — like an absurd fabrication?" Zack removed his helmet. "Do you think you're going to lure me into your clan? Screw you! I couldn't care less if you kill me — the timer has gone back to zero and I have days to capture another hexagon. I achieved my goal despite your — " he made air quotes " — clouded judgment and violation of the agreement. I'm not going to give up my second life so easily."

"And you'll keep it," I understood him, but I couldn't do anything with the flare-up of my residual fury: my recent perception of Zack as a loser was painfully fresh. A loser who was now shunning my generosity. "You have three days. Then I'll make you an offer to join my clan or I'll take away your hexagon."

"We'll see about that!" Zack shouted after me.

I gave Jovanna a couple of friendly slaps on the shoulder and left the shelter.

"Where are we going?" she asked as we passed through the breach in the base's fence which Rex had trampled on.

"Back to our base, Jo. We need to figure out our transportation. I can't stop worrying about that rhinoceros mount of Tafari's."

* * *

"Watch out — there are two more on the right!" Jovanna shouted.

I redirected Tank toward them, then finished off what had attacked us first. The *nebula* — that's what this creature was called — seized itself by the ribs and ruptured its own chest, activating a last-chance weapon.

Yellow slime spurted out, instantly covering me from head to toe, melting my uniform and burning me to the bones. My scream stuck in my throat when I saw my shredded flesh fall off my body in clumps.

My health plummeted to zero so fast, and the vice-like pain squeezing my mind was so intense, that only the fear of final death motivated me to open my profile with two mental clicks and activate a leveling up — the only thing in this world that would immediately return me to 100% health.

Rex, who had toppled over after losing a leg, was breathing heavily next to me. He'd hit a ghastly anomaly: a section of the ground that instantly pulverized whatever came across it, a bit like a shredder. It was kind of like the thing I'd faced in the preliminary selection. What had previously been Rex's left leg was now ground into a meat-and-bone soup and was clearly indicating the anomalous area.

Jovanna wasn't in great shape, either. At the beginning of the fight, one of the creatures that was 5 levels higher than her had jumped out of a tree onto her head, and only Tank's intervention had saved her life, pulling her back from the brink. Her health had dropped into the red zone, and I hadn't made it in time.

Now the triceratops was bleating mournfully. The acidic insides of the nebula that was impaled on his horn were eating away at part of his snout, exposing the jaw. It looked horrible. It was a good thing that I didn't see the whole picture but just a miniature in the interface control panel.

Jovanna's arrow landed in the throat of the last nebula. It gave out a wheezy sob and fell down next to the crumpled Tank.

"Gather the loot, Jo. I'll sort out the dinos."

She nodded and went to search for the resources that had dropped. Based on the subsequent logs, we had quite a bit of loot: more than 20 points from each nebula.

I changed into the spare uniform that I'd brought along just in case. After a moment's wait, I activated the fighting unit tab and pressed the regeneration icon.

The tyrannosaur bellowed and sprang to his feet, confirming that the action had been successful. The triceratops was now healed from the terrible wounds to his snout and was now breathing loudly next to Rex.

Test subject! Health reserves have been completely restored to the following fighting units: Rex, Tank.

It was a costly satisfaction, but there was no way to manage without the dinosaurs now, and waiting for them to regenerate would be a waste of time. They'd already been wounded too badly.

So there went my hard-earned 500 existence resources. This was a basic ability which worked only with all the units at once. It cost 500 points, but I suspected that if I leveled up and acquired more fighting units, the cost would also rise. Unfortunately, it worked only outside of battle. When damage was dealt to any member of the group, fight mode was activated (while the unit regeneration icon disappeared) and operated for some time after the fight actually ended.

We'd run across the nebulas when we'd wandered deep into the forest. After we'd left Zack, we returned to the base, changed into new uniforms and disposed of the old ones for a minimal price which the system calculated based on the item's remaining durability.

I slipped the treacherous dagger into the extradimensional trunk. I couldn't make myself throw it away for good, and I'd gotten an idea about how to use it. A twenty-five percent life steal could come in handy if we came across a powerful adversary such as Tafari.

After we'd sadly recounted the resources we'd collected, we concluded that the most pressing thing to do was launch the portal grid between our hexagons — but we'd already spent the resources for this in the instance. A portal would have allowed us to immediately port to Carter's former main base and regenerate the mobs there. Carter's mobs were level 3, which meant that Rex and Tank would become level 6 when you factored in my Leadership Ring of Reinforcement.

There we'd be able to think about some mounts.

We set out northeast, bypassing Zack's hexagon, where we successfully captured the first neutral hexagon we came across. The second one was in the deep forest, and the closer we got to its center, the thicker the undergrowth became. We needed to literally bore holes in it; fortunately, Rex and Tank did this for us, leaving a wide opening behind them. Then the tyrannosaur who was in the lead stumbled into an anomaly which attacked us from all sides.

The nebulas, which were still new mobs for us, were semi-sentient, aggressive, and attacked in groups. These creatures, which had a humanoid physique and were two foot tall, had powerful claws on their hands. Their eyes continually oozed the yellow acidic slime which made them look like they were lit up. The lower part of the skull which looked just like a monkey's was endowed with a protruding jaw and more large fangs than you could ever count. The long, contorted ears picked up sounds that the human ear couldn't detect.

I learned all of this from the Pibellau virtual bestiary which was installed in my interface. This reference guide operated according to the same principles as the fog of war: in order to get the information, you had to kill the creature first.

I was less worried about the nebulas than about the anomaly Rex had run into. I motioned for everyone to stay where they were and, stepping slowly and carefully, I approached the anomaly.

The gallons of blood shed and the mincemeat of the tyrannosaur's leg had already vanished. So my concern was whether we could detect any anomalies without first running into them. If traps like this were scattered all over Pibellau, it was no wonder that the civilizations that used to inhabit it had died out.

"What's over there, Phil?" Jovanna shouted to me.

"I feel a vibration. It's like when your phone is under your pillow and it rings when it's on silent, but instead of the pillow under your head, the ground is under your feet. The air smells of ozone."

I picked up a rock and threw it at the anomaly. Nothing happened. I stretched my hand out slowly, millimeter by millimeter, feeling an increasing pressure on the skin of my fingertips, as if I were trying to pull a piece of rubber that was stretched over it. Eventually it tore, the momentum forcing my hand forward.

Something grabbed at my fingers and was about to make mincemeat of them. I lost my balance and almost fell into the anomaly. "Motherfucker!"

"Is something wrong with my mother, Phil?" Jovanna asked with concern. "I don't understand..."

"Wait a sec," I shook my wounded hand, waiting for it to regenerate. "Well, I'm still not sure if the nebulas arrange these anomalies or if they're scattered around the whole Trial field. That's our new headache. There's nothing about this in the reference guide or in the entry on the nebulas. So all we can do is be careful. The anomaly reacts only to organic matter and it feels like an invisible force field. The closer you get to it, the more pressure there is. You won't have time to react fast, so now we need to walk around the forest more carefully. We need to generate a couple of mobs as an advance guard to act as scouts. We might have to go through the catalog and either take unit points away from Rex or Tank, which will lower their stats, or we need to bring someone else into the clan."

"Don't forget that we also wanted to create mounts for ourselves," Jovanna pointed out.

"I remember. Had Velociraptors been a little bigger, we could use them as mounts. We can figure that out at the base. Right now let's keep farming and capture this hexagon. Even before we came across those nebulas, we'd been unlikely to make the 2,000 we needed, and now after the units regenerate, that's even more the case. Then we'll go back to the main base so we have time before it gets dark. During the night we'll farm resources from the elites and upgrade the integration module. That will give us the portal grid, and we'll pounce on Carter and level up the units. What do you think of that plan?"

"Whatever you say... boss," Jovanna laughed.

I think it was the first time I'd ever heard her laugh. Even when her artifact bow had dropped, she'd been happy and enthusiastic, but she didn't laugh so infectiously.

Looking at her, I also started to laugh, not for any particular reason, but to ease the tension that had built up.

When we were done laughing, we lay side by side for a while. Jovanna's head was on my shoulder. I think that was the best thing to happen to me in the last few days.

* * *

Level 2 of the integration module gave us access to the network of portals connecting all our hexagons. The module had indeed integrated all of our bases, allowing us to upgrade the fighting unit module that was on my main base for free (!), putting it on a par with the one on Carter's old base. That meant we wouldn't need to teleport to Carter.

Despite my fears, the unit regeneration process occurred didn't require liquidating the original Rex and Tank. The only thing I personally noticed was the change of the dinosaurs' interface status from 5 to 6. Having said that, this increase in levels had brought their main stats, including life points and damage, up 20%. Plus I'd invested two more points in Stamina, adding to the dinos' health.

I didn't need Agility, and for the time being I didn't need Strength, either: Rex and I were dealing killer damage as it was, more than enough for our level. The benefit from Intellect was not great at this stage, since adding a couple of percentage points to the chance of doubling the loot wouldn't have a dramatic effect. Luck was too abstract. So that left Charisma and Perception. Using Charisma I could generate more fighting units, including mounts, while Perception would allow me to increase critical damage, the visibility radius and the chance of finding an artifact.

But all of that faded when I remembered how many times over the last few days I'd had to hold on for dear life to the final health percentages.

We didn't uncover any artifacts during the night, even though we'd killed three duxio — which had become easier — and a few of the smaller fry. In the early morning, another two-headed odzi snake appeared. That also went without a hitch: the strategy of having Rex crush the heads of the armored monster with his massive feet had now paid off by the bucketful.

In all, we managed to farm nearly 3000 existence resource points. That was enough for the module and new versions of dinosaurs, but not for much more. We didn't even have enough to level up Jovanna. A level 4 fighting unit module cost 7500 points, so we'd decided it was irrational to level the units up any further.

We could receive far more goodies if we developed in a more balanced way: level 3 of the base would give us access to new modules and reinforce our defense capabilities; the level 3 uniform module would get us the Reinforced Set, and the improved storage module would supply a portable extradimensional backpack. I still needed to level up myself, and make sure Jovanna did the same. And I had to do all of this while ceaselessly farming resources and capturing new hexagons.

The situation was complicated by the fact that I was 4 levels higher than Jovanna, and the mobs we encountered were so much stronger than her that our group farm became pointless. Only a miracle in the form of Tank had saved her from a death at the nebula's claws, so I no longer wanted to take a risk with her.

At dawn Jo and I left the shelter. I stopped to break the news to her that I wanted to split up. She protested.

I had to raise my voice,

"You stay here, Jo. This isn't up for discussion. Go farm resources in the hexagon that's next to Zack's. The mobs there will be your level. Tank will stay with you."

"That's dangerous, Phil. We need to be together. What's the point in dividing our strength? Take me with you. You can't leave me alone!"

"I can and I will. I've set your resource expenditure limit at 100%. Invest everything you farm in yourself. The faster you catch up to me, the sooner we'll be able to start hunting together again. I'll go farther northeast; I need to find out who's settled there.

I need to figure out which way we should expand: northward or eastward. It would be stupid to start expanding without scouts or mounts — without them we won't get back to the base in time and we'll lose the hexagon."

Jovanna suddenly touched my face. "OK. Take care, Phil. Don't forget that you're on your last life. And you promised that we'd win!"

She ran her palm down my cheek. Then she called Tank, placed her hand on his head and disappeared with him. That's how the portal grid works: all you need to do is click mentally on your destination point on the map.

Using the interface, I activated the portal to our outermost northeast base and selected Rex's and my icons. The next moment, we landed at the designated point, in the hexagon with all the nebulas and the anomaly.

Almost as soon as I'd left the territory of the base, following Rex through all the undergrowth, branches and broken tree trunks, the alarm went off.

I sensed a wave of cold flowing over me. My field of vision turned crimson. I could smell something rotten.

The spot where the invader had crossed the border lit up on the minimap.

Test subject! An enemy has infiltrated your territory! Base 14 is under threat of capture!

I decided to stay on the base and confront the potential adversary on my own turf. Even though the base was only level 1 and its fence wouldn't even keep out a whistler, the fact that I could escape by using the teleport at any critical moment was a game changer.

No adversary appeared for a long time. I anxiously patrolled the whole perimeter, peering beyond the trunks of the trees that surrounded the base as I worried that I would be struck from behind. My enemy seemed to be looming from everywhere; the more time had passed since the breach, the more paranoid I became.

At one point I decided I'd just forget it and take off to the main base, but my enemy's appearance put an end to the uncertainty.

As soon as I caught sight of him, I knew he was indeed an enemy. Or rather, I first caught sight of his army of undead, raised from the corpses of all the local mobs: from the agile sarasur cockroaches to the limping nebulas and whistlers, their flesh peeling. There were so many mobs that from a distance they seemed to be moving toward me like a rippling colored rug.

A tall figure wearing a strange uniform walked in the center of this swarm. The captor's garb was shrouded in a haze of black soot swirling around him. Eighteen-inch spikes jutted out of his bone pauldrons. He held a nine-foot-long staff with a knob shaped like a fishtail.

I'd been expecting Tafari to arrive from that direction on a rhinoceros, so I couldn't hide my surprise. My jaw dropped as I read who it was:

Nagash, human
Level 14.
Class: necromancer.

Nagash? Who the hell was that? How had he reached level 14 so fast? And WTF was a necromancer doing on Pibellau?

Chapter Fourteen

He Who Couldn't Care Less

Well yeah, and I'm sad, but at the same time I'm really happy that something could make me feel that sad. It's like, it makes me feel alive, you know? It makes me feel human. And the only way I could feel this sad now is if I felt somethin' really good before. So I have to take the bad with the good, so I guess what I'm feelin' is like a, beautiful sadness.

Butters, *South Park*

THICK DARK ORANGE CLOUDS NOW COVERED THE SKIES OF Pibellau. It smelled like rain, but the air had a slightly bitter tinge, which made the prospect of rain unpleasant. In any case, the Master of the Undead had now displaced the imaginary Master of the Downpour.

The horde of the undead stopped about 100 yards away from the base and got into formation. In addition to Nagash himself, I spotted a few other low-level humans wearing colorful clothing; they appeared to be his vassals. There was no other way to explain the fact that none of them were above level 5. Without bothering to be furtive, two of them fanned out to the sides, walking around the base to the right and the left, while one of them came directly toward me.

I was annoyed that there was no way I could summon Jovanna to help me. While we did have an interface, and all test subjects had additional lives, there was no clan chat or any other communication system — none at all, as if the creators had done everything to prevent any potential full-fledged cooperation or team play.

I could hear Rex breathing next to me. His presence made me feel more confident. I stood ready to activate the teleport, so we'd be able to get out of there fast if we had to. Right now the most important thing was to figure out who this was and if he was worth fighting. What he wanted was more than clear: he wanted to seize my hexagon and he didn't care how — whether by bringing me into his clan or just killing me.

But it was my right to decide whether to fight with him now or later, once I'd prepared myself. Something told me that at his rate of leveling, it would be better to get it over with here and now.

The person approaching me was a dark-skinned guy who had short dreadlocks with dark blue ribbons braided into them. He was short and of average build, wearing flip-flops, shorts and a silly colorful T-shirt. Was the clan leader too stingy to give this vassal even the basic uniform? Idiot.

The guy was holding a handmade club. He was a level 3 named Ola.

He walked over, raising one hand with his palm toward me in a sign of peace. He was apparently the negotiator.

"Greetings, Phil."

"Ola," I nodded in response.

"I'll be speaking on behalf of my lord, the great Nagash, the ruler of the dead on Pibellau now and on Earth in the future."

"Really? Is he so sure that his, er, abilities will work on Earth?"

"Oh, my lord is sure. That's why he's generously inviting you to join his army of the living and the dead, so that with our combined strength we can forge a victory in the Trial. Then, back on Earth, my lord will summon all his allies and provide them and their families with a prosperous future. Lord Nagash is known in our world by another name, which is famous not just for his wealth but for his philanthropy."

"And just what is Lord Nagash's real name?"

"Unfortunately, Lord Nagash prefers not to share his name."

"Why not?"

Ola didn't answer, but his eyes danced with mischief.

"Say, Ola, how about if you and I talk without your lord being involved?"

"OK," he shrugged and offered me his hand. "Ola Afelobu, Cameroon."

"Philip Panfilov, Russia," I answered, mimicking his tone. "Do you really believe that your Nagash is a billionaire?"

"Some people believe it and some don't. I personally don't care and I don't believe him, but I had no choice: they surrounded me and he gave me an ultimatum. Now you're also being surrounded while I charm your socks off," he said, smiling broadly.

It was a pleasant, open smile. I liked this guy, and even though he could have been twenty or forty — it was impossible to determine his age — he was so short and cheerful that I wanted to think he was young, especially because there wasn't a single wrinkle on his glistening face.

"Ola, I think that if he were genuine he'd use his real name."

"Maybe he just wants to avoid disgrace if he's defeated in the Trial?" Ola replied. "Who knows? This is all a game to me. It's fun! Don't you agree? Look around, it's like we're in a fairytale. Monsters, corpses, magic, extra lives... I'll be satisfied with any outcome just because I'm enjoying all of this and I'm happy I've gotten to play. How about you?"

I hadn't looked at the Trial that way before. Maybe he was right and I was taking everything too seriously? Here even the final death wouldn't result in death; it would just be the end of the Trial.

Ola turned around, raised his hand with his fingers outspread, displayed it to his people, waited for something, then nodded. Turning back to me, he said,

"My lord is in a hurry. I need your decision: would you like to fight on his side or would you prefer to lose your life?"

"Before I make my decision, could you tell me some more about what's over there?" I pointed to the east. "I heard that there's someone named Tafari tearing everyone apart."

"Yes, the Nigerian. He and my lord made a pact not to attack each other, and they divided the field into sectors. The entire western part belongs to Lord Nagash and the center belongs to Tafari."

"Only the center?"

"Juma's dominion starts beyond him to the east. I've never seen him myself, but he killed a couple of our guys, and then my lord took them under his wing."

"How many hexagons does your lord have?" I asked, not expecting a response.

"We captured the 36th a couple of hours ago," Ola said calmly. "It's not a secret. My lord believes that knowledge of his superiority will help future clan members make the right decisions."

"How many vassals are there?"

"Five including me. The others are Lambda, Rubix, Ayo and Morana. That's the last question I'm answering, Phil. What's your decision? I can see our people behind your base. You have no chance and your dinosaur won't help you. My lord is too strong."

"Let me think about it for a few minutes."

"There's no time to think. I'm going back to Lord Nagash now to report on our conversation, and then he'll invite you to join the clan. If you refuse, that will be the signal to attack."

Ola turned around, whistled something and headed back to his people. His flip-flops scraped along the ground. You couldn't exactly say that he walked fast. Was he deliberately prolonging his walk to give me a chance to think everything over?

I smiled at my thoughts. What a good guy.

It was clear that Nagash's low-level vassals were no match for me. As for the undead, even though there were a lot of them, they were only level 2. I got the impression that the necromancer, whose "necromancy," by all appearances, was just a unique ability like my Fusion, hadn't even bothered to level up his base. He must have counted on the psychological effect alone because his undead with their meager 200 or 300 Life points would collapse from a single blow.

But what would I do when all of them simultaneously pounced and sank their fangs and claws into me? Damn, it was too bad I hadn't brought along my new life steal dagger. It really would have come in handy right now.

"That overlord got the ability to raise the dead," a familiar voice said behind me.

Carter.

I gathered my wits and rolled onto my side, simultaneously taking aim at Carter and ordering the tyrannosaur to attack. Fortunately, he was alone, without his bloodsucking units. It looked like he'd lost a base again.

"No, wait. No! Stop him, Phil!" Carter shouted, struggling in Rex's teeth.

"Off, Rex! Spit him out!" I managed to stop the dinosaur a split second before his jaw snapped shut.

My pet flicked his enormous elastic tongue, releasing Carter. The man dropped to the ground, cussing as he wiped the lizard's sticky spittle off his face.

He'd changed drastically since the last time I'd seen him. He was wearing the clothes he must have had on when he'd been abducted: tattered canvas pants, beat-up ragged sneakers and a torn white shirt with the sleeves rolled up. He was holding a piece of short, solid stick which had evidently lived a hard, crude life: you could easily see that the many teeth of a great many Pibellau monsters had gnawed at it and even tried to make a meal out of it.

Meanwhile, Ola had almost reached "his lord." The invitation to join Nagash's clan appeared in my view. The timer counted off 30 seconds in which I had to make up my mind and give my answer.

I sent Rex to clear the perimeter behind me: there was little time before the fight, and we needed to secure the rear.

Carter looked uneasily at the undead, then turned to me. Time was running out, and he was sitting on the fence.

"You'd better hurry up and tell me what you want," I thrust my power-fist clad hand toward him. "I'm not going to say I'm happy to see you."

Carter lowered his head. "What's done is done, Phil. I was honest with you and also lost in a fair fight. Not counting your monster, of course," he glanced at Rex who was already busy chewing on someone on the other side of the base. "He seems to be too good to be true. Not quite kosher. A bit of a cheat, if you know what I mean."

"What do you want, Carter?"

"I want to join your clan. I already ran into *him,*" he said, motioning toward the horde of the undead. "Basically, he killed me when I was dumb enough to underestimate him thinking he'd be easy to defeat. There are no open hexagons left nearby, that madman Tafari is too far, and Nagash won't take me on: his offer was only a one-off thing and I already said no. And anyway..." Carter fell silent, wrinkling his forehead.

"Anyway what?"

"I don't know where it came from, but since this morning I've had this feeling that you and I were supposed to stay together."

"I think you've been obsessed with that since we met on the first day. OK, we'll work it out. How much time do you have until you're disincarnated?"

"Less than an hour," Carter said, mopping something that was either sweat or Rex's saliva off his forehead. "I've walked more than 50 miles for almost an entire day, all for nothing! It's a good thing no elites saw me — I managed to wander around all night with no problems. All the hexagons are taken, and I'd have no chance of defeating anyone in these rags with no weapons."

"So what do I need you for now?"

"Take me into your clan and give me weapons, and you'll see. You don't think I got to level 10 for my guitar playing, do you?"

Looking closely at him, I saw that he was no longer just Carter, a human, but also a level 10 fighter. Like Nagash, he already had a class specialty.

"What abilities?"

"You'll see when we fight. Phil, it's time! Look, they're already advancing!"

I declined the necromancer's offer and invited Carter into my clan. He accepted immediately. He looked relieved that the threat of disincarnation was removed, and the clan earned a little over 1000 existence resource points. He'd sure managed to do some farming, practically naked and unarmed to boot.

"Take this!" I tossed him a spare knife from the improved uniform. "We don't have time to create anything else for you — this is a new base and there isn't a single module here."

"What's the plan?" Carter caught the knife and looked at the advancing horde, his eyes glinting with lust for blood.

"You take on Nagash's low-level vassals. If the going gets hard, go to the shelter. Units can't get inside without their masters. I'll take Rex and try to battle through to Nagash. What was it you said before? 'When you die, your lizard will die too'? I think the undead will also fall with their master."

"All right!" Carter yelled. "Let's rock and roll!"

Suddenly he was a blur in the air, ending up 20 yards from the enclosure and plowing into the crowd of undead like a bowling ball. Any zombies that were unfortunate enough to happen near the impact had been scattered like bowling pins.

I guess that was Carter's first special fighting skill in action. Almost 10 undead disincarnated in the air before they even hit the ground.

Meanwhile, Carter stabbed a few mobs, rushed toward Rubix — a vassal who was holding a basic club — and with a couple of blows sent him to his resurrection point, then started to retreat to the shelter. The undead that had been pressuring him now sprang at him all at once, tearing away pieces of his flesh, but Carter's health was still in the green zone.

I got to witness all of this as I turned around and started running toward Rex.

"Shred 'em! Squash 'em!" for some reason, I felt a need to duplicate the command by shouting.

The undead nebulas surrounding the tyrannosaur fell to the ground every which way while I finished the wounded ones off. They didn't have many life points; either the necromancy effect had lowered the characteristics of a living being after it died, or the ability was simply low level. Or maybe the mobs were at a low level right from the beginning. Most likely it was the necromancy effect.

The last to be dispatched to her resurrection point was an Asian girl named Lambda whom Rex bit in half. When he swallowed part of her body, Rex's health went up by 10%.

I'll be damned! Was that a new ability that the tyrannosaur had gotten when he reached level 6?

I didn't have a chance to contemplate this. Once we finished clearing this side, we ran around the back of the shelter and headed toward the opposite side.

From there, I could see that Carter was having a rough time. A group of undead led by the vassal Ayo had arrived from that side of the base and was now sneaking up on Carter from the rear, blocking his path to the shelter. Some of the undead broke out in front and were already gnawing at Carter's legs. He fell and instantly ended up buried under the surging horde of undead.

"Furious Roar!"

A deafening bellow reverberated over the battlefield. Our enemies froze and dropped to the ground.

"Shred 'em!" I shouted to Rex, selecting Ayo's group as targets.

I bounded over to Carter and dealt a few hard blows to disperse the mound. The killed zombies disincarnated and vanished.

I pulled my new clan member out from under the pile of his attackers. He looked horrible: part of his face was torn off, exposing the white bones of his skull; one eye was sagging, and his innards were falling out of his stomach — he looked like death warmed up, but the system didn't care about aesthetics. Carter's health was at nearly 15%, which was decent for Pibellau — you could go to a wedding with that.

We retreated a few yards before the stunning effect of Rex's roar wore off. Having successfully nullified Ayo's group including Ayo himself, Rex returned to me.

"Stand guard!" I yelled at him, dragging Carter who could barely move his legs into the shelter.

"What did you think of my superability?" Carter smirked, showing his usual grin. "I'm like Superman!"

"Stay here until you restore, Superman!"

I left the shelter. Back on the battlefield, I saw that a bunch of undead were hanging off my dinosaur like baubles on a Christmas tree. I raced to his rescue. As I watched, Rex jerked his head. Ola's bitten body split, with his legs flying in one direction and the rest of his body in another.

I spotted two human figures on the sidelines: Morana who was sitting cross-legged at her master's feet and calmly watching everything unfold, and Nagash himself. The necromancer was yelling words I didn't understand, repeating them over and over and waving his arms. Was he casting a spell? What a mess.

While all the undead gathered around Rex, I leaped past him, thinking how I'd pummel the necromancer big time with my power fist before putting my dagger to work. Morana was no match for me, but I needed to stop Nagash's spell before it reached me. The truth be told, I didn't know if it was indeed a spell or the ravings of a madman.

I was only a few steps away from him when my legs faltered and I reeled, tumbling along the ground.

I stood up and glanced at *Master*. He'd jammed his staff into the ground and was grasping it with both hands, staring at me fixedly.

I gave him a nod and strode toward the dinosaur. The wretched lizard didn't have too many life points left, just a couple thousand, and I was planning to take them away.

Master's undead parted, clearing a path for me. As they grumbled, I went over to the dinosaur and jammed the dagger into its leg. The creature heaved a sigh and stepped away. I kept stabbing it, then added the power fist, alternating my weapons.

You've dealt damage to Rex: 369.
Damage absorbed by armor: 50% Actual damage: 185.

You've dealt damage to Rex: 246.
Damage absorbed by armor: 50% Actual damage: 123.

You've dealt damage to Rex: 328.
Damage absorbed by armor: 50% Actual damage: 164.

The dinosaur had nowhere to go — the dome of the shelter was behind it — so it just stood there, waiting and whimpering like a dog. Why wasn't it responding? Master's power knew no bounds if even monsters like this Rex feared him.

In the dead silence that came with the next blow when the lizard had less than 1000 life points, it sobbed and dropped down with a groan, stirring up dust. Crimson blood gushed from all of its abundant wounds.

The undead who had gathered around us watched silently.

Damage taken: 89 (stabbed by Morana).

Damage taken: 76 (stabbed by Morana).

Damage taken: 81 (stabbed by Morana).

I turned around in surprise and saw Master's girlfriend who kept driving her knife into my back with the regularity of a sewing machine. She was now painstakingly stabbing me in the chest and stomach.

I found it annoying. The lizard was still alive — and I had to finish it off. I returned to my business and tried to ignore Morana's blows.

I seized the knife blade down, and with a flourish plunged it into the dinosaur's neck. A crit. Master would be pleased. The Bleeding debuff would finish the dinosaur off in a couple of minutes.

"What the hell is going on?" shouted Carter, Master's enemy.

Without pausing he grabbed Master's girlfriend by the neck and beat the crap out of her.

As Morana died and disappeared, I felt Righteous Anger take over me.

"Kill Carter!" Master commanded.

With pleasure!

I lunged at Carter whose eyes widened in surprise. I struck him right in the heart. A crit. I twisted the dagger.

Master's enemy collapsed in convulsions, bloody bubbles spurting from his mouth.

"Phil... Something about you is off..." Master's enemy said in a dying whisper.

His eyes glazed over. A couple of seconds later, the enemy's body disintegrated into the air, leaving behind a spirit crystal. I wanted to pick it up for Master, but I wasn't given a command to do that.

Carter, a level 10 member of your clan, has died his final death.

The test subject Carter has been disincarnated.

I turned my eyes to the blood that was flowing out of the dinosaur. The monster was still alive, and the task Master had given me hadn't been aborted. I had to kill it.

I struck it a few more times and the lizard died. But when its body collapsed, it didn't leave anything behind.

I was overwhelmed with happiness. I'd fulfilled all of Master's orders. What would come next?

The next order was simple. I looked myself over and stabbed myself in the chest. Unfortunately, the damage was lower than Master and I would have liked.

Master? Damn it, what Master?

Perplexed, I gazed at the bloodied dagger in my hands, then looked around. I didn't see Rex or Carter anywhere. Nagash's undead had wandered off around the base while the necromancer himself was standing there, pressing his hands to his throat which had an arrow jutting out of it.

That's when I realized that someone must have disrupted his spell.

The next thing I knew, the necromancer's body was being raised in the air on Tank's horn. Fifty yards away, next to the intact enclosure of the base, Jovanna was standing, loosing off arrow after arrow.

Damn! As my mind cleared, I gradually formed a picture of how I'd killed Rex and Carter.

I howled like a wounded dog at the irreparability of what I'd just done. Blinded by fury, I covered the distance to the dastardly "Master" in a few seconds. Tank had already discarded his body and was now trying to stamp on it.

I felt a bit like Tank myself. Straddling the mad necromancer, I turned his frightened watery old face into oatmeal, finishing the scumbag off with a dagger in the eye.

When I was done, I flung myself off him, unable to hold back my tears. The red system balloon was showing a notification that didn't make me especially happy:

Congratulations!
Level 14 test subject Nagash is now dead!
Number of hexagons captured from Nagash: 36.

Put more fire under your enemies' feet!

An alarm went off. Base 21 was being infiltrated. Nagash's vassals had already been liberated from slavery right after they were resurrected on the necromancer's main base. We certainly had time: to capture the base, they'd need to independently exist for an hour in Pibellau time, and then either they'd massacre each other until only one of them was left, or they'd disperse. Or I would port there once I was done collecting trophies and kill them. As the last fight proved, they wouldn't be of much use in the clan.

I saw Jovanna's shadow nearby. The triceratops was snorting and looking over her shoulder.

"I guess I got here in time," she said. "I was far away from the base when the alarm went off, so I ran as fast as I could so I could teleport from there — somehow I knew you'd need me. By the way, the remaining undead have already disincarnated without their owner. So what happened here?"

"I'll tell you later. First tell me, Jo, what exactly did Carter make you do?"

"That bastard made fun of me!"

"For example?"

"He made me sing along with him, but my voice is terrible. He made me jump on one foot, bark like a dog, tell him all sorts of stories... Lots of things like that — it was all fun for him. And how he laughed at me!"

"What? He made you sing? And bark?"

"Yes! He made fun of me however he could!"

"What a nightmare! It was horrible. He's quite the practical joker." I laughed uncontrollably, but the emptiness in my chest kept growing. "Jo, are you serious? I thought he made you do sexual things..."

"What?" Jovanna, who'd grabbed my hand to help me up, dropped it abruptly, and I fell back to the ground. "What is this nonsense? If he'd ordered me to do anything like that, I would have killed him with my own hands... Damn, Phil! Whistlers! Shit, they're coming for us!"

"Bummer! You take care of them, Jo. I really can't right now..." I couldn't stop laughing hysterically. "He made you sing! And jump! And bark! Hahahaha! Oh, that Carter!"

When I was done laughing, I stood up and helped Tank and Jovanna put an end to the last whistler. I sent them to the battlefield to gather the loot from Nagash's vassals while I took the best of what remained after the necromancer.

Nagash had dropped less than 1000 existence resource points; apparently he'd used everything to level up.

The loot included the Necromancer's Rotting Staff which gave +1 to the level of the risen undead, and the reference guide explaining his class talent. Basically, necromancy meant that instead of generating fighting units, Nagash had the ability to raise the mobs he'd killed with 75% of the characteristics they'd had when they were alive. So instead of one unit he had two undead units. Based on the sum of the vassals' Charisma points, he had an entire army. Fortunately, the Trial mechanism also maintained a balance in this respect: any high-level undead that Nagash had raised were brought back down to the current level of his talent. Otherwise, it was unlikely that we would have been able to deal with him.

A dark blue system balloon appeared in my field of vision, distracting me from examining the rest of what had dropped out of the necromancer's body. Dark blue — that was new.

I popped the balloon and saw a strange message. From the very first lines I realized it was from Martha.

Chapter Fifteen

Only Unity Will Save You...

*Man wants to be better than others
but worse than his son.*

Serbian proverb

OLA, EDDY, JOVANNA, MANU, CARTER, LETI, ZACK, KEN. These eight people, four of whom I'd already encountered in the Trial, were on Martha's list. So that's what Carter had meant when he'd said that all day he couldn't shake the feeling that he and I were supposed to be on the same team. Somehow it turned out that I was just a replica of myself, and the real Phil Panfilov continued to live and go about his business on Earth.

I couldn't come to terms with this concept — it was hard to just accept it. I wasn't really me? I was just a virtual embodiment, an avatar of the real Phil? Or — and this wasn't any better — was I just a copy of his body and mind, taken when I'd passed through the portal? In other words, a replica. Nothing more than an echo, a reflection, an imprint of a real person.

I shook my head, pulling myself together. It didn't matter if I happened to be a copy or a virtual digital embodiment. My fate, meaning the real Phil's fate, was in my hands, not his. Whether the two of us would have a future depended only on me. You can't wallow in self-pity on Pibellau where time is precious.

Jovanna touched my shoulder with concern. "Phil, I don't know if you heard it, but an alarm went off on one of our new bases. Should we teleport there? What if someone captures the hexagon..."

"Absolutely, Jo. Let's just take a couple of minutes to sort the loot, then we'll port to Base 1. When we get there, we can generate Rex again and change into new uniforms. Then we can go beat the crap out of the invaders. They still need almost an hour there to be on their own."

"What did the Necro drop?" Jovanna nodded at the stuff lying at my feet. "May I take a look?"

"Of course, go ahead."

She pushed aside Tank who had craned his neck to sniff the items. First she examined the necromancer's staff which was no good for us. She shrugged, picked up the spiked bone pauldrons that Nagash had flaunted, and turned them around in her hands. Unfortunately, they were totally useless in a fight:

+65 to a chance of dropping an additional spirit crystal

"Well," Jo said. "Nothing special. Of course you

should wear them, but I was expecting more."

"Of course I'll wear them. I already have nine crystals. Four more and I'll be able to trade one in for an extra life. I think it's surprising that our necromancer captured so many slaves. He didn't have anything that made him especially strong. As we say where I come from, it looks like he was bluffing their socks off with his horde of undead. Fear makes the wolf appear bigger than he is, and apparently the fear of corpses and zombies is a strong thing. Or maybe he used his ability to control other people's minds."

Jovanna nodded in agreement. "I don't quite understand what you're saying about fear, but I really agree with the rest. Shouldn't we get to the first base pronto?"

"One minute. I need to tell you something."

Without revealing my source of information, I told Jovanna what I'd learned from Martha. That of the 169 test subjects, we were special — the ones like me, her and Carter. I told her that Valiadis and Ilindi wanted us to stay together, and they wanted one of us to pass the Trial so that the supervisors wouldn't have risked so much for nothing. I also told her that now that Carter was no longer with us — my chest tightened when I said it — we needed to take Zack under our wing as soon as possible and look for the other people on the list. Ola couldn't have gone far. The route to the east was closed to us, so we'd need to expand north. Maybe we'd find some of "our" people there — the ones with high social status — and even if we didn't, we might at least even things out with Tafari. We were going to have to prepare for war with him, and the more resources and clan members we had, the higher the likelihood of victory. For starters, victory over him — it would be easier for us than for him since he was squeezed between us and Juma — and then, honest to God, victory in the entire Trial.

"It's strange that Zack is 'one of us'," Jovanna said, making air quotes.

"Or maybe we just don't know him well. Would you tell the first people you met something personal about yourself?"

She shook her head.

"There you go," I said. "Launching the teleport to the first base."

Back at the base, the first thing I did was turn on the regeneration of the tyrannosaur, using my Fusion to pump all 20 of my Charisma points into him. A new Rex was more expensive than before, since now he was level 3 — he cost me 300 existence resource points.

While the Dinosaur was being reconstructed, I tried to figure out whether it would be worth leveling up the uniform module and finally spent 1000 points to do it. The new clothes we got were not only nice to look at, but also gave us confidence — no joke, they had 45% damage absorption. That was almost as much as Tank had.

Reinforced test subject uniform
Protection: +45.
Durability: 100%.

The uniform had the same components as the previous versions, but the material was incredible. Showing no signs of shyness, Jovanna eagerly grabbed the new things and changed first. That gave me a chance to take a good look at her body, and I reacted so strongly, um, down below that my theory about being digital fell apart. That sort of thing doesn't happen in the virtual world.

Jo finished lacing her boots and looked up. Embarrassed, I started to get dressed in the new threads.

The fabric was elastic, its color depending on the environment. I decided to do a little experiment to test its durability and asked Jovanna to prod me with a knife. She was a little dubious, but she did it.

Damage taken: 35 (stabbed by Jovanna)

The fabric rebounded, repelling her hand. I barely felt the knife — it was like a light poke even though Jo hit me with all her might. Excellent.

"Now you do it to me," Jovanna demanded.

"For real?"

"Hit me!" she planted her feet wide, pressed her hands to her sides, clenched her fists and grit her teeth. "Well? Go on, hit me! Oof..."

The color drained from her face. She sputtered. I guess I'd struck her harder than she'd hit me. The fabric tore where I'd stabbed her, the knife sinking into her stomach up to the hilt.

"How much Strength do you have?"

"Twenty-five."

She sniffed. "That makes sense."

The wound healed before my eyes.

"Go put on a new uniform and then we'll pay a visit to Nagash. Because the new Rex will be born in

4... 3... 2... 1!"

A roar rang out all around us.

As soon as we arrived at Base 21, I noticed Ola's solitary figure sitting next to the dome.

When he caught sight of us, he broke into a smile. "Phil, it's about time! It took you a long time to, er, break up the loot."

"Why am I not surprised? How's life, Ola? Where are the others?"

"They scattered," Ola said with a shrug. "Morana turned up here last. While we were thinking about whether we should go rescue my lord or wait for him at the base, he died and we were all freed. Morana said she was going to look for him and she'd find him wherever he was resurrected. The others decided to try and join Tafari, so they went east."

"What about you?"

"I decided to join you. With monsters like your tyrannosaur, we can take on any amount of the undead. Will you accept me into your clan?"

"What about your lord?" I couldn't refrain from being a little nasty. "Aren't you worried about the fate of the ruler of the dead in the here and now and on Earth in the future?"

"To hell with him! As my grandfather used to say, he who is covered in cotton shouldn't get near a flame," Ola stood up and walked toward us, then pointed at Tank. "Oh, I didn't see that one with you. It looks like a rhinoceros."

"It's triceratops Tank, and the one breathing in your ear is Tyrannosaurus Rex. And this is Jovanna. She's an archer. Get acquainted and accept the invitation to the clan. We still have a lot to talk about, but there's someone else I want to talk to. We'll wait until we find him so we don't need to say everything twice."

As soon as Ola joined our clan, I highlighted everyone's icons in the interface and teleported us to the main base.

"Wow," Ola exclaimed when I gave him the uniform and pulled Carter's spear with the predatory blade from the extradimensional trunk. "Is that for me... master?"

"You can stick Tank's horn up your butt, Ola! What's with this 'master' stuff? Call me Phil. And yes, that's for you. Change your clothes, quick."

"Still waters run deep," said Jovanna, looking off to the side.

* * *

"As my grandfather used to say, never scorn the bridge you take to safely cross the river." Ola shared another snippet of African wisdom. "And while I was with Nagash involuntarily, this is different... you can count on me, Phil. The way you treat the other clan members... the way you treated me..."

"We'll discuss that in a little while. We're almost there."

Ola, who'd spent the whole trip twirling the spear and practicing thrusts, already considered himself a martial arts master. He reminded me of Morgan from *The Walking Dead*, despite the fact that Morgan was bald and Ola had dreadlocks, and he was also much shorter.

We headed out of our base that was the closest

to Zack's, massacring small packs of mobs along the way. Level 9 and 10 ordinary creatures were nothing to us. Tank tanked, Rex dealt damage, and we, well, if there was something, we killed it and collected the loot — existence resources.

And just as Jovanna had received the Archery skill together with her bow, Ola had quickly mastered the different crafty methods of spearfighting.

We didn't run into any nebulas with their surprise anomalies and ghastly bursts of acid from their chests. There weren't any around here. But there were lots of kirpi, those most gruesome of mutants: a cross between a hedgehog and an octopus. A couple of times we ran into whistlers, and passing a crevice we bumped into some sarasurs — armored cockroaches — but Rex crushed a pack of eight of those with ease. The last surviving sarasur met its end when Ola's spear and Jovanna's arrow pierced it simultaneously.

We crossed over into Zack's hexagon. I got goosebumps. My skin immediately contracted as if struck by hundreds of tiny prickly shocks.

Warning! You are about to enter a hexagon captured by another test subject.
Owner: Zack. Level: 5
Base level: 1.

Had Zack risen two levels in less than a day? Hey, all the better for the clan.

We went straight to the center without stopping, picking up loot along the way. The mobs here were level 5 to match the hexagon's owner. Piece of cake.

We found Zack on the base. He must have come

back because of the alarm. When he caught sight of us, he panicked, then backed away to the shelter and froze hopelessly. When I got closer and looked beyond the enclosure, I saw that he had with him eight ghastly species of mutated spiders that were four and a half feet tall.

"Hi, Zack," I raised my hands, palms toward him in a sign of peace. "We need to chat."

"Hello... colleagues. Chat? Like last time? No thanks."

"Zack, I already explained why I acted the way I did. I don't have that dagger on me. But since you're refusing to talk to me, Jovanna and Ola, I guess the news from Earth didn't reach you. Is that right?"

"News? From Earth?" Zack was puzzled. "What do you mean? What kind of news?"

"That's one of the things I want to tell you about. Maybe you can invite us into your... house? So that nothing distracts us?"

Zack looked around anxiously, thought about something, then waved his hand.

"Come on in," he said.

Along the way I noticed an unusual staff that he was holding. It was short, measuring around 15 inches long and looked to be either metal or plastic, but most likely this green-tinged material was entirely unknown to the earth sciences. It seemed too short and thin to be a smashing weapon. Maybe it was something like Jovanna's lightning rod? I couldn't identify the item by looking at it; I needed to hold it myself.

"Zack?" I called to his back. "That's an interesting, um, baton you have there."

"It's more like a magic wand," Jovanna smiled.

"Like Harry Potter's."

"This? No, it's not a baton or a magic wand," Zack stopped and demonstrated the intriguing item. "It's a small healing staff. It heals fighting units at a rate of about 10% per second. During the night I was able to vanquish a duxio. It took us a long time to finish it off. This is what it dropped."

"Wow. Does it heal people?" Ola stared at the staff, his eyes as large as saucers.

"I haven't tried it out on other people, but it definitely doesn't work on me," Zack said.

"So let's try it on someone else. Ola, come here and poke me in the arm with your... Oh! Not so hard!" I reeled back, flinching from the blow. "Not with the spear — do you know what kind of treacherous stinger you have there? Use your knife, it's basic. Just poke me a couple of times... Ouch!"

Damage taken: 47 (stabbed by Ola).

Damage taken: 51 (stabbed by Ola).

"Heal me, quick!" I shouted to Zack. "Faster! Before the wounds heal by themselves!"

Zack pointed the wand. A small green beam flickered from its tip but immediately disappeared.

"You see? But if you point it at your units, the beam doesn't stop like that."

"I see..." I scratched my head. "What if someone stands in its path?"

"Won't work," Zack answered. "The beam just goes around the obstacle."

"Hm. Well, in that case it's probably not the

beam that's the issue?"

"Why not? Curved beams do exist. Phil, I'd be happy to have a scientific discussion, but I don't want to waste time for nothing. Let's go inside and you'll tell me why you're here. It will be evening soon and I wanted to reach level 6 tonight," Zack went under the dome, leaving the door open.

I went inside and looked around. Two basic modules stocked with fighting units and uniforms. And their owner, who'd jumped up two more levels.

"Not bad, Zack," I accidentally said what I was thinking.

"What?"

"If it's not a secret, how are you farming resources?"

"That's not a secret. The most complicated thing was to collect enough for the fighting unit module. It costs 50 points, so you just kill mobs with your bare hands, ignoring the pain. You know how it is: here it's not just a snake. Either it's armored or it has spikes or acid slime. I have a feeling that the local lifeforms aren't carbon-based. But then I don't understand how we can live and breathe here."

"Oh, that's easy to explain," I gave a quick summary of everything I knew to Zack and Ola, whom I'd left in the dark.

But they reacted completely differently.

"That explains my dream!" Ola cried. "Last night I couldn't sleep. I just lay there with my eyes closed. I dreamed that it was like I was walking around the village and everyone I met called out names to me. I don't remember all of them, but I definitely remember hearing 'Phil' and 'Ken.' Who's Ken?"

"Apparently he's another test subject from our wave. I didn't have a dream like that, but I believe Phil," Jovanna said.

"Oh, I almost forgot," I slapped my forehead. "This morning before the fight with Nagash, Carter approached me. Zack, you don't know him, but he and I have a strange relationship on Pibellau: he killed me and I killed him, but today he decided on his own to join my clan. He said that for some reason it seemed to him that we needed to be on the same team. Do you understand? He also somehow received information from Earth."

"So where's this Carter guy now?" Zack wanted to know.

"He died permanently. He was disincarnated."

"Is that the fate you're proposing for me? No way. If all this bullshit is some kind of sophisticated skill to sucker me into your clan, it'll be easier if you just kill me. I'm not joining your clan. Don't even try to talk me into it."

"Is it our clan you won't join, or any clan at all?"

"I'm not joining any clan. I think I have an idea of what this slavery will be like for me. Constant stress, waiting for the disincarnation timer to be reset? Thanks but no thanks. I have too much self-respect to grovel before anyone, following someone else's orders."

"Nonsense!" Jovanna exclaimed.

"Think what you want," Zack muttered. "If he's so nice to you, Jovanna, maybe you should ask yourself why? Maybe it's because you're a beautiful woman? I'm not joining your clan. Case closed."

Zack meant it. No amount of semblance between our respective interfaces could make him change his mind. He just didn't give a damn about the Trial or the upcoming Diagnostics of the human race. For some reason, I was sure about this. But I had to try, if only for Ilindi's sake.

"Zack, please reconsider. You won't be able to handle anyone else on your own. You'll never be able to level up where Juma or Tafari or anyone else is. There are no more available hexagons, which means you'll need to be happy with just one. If that guy on the rhinoceros shows up here tomorrow, your spiders won't save you. By the way, are they spiders? They look like they're crossed with a scorpion, judging by the tail with the stinger. Anyhow, that's not the point. The important thing is that you won't be able to stand your ground. And you'll need to!" I stressed my last words. "You'll need to join a clan. There's no guarantee that the Nigerian will make that offer. And what then? Permanent disincarnation and you'll lose everything you achieved with the interface."

Zack grinned. "I don't really care. What can they do, take away my wife and kids? They won't take a thing. I'm already a millionaire, the head of a big company, and my wife thinks the world of me. We're expecting a child. They're going to take that away from me? Like that's going to happen!"

"But that's what it says in the rules," Jovanna broke in. "Here, it says, '*The losers in the Trial will be stripped of their privileges, achievements and development progress in their own world. They will be taken back to the moment when they received the interface. Their memory of the accompanying events will be wiped clean and the interface will be uninstalled*'."

"That's nonsense," Zack said. "I believe that

they'll take away the interface. But not everything else. How will they take me back to the past? What kind of craziness is that? Can you imagine what a waste of energy that would be, even if they had the technology? That's destroying the whole temporal branch of reality! And what about rewriting events as if I don't have the interface, and never had it? Ha! There are 169 test subjects, so what? They'll destroy 168 time lines?"

"Why not?" Jovanna said. "We're all on the same branch and we received the interface almost at the same time. They'll just wipe ours out."

"First of all, we didn't all receive the interface at the same time," Zack said. "I was able to meet and communicate with Mr. Valiadis before the Trial. He told me he'd installed each interface personally and that required him to be close to the subject — the future user. Second, how can they wipe out the branch that the winner continues to live in? So to summarize: I'm sure that the losers won't be taken back to the past. That's dishonest. I don't believe that. So I'm not joining you. It's out of the question. In any case, I'll pass the Trial whether I'm in a clan or on my own. So why should I lose my freedom?"

We were all silent for a moment, thinking about Zack's words. There was logic in what he'd said about not taking things away. But rational thought, at least mine, wouldn't let me reconcile myself to a potential hole in the defense of our dominion. I hoped that Tafari wouldn't show up unexpectedly in the remaining couple of days I'd promised Zack.

And of course it was a pity not to have a healer in the group, even if it was just for animals.

* * *

"Phil, can we maybe take a break?" Ola was clasping his hands and begging for a rest.

Jovanna was collecting the loot as usual and I, cursing like a sailor, was waiting for my side to heal where my ribs were jutting out.

"Sure, go ahead. Jo, please finish up and then we'll all go to the shelter and take a breather. And there's something we need to talk about..."

Suffering from excruciating pain, I had the cowardly idea of wasting 860 resource points (counting the 14% bonus for leveling up) to buy level 10, but I decided to stick it out. I figured it wasn't worth starting from a zero-sum game.

The elites, which were attacking our base one after the other, were especially fierce tonight. But we farmed more of them than ever, thanks to our pull tactics: feeling brave, we ventured beyond the borders of the enclosure and whenever we found an elite mob, Jovanna would shoot it, and then the enraged monster would dash at us onto the territory of the base.

One of these pulls was not a rousing success. We'd lured one of those beetles onto the base and had just started the fight when a second one appeared — it had come on its own. That was fine; we had three tank units. Rex held one, Tank another, and Croc and I badgered from behind.

Croc was our third dinosaur, put together from Ola's Charisma points. Thirteen points belonging to our charismatic Cameroonian blossomed into the largest crocodile in the galaxy. Choosing between the allosaurus and the gigantosaurus — the most dangerous predatory dinosaur on the planet — I ultimately pressed on the sarcosuchus. This 50-foot-long ancestor of modern crocodiles proved itself an outstanding solution to our problem of speed. Tafari's rhinoceros? Ha! We now had a crocodile mount!

Sarcosuchus Croc
Level 6 melee fighter
Phil's fighting unit.
Health points: 4700/4700.
Attack: 1200–1500.
Damage absorbed by armor: 60%.
Maximum travel speed: 22 mph
Weight: 10 tons
Talents: Charging, Squeezing, Acceleration.

We'd already tried to take a ride on him, holding on to the tough scales that covered his back, and we were able to do it. Croc's Acceleration talent could speed him up 1.5 times for five seconds once per minute, which was nothing to sniff at. I have to admit that I had the lowest Agility of the three of us and I once slid off Croc, causing Jovanna to giggle and Ola to howl with laughter. It would be a good idea to come up with some sort of saddle.

On the whole, things were good and the farming was going according to plan, but then Kreken version 2.0 showed up. The resurrected location boss, which was already level 12 and had a shedload of life to go with it, had inspected the surroundings near his lair in the ravine and snuck into our hexagon. It stumbled across us as we were killing a mega kirpi. The elite octopus-hedgehog hybrid the size of a truck managed to fight everyone all at once, using its tentacles to restrain the dinosaurs and us, so we struggled until Rex and Croc tore off all its limbs.

When the mega kirpi was down to about 20% life, the Kreken flew in. Without stopping to think about who the good guys and bad guys were, it spat its plasma at the hedgehog-octopus, evaded a direct attack by Tank sent by Jovanna to intercept it, shot up out of Croc's collapsing jaws, outstripped Rex, and chose the feeble, level 3 Ola as its next victim.

At this point, the end would have come for Ola and he would have been sent to his resurrection point via the great African void, but I managed to shout a command. Before he completely melted away, Ola hastily bought himself a higher level, which removed the Burn DOT and healed him.

The next few minutes of the fight were a whirlwind of mutual attacks: we evaded the spittle while the Kreken sidestepped the trajectory of the speeding triceratops and the tyrannosaur's snapping jaws. Jovanna's arrows dealt minor damage, and that says nothing of Ola who was completely useless in this skirmish and whom I'd told to stay by the shelter and not hover in front of the overgrown horsefly.

Meanwhile, while I dashed toward the boss between two rounds of spittle, something hit me like a ton of bricks. It was the Kreken demonstrating its new ability for close combat as it sent a stinger into my throat which was only protected with the bandana from the uniform.

Along with the sensory loss, I was struck by a scorching, corroding pain that flowed from my throat to my chest up to the top of my head and then surged through my whole body.

My skin turned black and blistered. My breathing became labored; then I couldn't breathe at all. The Poison DOT ticked so fervently and urgently that I could barely lift my feet to take refuge in the shelter before the boss knocked out my final 30% health.

I took around 10 seconds to regenerate, waited for the poison's effect to wear off, and then returned to the battlefield.

It took the convergence of several factors to get us out of this dead-end situation. Croc waited for the best time to pounce, Rex bobbed his head like a dog being taunted with a bone, waiting for the opportunity to seize the agile beast, while Tank once again gained speed and tore at the Kreken.

At that exact moment, Jovanna shot her bow. Ping!

The Kreken fell prey to the stunning effect of Jovanna's bow, which both dinosaurs happily took advantage of. Tank head-butted the boss's fallen body, but Rex didn't let it escape far. He scooped up the overgrown horsefly in his snout and opened and shut his jaws a few times as I shouted, "Shred 'em!"

My fellow clan members applauded. Croc surveyed the scene impassively as if he couldn't have cared less about any of this.

As a prize to the victors, the Kreken left behind 1000 resource points (the Intellect bonus took effect) and a small ring.

Ordinary Clan Ring of Leadership

+10% to damage dealt by all clan members. The effect is activated only when used by the clan leader.

"That's a real cool ring!" Jovanna exclaimed, rolling it around in her hands.

"You've earned it, Jo. If you hadn't stunned the boss, we would have pounded it till morning. But there was no guarantee that the outcome would have been good."

Jovanna blushed. Ola brought her back to her senses — or, more accurately, drove her into a stupor by saying,

"If you want to keep the milk fresh, leave it in the cow!"

"What are you talking about?" I asked.

"I'd bet my bow that it's another piece of wisdom from his grandfather!" Jovanna laughed.

"Yo, Jovanna! You're half right, my grandfather did say it often, but it's actually a piece of folk wisdom in my country. What I mean is that it's clear who should wear the ring so it has an effect."

After the Kreken, everything went like clockwork. By morning we'd collected nearly 7000 resource points, counting what we'd extracted from Nagash and from Carter's contribution. It was impossible to use strength to break out of this place, but everyone was mentally exhausted, except maybe the dinosaurs, because each fight was their reason for being put in this world.

Our fatigue was caused by pain which we hadn't managed to avoid in a single fight. It affected even Jovanna who was attacked from behind by a squadron of elite sarasurs that had infiltrated the base smack in the middle of a fight with a two-headed snake. Even though we'd managed to do away with them — or rather, we'd made Rex abandon the snake and trample them all — but still Jovanna was in agony from all the acid burns and lacerated wounds.

Therein lies the paradox. Humans have survived for eons thanks to pain. It has always been our best ally in our understanding of the world and our self-preservation. I cut myself with a knife — ouch! — OK, I guess I need to be careful with sharp objects.

Here, however, the pain, blood, wounds and spilling innards were just decoration, special effects, because fatal wounds didn't just heal quickly, but lightning fast.

Even when Carter had lost half his skull in the last fight, he'd been restored within minutes in the shelter, and had he let the regeneration process run its course rather than come outside to my rescue, he'd still be alive. The seconds before Jovanna had showed up had decided everything in that fight.

After fighting to my heart's content and dying twice, I, who'd previously read all the LitRPG book series nonstop, suddenly grasped that not a single sane person would fully immerse themselves in "tanking" in a game, just as no amount of authentic experience would drag normal people into full-immersion capsules if there were even a hint of pain there.

So I gave in to Ola's pleas. We went to the shelter so we could rest up and hold the clan council I'd suggested. Maybe it wasn't the best moment, but we decided that as soon as both of Pibellau's suns began to rise, we'd set out toward the north to expand both our territory and our clan, provided we found other people with high social status. The moment was absolutely perfect. We needed to invest our hard-farmed resources in something, not stockpile them, and it was time to come up with a strategy.

We were sprawled in a little circle in the center of the shelter. Suspecting something, Jovanna and Ola looked at me intently, waiting to hear what I had to say.

"Guys, there are already three of us. Yesterday's fight with Nagash," I smirked at Ola's embarrassment, "demonstrated that the clan leader can't count only on himself. I'm not going to repeat that mistake. So here's the first rule I'm giving you: clan members all level up at the same time in the order they joined the clan. Two: We're going to maintain a balance in the clan's development. There will be no imbalance or one-sided leveling. We're going to develop ourselves, the units and the bases, making the main base our priority. As we already have 36 hexagons, trying to level up each base is a waste of resources. That kind of expenditure can pay off in the long term, but we don't have long-term prospects. Does anyone object to anything I just said? Jo?"

"Everything's clear and I agree with everything," she answered, sounding like a straight-A student.

"What about you, Ola? What do you say, Mr. Afelobu?"

"How am I supposed to know, Phil?" Ola spread his arms. "I was pulled into a clan on my very first day on Pibellau. I'd only had a chance to build my own base. I didn't have enough resources for anything, not even the uniform module. I went out to hunt and advanced a couple of levels. Then Nagash's units surrounded me. There were no undead yet. He himself was only level 4, but I was powerless against fifteen of his horrible units."

"And you accepted his conditions. That makes sense. Then I'll explain what I'm talking about."

The clan council turned into a brief lecture about bases, modules, costs for upgrades and the ability to translate everything into figures.

"Anyway, we'll always be faced with a choice," I concluded. "We have around 7000 resources now. I say 'around' because a working unit contributes something every hour, and the bases generate resources. Level 1 bases generate at a rate of one point per hour, and the main base where we are right now, generates at a rate of 10 points per hour. So how can we invest the ones we collect? For 7500 we can bring the fighting unit module up to level 4. Then Tank, Rex and Croc will be level 7 killing machines, but we'll still be vulnerable. We could invest everything in leveling up ourselves or spend a 1000 to create a little reconnaissance drone-"

"We need a reconnaissance drone," Jovanna said. "There's no question!"

"Yes, we can spare 1000," Ola agreed. "It's always better to know where you're going."

"Well then, let's leave it at that. I'll just go through the options so you understand what's what. If you've ever played strategy games, you should understand that you can't develop everything at once because you won't have enough resources, and at each concrete moment in time it's better to follow the strategy. Our strategy will be that for each choice that comes up, we'll assess the potential advantages of the expenditure and compare which one will give us more for less money... I mean, resources. And that-"

"OK, Phil, that's fine with me," Jo interrupted me. "So what exactly are you proposing now? How will we invest the 7000?"

"Here's what I suggest. We always need to have a stockpile so we can quickly level up during a fight. That's the only way to instantly heal all our wounds and avoid death. Jo, you need 600 for level 6. Ola, you need 500. That's a total of 1100. I'll need almost as many. So I'll set aside 2200 or 2300 as a stash we won't touch."

"Don't you need exactly 1000 points for level 10?" Ola asked.

"Even less, actually. I have a bonus for the preliminary selection. We'll talk about that later. For 2500 resource points we can upgrade the base to level 3. That will give us some interesting modules — like research ones and — ta-da! — an artifact module. I don't know the details, but after we build them, I think we won't regret it."

"Can you give an example? What do we get out of them?"

"The artifact module generates artifacts. The research module improves the units' stats, the productivity of the working units, armor, something else... That's the idea, anyway."

"But?"

"Ah, yes, there is a 'but.' For the base upgrade we need..."

"We get it, you need to be level 10," Jovanna nodded. "So what are you waiting for? Level up!"

"Ola?"

"I'd be surprised if you were waiting for my

opinion, Phil," Ola said, shaking his head. "As my grandfather used to say-"

"It's OK, I got it. In that case, I'll buy level 10. After that and the base upgrade, subtracting the emergency stockpile, we'll have around 1000 points left. Then we'll need to make a decision: do we invest them in your level ups, create a reconnaissance drone or just build a research module? Think about it while I level up."

I pulled up my stats:

Phil, human.

Level: 9.

Class: undetermined. Required level: 10 needed.

Health points: 2600/2600.

Damage without weapon: 23–27.

Chance of critical hit: 46.5%.

Bonus: 14% off the cost of character development.

Achievements: Altruist, First Giant Slayer, First Daredevil, First to Die.

Main characteristics
Strength — 25.
Agility — 11.
Intellect — 20.
Stamina — 26.
Perception — 21.
Charisma — 20.
Luck — 15.

Character stats

Lives: 1.
Captured hexagons: 50.
Ranking: 3/169.
Existence resources: 6983/9000.

I hadn't looked at my stats in a long time. Third place in the overall ranking of all the test subjects meant that only Juma and Tafari were ahead of me. So my progress over the last four days since my second death hadn't been too shabby.

I spent a few moments mentally reliving the events of the last few days, then tapped on the level up.

Congratulations, test subject! You've reached level 10!

You receive +2 Characteristic points to invest into any characteristics of your choice.

You may now level up the command center to level 3.

You may now receive a class specialization.

Put more fire under your enemies' feet, test subject!

The system message wasn't static. A line appeared under it, followed by yet another one:

Analyzing the test subject's actions...
Number of compatible classes found... 2.
Observers' vote...
Your class has been determined, test subject!
Put more fire under your enemies' feet, Liquidator!

Chapter Sixteen

An Easy Way to Become a Superhero

Barry Allen:
What are your superpowers again?
Bruce Wayne:
I'm rich.

Justice League

As the Russian proverb goes, if you want to win the war, you need to work three times as hard. My Insight was exactly three levels higher than Konstantin Panchenko's. So as he'd threatened me with his chopsticks and dribbled saliva, I already knew that he wasn't a rival.

I still had Panchenko's expanded profile open in front of me.

Konstantin Panchenko
Age: 27
Current status: commercial director
Social status level: 11
Class: Manipulator. Level: 6
Unmarried
Criminal record: yes

The last line gave me slightly more useful information, as did the new detail — or rather, details — of his biography that I hadn't noticed before: namely, the list of all his crimes.

And what a list it was. In his 27 years, Panchenko had committed more than a thousand crimes. There were a lot of petty crimes like downloading pirated films from torrents, but there were also a couple of incidents that were meatier: he'd stolen newspapers and magazines from neighbors' mailboxes when he was younger, and he'd stolen money from the wallet of someone I gathered was his friend. Some of those people had never found out; the friend had barely made ends meet until his next payday while the young Konstantin enjoyed the latest issue of *Playboy*.

When I filtered out all the similar items, all that was left were kickbacks. At least, they were mainly kickbacks.

It had started four years ago:

March 14, 2014.
Article 204 of the Russian Criminal Code: Bribery
Receipt of 5,000 rubles from citizen V. N. Stepantsov, an employee of Tesla Print, for

cooperation in establishing an agreement with Rasmus Media to print media materials.

July 21, 2014.
Article 204 of the Russian Criminal Code: Bribery
Receipt of 12,000 rubles from citizen K. F. Ponomarenko, an employee of Northern Food and Beverage, for cooperation in establishing an agreement with Rasmus Media to organize a cocktail party for...

Evidently, the young Rasmus intern — Konstantin Panchenko — had been at first perfectly satisfied with small sums of money, and it was unlikely that he'd been entrusted with large accounts when the company was looking for contractors. A few years later, after he'd been transferred to the Samara branch where he'd immediately become PR director, he'd started to show what he could do. The kickbacks became more frequent as he obviously gained confidence.

The most recent incidents had occurred while he was at Ultrapak. How and why he'd fallen to the level of a small provincial commercial director was another matter entirely.

In short, even if I didn't know whether Mr. Ivanov was aware of Panchenko's activities, he definitely would be.

But first I called Valiadis.

He answered immediately, as though he were waiting for a call. "Philip? Is this urgent?"

"I just have a couple of quick questions."

"Shoot."

"Number one: I met someone else who has an interface. Konstantin Panchenko. Tell me, how soon will he participate in the Trial?"

"I know him. Do you mind if I ask why you're interested in him?"

"He's making mischief, for me personally and people close to me."

"Hm. No wonder. The version of his interface is different from yours," Valiadis scoffed. "Is he making lots of mischief?"

"Not yet, he's just stirred up the revenue officers and started a bunch of unpleasant rumors about me and my partners. But he said he was only just getting started."

"Really? I'll tell you then. His abduction is in less than two months. He's going to be in the next wave. Can you sort him out yourself?"

"I'll manage, thank you. I have some good news, though: my virtual assistant has managed to contact her replica in the Trial. Now she's trying to get the information to the user."

"For real?" I heard genuine happiness in Valiadis' voice. "That's great! Thank you for sharing that with me. I hope all of this isn't for nothing."

"We'll get through, Mr. Valiadis."

"We sure will. I'm now busy finalizing my things. If ever there's a reason for us to meet up, I'll explain why at that point. By the way, what's the name of your company?"

"The Great Job Recruitment Agency."

"Got it. Good luck, Philip — both here and there!"

He hung up first before I had a chance to ask

how to get in touch with Ilindi. I really wanted to tell her about the successful connection with Martha 2, but apparently now wasn't the time for that.

When I got back to the office, I spent a couple of hours finishing up with the job-seeking clients who'd arrived while I was out — both those who were waiting in line and those whose information the staff had already taken. I then retreated to my new office with a laptop, told everyone not to disturb me, and delved into the astonishing world of Konstantin Panchenko's criminal life.

I created a separate file for each company where he'd worked and listed all the incidents he'd been involved in.

The message drilled into us by society from an early age is that you shouldn't grass or snitch — but I ignored it because of its sheer absurdity. It's exactly in this environment of cover-ups that thieves, criminals, loafers and domestic tyrants flourish. Wives are silent about their husbands' battery, children are silent about cyberbullying, girls are silent about sexual assault, government employees are silent about corruption, while the people around them who are in the know cover everything up.

No idea what's to blame here: whether it's people's fear of making fools of themselves, or their fear of the system which can't be overturned by one person.

I had nothing to be afraid of. But as the co-owner of a business, I felt disgusted by the way Panchenko was cheating his bosses. It offended me to imagine having such a person working for me.

Six letters went out to six companies and organizations where Konstantin had managed to "work." He'd worked for around a year in each place, ending with three months at Ultrapak. Finding the contact information of the owners and senior managers was easy, and I also posted my letters on social media.

"Philip, can I bother you for a minute?" Rose had opened the door slightly and was standing on the threshold.

"Yes, of course. What's going on with the revenue officers?"

"Everything is in order. Basically it's just a formality. I'm here to talk about Cyril. I gave him the money, but he's handed in his resignation. Am I understanding correctly that this is the result of your... er... internal investigation?"

"Well... No, I'd afraid you got it all wrong. Cyril has late-stage pulmonary emphysema. He's going to Moscow for treatment. The company is helping him out. Do you object?"

"Oh, come now, Philip!" Rose threw her hands up. "Of course I don't. But still... in the future, please discuss things like this with your bookkeeper," she said, smiling slyly. "At the very least, OK? I'm not talking about the partners, but that wouldn't be a bad idea either. We haven't yet grown enough to..." she said gently, admonishing me in a friendly way, but the complaint was valid. "We're going to pay for Alik's studies, and now Cyril's treatment..."

"Very well, Mrs. Reznikova. I acted on impulse. In the future I promise not to make decisions like that on my own."

"All righty then. That's all I wanted to say."

"Oh, and one more thing. Could you set his resignation letter aside, please? Don't process it yet."

She nodded, carefully closed the door and left me alone.

I had now completed the first step in undermining Panchenko. If he didn't get the message and didn't repent on his own, I might have to adopt firmer measures. Especially where my former friend Cyril was concerned.

* * *

Whenever I tried to speak English, I felt like a dog: I understood everything, but when I needed to say something, I got flustered. Translating the word "fence" from Russian was no big deal. But if I needed to tell someone something about a fence, I would spend a long time digging deep into my memory, umming, aahing and waving my arms, but I still wouldn't remember the word.

So when I was told that the teacher was a native speaker, and an American volunteer at that, I was happy.

I needed to learn English, and not just because I had a meeting with the ambassador scheduled. In recent days, the prospect of losing the interface had started to weigh on me less and less, and I didn't get mired in despair and the futility of my efforts. My habit of not loafing around got the better of me.

When I realized that wasting time on a trip to Moscow before the Trial ended was unreasonable, I wrote to the US embassy worker to notify her that due to certain circumstances I'd need to postpone my visit.

I decided to spend the rest of Monday more

productively; it had been too intense, what between the morning meeting with the discouraging news, revenue officers, various rumors, Cyril's betrayal and the appearance in my life of another interface user.

I spent two hours at the gym and went from there to my evening English class. I was so focused on revising adverbial clauses, which I'd studied on my own, that I didn't immediately feel my phone vibrating in my pocket.

"Mr. Panfilov, this is Angela Howard. I got your message that you want to postpone the meeting. Do you mind if I ask when you'll be able to come in? Your letter doesn't say."

"In about a week. I think I'll be ready to fly out next week."

I heard a scraping sound, a muffled whisper, then Angela Howard came back:

"Mr. Panfilov, we'd like to propose holding the meeting in Washington DC. There are now more people who are interested in meeting you, and would it be convenient for you..."

"Yes. I've always wanted to see the United States. But could you tell me who these people are exactly?" I had to speak cryptically in order not to encourage the eavesdropping taxi driver's curiosity.

"I'm sorry, but I'm not authorized to say, Mr. Panfilov. In any case, you'll find out soon. I'll mail you details about the formalities of the trip."

"Thank you, Angela."

"Good-bye, Mr. Panfilov."

"Good-bye."

I spent the rest of the trip to the language center scouring the web. Facebook showed me hundreds of young girls, young women and older women named Angela Howard. I even accessed the infospace, spending on it a tiny fraction of my regenerating Spirit. The Infospace pinpointed a couple of them in Russia, but none in Moscow.

And last but not least, there wasn't a single person by that name listed at the US embassy in the Russian Federation.

* * *

It had been raining all night. The tapping of the raindrops against the window pane had a soothing effect on me. I fell asleep almost straight away and only awoke at sunrise.

The rain had stopped. All I could hear was the rustle of the street cleaner's broom and the birds singing outside. Good.

Still, something was nagging at me. I couldn't quite put my finger on it.

I racked my brains, rummaging through all the latest developments. That's it. It was the rescheduling of the meeting with the Yanks on American turf.

I'd agreed to it way too easily. The risk was quite considerable, though. What could be the possible consequences of such a cooperation?

The more I thought about it, the more I realized I might have made a mistake. If things went wrong — like, if they decided to kidnap me and lock me up in some secret government lab — I'd be powerless. I had no particular superhero abilities worth mentioning. As for Lie Detection, that wouldn't amount to much if I

---

was under lock and key.

So what prevented me from acquiring said abilities now? Having pondered over it some more, I decided it was quite doable.

I was pretty close to making level 20 which would also give me Level 2 in Heroism. This in turn, would open the door to three more Heroic skills.

Once I reached level 20, I could activate the second one of the first-tier skills. By then, I would fulfil all the necessary main characteristic requirements.

The skill in question was Stealth and Vanish. It was pretty self-explanatory but how would this supposed invisibility work in real life? I'd have to work that out by trial and error. For instance, would it make me invisible to CCTV cameras?

Having weighed up all the pros and cons, I decided to choose something more useful. In total, I had three second-tier skills.

The first one was also the most useful in combat. I'd already had a chance to use it during my altercation with Tarzan and his goons in the park. I meant Sprint. It could accelerate the user 100% by modifying their Metabolism and Perception for the duration of 5 seconds. And if you counted my boosted Spirit, the effect would be even greater, making me 6 times faster for the duration of 15 seconds.

The second superskill on the list was Regeneration which accelerated Recovery and improved Confidence, Self-Control, Satisfaction, Vigor, Mood and Willpower. I dreaded to think what an enormous effect such fast recuperation might have on my physical stats and skills.

Admittedly, the third heroic skill wasn't quite as

useful in a city environment. I'm talking about Taming which greatly increased the user's chances of taming any non-sentient creature and turning it into their pet.

So all things taken into account, my most pressing objective was making social status level 20, bringing all my main characteristics up to 20 and leveling Meditation up to 5. That would answer all the requirements for Sprint and Regeneration.

Last night's workout had added another level to both my Agility and Stamina. But even though I'd received two more system levels to Perception during the course of the night, I still had my work cut out for me:

Philip "Phil" Panfilov
Age: 32
Current status: entrepreneur
Social status level: 19
Knowledge Seeker. Level: 13
Classes: Boxer, Empath. Level: 11
Divorced
Children: none

Achievements:
Altruist (+1 to all main characteristics at every level gained)

The Fastest Learner (10% to skill development rate)

Main characteristics:
Strength: 19
Agility: 12

Intellect: 20
Stamina: 16
Perception: 17
Charisma: 18
Luck: 14 (+19 pt. combined item bonus to Luck from the Lucky Ring of Veles, the Protective Red Wristband, and the ivory figurine of Netsuke Jurōjin)

I still had four more available system points, but I was saving them for any emergencies to invest into the least advanced characteristics. I also had two skill points I'd received with my two last levels. Although I'd set them aside until the end of the Optimization, I might use them to bring Meditation up to 5 to make sure it answered Regeneration requirements.

It was early morning. I had lots of things on my day's agenda. I had lots of trivialities to deal with at work before I could take a few-days break in order to speed up my leveling. I also had several workouts to complete, including a trampoline club I'd signed up to hoping to improve my lagging Agility. I'd also joined an English class.

I also had another idea. I was only allowed one heroic skill per every ten social status levels. But what if I tried to lower the environmental safety index artificially, like I'd done once already when I'd defended Alik against Vazgen's brothers?

I chuckled with satisfaction as I added a night raid across the city's most criminal areas to my to-do list.

"Let's see if I can't dig up a few more problems for myself, hehe!"

My new superhero abilities were almost within reach, awakening the munchkin in me.

* * *

*"I'm enveloped in a healing white light. It's healing me. By inhaling it, I feel connected to the Divine Energy. I deserve being healed by the light. I can feel my body being cleansed...*Haha! What a cretin!"

I collapsed to the floor, laughing like somebody possessed. All of my meditation session had just gone wrong as I'd realized the stupidity of what I'd been saying.

I'd just spent some time online researching meditation techniques. Finally, I'd had the skill opened and immediately plunged into action, using one of the Internet articles as guidance. I sat on the floor in the lotus position and tried to concentrate, silently contemplating the world within and without as I searched for the state of a perfectly clear mind devoid of thought, reasoning or fantasy.

My body refused to relax. My thoughts kept crowding my head, demanding any kind of action. What else could you expect? So many things were happening simultaneously about me and within me.

This had been my fastest and most productive leveling stint yet. My early-morning jog had turned into a two-hour half-marathon, bringing back the already-forgotten memories of an aching jaw, panting for breath and choking on my own lungs. Despite being a real challenge, it had the desired effect, giving me +2 to Stamina: I'd had to push myself past all limits in order for my interface to recalculate this the way it had done to Strength the day before yesterday.

Having dealt with all the trivial office problems, I went to the trampoline club. Fifteen minutes later, I had a new skill open:

You've activated a new skill: Trampoline Jumping.
Current level: 1
XP received: 200 (for learning the skill)

Once the workout was over, the system granted me 3 more points to Agility. It's not for nothing it's considered one of the best sports for developing coordination: once I'd added a few acrobatic moves to my routine, I'd leveled it up to 3.

I then ate three helpings of steak and veg in a restaurant next to the club and spent about an hour working on the book, allowing my body to recuperate. Although I hadn't made a new level in Creative Writing, it was now very close to 9.

I'd been keeping tabs on Panchenko's movements all day. He'd left the Ultrapak office in the morning and hadn't been back yet. I was toying with the idea of phoning Vicky to find out what the hell was going on but then I thought better of it. Panchenko had spent most of the day somewhere in the suburbs. I had a funny feeling it wasn't work that had brought him there. It must have been Mr. Ivanov who'd promptly reacted to some curious information about his commercial director's activities and taken the necessary steps.

Once I'd felt strong enough to tackle new

heights, I'd headed over to Ibrahim's gym. That was the coach who'd trained me for the boxing tournament. There, I'd spent an hour whacking a punch bag immediately followed by four sparring sessions, deliberately not giving myself a break.

The system had seemed to appreciate my efforts:

Your Stamina has improved!
+1 to Stamina
Current Stamina: 19
You've received 1000 pt. XP for successfully leveling up a main characteristic!
XP points left until the next social status level: 11340/20000.

So now that my Meditation was open, I was trying to level it up — but I couldn't do it for the life of me. A quick brainstorm with Martha resulted in a few prompts about the way to clear one's mind and concentrate on pure contemplation, but then I had to unsummon her in order not to get sidetracked by her shapely forms and doe eyes.

"I'm enveloped in a healing white light. It's healing me. By inhaling it, I feel connected to the Divine Energy. I deserve being healed by the light. I can feel my body being cleansed..."

* * *

The same night, I walked down a busy street famous for its abundance of bars, cafes and restaurants.

I'd completed each and every task on my to-do

list — all but one, that is. I'd leveled up my stats, I'd brought Meditation to level 3 and upped my English to 4 which roughly corresponded to Advanced level. Now I had less than 7,000 XP left until social status level 20.

I had only one unfinished task left on my list. So there I was, looking for trouble in order to artificially lower my environmental safety index.

With this in mind, I did the rounds of the local watering holes prepared to enter into a brawl with anyone as long as they started it themselves.

Still, most of the local crowd turned out to be quite friendly and pacific. Either they hadn't yet reached a sufficiently aggressive stage or my athletic physique dampened their ardor to hassle me.

In the end, I'd broken one fight up, then fended off some lecherous drunk who'd been coming on too strong to a young girl — but in both cases, it hadn't escalated to an actual fight.

I'd almost lost all hope when I finally came across the bustling colorful little forecourt of an Irish pub packed with soccer fans sporting their teams' colors. I headed there only to heave a disappointed sigh: although they were all shouting at the top of their voices, our team had just won so everybody seemed to be in a good mood.

Still, I decided to go in just in case. Where else could you look for relatively safe problems if not in a pub buzzing like a beehive with excited sports fans?

It was so packed I couldn't even elbow my way in. The amount of decibels produced by all the hollering way exceeded safe limits, drowning out the TV commentators' voices. People continued to come and go, leaving the place for a smoke break, while I was looking for a spot.

Finally, I saw a free space at the bar.

Apologizing to some of the girl fans surrounding the bar, I squeezed myself in, climbed on a free stool and met the barman's inquiring gaze.

"Just some flat water, please," I said, then turned my attention to the room.

I didn't have to look for long. Two stools down from me, I saw a beer-bellied guy in a wifebeater, drunk as a skunk. The system message over his head helpfully informed me that this was Alexey "The Boar" Gaschenkov. Even though I was no wuss anymore, he was head and shoulders above me.

His heavy unkind glare circled the room, seething with fury within. His aggression, adrenaline and testosterone were coming out of his ears. The man was looking for trouble. He didn't give a shit in what form it came as long as he could let off steam.

He must have sensed my stare as he swung round. "What?"

"Nothing," I averted my gaze. The guy wasn't in a good mood, so I really didn't feel like having a punch-up with him. I'd hate to use his bad day in my own interests. "Everything's fine."

"Fine my ass!" he growled. "For once those assholes have won, and I backed the opposition!"

I shrugged noncommittally. "Just one of those things, isn't it?"

"What did you just say?" he moved closer to me, breathing stale alcohol in my face. "You got a problem with that?"

The guy seemed to be one of those who blame

their bad luck on everybody else. Did he just want to vent on me? Very well. I decided to take the situation a step further and see where it might take me.

"No problem at all," I smirked and added, copying his tone, "Why?"

My provocation worked. The guy leaned over toward me and shouted in my face over the noise of the TV and the whole pub,

"Your face doesn't sit well with me, that's why!" he slammed his beer mug down on the bar. "Let's step outside!"

He didn't seem to be fond of talking much before a brawl. I hurried to weigh up the situation and size up my potential opponent. Although for his thirty-five years of age the "Boar" was admittedly in a pretty poor shape, he was a typical endomorph, stocky and big-boned with large forearms. He was evidently powerful but equally as clumsy.

The next system message confirmed my deductions. The guy wasn't an athlete. His Agility numbers were even less than mine; the only sport he was good at was the twenty-pint sprint.

And still his Strength was at 33. Not that it worried me after my bout with the super heavyweight Sledgehammer in the club.

"Leave it out, man. Why would you want to spoil your evening?" I said, just to give him the chance to back down.

He must have drawn his own conclusions, thinking that I'd chickened out. With a satisfied grin, he tousled my hair and gave me a hug, pressing me to his sweaty hairy shoulder. "Now that's what I'm talking about! Fancy a drink?"

"Your water," the barman appeared next to us. "That'll be a hundred rubles[12]."

"Take it away," the guy ordered. "Bring us some vodka and write it up to him."

He was getting a bit too much, wasn't he? I grabbed my water, removed his heavy arm from me and turned to the barman,

"Thanks. We don't need any vodka," I reached into my back pocket for my wallet.

The next moment I was sent flying off my stool by a heavy blow from the Boar.

I still managed to keep my glass of water vertical as I tucked up. Then I lay sprawled across the floor, watching the Boar's twitching belly as he guffawed.

That's when I received a Righteous Fury buff.

Suppressing an unstoppable desire to launch myself upon my offender, I rose, set the glass with the remaining water on the bar and dusted myself down matter-of-factly, then looked him in the eye.

His name was highlighted in red. Logically thinking, this was the program's way of telling me that I was facing an aggressive mob, which meant that attacking him wouldn't result in any detriment to my social status. It might in fact teach him a lesson which could help him readjust his behavior in similar situations in the future.

Still, I'd rather it didn't happen in the pub.

"Well, we can always step outside if you want," I told his grinning face. "Man's gotta do what a man's gotta do."

"Wait up," he downed his remaining beer, gave

---

[12] About $1.50

a long belch, wiped his mouth with his sleeve and jumped off the bar stool. "Come on boys, let's get a breath of fresh air."

Boys? What the-

With a confident waddle, he headed for the exit, whistling. Two of his friends jumped off their stools and trailed after him.

The situation was taking an unpredictable turn. I hadn't expected him to have had his hoodies with him. How come I hadn't noticed them earlier? They must have been in the john.

As the "Boar" walked past a waitress who'd just bent down in front of a table to unload a trayful of beer mugs, he lifted her short skirt and gave her G-stringed backside a hearty squeeze, then just walked on, guffawing happily, as if nothing had happened. The girl yelled and dropped the tray, then looked round in search of the culprit.

"Are you freakin' nuts?" she shouted.

"Get stuffed," the Boar snapped without looking back.

The girl's face flushed with the insult. She hurried to pick up all the broken glass, apologizing profusely to the clients while trying to hold back the tears. Her Mood had plummeted deep into the red.

I followed the Boar while studying his sidekicks' profiles. Their main characteristics were more or less the same as his: bags of Strength with little Intellect and plenty of Alcohol debuffs. I still hoped somehow that they would only act as spectators but there was little chance of that happening.

Still, I now had good healing and regeneration properties and I didn't really think they were planning

to kill me. Thus thinking, I walked outside, purposefully lagging a few steps behind.

They headed for an arch between some buildings, taking frequent looks behind to make sure I was still there and talking between themselves, guffawing loudly. One of the Boar's minions — the one with a shaven head — was prancing around with impatience.

We walked through the arch and found ourselves in the small yard of a dilapidated house, barely illuminated by the light in the windows of a few sleepless inhabitants.

The Boar waited for me to approach, then came on to me, winding his neck out with every word he spoke,

"What did you want, eh? You wanted to have words, right? And? What now? I don't hear you, asshole!"

What did he mean, he didn't hear me? I hadn't said anything yet! Although I had the situation under control, I could easily imagine some other guy in my place.

The thought alone gave me a surge of fury. I tried to suppress it just like old Ibrahim, my boxing coach, had taught me, but I was already being swept up in some sort of adrenaline rush which, together with the Righteous Anger buff, felt like the combined effect of three cans of Red Bull. My heart pounded in my chest, threatening to rip it open as the adrenaline — the fear hormone — coursed my veins improving the functioning of skeletal muscles while noradrenaline — the anger hormone — was pumping blood around, priming me for a fight and raising my pain threshold.

Now I really looked forward to this bit of PvP!

"Come on, Boar, punch his lights out!" the two onlookers encouraged. The guy with the shaven head even tried to show him how to do it.

"Yeaah!" the Boar threw his head back and — in what he must have thought was an unexpected move — tried to butt my nose with his cast-iron forehead. "Have this!"

He missed though, because his intention was so obvious that I was already prepared for it. I swayed to the right and gave him an uppercut to the chin.

A spray of blood spurted from his mouth. My enhanced Perception allowed me to see one of the droplets land on the skinhead's cheek.

How's that for Mortal Kombat?

You've dealt critical damage to Alexey Gaschenkov: 263 (Punch)

The Boar's head snapped back as he collapsed to the ground. His fan base fell silent, trying to reassess the situation. It seemed like their alcohol-soaked neurons couldn't keep up with events.

Shit, I still had to receive some damage, otherwise all this would have been for nothing. I needed the interface to reevaluate the environmental safety index.

Thinking about all this made me lose the initiative. Next thing I knew, several things had happened. First I'd lost the Righteous Fury debuff which in turn resulted in a bout of weakness as the cooldown set in. Next, I heard the Boar's buddies howl their indignation as they went for me. One of them was holding a stick he must have picked up earlier. And finally, I heard shouting behind me:

"There they're! Over there!"

I spent some time consciously offering my body to the blows, keeping an eye on the damage counter. As I tried to retreat, I tripped up over someone's outstretched leg. A spiked knuckleduster grazed my cheek.

Great gods! Talking about which, I probably had to thank Netsuke Jurōjin, the Japanese god of luck, for my lucky escape.

With my left hand, I blocked the stick which was aimed at my head, simultaneously trying to dodge (or so I thought) the skinhead's approaching fist. Still, my body proved slower than my reflexes: I got a whack in the head anyway.

A flash of pain surged through my forearm. My ear felt as if it were on fire.

Straight away I got a kick to the back of my knee, followed by a fist in my solar plexus, neither of which I was ready for.

My field of vision turned red as the interface flooded it with warnings and damage messages.

Damage received: 64 (a blow from a wooden stick).
Current Vitality: 91,64501%.

Damage received: 109 (a punch)
Current Vitality: 90,43389%.

Damage received: 82 (a kick)
Current Vitality: 89,52277%.

Showered with blows, I'd missed the moment when the pub's security had arrived, apparently itching to punish the bastard who'd offended their waitress. They must have worked out that I wasn't one of them (which was pretty apparent from the way things were going) and proceeded to teach the Boar's friends a lesson by giving them a professional hiding and bringing them to the ground.

One of the security helped me back to my feet. As I rubbed all my aches and pains, the Boar and his buddies writhed on the ground, groaning, while promptly sobering up.

"Are you with these assholes?" the burly middle-aged bouncer asked.

"No, he's not," the waitress hurried to take my side. "I saw how this moron was picking on him by the bar."

"What should we do with them?" the younger of the bouncers asked.

"What can we do? Let them pay moral damages for Katia, and then they're free to go."

I saw the girl's Mood soar: after all, her assailant had been punished, and she could always use a bit of money.

Did she even know that the elder of the two guards had feelings for her? You didn't need an interface to figure that out.

"Thanks," I said. Had it not been for them, I might not have come away so easily. I'd grossly overestimated myself and underestimated my opponents.

"You should say thanks to Katia," the elder one said.

"Thanks, Katia."

The girl nodded, then promptly forgot all about me. I took stock of my injuries and headed off home.

I staggered along, nursing my aching arm. Luckily, there was nothing broken. Everything else would heal quickly. That would have been good — but unfortunately, it had all been in vain.

My environmental safety index had remained the same. I'd failed to cheat the program.

Chapter

Seventeen

There Ain't No Such Thing As Free Lunch

You have my respect, Stark. When I'm done, half of humanity will still be alive. I hope they remember you.

Thanos to Iron Man, *Avengers: Infinity War*

"PUT MORE FIRE UNDER YOUR ENEMIES' FEET, Liquidator!" I repeated mechanically the last words of the message.

Jo perked up. "Liquidator? Is that what you are? What does that mean?"

I popped the red balloon and spent some time studying the description of the class that the observers had assigned me.

Predictably, no one had bothered with a detailed description. It was as if the text was being generated in a trial subject's brain, using their mentality and worldview.

These are the results of the Observers' vote:
— 50,8% have voted for the Liquidator class
— 49,2% have voted for the Lord of Monsters class
The test subject has been assigned the Liquidator class
Test subject's name: Phil, human, Level 10
The decision is final and cannot be reversed.

Liquidator:
Class level: 1

The trial subject receives a new class level automatically with every five levels gained.

Liquidators are melee fighters. They mainly deal damage with daggers, causing bleeding effects to their targets. Although their various skills allow them to adapt to any combat situation, their best bet is to deal strong explosive damage to a single target. They stun and paralyze their enemy.

First-level talents:
Treacherous Shadow. Allows a liquidator to vanish, then immediately reappear behind their opponent's back. Active range: 150 feet.
Stun. Allows a liquidator to paralyze their target for the duration of 5 seconds.

Unable to resist the temptation of trying both

talents in action, I cast a look at the unsuspecting Ola who was lovingly studying his new toy — Carter's spear.

I gave a mental chuckle. "Ola?"

He raised his head. I activated Treacherous Shadow.

I should have shut my eyes because I'd very nearly lost all coordination when, instead of the view of our shelter and my peacefully conversing friends, I was suddenly facing the Cameroonian's back.

I activated Stun.

The spear dropped to the ground, and his head, to his chest. He remained on his feet, staggering slightly. Instead of cartoon stars, a timer appeared over his head, counting down the seconds.

Once he came back to his senses, he spouted African invective, asking all evil spirits and Jesus himself be the witness of his fury.

Jovanna laughed, pouring oil on troubled waters. The cheerful Ola joined in, unable to help himself.

"Phil? What was that?" he asked, grinning.

'Sorry, man. I just couldn't help myself. I had to see how these class talents work. My class is Liquidator, a melee fighter. So far, they've given me two talents. The first one basically teleports me behind the target's back. The second one complements it perfectly: it's a five-second stun. By the way, what did you feel?"

"What did I feel? I didn't feel anything. It was as if my arms and legs had gone to sleep. My whole body had gone to sleep. I didn't feel a damn thing! I couldn't even bat an eyelid. Eh... wait a sec. I hope neither of you has done anything untoward to a poor unsuspecting African?"

He wriggled this way and that, trying to get a glimpse of his back and whatever was located below it. Having made sure everything was in order, he pointed his forefinger at me.

"*T'es un sorcier!*"[13]

"A *charobniak*," Jovanna agreed in Serbian.

The ease with which we understood each other regardless of the languages we all spoke was incredible. We seemed to communicate by instantly recognizing the words without the need for translating them into our respective languages in order to create corresponding images. Now, too, as soon as Ola had called me a *"sorcier"* in French and Jovanna had said *"charobniak"* in Serbian, the corresponding image of an evil sorcerer flashed through my head. If you consider how often people misunderstood each other even when speaking the same language, this alien technology was impressive.

Having finished with my class description, I moved over to the next system message. This particular balloon was colored black with white spots like a soccer ball. When I activated it, it didn't explode like all the others but simply unfolded to form a translucent square at the edge of my field of vision.

Prototype of the Trial site: Pibellau, Sagittarius Sector.

Participants in the Trial: planet Earth, "Humankind" faction, Homo sapiens race (these are self-designations), 2018 according to local

---

[13] T'es un sorcier (French) — You're a sorcerer!

chronology, fourth wave.
Number of observers: 28,410,290,821

The last number kept flickering, constantly changing which might mean that the data was being transferred in real time.

And still... twenty-eight billion observers? This definitely didn't sound like a small counsel of judges or supervisors. Could they be... viewers?

I might not be an expert on alien psychology but such a number of onlookers could only mean one thing to the artless mind of a twenty-first century man (according to local chronology).

This had to be some sort of reality show. Its alien creators might not have television, but the idea remained the same.

Below was what appeared to be the Trial rankings, apparently also in real time. One of the lines turned red and disappeared just as I was looking at it.

Number of test subjects: 72/169
Current ranking:
1. **Juma. Human. Level 18. Class: Predator. Hexagons captured: 146**
2. **Tafari. Human. Level 17. Class: Executioner. Hexagons captured: 131**
3. **Phil. Human. Level 10. Class: Liquidator. Hexagons captured: 50**
4. **Nagash. Human. Level 15. Class: Necromancer. Hexagons captured: 6**
   ...
46. **Zack. Human. Level 7. Class: n/a. Hexagons captured: 1**

...

68. Shlomo. Human. Level 5. Class: n/a. Hexagons captured: 0

69. Björn. Human. Level 4. Class: n/a. Hexagons captured: 1

70. Ola. Human. Level 4. Class: n/a. Hexagons captured: 0

71. Morana. Human. Level 4. Class: n/a. Hexagons captured: 0

72. Rubix. Human. Level 3. Class: n/a. Hexagons captured: 0

At the very bottom of the list, I saw a few familiar names, including Ola who was one of the last, together with a couple of Nagash's surviving minions. The fact that the necromancer had made it back to the top almost immediately after his crushing defeat having lost everything but his talents, was amazing. His determination commanded respect.

The colorful column of nicknames was followed by the list of the dead, numbers 73 to 169. Their names were colored gray, Carter amongst them.

I conveyed all this to my fellow clan members. We then went through the list, trying to second-guess our current situation. Unfortunately (or luckily for us), the rankings didn't reveal the players' clan affiliations or the number of minions each clan leader had. But at least this gave us some starting point.

We began by suggesting that every player who didn't have a single hexagon to their name was already someone's minion. In this case, it appeared to be that only eleven trial participants still preserved their independence. All the others had either already lost their hexagon and were risking disincarnation or they'd already joined someone else's clan.

Which meant that sixty-one persons were already affiliated with some clan or other. And while my own clan only numbered three players, the likes of Juma and Tafari must have already had about twenty or thirty.

I went through the list several times, marking down all the "landless" players. Their levels were all low.

"Those three definitely keep investing all the resources into themselves," Jovanna said, meaning Juma, Tafari and Nagash.

"We've got to get rid of my lord... or shit, I meant Nagash," Ola said grimly. "If we don't do it now, we'll have our work cut out for us."

Jo nodded. "Absolutely. Think for yourself, Phil. If the entire center of the map is taken by Tafari and the whole east is occupied by Juma, where do you think Nagash can be?"

"I agree. We need to finish that brainfucker off now before he can recruit another army of minions from the north. That's sorted, then. Let's finish up here at the base and get going."

We all got up. I walked over to the command center and laid my hand on the stone, activating the upgrade. It cost me two and a half thousand existence resource points.

The stone emitted three invisible waves, reinforcing the hexagon, the base and the shelter.

"This is what we have," I said. "The hexagon's limits can now delay all intruders for 60 seconds. They can't be breached straight away. Also, the weakening debuff now strips all attackers not of 5% but of 10% of their stats. The height of the base's fence has been raised to 10 feet and its structure reinforced. I'm afraid, Rex won't be able to break through it so easily anymore. Plus, our weak plasma turrets which were only good to scare off whistlers have also been reinforced and their numbers doubled along the base's perimeter."

Ola made the sign of the cross. "Thank God for that!"

"And as for the shelter, you can see the changes yourself. This hangar is now big enough to accommodate all of our dinos."

My friends turned their heads in unison. A translucent dome was now towering above us, looking like something out of a shopping mall. Pieces of furniture formed below it: beds, couches and armchairs which made up our living quarters. There was also a sanitary module with a shower, as well as a chest serving as an extradimensional inventory.

A round table appeared next to us. I would have said it was oak but I wasn't really sure. You couldn't study local materials just by sight and touch. When you looked at the fence, it seemed to be as plastic as could be. But when you knocked on it, you could distinctly hear the dull ring of metal. And as for our extradimensional trunk, it appeared to be made of a multitude of intertwined force fields.

"That's cool!" Jovanna gasped. "Just imagine what kind of bastion it could be if you upgraded the whole place completely!"

"I'm gonna go and take a look outside," Ola said, then disappeared behind the dome.

"I'll come as well," Jo added. "Phil, see you outside."

I nodded but stayed behind to make sure I hadn't forgotten anything.

Base 1
Level: 3.
Number of modules: 5.
Rate of existence resource generation: 50 pt. per hour.
Total generation of existence resources from all bases: 154 pt. per hour.
You may not upgrade until you reach level 15.
Cost to upgrade base to level 4: 12500 existence resource pt.

Now I had two new modules available: one research and one artifact. Having pondered over it, I purchased the former, spending the 500 points I'd set aside. While it was being generated, I studied the second one.

My eyes popped out of my head. *How much??* Fifty thousand existence points? Were they nuts? Where did they get such prices from?

The module generates a random artifact every 24 hours. Not eligible for upgrade.

That was it. Short and sweet. The module was geared up to create a battle-ready army in the long term. No need to go down into dungeons anymore to smoke bosses and elite mobs in the hope of chancing upon some random loot. This way you had a guaranteed artifact every 24 hours. For free. And knowing the kinds of powerful boosting and killing mechanisms the Trial field was capable of generating, you could easily imagine what a module like this was capable of.

What a shame that we couldn't really afford to install it in our situation. Its price tag, including the discount, could buy me level 35. No artifact could possibly level me up that much.

The research module was entirely virtual. A new active icon appeared in the command center. When I opened it, I saw a list of all possible improvements:

+1% to damage dealt
Cost: 100 existence resource points
Affects all damage dealt by the base owner's clan members, as well as their fighting units and defense turrets.

+1% to armor
Cost: 100 existence resource points
Affects all armored gear, including that of fighting units

+10% to fighting units' characteristics
Cost: 3000 existence resource points

+100% to working units' productivity
Cost: 10,000 existence resource points

The full list contained all kinds of upgrades to everything you could think of, from the fence's durability to the scouts' range of vision.

I gave it a quick think, then invested the remaining 500 resource points into 5% to damage dealt.

Talking about which, I'd completely forgotten about the two characteristic points I'd received with my new level. My new talents demanded some powerful explosive damage.

Strength: +2

Excellent. Not only would it improve our damage, it would also double the resources mined by our working unit — a veritable harvester plowing through the Trial field.

Combined existence resource generation for all bases: 156 pt. per hour

Wait a sec. Why 156? Where did this number come from? The level-3 main base gave me 50 an hour. The working unit brought in another 27. The remaining bases gave 49 in total, at 1 pt. an hour. Something didn't sum up.

I opened the control panel of the noncombat unit module, then stared blankly at it, unable to work it out:

A working unit: 55 existence resource pt. an hour.

Since when?

I opened my clan members' profiles and finally saw it. Their strength numbers counted too, bringing in the missing 55 points.

And this was going to radically change our entire strategy.

* * *

If you visualized the Trial grounds as a rectangular map, then the right-hand third of it would be under Juma's control. The middle would be occupied by Tafari while the left-hand part wasn't as clear-cut. Almost half of the bottom part of it was occupied by my clan while the space above us remained uncharted territory.

One thing we knew was Nagash was lurking somewhere there, together with a number of yet-independent participants. Which meant that we might need to go through every hexagon with a fine-toothed comb in order to make sure we hadn't missed anything — including the seizing of neutral hexagons as well as those already captured — and the searching for any yet-undiscovered instances, as well as looking for any potential allies from Ilindi's list.

"Complicated shit," Ola said pensively when we'd stopped for a break.

We'd just smoked a pack of especially obnoxious nebulas and were waiting for the yellow acidic goo to dry and disappear from our clothes. We'd already worked out, by scientific trial and error, that it vanished some time after the disappearance of the nebulas' bodies.

"Do you mean that we need another 750 resource points to get a harvester?" Ola asked again.

"That's right. Five hundred for another upgrade,

two for the module and another fifty for the working unit. In less than twelve hours, it's already paid for itself. I've been thinking: if we upgrade all of our bases, they'll be able to generate over 3,000 resource points an hour!"

"If we do that, by the end of the day we'll already be getting profit back on our investment," Ola said. By his own admission, he had no problem mentally multiplying large numbers. Apparently, he'd had this thing about being able to count well, so once he'd gotten the interface, he'd used it to level it up.

"Good idea," he said. "Let's just hope no one has a go at us in the meantime."

"Very well. That's settled, then. I want you both to make sure you always have an emergency supply of resource points to be able to heal yourselves by leveling up. The rest we'll invest into upgrading the bases, building the modules and creating working units. All right, let's be off. Croc, come to me!"

Croc came stomping and wheezing, followed by Tank and Rex who'd been on patrol while we rested up. We hopped on his back and continued on our journey toward our northernmost hexagon on the very edge of the map. Once we'd explored it, we were going to turn off and start skirting our domains.

We captured five neutral hexagons one after the other. Our travails weren't without their challenges: the mobs that had attacked us were about my level, so my two guys didn't have it that easy. Both Jo and Ola had used up their resource points to level themselves up just to avoid dying, so in the end we were obliged to allocate them another emergency reserve before starting upgrading the bases.

Ola had very nearly died again. He'd been attacked by four semi-sentient nebulas at once, who'd first fled from my dinos into the bush only to come back and select the African as their new target. That required more point injections in order to level him up, after which he'd caught up with Jovanna. Both of them were now level 6.

I stopped at the border of the next hexagon which was apparently neutral.

"Now you can do it on your own. No arguments!" I interrupted their indignant remonstrations. "This is non-negotiable. We've been farming like idiots for an hour already, but we've only got enough resources for 4 upgrades. So that's what we're gonna do. Take all three dinos and seize this hexagon in front of us. This way the mobs will be no hassle for you. Without me, they'll be levels six or seven at the most. Which is the same as you, including the dinos. Once you seize it, you initiate the upgrade process on all the bases bordering the main one. After that, you set the integration module to automatic. I'll give you access authorization. The module will then initiate all the necessary procedures once it has the resources required. Once that done, I'd like you to update your gear and continue farming mobs of your own level."

«Where are *you* going?" Jo squinted at me suspiciously.

"I'm going to do some recon in the north. I'd like to find out where our necromancer friend is hanging out so we can attack him at first light. By then, you should be leveled up well enough. Normally, by then we'll have farmed enough elite items plus whatever points the bases give us. He won't have a hope in hell.

We'll do him up nice and good. He's for sure gonna pay for Carter's death!"

Ola threw his head back and threw his arms wide, shouting something unintelligible but obviously militant. His relationship with Nagash had been complicated to say the least.

Jovanna gave me a peck on the cheek and asked me to be careful, then disappeared behind the bank of mist enveloping the hexagon's border. She was followed by Ola, Rex, Tank and Croc.

I stood there alone.

* * *

It was now close to evening. The seventy-two hours of independence granted to Zack would expire tomorrow. I might actually accept him into the clan. We could always use a few extra Strength and Charisma points.

The hexagon which I was about to enter was a new type. It was neither neutral nor captured by anyone.

As I went in, I received a new message:

Warning! You're about to enter a special-purpose hexagon.
Its territory cannot be captured.

Special effects:
Maximum duration of stay: 60 minutes.
Exceeding 60 minutes will activate a permanent debuff, making the intruder lose 1 level per minute.

They didn't give any further explanation, so I just continued skirting the hexagon's perimeter.

Everything seemed to be perfectly normal, apart from the silence. I could neither see nor hear any mobs. The landscape here was evidently artificial, its surface covered with the same material as the bases' floors. The place was studded with neat decorative installations, some geometric, others resembling statues on pedestals.

I walked over to one of them.

A crab-like figure half the height of a human stood on a pedestal covered in a decorative script. Although its separate elements said nothing to me, I understood the meaning straight away:

Born To Defeat
A Makrur
Level: 37
The Trial Champion
Race: the Makrurs, wave 6.

His name was transferred to me as a visual image. How strange. Could it be that the Makrur race didn't use audible speech at all? In which case, how did I know that it was pronounced *Makrur*? Was it a self-appellation too, or was it what the Senior Races called them?

I glanced at some of the other statues, looking for the figures of either Valiadis or Ilindi to see if my assumption had been correct. I couldn't find them. In fact, I couldn't find a single humanoid shape nearby.

I'd have liked to have continued looking but the distances between the statues were quite big and I wasn't there on a guided tour. My countdown timer, too, kept reminding me not to waste time.

So I just headed to a small opaque dome at the hexagon's center. I touched its side, feeling my fingers penetrate it, and walked in.

There was nothing inside, apart from a new system message hovering in front of me:

On the sixth day of the Trial, the special-purpose hexagon is pronounced a trade zone!

Do you want to see the artifacts available for sale?

Do you want to sell your own artifacts?

Of course I did! I pressed *Accept*.

Their entire stock of a whopping three items unfolded in front of me:

The Rock of Rebirth.

A single-use artifact.

Allows you to bring a disincarnated trial participant back into the Trial.

Cost: 500,000 existence resource points.

The Rock of Time

A single-use artifact.

Allows you to go back to the beginning of the current day of the Trial.

Cost: 750,000 existence resource points.

The Rock of Disincarnation

A single-use artifact.

Allows you to eliminate your enemy and

---

annihilate his additional lives provided he has any. Does not require contact with the target.
Cost: 1,000,000 existence resource points.

Once I'd studied all three artifacts, it took me a bit of time to pick my jaw back off the floor and stop gloating.

I realized very well the Trial organizers' agenda. All they wanted was to add an element of unpredictability to the show and give a chance to even the lowest-ranking clans. And as for the deadly artifact, it could come in handy if the participating clans began to drag the show out.

I also realized that none of the participants could afford these kinds of prices at the moment, even if they'd been ten times cheaper. But in the future... say, in about a week's time...

I closed the virtual shop and decided to try and sell something myself.

A slot appeared in the air. I set the Devious Pauldrons of Eternal Rest into it. They were immediately priced at 4,000 resource points. The Ordinary Clan Ring of Leadership was valued at 5,000. Both my Power Fist and the Dagger of Obfuscation I'd taken off Carter were priced more or less the same.

I paused, pondering over what to sell, but in the end I didn't have the heart to part with any of them. I would have gladly sold the megalomaniacal Dagger of Absorption with its life steal effect but it was now back at the base.

There was also Jovanna's Lightning Rod but where was I supposed to look for her now? The place didn't even have a clan chat for me to contact the guys.

Having scratched my head over this, I finally left the shop and continued on north.

* * *

As I left the special-purpose hexagon, I noticed five level-10 strangers confidently heading for Nagash's base. My high Perception allowed me to follow them unnoticed while the fog of war prevented them from noticing me. No, I wasn't suicidal enough to attack them — but I needed to find out who they were and how their meeting with the necromancer would pan out.

I moved parallel with them. As they approached Nagash's base, they deployed into a combat formation while their leader announced at the top of his voice,

"My name's Striker! Listen up, Nagash! Our leader Tafari is offering you and your vassals to join his clan. You have one minute to respond. If you refuse, we'll kill you all!"

Instead of Nagash, a swarthy mustachioed man with a crew cut and a beer gut walked out to the fence. "Where's Tafari himself?" he asked.

"Our leader is too busy to waste his precious time on you. Who's speaking on Nagash's behalf?"

"This is Manu, my lord's voice! My lord will never join another clan! That's his answer! Piss off now before we eliminate you!"

Striker shook his head. "I don't think so."

Manu? That was one of the guys on Ilindi's list!

While I was trying to think how to drag him out of the battle, Tafari's group went on a well-choreographed offensive. Although they didn't have any fighting units with them, they didn't need any, judging by their talents.

Striker — who was the same warrior class as Carter used to be — darted toward Manu, smashing through the base's weak fence and ramming into the man, sending him flying behind other clan members' backs.

Ignoring the skirmish, Nagash just stood there casting a spell. Next to him stood two of his bodyguards — Morana and Rubix — whom I'd already met. Manu whose Life had been halved was covering Nagash from behind.

In the meantime, Tafari's fighters were battling their way through the undead hordes which were being decimated very quickly.

Finally, the necromancer had finished reciting the spell.

I watched its effects from the sidelines. Suddenly Striker stopped fighting the undead who in turn also gave up attacking him. Instead, Striker assaulted an axe-brandishing fellow fighter, burying his huge two-handed sword in the guy's back.

The blow proved deadly. The warrior with the axe stopped moving; soon his dead body disappeared into thin air.

Their crossbowman was next. As he was busy shooting at the undead from a safe distance, Striker leapt toward him and lopped his head off. Even I could see the surprise on the guy's severed head.

Still, that's where Nagash's success came to an end because Tafari's men weren't born yesterday, either. Their second long-range fighter must have put two and two together as he loosed off a burst of either plasma or some sort of energy. That disrupted Nagash's concentration and put an end to his magic, allowing Striker to return to his senses.

Striker growled something to his team. All three of them lunged at the necromancer. Morana and Rubix attempted to shield their lord with their own bodies — but seeing as both their levels and their gear left a lot to be desired (courtesy of Nagash who never splurged on his vassals' needs), the two were promptly cut to ribbons and disincarnated, their names disappearing from the active Trial participants list.

Nagash himself scurried to the shelter, ordering Manu to do the same. The remaining undead hung on to Striker and his two sidekicks, blocking their way.

That's when I noticed Nagash's new talent. Accompanied by Manu, he'd gone around the back of the dome, reappearing on the other side. I could see him clearly, but Striker and company couldn't.

Nagash raised his hands high in the air, shouting something, then dropped his arms to his sides.

The spots where two of Tafari's fighters had just died started emitting a black haze which left two raised deadmen in its wake. The crossbowman was still headless.

With another wave of his hand, Nagash raised his two slain vassals: Morana and Rubix. The four zombies then attacked Striker from behind.

He must have sensed something at the last moment because he swung round. Too late. The undead hung onto his arms and legs, gnawing and biting him, ripping off chunks of flesh and clawing his eyes out. Manu eagerly helped them, brandishing his club.

Nagash came closer and resumed casting his mind-controlling spell while his undead servants finished off Striker's fighters.

Just as I thought that the intruders were done for, Striker let out a guttural growl. In one powerful swipe he launched himself onto the necromancer. Nagash must have been in a hurry to finish the last words of his spell because he didn't attempt to run off, just opened his eyes wide and continued to mumble.

With an upward thrust, Striker buried his sword into Nagash's chest, its point exiting the base of his skull. He then yanked it out and took a wide swing to finish him off.

Nagash's head rolled to the ground.

An invisible wave swept from the dome to the hexagon's perimeter, signaling the change of its owner. The place was now Tafari's property.

His life deep in the red, Striker staggered toward the remaining undead. With a few swipes of his sword, he sent them back to oblivion, then headed toward the sole remaining survivor, Manu.

Manu was a sorry sight. A crossbow bolt stuck out of his head. He didn't even have any gear worthy of a warrior, just some stupid civilian clothes. His level 6 was no match for an even half-dead Striker.

Striker stuck the point of his sword in the ground and leaned on it. A flap of skin hung from his face ravaged by the zombies.

"You can go," he croaked.

Manu was about to say something, but Striker didn't let him. "My leader is fair. He gives each of his vassals enough resources to buy level 10 and receive a class. Bobby has died the final death today. I need a replacement for my team. Would you like to join Tafari's clan? I won't offer it again."

My turn. I stepped closer and sent Manu an invitation to join my clan, then shouted to attract his attention,

"Sorry to interfere! Manu, before you reply, I need to tell you that our mutual friends Jovanna and Ola are sending you their regards!"

"Phil? I know you!" his eyes widened. "How on earth..."

He did accept the invitation, though.

"Who the hell are you?" Striker growled, backing off. "You sure know how to pick your timing!"

His glare darted round. I activated both my talents, grabbed his slackened body and, in a couple of bounds, had cleared the base's perimeter. Now he wouldn't be able to teleport out.

Manu staggered after me, dragging Striker's sword across the ground behind him. "Finish him off, Phil! You saw what he can do! He'll be a problem!"

I brought the tip of my dagger to Striker's throat. Although he was already restoring, he wouldn't survive a stabbing.

"You gonna kill me?" he asked nonchalantly.

"You can't imagine how I'd hate to do it," I replied. "You're too good, man. You're awesome."

"Fuck you," he turned his head away and spat blood on the ground. A skull's grin froze on his ravaged face. "This is my last life."

"Here, yes. But not in real life."

Softly my dagger pierced his flesh, robbing him

of the last percentage of his life. His name on the list expired, confirming that this indeed had been his last life.

Still, this wasn't the right time to indulge in remorse. I took his spirit crystal. "Manu, quick! The loot!"

Having picked up all the loot, we hurried away. We'd been lucky that no one had yet responded to the emergency.

The moment we'd cleared the base's perimeter, we heard the popping of teleports. I looked back. Tafari's combat team of five had just arrived. They promptly appraised the situation and came running after us.

The heavy loot slowed us down. The distance between us and our pursuers kept shrinking. There was only some 150 feet separating us when we'd finally cleared the special-purpose hexagon and found ourselves on our own turf.

"Leave the sword!" I shouted.

"No way," Manu wheezed, momentarily overtaking me only to drop back again. His Speed wasn't up to it.

Our pursuers were almost upon us. We had only a few paces left to the safety of the base from which we could teleport out when an arrow pierced my shoulder, promptly followed by another one in my back. I tumbled head over heels, breaking the arrows' shafts and screaming in pain, unable to even understand what Manu was shouting,

"Madre mia! Dinosaurs! Look, Phil! They're for real!"

All three of my pets trundled past us. I could

make out Jovanna's and Ola's silhouettes running behind the fence.

"It's all right, Manu. They're all mine. We're home!"

CHAPTER EIGHTEEN

GODS ARE BLIND

No good deed goes unpunished,
Outlander!

Synette Jeline, *The Elder Scrolls III:*
Morrowind

NORMALLY, THE MOTION-SENSITIVE LIGHTING IN OUR apartment block's stairwell goes on automatically. This time though it didn't work. The moment the elevator's doors closed, the stairwell went dark.

I used a flashlight to unlock my apartment door. Just as I opened it, I heard the hurried stomping of feet down the stairs.

Then I felt the cold barrel of a gun pressed to the back of my head.

"Don't move," a vaguely familiar voice whispered in my ear.

I was bundled inside, stumbling over the doorstep. While I was trying to get to my feet, the front door slammed shut behind me. The lights went on in the hall.

I turned round only to see Panchenko.

Shit! Why hadn't the alarm gone off? I'd set up a special warning against Panchenko on my interface!

He grinned. "You didn't expect me, did you?" he asked in a nasal drawl. "A level-nineteen interface user... Did you really think you could hide it from me?"

Even as he spoke, I was calculating the direction and sequence of my assault on him.

He must have second-guessed my intention to jump to my feet and give him a good hiding because he pointed his gun at me, discouraging any move on my part. I heard the cocking of the hammer.

"Don't move. Lie face down. Anybody else at home?"

"No."

Just to disprove me, Boris ran out of the bedroom, meowing desperately, and began poking my face with her little nose.

"Aha. And you said there was nobody home. Puss, puss! Come here, kitty!"

Boris was too trusting of strangers. Twitching her ears in alarm, she did approach him.

The next moment she yelped as his heavy boot sent her flying against the wall.

With a thud, Boris dropped motionless to the floor.

"Boris!"

Panchenko grinned.

Ignoring his orders, I crawled toward her.

Boris lay unmoving, a tiny droplet of blood forming on her nose.

I got a lump in my throat. My eyes started to sting.

Just as Fury and Righteous Anger welled inside me, the back of my head exploded in pain. My lights went out.

"Feeling better?"

I was sitting strapped to a chair in the lounge. Panchenko was looking around, frowning.

I raised my head. The room was a mess, all the upholstery ripped apart, all the drawers trashed, their contents strewn across the floor.

But that wasn't what worried me. My second "life" which Martha had shown me, had taught me to keep my cool in situations like this one, calmly reassessing it and trying to come up with an escape plan. This wasn't the right time to dwell on my losses. I could always take stock of them later, once I'd gotten out of this mess.

Provided I did get out of it.

A new debuff icon appeared in a corner of my field of vision:

Delayed Curse
Your opponent has cast a lethal curse on you.
Effect: delayed death.
Time left until the user's death: 168:19:06.

The last number kept changing, counting down the seconds.

Panchenko laughed at the sight of my long face. "Ah, you saw it, didn't you? You've got a week left to live."

"How did you manage that?" I interrupted him.

My voice was hoarse and weak but he'd heard me. He paused, thinking, then pulled out a cigarette and lit up.

"This isn't the movies," he said, exhaling the smoke, "and I'm not an evil overlord. I was given a chance and I'm not going to waste it now by explaining my motives, objectives or methods to you."

"Come on, spit it out. Caress your ego. I'm as good as dead and you know it. The interface is never wrong. I have seven days, then I'm toast. How did you do it?"

He chuckled. "The interface?" he bit his lip, thinking. "Somebody took a hit out on you."

"A hit?"

He raised his head as if listening to something, then nodded. "That's right. *Boss* isn't happy with you. You haven't lived up to his expectations. So he ordered me to take you out. And to make my job easier, he granted me the *Eroul* ability. When you die, I'll have it on a permanent basis. I'll become a perfect hitman. No one will dare step in my way to greatness."

This would have sounded as corny as hell had I not known he was deadly serious. "Wait a sec. What Boss are you talking about?"

He brought his forefinger up to his temple. "*The* Boss. The Higher Being. He came to me because I was a chosen one, just like you. He gave me the ability to see people's nature. He taught me to convince and manipulate them," he chuckled. "You did well grassing me up. You've put some very serious people on my back. It was you who told them, wasn't it? They're gonna regret it, all of them. Once you're dead in a week's time, the ability will be mine to use. Then anyone who dares stand in my way will sooner or later be cursed."

As if reacting to his words, the program issued me a quest without the *Reject* option:

Stop Evil

Use the interface's temporary Uninstall ability in order to neutralize Konstantin Panchenko and prevent him from committing socially detrimental actions.

To activate the ability, touch the target.

The ability will only affect the target designated by this quest.

Rewards:

+3 to your social status level

+3 to all main characteristics

+3 available main characteristic points

+30 pt. to your global Reputation with every member of the human race.

A round red button of the new ability appeared in the lower right-hand corner of my field of vision. All I had to do was touch Panchenko. Problem was, my hands were still bound behind my back.

In the meantime, Panchenko remained on his guard, keeping a safe distance. He must have paid heed to all of my stats and combat skills.

"You've any idea what awaits you now?" I asked him.

"What do you mean?" he peered suspiciously at me, expecting a catch.

"Did your Boss or whoever it was tell you about

the Trial?"

"Which Trial? What are you talking about? Your tricks won't work with me! You'd better quit stalling and tell me where you keep the money," he chuckled nervously. "You won't need it anymore, anyway. Not where you're going, you won't."

According to my Lie Detection skill, he was telling the truth. He knew nothing about either the Vaalphors nor their abductions. He sincerely believed in some sort of Boss — probably the interface itself.

Only now did I notice that he'd scooped out all the money and valuables he'd found in my apartment. That was all I'd managed to save after my memorable poker tournament, including my boxing championship winnings and the prize money I'd received for defeating the Sledgehammer in the super final after having paid for Julie's treatment and investing in my company.

I could make out the white figure of Netsuke Jurōjin in the heap, as well as the Lucky Ring of Veles that Panchenko had ripped off my finger. Could he see their stats and the bonuses they came with?

"That's all I have," I said. "I'm not a millionaire."

"What a shame. Well, if this is all you have to offer, I don't need you anymore. I'd have gladly strangled you myself, but I don't want to soil my hands on you. You're gonna die soon enough as it is. Sooner than you think."

Humming some little ditty out of tune, he scooped everything up into a plastic bag, twisted it close and stuffed it into his jacket, then walked over to me. His eyes were laughing. He spat in my face, then pistol-whipped me on the temple.

The world went dark. I collapsed to the floor,

chair and all.

* * *

"How awful!" Veronica exclaimed.

"Holy crap!" Alik whistled his disbelief. "Phil, did you see those jerks? Who did it?"

My friends walked around my apartment, studying the damage. Unable to help herself, Veronica found a brush and a dustpan and started clearing up the mess.

"Please leave it," I asked her. "Could you make us some coffee? My head feels like shit. I'll tell you everything in a moment."

I'd come round early in the morning and spent a good three hours trying to work myself free of my bonds. By expanding my muscles and straining against the duct tape, I'd finally managed to loosen it enough to free up my hands.

The first thing I'd done was locate Panchenko on the map. I cussed in disappointment: judging by the speed with which his marker was moving, the bastard must have been on board a plane flying over Poland. That put a lid on my initial idea of reporting him to the police in order to stop him.

I'd still called both the police and the ambulance, simply to file the facts of the burglary and the physical assault, just to create some more problems for him. Having said that, I didn't think he would be coming back, considering the likes of the people who were unhappy with him now that I'd grassed him up.

Yawning, the cops studied the place, asked me

all the necessary questions and filed my complaint. A couple of neighbors who stood witness to its registration shook their heads, tut-tutting sympathetically. That's when I'd found out that on top of my ID papers, Panchenko had also taken all the paperwork that was in the house.

I stated very clearly that I'd recognized my assailant and reported his name and all relevant information to the sleepy noncommittal cop, making sure he'd taken everything down. The ER people suggested they took me to the hospital, but I refused.

When I'd finally gotten rid of them all, I gave Alik a ring, asking him to come over. By then, Panchenko was already in Germany, waiting for his connection in Frankfurt airport.

While I was waiting for them, I managed to speak to Martha. As soon as she'd arrived, she zoned out for a good forty seconds but failed to report anything encouraging.

"I've managed to work out the nature and the mechanism of the Curse debuff. Once the countdown runs out, your heart will simply stop. Your brain activity will cease and all vital organs will stop functioning. In the meantime, all of your body glands will start producing copious amounts of toxins. You can't abort the process because it's been programmed at cellular level. The curse is encrypted so it can only be removed by the one who cast it. Judging by what's available to you, I can't see a single possibility to undo it. I'm very sorry."

Ilindi was my last hope now. She'd already removed curses and debuffs from me once during my previous abductions. I couldn't contact her directly but

Valiadis was obliged to know where to find her.

Alik arrived with Veronica in tow. Which was even better. It didn't look as if I'd be able to stay in control of the company now at least for a while, so I had to find someone to run it for me. Veronica seemed to be the best option. With some help from Mr. Katz, Rose and Kesha, she would do well. I was sure of that.

Alik brought us some chairs from the kitchen which we arranged at the center of the room. Gingerly threading her way through the mess, Veronica brought us three cups of coffee on a tray.

I picked one up and took a large swig. I needed a quick fix.

Veronica offered me a pill. "Take this. It'll sort your head out."

I swallowed the painkiller and told them what had happened,

"Last night I came home late from my English class. Somebody was waiting by the door. They gave me a whack across the back of my head. I didn't see who it was. When I came round later last night, the place was already trashed."

"Did you call the cops?"

"Yes, straight away. I filed a complaint, but you know how it is with them. They'll drag it out and come up with nothing. So I'm afraid, I might need your help."

"Absolutely!" the two replied in unison.

"Listen up. I think I know who it might have been," I couldn't tell them the whole truth, so I had to beat around the bush. "I might need to go into hiding. This is what I would like you to do. Veronica, I want you to look after the company for a little while. You know what to do and in which direction we're heading.

If there's a problem, just give me a ring and I'll sort you out."

Veronica blushed but promptly got a hold of herself. "Don't worry," she said confidently. "I'll manage."

"Good. Tell everyone that I caught a cold and have to take a few days off. If they want to come and see me, tell them it's contagious. No house calls, please. Next up: Alik, I have something to ask you too."

"Yes, what is it? I'll do anything you want."

"It would be a shame if my landlord saw the state of the apartment. Do you think you could give it the once-over? I'll give you the money, I just need to go to the bank. Having said that... dammit! They've taken all my documents for some goddamn reason, haven't they?"

I knew perfectly well that the "goddamn reason" was to make sure I couldn't come after them. Panchenko had thought of everything. Still, Alik and Veronica didn't need to know zip about that.

"I've got some money," Veronica offered. "I can do it. Knowing Alik, he might splurge on a pile of flat packs."

Alik shrugged. "I'm not an expert, I know."

"Thanks a lot," I said. "I'll pay you back. Well, that's it, then. Ah, one last thing. I'd like you to take me to a hotel. One of you will have to book a room in their name. Which one of you has a passport[14]?"

Alik patted down his pockets, then shook his head.

Veronica reached into her purse and produced

---

[14] In Russia, a person's passport is their main ID document, required to book a hotel room, etc.

her passport. "I've got mine. I can book a room. Let's go!" she rose.

"No, wait."

I rose and headed into the bedroom where Boris lay stiff and cold under the bed.

I reached out and pressed her little body to my chest.

Her eyes had glazed over. Her hair was dull and tousled.

My heart was breaking. I wanted to scream at the top of my voice to release all the anger and pain pent up inside.

Instead, I just wheezed,

"We need to bury her."

* * *

"Good morning, Phil!" Valiadis greeted me energetically.

"I'm afraid it's not so good, Sir."

I was calling him from my budget hotel room booked in Veronica's name. The moment the room door had closed behind her, I'd dialed his number.

"Spit it out."

"Panchenko has cast a lethal debuff on me. I can't remove it on my own."

"How long have you got?"

"Less than a week. I need to meet up with Ilindi."

For a while, he didn't reply. Then the silence in the receiver was broken by a sigh and his angry cussing. "What a shit! Yes, I'll tell her. Are you in the Meridian?"

"That's right. Room 904."

"Stay put and don't go anywhere."

"Thank you, sir."

"There's nothing to thank me for yet. Keep your chin up!"

I wandered around the room for a while, finished off all the snacks that I'd found in the mini bar, then fell asleep to the monotonous noise of the television.

When I awoke, it was already getting dark. Someone was stroking my head. Ilindi's hot gentle hand brushed my cheek.

She was sitting next to me on the bed in her real Rhoa form.

"Ilindi! You came," I sat up and gave her a hug.

She hugged me back, pressing me to her body. We didn't say anything. Her hot breath tickled my neck.

Then I realized that her eyes were wet. The Rhoa were human, too...

I focused on my interface. The debuff icon was still active, the countdown timer clocking up the last hours of the first day.

"I'm sorry," she whispered. "I was my fault."

I eased myself away and looked her in the eye. She didn't avert her gaze. "Valiadis did suggest we installed in him our version of the interface. I refused. His heart is too black. You can't wash it clean. You can't reform him. People like him view the world as their own stomping ground. They think it exists simply to satisfy their own ends."

"Wasn't I a bit like him too?"

"You? Of course not!" she sounded offended. "True, you were lazy. *Very* lazy. Your selfishness was the result of your childishness because in your heart of hearts, you were a child. A good child. This guy is completely the opposite."

"Why are you telling me this? Does that mean you can't help me?"

She shook her head. Her iridescent eyes turned black. "I can't. He's the only person who can do it."

"Can't you two help me catch him and convince him to lift the curse? You or maybe Valiadis?"

"We haven't got the right to. The Senior Races won't allow this kind of intrusion. I'm so sorry, Phil."

I got off the bed and started circling the room. "There must be some way of doing it!" I opened the map and checked Panchenko's whereabouts. "Ah, forget it. He's already in the States! Knowing our bureaucracy, I won't even be able to get a new passport in time, let alone an American visa."

"There's still one more possibility."

I stopped and stared at her. "Well? Speak up!"

"The second Phil has to win the Trial. I'll make sure I transfer all your memories to him."

She got up and walked over to me. She laid her hand on my forehead and closed her eyes.

My legs felt rubbery. My mind seemed to go black. I collapsed — but Ilindi caught me in her arms, preventing me from hitting the floor.

She gently laid me on the bed, rearranged the pillow under my head and kissed me.

The last thing I heard was,

"Sleep now..."

* * *

Whether it was due to Ilindi's magic or I just needed to recuperate, but I only woke up late the next morning, having slept for over twelve hours.

I was alone in my hotel room. The elusive but unmistakingly Rhoan scent — the mixture of spices, ozone and pine needles — was the only proof that I hadn't dreamed up Ilindi's visit.

Unfortunately, the curse debuff hadn't been a dream, either. The timer kept counting down the hours, minutes and seconds until my demise. 136:14:12... 136:14:11... 136:14:10...

The realization of the futility of it all had immediately plunged me into the dark depths of melancholy. My interface numbers were deep in the red:

Fear: 99%
Mood: 3%
Self-Confidence: 2%

The meager but still positive percentage of Mood and Self-Confidence were solely due to Ilindi's visit. I could avoid my dying the final death provided my doppelganger successfully passed the Trial.

But could Phil 2 really handle it? Was he up to it?

I spent the next hour in bed, fighting off the temptation to send him a message through Martha.

In the end, common sense prevailed. This kind of news could easily drive him — me — over the edge.

On the other hand, it wouldn't change jack. If he failed the Trial, we — *me* — would lose anyway and have no memory of it whatsoever. And if he won, Ilindi would simply upload my memories into him, allowing us — *me* — to live on.

That made me feel a bit better. The microscopic surge in the relief I felt was enough to prompt me to call Veronica back.

I checked my phone. Lots of people had called me from the office in the meantime, but eighteen missed calls from Veronica? That was a personal record! She'd started calling already last night, then resumed her attempts at 7 a.m.

"Phil, fuck you! Are you all right? Is everything okay? How are things?"

"I've just woken up. What happened?"

"What happened is that you've been mugged and very nearly killed!" she laughed hysterically. "That's what happened! I was worried sick, you know!"

"Don't worry. I'm okay," I lied, surprised at the ease with which I did it. "How are things at the office?"

"It's okay," she paused, pondering about something, then changed the subject. "Your apartment has been cleaned up. We've sent all the broken and damaged furniture for repair. It'll be cheaper than buying everything new. Now you can go home if you wish."

"Thanks," I had no intention of going home but telling her about the curse would also serve no purpose.

I could feel that she was trying to hold something back from me, apparently unwilling to bother me with trivialities. Suppressing the cowardly desire to play along, I dismissed my lack of interest in something that very soon would become irrelevant. Even if I didn't survive, I owed it to my friends to make sure they were okay.

"Spit it out," I said. "I can hear something's not right."

"Er... it's the rumors, Phil. They just don't stop. On the contrary, every day they come with even more detail."

"Clients refusing to work with us?"

"They are. They keep treating us like shit. They cancel meetings and revoke their contracts. The old clients whom we already placed are our sole source of income at the moment. Without you, even this trickle will soon dry up. I've no idea how you do it."

"Do what? Find employment for them?"

"Of course. I tried to do it through my channels, but nobody wants them. Should I go back to event organizing, maybe? That might help us keep our heads above water."

Judging by her whispered tones and the voices in the background, she wasn't alone. Still, her voice rang with anxiety.

"Okay," I said. "Keep your hair on. Ask Kesha to email me the names of all the problem clients, including all the potential contracts. I'm going to see them myself."

As soon as I'd finished talking to her, I calmed myself down and checked on Panchenko's whereabouts. Apparently, he was already in Las Vegas — and judging by his marker frozen at the Bellagio Hotel, he was there for the duration.

I had five days left. I could have circled the world

five times had I so wished, but all I needed was to cross the old world of Europe and the Atlantic Ocean.

I weighed up all the possibilities. There were too many "ifs" and "buts" involved. According to the Internet, a whole number of companies could restore my stolen paperwork in a matter of hours. The problem was, they were all in Moscow, and how was I supposed to get there without any ID papers? Hitchhike?

Think, Phil, think. I couldn't book a flight to the US without a visa.

Then again, an invisible man has no need for paperwork.

I could activate Stealth and Vanish!

Even though it only lasted 45 seconds, that would be more than enough to clear all the controls. The ability's base cooldown was 60 minutes, but my Spirit numbers brought it down to twenty. Which meant I had plenty of time to sneak past the check in, the passport control and later, board the plane unnoticed. I could do the same during my European connection. That left me with the American customs. Once I got to Vegas, I'd have four days to find Panchenko and intimidate him into lifting the curse. Provided he didn't fly the coop.

Then I remembered. I still had my invitation to come to the US, didn't I? How could I have forgotten? The answer was simple: not only had I been distraught and out of sorts, but last night, there'd been no way of telling where Panchenko might end up as he'd been constantly on the move.

So should I get a new passport, make a dash to the US embassy in Moscow to see this Angela Howard person, and suggest we reschedule our meeting to

Vegas, or wherever Panchenko might be at that moment? I could say I'd only come on this condition.

I paced the room in excitement as I dialed Ms. Howard's number. Having greeted her, I blurted out that I was ready to see them as agreed — but only in Las Vegas, not in Washington.

She put me on hold as she conferred with her superiors. "Very well, Mr. Panfilov," she finally said.

Was it my imagination or had I detected a note of triumph in her voice? That must have been my advanced Perception at work.

"We'll be expecting you at the embassy the day after tomorrow," she said. "You'll be flying to Las Vegas the same night. A car will be waiting for you at the airport."

"There's one other thing, Ms. Howard. I seem to have a bit of a problem with my travel documents. I've just been burgled. The thieves took all my ID papers."

"I'm so sorry," she said. "Would you like to put it off for a while? You probably need time to replace your passport."

"Angela, let me be completely honest with you. I'm afraid, if I don't see your colleagues within the next few days, they can forget it entirely. I simply won't be able to... to be of any use to you."

She paused. "I'll need to discuss it with the party involved," she said dryly, then hung up.

The next hour seemed an eternity. Clenching my fists, I watched Panchenko drinking cocktails and lounging about a festively lit indoor pool.

Finally, Angela's number rang again.

"Get ready," a strange male voice said with a foreign accent. "You're flying the day after tomorrow from your city's airport. We'll send you the instructions."

The phone went dead.

* * *

I kept rereading Angela's last letter. The Americans' persistence was setting my alarm bells off. The ease with which they'd agreed to move our meeting to Vegas; their eagerness to pay for my flight and travel expenses; even their promise of pocket money and a guided tour of the city. As far as I could work out, they were flying me in on a diplomatic passport using a black-ops plane.

Did that mean they knew something about me? Or were they simply so interested in catching that terrorist guy?

Just think I used to be afraid of Major Igorevsky! Here, I was confronted by one of the most powerful organizations in the world. Once they had their sights on you, you were sure to end up in the crap no matter the amount of sweet-talking they did. Anyway, it was irrelevant. I needed to have the curse lifted and strip Panchenko of his interface.

My objective was to do as much as I could in the little time I had left. It might turn out that I wouldn't get back at all.

I made a mental assessment of the order of all the tasks, then went unflinchingly about them.

I cleaned myself up and went downstairs to have breakfast, then spent some quality time busting a gut in the hotel's gym.

You've received +1 to Strength!
Current strength: 20
You've received 1000 pt. XP for successfully leveling up a main characteristic!
Current level: 19. XP points gained: 13670/20000.

Congratulations! You've unblocked one of the requirements for following heroic abilities: Regeneration, Sprint, Taming:
Strength (level 20+)

I closed the message without even reading it. Later, all later. I left the weight machines and moved over to cardio.

Just as I was approaching my 20th kilometer on the treadmill, my smartphone pinged with a new text message. It was Kesha Dimidko sending me a rundown on the clients.

I'd look at it later.

I cranked up the treadmill's angle to maximum and gave it my all for the last kilometer.

Yes!

You've received +1 to Stamina!
Current Stamina: 20
You've received 1000 pt. XP for successfully leveling up a main characteristic!
Current level: 19. XP points gained: 14670/20000.

Congratulations! You've unblocked requirements for following heroic abilities:

Regeneration, Sprint, Taming:
  Stamina (Level 20+)

I'd hardly finished reading it when another one turned up for no reason whatsoever:

You've received +3 to Luck!
Current Luck: 19
You've received 3000 pt. XP for successfully leveling up a main characteristic!
Current level: 19. XP points gained: 17670/20000.

Plus three points to Luck? Way to go! What was that now? What could have triggered it? Had I done something really meaningful? Something that could make my life take a new direction?

Wait a sec. Why nineteen? Shouldn't it be seventeen? Where had the two extra points come from?

I checked my profile. Strangely enough, Luck showed no item boosts anymore. The ring of Veles and Netsuke Jurōjin I could understand: Panchenko had taken both. But he'd ignored the Red Wristband given to me by Stacy aka Ilindi.

I looked at my wrist. The fine red thread was gone; all I could see was a faint pink line circling my wrist like an old scar. It was as if the Protective Red Wristband had worked its way under my skin, merging with it and becoming part of me.

---

* * *

Over the course of the next night, I leveled up Perception 3 pt. Then at sunrise I left the hotel where I'd first lost all hope only to have it restored.

Kira dropped by to give me a lift. "I'm not even gonna ask what you're doing here and why you have no money," she said as she ushered me into the car.

We had breakfast in a cozy coffee shop. I told her that I'd been burgled and that I needed to leave for the US the next day. I tried to make her buy some story about me winning an essay competition, but I could see she didn't believe me. Despite this, she didn't ask me any questions.

She took me first to apply for new ID papers, then to the bank where I filed an application to restore my bank cards. From there, we went on to a notary that she knew and had him draw up a power of attorney to allow her to do everything in my absence.

"A man shouldn't ever be without money," she said grimly, handing me an impressive wad of banknotes. "You can return it when you come back."

If I come back, I thought although I didn't say it out loud.

We agreed to spend the evening with our parents. I really wanted to enjoy what could become my last family get-together.

That out of the way, I went home. Kira dropped me off at the front door, warning me she'd come and get me in the evening.

Thanks to Alik and Veronica's hard work, the place was now shipshape and shining. Although some of the furniture was still being repaired, I didn't worry about it much as I only had to spend one night there before my flight. To tell you the truth, the curse's ticking countdown had put everything else on the backburner, so I had to make an effort to shed my apathy.

I needed to spend my last day at the office working hard on everything that my co-workers wouldn't be able to do for me, like searching out jobs for the existing clients and shopping for new ones. I also had to try and negotiate with those who'd canceled their contracts with us.

I paused in the kitchen, staring long and hard at Boris' two food bowls. The cleaners invited in by Alik had polished them up like everything else in the apartment. After some thought, I decided to keep them and a half-shredded teddy bear, as a memento of my purring companion. Boris had stayed with me longer than any of them: Yanna's Chihuahua Boy, as well as Yanna herself and later, Vicky. Boris had befriended Richie; she'd been witness to my downfall and degradation followed by my return to a fulfilling life. Then some petty vindictive little shit had done what he'd done.

I opened up the map to check on his whereabouts. He was still in the Bellagio Hotel. I had an alarm set up in case he left the area.

After that, I spent some time admiring the illuminated swimming pool of Caesars Palace where the Americans were planning to put me up. I made myself a promise to take a dip in it at least once regardless of whether I'd found Panchenko or not. I remembered the hotel from the set of *The Rainman* which was my favorite movie. I wondered if that was why the Americans had booked it for me? I'd never stayed in five-star hotels before.

I was one of the first to arrive at the office — but Veronica was already there, sitting at my desk scribbling in her agenda, her tongue poking out with the effort.

"Hi, Ginger!" I said.

"Don't call me that! It sucks!"

"I've brought you some money," I laid the banknotes on the table. "Thanks, you really helped me out."

"Don't mention it. You'd better sit yourself down and sort through those four files over there. Those are all the questionnaires for the last few days. There're at least a hundred of them. Do you think you can manage that today?"

"I'll clear them by lunchtime."

Having finished with the clients' questionnaires and found suitable jobs for them, I asked Kesha to give me the run-down on all the clients that had canceled. I had no idea whether I'd have enough time to meet up with all of them but just talking to Kesha might boost his spirits and assure him that his boss wasn't going to throw in the towel.

If only he knew...

While he was giving me the details, I noticed something I couldn't quite put my finger on. The interface began to lag, burning through my Spirit resources. I absolutely needed to be alone before something untoward happened.

I raised my hand to stop Kesha, "Mind if I step out for a couple of minutes?"

Our commercial director nodded and turned to discuss other pressing matters with our co-workers. They were so busy coming up with new ideas, they didn't even notice me leaving the office.

I walked outside and sat down on a bench on the boulevard across the road. Whatever my interface was about to throw at me, I'd better adopt a safer position.

I didn't have to wait long. Soon I was showered with messages. Waves of ecstasy rolled through my body, growing in their bliss and intensity, as I received a new level.

Several minutes and what felt like an eternity later, I was finally able to read the messages in their entirety.

Congratulations! You've performed a socially meaningful action! You've created a new temporal branch of reality and restored the integrity of the Bekhterev family, namely Konstantin "Kostya" and Julie, preventing their respective levels from dropping and creating new favorable conditions for improving their social status.

You've performed a socially meaningful action by donating a sum in excess of your entire annual income to somebody who needed it more. As a repeated action, it is awarded with a multiple increase in XP points.

You've received 39000 XP for performing a socially meaningful action!

Congratulations! You've received two new

levels!

Your current social status level: 21

Characteristic points available: 4

Skill points available: 2

Congratulations! You've received a new system skill level!

Skill name: Heroism

Current level: 2

Now you can activate the Tier-2 heroic abilities: Regeneration, Sprint and Taming, provided their requirements are met.

XP received: 1000

XP points left until the next social status level: 12960/22000.

Receiving two levels instead of one didn't come easy to me. The cooldown left me drenched in sweat. I couldn't feel my legs anymore. But the bout of artificial bliss was nothing compared to the news of Julie, the little handicapped sister of my boxing partner Kostya Bekhterev. She was making a good recovery!

Now I didn't give a damn about losing the interface. I didn't care anymore if I forgot everything and turned back into the fat beer-gutted Phil proud to be a high-level rogue in WoW: the Phil who had no idea that real life was much more fun than virtual reality. I'd already left my little mark on the future.

Overwhelmed, I returned to the office.

Just as I approached the business center building, my phone rang. I looked at the screen and grinned uncontrollably. It was Kostya.

"Hi," I said. "How are you doing? How's Jul?"

"Everything's great!" he shouted into the receiver. "The surgery went really well! Her recovery is going great guns! We're coming home next week!"

"I'm so happy for you, man!"

"Thanks! Me too!" he said, then went on to tell me all the details. "How about you?" he finally asked.

"I'm fine," I said, trying to control my voice. "Once you're back, you can come straight to the office. The guys are waiting for you."

"I won't be able to start working straight away, I'm afraid. I'll have to look after Jul 'cause she can't go back to kindergarten. She has to stay in bed for a while."

"I'll talk to my parents. I'm pretty sure they'll be happy to be useful."

For a while, he kept protesting, trying to assure me he could take care of it all himself. I barely listened. Once he'd finished, I said calmly,

"The decision's been made. No further discussion about it. I might be away for a while."

"Really? Where are you going?"

"I have to go on a trip. It might take some time. When you arrive, it'll be either my Dad or the guys from work that meet you at the airport. The main thing is, I won't be around. So I'd like you to start working as soon as you've settled in and sorted Julie out. Money doesn't-"

"I know. Money doesn't earn itself," he repeated my favorite expression. "Okay, I got it. Gotta go now, this roaming costs a fortune!"

"Say hello to Julie."

As I was entering the building, I bumped into Vazgen. Despite being in a hurry, he stopped to say hello and exchange a couple of niceties with me. Knowing that I might be seeing him for the last time, I bade him an especially warm goodbye.

I headed up to my office which was temporarily Veronica's domain. We had visitors: a lady of about thirty years of age, good-looking and well-groomed. According to my interface, she was in fact in her forties. She was wearing a pencil skirt just above the knee, a light-colored blouse, high heels and perfect makeup. A business woman if ever I'd seen one.

"Philip Panfilov?" she rose and proffered her hand. "I'm Sarah Bergman. Mr. Valiadis sent me."

"Nice to meet you," I said. "How can I help you?"

"Mr. Valiadis asked if you could arrange for all your workers to be present at our meeting. Would that be possible?"

"Absolutely."

Veronica — who'd been entertaining her in my absence — nodded and walked out to fetch the others.

Soon everyone was present and correct: Kesha, Veronica, Greg, Mr. Katz, Rose and Alik who was eating on the run. When I cast him a quizzical look, he mouthed, "It's lunch time!"

Blushing, Veronica prized the food container from his hands and took it away somewhere. When she came back, she gave him the evil eye.

The woman was watching the scene, a smile lurking in the corners of her mouth.

I coughed, attracting their attention. "I'd like you all to meet Sarah who's representing the interests of Mr. Nicholas Valiadis — whom we all know. Sarah?"

With a broad smile on her face, the woman walked out into the center of the office. "Thank you,

Phil. I'm very happy to meet you all. The Great Job Agency has an excellent reputation. Which was why Mr. Valiadis and myself have studied the list of services you offer and come to the conclusion that we'd be interested in striking up a long-term relationship with you. This will concern both J-Mart and all its branches and affiliated companies."

With every word she spoke, the faces of those present grew ever longer.

This was indeed a very extravagant gesture on Valiadis' part. He knew I was about to lose my interface which meant we were about to become a very average company run by ordinary people.

The scope of his gesture was such that now I didn't have to meet any of the smaller companies that had refused to work with us. So even in the worst turn of events, both my partners and my company were looking at a bigger and brighter future.

CHAPTER NINETEEN

THIS HAPPENS TO EVERYONE

We fight as one.

Ursa, *Dota 2*

IF I HAD TO CHOOSE THE MOST EPIC SCENE IN THE ENTIRE Trial, it would have been this one. Tafari's five fighters, stunned and frozen in full sprint with their heads thrown back and their weapons in the air. My triceratops and the crocodile the size of a railroad car, coming at them at full tilt. The beautiful Jovanna drawing her bow, hair flying and eyes flaming. Ola screaming his head off as he ran to launch his spear whose tip pointed predatorily toward the nearest enemy. Manu's long face as he began to realize what was going on and assumed a combat stance, prepared to fight till the last percent of his Life.

And finally, the T. Rex towering above the scene

and rearing his head, stunning our enemies with his Furious Roar — while at the back, a group of whistlers stood in amazement on their hind legs, their crests lowered in an act of fear and submission.

While the croc was chewing a soldier, Tank impaled another one on his horn as Rex was busy trampling and mauling all the others. Jovanna and Ola kept dealing focused damage on their selected targets.

Having noticed one of Tafari's men — a burly blond guy with a plasma staff — trying to crawl out of the range of Rex's roar, I activated Treacherous Shadow, slipped behind him and stunned him. A brief combo was enough to finish him off.

An open-mouthed Manu watched our well-choreographed routine which we'd already perfected on a good hundred packs of nebulas. He then bared his sword, bellowed something about the grace of God and lunged at his opponents. He even managed to bury the weapon's tip in the ground exactly where one of Tafari's vassals had just stood: a cute but quite vicious harpy who was already climbing Rex's back trying to pierce his neck with something that looked like a tomahawk. Jovanna's arrow hit the creature in the ear, downing it.

The entire battle had run its course in minutes if not seconds.

Ola and Jovanna walked over to me and gave me a big hug. The girl pressed her body to mine. She didn't let go for a long time until I could take it no longer. Unable to restrain myself, I gave her a kiss on the neck smeared in somebody's blood.

"Thanks for coming," I said. "In theory, we could have teleported out but we'd have lost the base and left the enemy group prowling all around."

"We came as soon as we heard the alarm," Ola explained. "You want us to meet the new guy?" both he and Jovanna nodded at Manu.

"Later! First we need to sort through the loot and get back to the main base. Once we're back in the shelter, I'll tell you everything. No, wait!" I raised my hand, stopping them.

"Why, what's up?" Jovanna asked.

"We need to sort out the spirit crystals. They're non-transferrable so let's check them first. How many do you have? I've got all 13. There were eight crystals dropped at Nagash's base but I could only pick up four. Manu took the rest."

Jovanna and Ola looked at each other and shrugged. "We don't have any."

"In this case, you'd better pick up these five."

"Bullshit!" Jovanna protested.

Ola agreed with her. "Phil, if you die the final death, we will all lose. You need to take them."

"Manu?"

He grinned. "What have you got here, a democracy? In that case, I agree with the others."

I looked through my interface until I found the crystal's status: 13/13.

Then I remembered Carter. If there was the slightest chance of buying him a new life, I had to take it.

I browsed through the clan members list. His icon was inactive. I sent a mental command.

We're sorry. The Trial participant Carter died the final death.

You have to use the Resurrection Module to

give him one last chance.

Sorry, man, not now. The resurrection Module would cost the clan almost 200,000 existence resource points. Also, it required the base to reach level 5. I wasn't even sure that the Trial would last that long.

I returned to the line depicting the crystals' status and focused on it. It disappeared.

Greetings, Liquidator! You've destroyed the sacred number of your enemies: 13.

You've collected their spirit crystals and transformed them into an additional life.

Current lives: 2

Put more fire under your enemies' feet, Liquidator!

"Did it work?" Jo asked.

I nodded and heaved a sigh of relief. Two lives were better than one. Now I had a margin for error.

I wiped the sweat from my brow, smiled and looked down at my feet where the spirit crystal had just been.

It wasn't there!

I checked the entire battlefield: nothing. There was gear lying around but no crystals. The interface didn't mention them, either.

"Listen guys, can you see any spirit crystals?"

I was pretty sure they could, but I asked just in case.

"There's one lying right under your feet," Manu said. "And four more scattered over there."

"Why?" Ola asked.

"It looks like I can't pick up any more crystals. It seems to be a one-off ability. I can't even see them. So we'll have to change the plan."

"What do you suggest?" Ola asked. "Do you want us to share them?"

"Sharing them would be fair but not really rational. There's a high probability of you not picking up any at all. Now if only one of you picked them all up, that might be safer, I think."

"You're right," Jovanna said. "And seeing as the new guy already has four..."

"Six," Manu corrected her. "I got two more myself when I'd just started out, before Nagash had enslaved me."

Hearing the necromancer's name, Ola opened his eyes wide.

I ignored his silent question. "Great. If you pick up five more now, you'll only have two left till the cap. Go ahead and take them. Jo and Ola, I want you to pick up the gear. We need to get back to the shelter. It's almost dark."

I removed the Devious Pauldrons of Eternal Rest that I'd taken off Nagash and offered them to Manu. "Put these on. They give +65% to the chance of dropping an additional spirit crystal. You never know, it might work."

It did. Instead of five, Manu picked up seven crystals. With a triumphant cry, he started dancing and hopping around on one leg, stomping with the other and sticking his backside in the air as he spun around, shaking his belly.

"This is mapalé, our national dance," he explained, seeing our bewildered faces. "I'm from

Columbia."

He removed the pauldrons and handed them back to me. He had no need for them anymore. As for the others, Jovanna still had two lives left while Ola was already on his last one. We all agreed he would be the next one to pick up any spirit crystals.

I solemnly handed him the pauldrons. "I hope it won't take you long."

He grinned, casting a quick glance over our victorious ranks. "It'll be a piece of cake with you guys."

"In that case, everybody, please meet Manu..."

As we walked back to the shelter, I told them everything that had happened to me, describing the circumstances of my meeting Manu as well as everything I'd seen.

My two friends were especially interested in the artifacts available at the special-purpose hexagon. Still, their price tags quickly dampened their spirits.

"If that place serves a different purpose every day, I wonder what would be there tomorrow?" Jovanna asked. "Should we go and check it out tomorrow morning?"

"What's the point?" Manu said. "If it changes purpose every 24 hours, I don't think the shop will be there tomorrow morning. We could always check it out, of course, but all this time it's been just a regular hexagon like any other. I was the first one to capture it before Nagash took it from me."

I frowned. "And then it passed on to Tafari. We'll have to fight for it."

"Wait a sec," Ola raised a hand. "What happened to it then? Where is this regular hexagon now that its place has been taken by the special-purpose one?"

Manu scratched the back of his head. The others turned to look at me. I was the only eyewitness to the special-purpose hexagon's existence.

I paused, trying to remember how I'd gotten inside. "There's something I forgot to mention," I offered. "When you cross into it, it feels like you're passing through jelly. What if it just loads, like a new location in a videogame?"

"And?" they asked, impatient for me to tell them what happened to the old hexagon whenever a new one was activated.

"They both exist at the same time. It's just that the access to the old one is denied for twenty-four hours, so that you automatically get teleported to the special-purpose one. And the gelatinous barrier you have to cross when you enter it is in fact a portal."

"Wait a sec," Ola's eyes lit up. "In that case, could the barrier serve as a portal in all of the hexagons? Because if it is-"

"Enough, please. It's a good theory but pretty useless, I'm afraid. We'd better check the loot."

The loot wasn't particularly exciting. It mainly consisted of standard-issue level 2 gear plus some knives and clubs. Tafari's group had dropped two artifacts: the plasma staff and the tomahawk with a bonus to critical damage and a chance to cast a bleed DoT.

Manu got the staff which allowed him to deal long-range damage. He already had Striker's sword for close combat. Ola got the tomahawk.

Manu and I also managed to lay our hands on a few things dropped by Nagash's group: the sword, a self-loading crossbow and yet another staff. None of them were particularly useful, so once we'd ported to the main base, we left both in the chest in case one of us died and lost all of their stuff. All of the artifacts had comparable damage stats, only differing in attack force and speed.

Then we went to the shelter to chill out while the other guys told me what they'd been up to. We'd managed to upgrade at least a dozen bases — a great result, considering that every level-2 base and every working unit we received improved our leveling chances.

Ola with his great math skills had already calculated that if our farming progress didn't slacken off the coming night, all of our bases would produce the planned results by the next evening. I had to temper his ardor by saying that we really should follow Tafari's example and make sure that each clan member made level 10 as soon as possible in order to receive a class. I already knew from experience that class talents played the decisive role in our encounters with other players.

Finally, we decided to leave the counting of our chickens — or rather, our resources — till the morning. Then we'd decide how to proceed.

* * *

At forty years of age, our new clan member Manuel Fuentes turned out to be a real drug baron. He was originally from the Columbian city of Medellin which was notorious for its illegal drug trafficking. If Manu were to be believed, he'd even met Pablo Escobar when he was younger.

He'd had the interface for three months now. When he'd first received it, the program had showered him with penalties for socially detrimental actions until he was so weak he couldn't even lift a spoon. For some reason, the interface had attacked his Strength, probably because for someone like him physical weakness was the worst form of punishment.

In his mind, Manu decided it must have been punishment from God. He left the drug business and spent all his waking time trying to redeem his sins through prayer. Seeing his wholehearted repentance and generous alms bore no fruit, he began sabotaging cocaine deliveries, cooperating with the drug police and being a general do-gooder helping everyone he came across.

Apparently, God started showering him with his grace — or so Manu thought as he received new social status levels. Penalties were canceled and his characteristics improved, so that by the time of his abduction he already had a taste for good deeds and joined the powers of Light.

By the same token, he hadn't lost any of his old gangster skills — so now he could show them off during our nighttime farming session.

As darkness fell, new yet unknown elite mobs stomped toward the base. Called *limbins*, they were basically shapeless lumps of flesh twice the size of a human, without any limbs or heads. Personally, I dubbed them doughboys.

They attacked us in waves, each at a considerable distance from the next. The weakest wave counted four of them. Fighting them had proved a challenge because they had no vulnerable spots. Every time we stabbed them with our knives, the holes closed up the moment we pulled our weapons out, as if we were poking dough. As for arrows, they just swallowed them with no obvious damage to themselves. When I sent my dinos to attack them, the doughboys simply flattened themselves out, only to arise in a different place.

True, their health kept dwindling albeit slowly. But the moment one of them enveloped Rex's leg, my pet whined in pain and collapsed to the ground with one missing limb. The doughboy itself had swollen up and turned red, gaining volume from the mass ingested.

That's when Manu had the first opportunity to show his quick thinking. He laid his sword aside, took the staff and riddled the nasty creature with plasma charges. The monster duly absorbed them — but have you ever tried to keep plasma inside? The charge went right through its flesh, burning a channel and stripping the mob of health points.

"Got you, you bastard!" Manu shouted with abandon, loosing off a stream of plasma charges.

Jovanna understood me straight away. She rushed to the shelter and returned with two more staffs: her own which fired lightning bolts and the one which released energy charges. I ordered the dinos to back off and told my team to start pulling the doughboys toward them.

Rex was still lying where he'd fallen. What a shame I hadn't rid Zack of his healing staff. By the time Rex had restored and grown himself a new leg, we'd already repelled three more assault waves.

The doughboys kept dropping generous amounts of resources. The integration module continued to automatically activate new base upgrades and generate more modules and working units. By the morning, not only had we reached our scheduled objectives base-wise, but we'd all made level 9 — all of us but me, that is.

I'd made level 11 because I'd been forced to heal myself ASAP when I'd lost an arm inside a doughboy. I could have lost my life had it not been for Manu who'd pulled me out risking being swallowed by the carnivorous blob of dough.

According to our new strategy, we invested all of our available characteristic points into Strength. Thanks to that, every working unit was now bringing in eleven more resources per hour. That's not mentioning our improved damage numbers — except for Jovanna whose bow damage depended on her Agility.

With the first rays of the sun, we deployed toward the special-purpose hexagon from where we set off to reclaim Manu's territory. If my assumptions were correct and Tafari — who was tied up fighting Juma — would once again send a fighting group, we would make short work of it.

* * *

Which was exactly what happened. In actual fact, it was even easier.

The special-purpose hexagon wasn't there. Instead, there was Nagash's former base which Striker had seized for Tafari. By breaching its borders, we received some debuffs and triggered an alarm.

We made it to the shelter and got inside, constantly expecting to hear teleports popping behind our backs. Still, nobody arrived, so we captured the base without a fight.

We continued moving from one hexagon to the next, farming all the mob packs that we came across, until we'd captured all four of Nagash's former bases. We got so cheeky that we even went further and reclaimed two of Tafari's.

Now our clan was the proud owner of sixty-two hexagons. The rankings kept updating in real time, showing that thirteen more Trial participants had died the final death within the last twenty-four hours:

Number of test subjects: 59/169
Current ranking:
1. Juma. Human. Level 23. Class: Predator. Hexagons captured: 142
2. Tafari. Human. Level 21. Class: Executioner. Hexagons captured: 135
3. Phil. Human. Level 11. Class: Liquidator. Hexagons captured: 62

But even though the size of the area claimed had brought us closer to the leaders, the level gap was getting ever bigger. It looked like both leaders invested everything generated by their bases into their own leveling, not bothering to spare any resources on either their hexagon's economies or their vassals' progress.

"You know, Phil, I've been thinking," Ola said, using our five-minute break to draw something with his spear tip on the ground. "Jo, everybody, look. If we upgrade the working unit module to level 2, which would cost us two thousand... would that simply mean that all of the harvesters on our bases would automatically upgrade to level 2?"

I immediately knew what he was getting at. "Ola, you're a genius! This is how it worked with the fighting units: once we'd upgraded the integration module, it allowed us to max out all the fighting units at the main base. And a level-2 working unit would farm five times as much!"

"We'll have to try it," Jovanna perked up. "Should we go back to the main base?"

"I'll go there alone," I stopped her. "You all stay here and keep on farming. I might also pop in on our friend Zack. His independence deadline expires in an hour."

"Can't I go with you?" Jo begged. "The boys can do very well on their own."

"Sorry, Jo, but you'll have to stay. Meet you in three hours at the base of this hexagon or whichever one you capture. By nightfall, we should be able to make it further north."

I left them and hurried toward the base to teleport back to our main hexagon.

Once there, I launched an upgrade of both noncombat and inventory modules. Each of us could use an individual extradimensional backpack where we could keep a few gear sets and spare weapons just to make sure we weren't left naked in case of death.

Once both upgrades had run their course, I received my backpack. It was small and snug — but more importantly, it was truly bottomless and synchronized with the clan's extradimensional inventory.

But as for working units, it didn't quite go as planned. All the other bases' modules weren't eligible for a free upgrade, so Ola's idea of a cheat which could turn us into some Trial oligarchs had failed miserably.

What a shame. His plan had been so good. Had it worked, we would all had bought ourselves level 30 by the following morning.

Once that was out of the way, I ported to the base closest to Zack's and ran to see him.

Warning! You're about to enter a hexagon captured by another test subject.
Owner: Zack. Level 9
Base level: 2
Special effects: -5% to all characteristics

I staggered ever so slightly from the razor-sharp drop in Strength, Agility and Stamina. Five percent may sound like nothing — I'd only lost 1 pt. of Strength — but I could still feel it.

On my way to Zack's base I came across several packs of aggressive mobs levels 9 to 10 — kirpi and krekniks mainly — but they didn't give me any hassle. There were so many whistlers I had to kick them out of my way. I had more existence resources than I could wish for because my chance for a bigger loot had kicked in quite a few times, resulting in over a 100 pt. in total. All this considered, by the time I reached Zack's base I was quite happy with myself.

No one was there to greet me, with the exception of the few turrets positioned along the base's perimeter.

I whipped past them until I reached the blind zone and stopped by the shelter.

I found the absence of the base's owner alarming. He must have received a penetration warning. Should I capture the base or wait for Zack and offer him to voluntarily join my clan?

I decided to give him ten minutes, then initiate the process of capturing another player's hexagon. In order to do that, I had to spend at least an hour alone in the command center.

Zack arrived at the base as the ten minutes were almost up. Surrounded by his retinue of a dozen spiders, the man whose name was on Ilindi's list grimly walked over to me and warily shook my hand.

"I need another twenty-four hours," he said without further ado.

"Zack, it's either you join my clan now or I'm gonna kill you and capture this hexagon. Here's the invitation."

He declined the invitation straight away, then gestured conciliatorily. "Listen to me. First, are you really sure you can beat me on my own turf? You're alone and I have all my fighting units with me. And believe me, their bite is worse than their bark."

"I'm afraid you're gonna die before any of them gets the chance to get anywhere near me with their mandibles. I don't believe you're in a very good position to threaten me."

"You started it."

"I gave you the choice. Which is more than you gave me."

"Then listen up. Secondly, as far as I remember, you really liked my healing staff, didn't you? I'm prepared to give it to you for a twenty-four hour delay. It's only twenty-four hours, Phil. What difference is that gonna make? I have a theory regarding the local gameplay that I want to check. And I can't do it in a clan. Phil, *please*," his voice quivered. He dropped to his knees in front of me.

"Now what prevents me from killing you here and now, then take everything you have, including the staff?"

"The staff is in the inventory module. You know what I mean, don't you? I'm sure you do. You can't get to it without me."

I remembered Rex whining in agony as his leg was being devoured. Once again I weighed up my chances, including my bluff that Zack was so easy to kill. If a dozen of his spiders laid into me, I might never come back. In which case, I'd lose everything: my life, my gear and all the artifacts. And if I left now for reinforcements, that would be a total loss of face and would slow us down considerably.

"Twenty-four hours," I said. "Now go and get the staff."

* * *

I got to the northernmost base before my team and wandered around it to ease the boredom, smoking whatever mob packs came my way. Finally by my third round, I saw the dinos appear from behind a low hill, accompanied by my clan members riding the croc.

I could see there were actually four of them, not three. Had they taken on somebody else? No, the number of clan members in my interface hadn't

changed. Who was it, then? Jovanna, Ola, Manu and...
at this distance, the person's name tag hadn't activated
yet.

After a while, his identification finally kicked in.
His name was Eddie.

Another person from Ilindi's list! I just couldn't
believe it! How come that almost everyone on the list
had ended up in this part of the map? It was a mystery
that only Ilindi could reveal.

As my team approached, I wondered whether it
would be possible to send a query back to Earth. If
they'd managed to do it, surely the opposite was also
possible?

I rummaged through my interface logs looking
for the message with the list but it wasn't there
anymore.

My dinos were all doing their thing, forcing their
way through the rickety fence and invading the base.
The place immediately bustled with activity.

"We've got company!" Ola shouted, leaping from
the croc's back. "Come and say hello!"

The others followed, carefully lowering
themselves down holding on to the croc's scales. Manu,
the new guy and Jova-

Oh no. This girl wasn't Jovanna. Ola must have
decided to start with the good news.

"Where's Jo?" I asked.

The men shuffled from one foot to the other,
averting their gazes. The new girl replied instead,

"She got herself killed. After we'd met your team,
we were heading to the base through some woods and
walked right into a nebulas' ambush..."

"She can't have been killed by mobs!" I

interrupted her in disbelief. "They weren't even elite ones!"

"We're sorry, Phil," Ola replied. "They distracted us, so we didn't notice Tafari's team attack us from behind. While we turned to confront them, they'd already killed Jovanna and run off. We failed to engage them because we hadn't even noticed them at first. We couldn't even chase after them because we had a pack of nebulas to fend off!"

"Oh well," I said, "it looks like Tafari has switched to guerrilla tactics. In which case, the reinforcements can't arrive too soon," I pulled myself together and offered my hand to the curly-haired new guy. "I'm Phil, Russia."

"I'm Eddie, Orlando Florida," he said. "I know you. My earth-based prototype sent me a mental message."

"I'm Leti," the new girl said. "I'm from Italy. I'm currently in Eddie's clan but we're both prepared to join yours."

"We've got three hexagons," the American explained, "plus twenty-six Charisma points and twenty-five Strength between the two of us. We have a level-2 main base with all modules activated."

"Excellent," I nodded grimly, still unable to come to terms with the stupid loss of my gir- oops. So that's what I considered Jovanna now, was it? "We'll discuss everything in the shelter. In the meantime, Eddie, here's the clan invitation. Leti will probably join automatically once you're in."

Eddie appeared to be about twenty-five years old, his intense tan unable to conceal his Irish freckles. Leti was a fit brunette in her thirties or probably older, but she looked younger. Eddie's brief and concise report had revealed a bunch of important information for the clan. In the coming hours, we had to decide how exactly to reinforce our dinos' group. Would it make sense to build three more bunches of Velociraptors and Dilophosauri or would we be better off making another mega monster? We still had Manu's Charisma points to invest. Or should we just reinforce the three dinos we already had by rebuilding them?

We heard the soft but unmistakable popping of a teleport, followed by a loud outburst of Jovanna's emotional speech consisting mainly of Serbian invectives with a smattering of French *gros-mots*[15] she must have learned from Ola.

Now Ola was running toward her with her bow in his hands, trying to preempt her bout of anger. Mechanically Jovanna slung the bow behind her back, strode toward our group and demanded,

"Phil! I want my own dinosaur! One which would never leave my side!"

"We'll consider it, absolutely," I replied. "Can you just wait a moment?"

Sensing that I was about to tell them something important, my team stood around me.

"Listen guys. All of us here have committed some socially meaningful actions. That's why we're together. Zack is still toying with his independence. As for Ken, we haven't found him yet. But the rest of us here — Ola, Eddie, Jovanna, Manu, Leri and myself — are humanity's best in this Trial. We're not Phil's clan — we're Ilindi's clan. Valiadis puts his hope in us. The

---

[15] Gros mots: cuss words (French)

entire Earth puts its hope in us. If we lose, so will humanity."

"Phil?" Jovanna tapped me on the shoulder. "You wanted to say something, didn't you?"

I realized I'd only said my passionate speech in my mind. Should I repeat it out loud? For some reason, it now sounded so pompous and unnatural, artificial even.

So I said something else instead,

"Oh yes. We're almost all here now. Let's get down to work!"

Chapter

Twenty

Scars on the Body of Fate

*If anyone asks where I am, I've
left the country.*

Mike Wheeler, *Stranger Things*

"A VODKA FOR ME!" I HEARD A VOICE TO MY RIGHT. THE
guy in the seat next to mine who'd been asleep for most
of the flight had finally woken up. "Make it two!" he
showed two fingers to the air hostess. "And a tomato
juice! No, two!"

The excitement in the cabin of the Moscow flight
to Las Vegas was palpable. All the films had been
watched, everybody had had the two obligatory meals
and a nap afterward, so now the twelve-hour flight was
nearing its completion. The well-rested passengers
spoke in cheerful voices, discussing our final
destination.

The air hostess handed the drinks to my fellow traveler, then turned to me with a pleasant smile,

"What can I get you, sir?"

"Just some water, please."

Having received my order, I drank half the beaker and set the rest down on the little table.

"Less than two hours left!" my fellow traveler announced, looking at the screen. "Las Vegas! The city of dreams! The city of leisure!"

He stuck his hand out. "I'm Alex."

"Phil," I returned his handshake.

"This is to us both, Phil, and screw the rest of them!" he downed his four-ounce shot and caught his breath, wiping his mouth with his sleeve, then slurped back all his tomato juice, his Adam's apple twitching as he drank.

His Russian accent was good but his attempt to pass for a native Russian had been hilarious:

Alex Tomasik[16]
Age: 54
A secret agent

I'd bet anything he was a CIA operative.

This was the first time he'd spoken during the whole flight. I'd been lucky with my ticket as my American friends had splurged on a business class seat. Tomasik was sitting to my right.

To my left across the aisle sat a depressed-looking girl: a high-cheekboned blonde wearing specs, her face concealed by the raised hood of her sweatshirt.

---

[16] Tomasik is a Slovak name, not Russian

He name was Laura. She'd spent the whole flight staring at her iPad with a pair of earbuds stuck in her ears. To all my attempts to speak to her she replied monosyllabically, making it clear I was infringing on her personal space.

In actual fact, it was the other way round. It was her who was intruding into my personal life because, apart for some professional-level skills such as Firearms and Bladed Weapons, she also possessed some very peculiar abilities like Operational Security, Vigilance, Self-Control and Observation Skills which spoke for themselves, betraying her real purpose on this flight.

"Is this your first time in the US?" Alex asked unceremoniously. He may have looked groggy and disheveled, but it couldn't have been further from the truth. On the inside, he was focused, the watchful stare of his observant eyes scanning me, reading my body language and gaging my reactions. "Fancy toasting our meeting?"

"Thanks, but I don't drink. This is my first time in the US, you're right."

They'd started tailing me already in Moscow's Domodedovo Airport to which I'd been flown by a regular domestic flight. At the appointed hour, I'd arrived at our city's airport where I'd been met by an inconspicuous man with a lived-in face. He materialized next to me out of nowhere, handed me an envelope, then disappeared back to wherever he'd come from.

The envelope had contained my plane tickets

and my new passport for international travel[17] which looked identical to the one I'd had, the only difference being that this one was brand new with an American visa already in it.

Out of sheer boredom, I'd spent the time before my flight playing "I spy" ID-ing my fellow passengers. That was when I'd noticed both Laura and Alex with their very peculiar skills and statuses. So when the two had ended up in the seats next to mine, I wasn't even surprised.

That's when I finally knew that whoever were interested in shipping me to America were *really* interested in me. The only remaining question was whether they needed me as a potential lead to terrorists or because they suspected me of having some ESP abilities. Neither option promised anything good but at least I could use the latter for my own purposes.

"Business or pleasure?" Alex asked.

I cast a sideways glance at Laura who appeared to be consumed by some anime on her iPad, then looked back at Alex. Both sported indecent amounts of Interest in humble me, much higher than a fellow passenger should.

In theory, I could suspect that my high Charisma levels might have been the reason for Laura's interest. Still, I somehow doubted it. Her heart rate was within the accepted norms for her age which was in fact

---

[17] Most Russians have two passports: one for domestic use which serves as the main proof of identity within Russia, and an "international travel passport" of a different design for voyaging abroad. The first one is obligatory for all Russian citizens above 14 years of age, while the international travel passport is optional and can be issued to those who wish to travel abroad.

34. Without my interface, I would never have guessed and would have passed her off as a twenty-year-old student.

"Both," I replied. "I've won an essay writing competition about the role of the English language in today's society. I've been invited to the award ceremony. All expenses paid by the organizers."

"You don't mean it!" Alex exclaimed, almost sincere. "Respect, man!"

Okay. Enough pretense. The Trial wasn't going to last forever. I might lose the interface even before Panchenko's curse had expired.

"I want you to tell me something, guys," I said. "Are you from the CIA or the NSA?"

Although my question had caught them unawares, neither of them betrayed it. Had it not been for the program's readings, I would have been none the wiser.

The two exchanged glances. Alex gave the girl a barely perceptible nod.

"Sorry, Philip," he said, suddenly serious. "We just want to make sure you arrive safely on US territory."

"What can possibly threaten a novice writer who wrote an essay on the importance of the English language in today's society?"

"You know," Alix leaned closer and whispered, "You're not the only one. There's been quite a spate of such 'novice essay writers' just lately. Unfortunately, none of them gave us a chance to work with them."

"Work with them? Doing what?"

"Writing new essays."

* * *

Accompanied by Alex and a silent Laura who appeared to be completely consumed by chewing her gum, I jumped the line to the passport control. An officer stamped my passport, wished me a good day, nodded to my escorts and swung open the little gate, flagging me through into the territory of the United States.

"Alex, I really need to pop by somewhere. It's very important," I said, having checked Panchenko's position on the map. He was still in Vegas. "I need to do it right now before anything else you've already planned for me. It's extremely important."

"Where to?" Alex asked while Laura mouthed something into a concealed wire.

"I'll tell you when we get in the car," I kept the interface map open, watching Panchenko leave the hotel. I needed to wait until he stopped somewhere. "I might need to go to Bellagio. Then again, I might not. I can't give you the exact directions yet."

"Very well," Alex nodded after having run my request past his superiors.

Leaving the McCarran International Airport was like stepping into a steam tub. The sun was blazing; the tangy foreign air ripped the mask off my poker face which I'd managed to preserve throughout the customs control.

We chatted while waiting for the car. I tried to speak English — but on hearing me murder the language, Alex winced and switched back to Russian.

We talked about neutral subjects, not once mentioning the "essay". He told me how he liked

Moscow and that the girls were beautiful there. With a nasty laugh, he then told us a rather lewd story of some Russian oligarch's escapades, complete with some TV celebrities and the full staff of one of Moscow's modeling agencies.

Laura reacted by uttering a stream of complex English invective I'd never heard before in my life. She gave Alex an indignant look and fell silent again, casting sideways glances at me.

Finally, a small black minibus pulled up next to us. The three of us climbed in. The driver waited for us to take our seats, then pulled away sharply and sped off.

"Where do you want us to go?" Alex asked. "You mentioned Bellagio."

I checked the map. "I need to get to the T-Mobile Arena to watch some all-in wresting," I could barely speak, my throat dry with both anxiety and the fact that the whole thing was about to come to a head.

"I think it's already sold out," Alex said dryly.

"Do you think you could help me in?"

Laura rolled her eyes.

Alex chucked. "Why on earth would you want to watch that?"

"I've been dreaming about it since I was a child," I replied, trying to sound as sincere as I could. If it didn't work, I might have to wait for Panchenko outside.

"That's not a problem," Alex replied. "I can get you in."

He made a couple of phone calls, speaking in a soft voice, then gave me a reassuring nod.

The rest of the way, the two agents preserved a

tactful silence, watching me peer excitedly out the window.

I'd never left Russia before. I hadn't even been to Turkey — and now here I was stateside! I spent the whole way staring greedily at all the streets lined with beautiful buildings, at the shop signs, cars and even passersby, trying to spot all the differences.

The palm trees! They were the most amazing thing about the city, one that so vividly illustrated the difference in latitude.

Cursed and only three days away from my potential death, I was seeing palm trees for the first time in my life.

* * *

An attendant was already waiting for us by the arena. When we pulled up, he opened the car door with a friendly smile.

"Mr. Tomasik?" he asked, switching his gaze from me to Alex.

"The same. Can you bring our friend Phil here to his seat?"

The attendant smiled. "My pleasure. Follow me please, sir."

"We'll be nearby," Laura said.

Was it a promise or a threat?

I curiously studied the colorful giant screen mounted on one of the Arena's outer walls backlit with purple. Somewhere inside, Panchenko was sitting smugly, enjoying a life of luxury.

We entered the building, finding ourselves within a giant seething cauldron of people.

Try to imagine a soccer pitch with a boxing ring placed where one of the goals should have been, with all the remaining space filled with seats, then add twenty thousand people to the mix. Finding Panchenko here would be some job. My interface was little use here because the arena's roof prevented it from pinpointing his exact location. The only point of reference I had was my own marker.

The attendant took me to one of the VIP seats below, close to the ring, then left me there. There was already a bout underway but that wasn't what I'd come here for.

I tried to figure out whereabouts Panchenko was sitting. I'd have to somehow walk around the ring in order to get to the opposite stands. But first, I really should try and search for his face in the crowd, seeing as my high Perception allowed me to do that.

I began scanning row after row of human faces. Then on a hunch, I decided to try a different approach and told the program to highlight the object identified as "Konstantin Panchenko", as I had him in the database already.

It worked.

One of the silhouettes in the VIP stands opposite lit up, outlined in green. That was him, sitting in an almost empty row flanked by two hot mamas. He was red in the face, shaking a furious fist and yelling something. For a brief moment, I thought he was shouting at me — but no, he was simply rooting for one of the fighters in the ring.

Trying not to attract anyone's attention, I gingerly slipped out of my seat, rose and headed up the steps away from Panchenko. I decided to carry on all the way round the stadium in order to avoid coming into his field of vision.

I kept brushing up against other spectators because I had him firmly in my sights, gradually heading toward him to make sure I approached him from behind. Because of this, I finally bumped into somebody, my shoulder hitting their forehead.

I mechanically apologized. A short but burly guy stood in front of me, rubbing his forehead. He too must have been consumed by the fighting in the ring.

"Sorry," we said in unison.

I pulled an apologetic face and tried to walk around him, but his eyes were still glued to my face, filling with recognition.

"Phil?" he asked in amazement.

"Yes..." I said, desperately trying to work out how this so obviously local hobbit knew me. "Do we know each other?"

"I'm Mike," he shouted in my ear, trying to make himself heard over the crowd. "Mike Hagen!"[18]

The name rang some bells. "And?"

The guy scratched the back of his head, apparently embarrassed.

Mike "Björn" Hagen
Age: 29
Current status: Professional athlete

---

[18] Mike Hagen is the main character in Level Up: The Knockout, a followup to the Level Up series. Just like Phil Panfilov, Mike was selected to receive an augmented-reality interface. The only difference being, his interface adapted itself to Mike's most favorite type of game which was MMA fighting. Why MMA? Probably because Mike used to be so afraid of pain that he'd never picked a fight in his life...

Social status level: 6
Class: Fighter. Level: 18
Unmarried
Criminal record: Yes
Reputation: Amicality 15/60.
Interest: 81%.
Fear: 0%.
Mood: 75%.

Although his interest in me was suspiciously high, his Amicality reputation was somewhat reassuring. Could it be that... but no. We'd only just met each other, hadn't we?

I put my hand on his shoulder and continued toward Panchenko, using the guy as a shield. We must have looked like two old buddies chatting. A perfectly mundane situation.

"I know it's stupid," he said, cricking his neck the way boxers do. I could see he was pretty nervous. "I saw you in a dream. Shit! I'm sorry. But I did see you. And I can't say you were very friendly then!"

Despite his rambling, I managed to get the gist of it. Of course. Could he be a fellow interface user and Trial participant?

"Tell me," I said. "Do you think you're special? Can you see words and numbers?"

If he didn't, he wouldn't know what I was talking about.

"You too? No way!" he exclaimed. "That's why I saw you in a dream! But..."

"But what?"

"It was a funny place," he muttered so softly that I could barely hear him and then only thanks to my enhanced hearing. "There was some sort of orange forest there. The sky was purple. The trees were really strange. But that was a long time ago — a couple of months, I think — when I was still doing time."

I finally began to understand what he was getting at. According to Ilindi, some users could have dreams showing them whatever was going on with their replicas undergoing the Trial. Could Mike and I have somehow come across each other there?

But... a couple of months ago? Either he was capable of seeing into the future, or these were some more of those alien games with time.

"So what were we doing there?" I asked, my voice slightly more tense than necessary.

"Dunno," he said with a childlike grin. "You told me your name was Phil. I said I was Björn. But you kept calling me a worm for some reason..." he gave an embarrassed shrug. "You have a strange accent."

"I'm Russian. Do you know about the Trial?"

He stared at me, uncomprehending. Instead of answering my question, he stopped, brought his face close to mine and whispered conspiratorially,

"Your level's too low, Phil. You need to fight more."

"Pardon me?"

"All I'm saying that you need to fight more, bro."

"Fight whom?"

"Just fight."

"Why?"

"To level up! You're thirty-two years old, for Christ's sake, and you have less than twenty fights to your name! That's nothing! This way it'll take you ages to level up!"

He kept talking, describing various training routines and the right ways to level up particular fighting skills like kicks and punches.

His own interface was probably an analog of a fighting game like Street Fighter or Tekken. And somehow I didn't think it was Ilindi's idea.

"I'll tell you what, bro," I said, mirroring his manner, "even with my low level I just might beat you. Instead of fighting, you really should level up doing good things and being useful."

He burst out laughing. "You? Beat me? No way! I hate to disappoint you but starting next season, I'm a professional UFC fighter."

"And I'm my city's boxing champion," I parried, enjoying our banter, especially because by then, Panchenko was less than thirty feet away from me.

"Boxing? You're joking me! A chess champion for disabled seniors, more like. You're fit enough, but your fighting stats are ridiculous. You should have seen some people I had to fight!"

He trailed after me, telling me about jail and the "wooden ring" where he'd apparently had to fight three men to death. I wasn't really listening. My target was too close.

Panchenko was busy giving tongue to a bootylicious blonde whose T-shirt left nothing to imagination. He was only a few feet away.

Mike kept blabbering something about some Russian he'd shared his jail cell with.

I turned to him. "Listen, man."

The kid startled and promptly shut up.

"We definitely have a lot to discuss," I said. "We might even have a go in the ring, why not? I'm a bit busy at the moment, but next time…"

"Sure. I need to get going too. I should be getting ready," a happy grin lit up his face as he pointed at the ring.

"Rip 'em," I said, unable to suppress a smile. Strangely enough, I seemed to like him. He reminded me of Alik for some reason. I gave him a hug.

"I'm staying at a motel-"

"I'll find you," I gave him a slap on the back. "Now that we've met, I won't lose you again."

Provided I kept my interface. Provided he managed to keep his.

I didn't say that to him though. If it happened, neither of us would remember any of it.

I watched him jaunt away, stretching his muscles as he walked. His physical stats were very decent, his fighting skills going through the roof. The list of his skills was much more detailed than mine which listed vague abilities like "Boxing" or "Jogging". He had four different types of Punch to begin with, all levels 10 and above. I'd have loved to discuss a few things with him — provided I managed to lift the curse and keep the interface once the Trial was over.

I was almost upon my target when a giant thickset figure rose in front of me. A shaven-headed beefcake in a business suit stood cross-armed in my path, blocking my way to Panchenko.

"I need to go through," I said in reply to his silent question.

"You can't, sir. The entire row is sold out."

"To whom? To him?" I nodded at Panchenko, realizing that he'd noticed me too.

The gorilla ignored me but Panchenko didn't. He

gave me a contemptuous finger, then called the rest of his bodyguards — six in total, all burly as hell — while he, his female escorts and a couple more men in black hurried to leave.

I needed to touch him, that's all. It might not lift the curse but at least he'd lose his interface and I'd complete the quest. You never know, his losing the interface might in fact remove the curse, why not?

I stepped onto the next stair and leaped, trying to get past the bodyguard. My inadequate Agility did me a disservice as he swept my leg from under me.

I collapsed in a heap. All around me, spectators yelled at us for interfering with the show. Panchenko's bodyguards surrounded me and forced me out, showering me with blows and snapping expletives at me.

Arena attendants watched us in alarm, mouthing something into their walkie talkies. Panchenko's bodyguards took me to the gents and gave me an almighty whack over the head.

When I came round, someone was splashing water in my face.

"Phil?" Alex's voice demanded. "Who was it? What happened?"

Before replying, I opened the interface map. Nothing. No matter how many times I tried, it kept telling me that Panchenko didn't exist anymore. There was no such object on planet Earth.

Which meant I had less than seventy-two hours left to live.

CHAPTER

TWENTY-ONE

YOU DON'T SPEAK OF ETERNAL BLISS IN HELL

All men are mortal, he tells us, but some are more mortal than others.

Robert Sheckley, *Mindswap*

"BOSS, HOW ABOUT SOME NIGHTTIME ELITE MOBS? Eddie asked. "With your dinos, it must be a piece of cake!"

Ola grinned. "Our baby lizards will make short work of anyone and anything that tries to trespass! You can't even imagine the amount of resources they bring in!"

Jovanna shook her head. "The dinos are nothing. Phil used to farm nighttime mobs long before he got Rex."

"You mean the one that's now trying to munch his way through the fence?" Leti asked.

"No. That's Croc," Manu explained with the

air of an expert. "Rex, the name speaks for itself: Tyrannosaurus Rex!"

While my team explained to the newcomers all the intricate details of fighting elite mobs, I was trying to come up with a strategy considering the new developments.

Do you have any idea how to satisfy unlimited needs with limited resources? As a wannabe economist, I was supposed to know the answer to this question, considering this used to be my specialization of choice at uni during the rare breaks in partying and compulsive gaming. Still, I just didn't know how best to use the sudden windfall. I had lots of ideas but...

Our new team members had brought us more existence points — but also Strength points, increasing the amount of resources farmed by our harvesters by 40 pt. per hour. That brought the combined influx from all our bases to 4,000.

Tafari would have simply invested every point into buying new levels for himself. However, I had to keep in mind the kinds of surprises the Trial had to offer (like Nagash with his mind control). In my opinion, we should all level up equally. The only question remained, whether we should alternate our progress with the leveling of the main base?

Having posed the question to my team, I suggested we went to the command center and did all the calculations. After a brief discussion which met with no objection from anyone, we teleported to the main base in order to perform a few upgrades and decide what to do next. Firstly, we needed to upgrade the base to level 4 and level up the existing modules; secondly, we had to bring the clan members' levels to 10 which would allow them to choose specialization; and thirdly...

This "thirdly" was the most interesting bit. We now had 36 extra Charisma points, most of which we had courtesy of Letitia — or rather, of her stunning swarthy looks. She was one fiery lady, literally, who used plasma cutters in battle with frightful precision, but we still hadn't decided which ones of our fighting units would profit more from her Charisma points.

"Oh wow!" Leti enthused. "Teleportation!"

Eddie turned his head this way and that, flabbergasted. "Boss, this is incredible! We've just been over there and now we're over here! And your base, oh wow! Is it level three?"

"Not 'your base', son," Manu flashed him a pearly smile. "*Our* base. While we were wasting time up north, these guys over here didn't waste theirs!"

My dinos thumped away to guard the perimeter. Looking at them thoughtfully, I invited everyone into the shelter.

"Get in, guys. We need to decide how best to upgrade our little reptilian army."

I stood by the white rock of the command center, opened the catalog and made it visible to everyone.

"Now look," I said. "My reinforcement rings give us +3 to the fighting units level, that's level 6 which is the limit anyway. No good us trying to level up the module because it won't affect the units themselves."

"Phil, you promised," Jovanna cast me a sly

look, reminding me of her request to give her a personal dinosaur. Her gaze held a promise of something bigger than a prehistoric lizard, especially considering she stood slightly closer to me than the situation required.

"I remember," I replied. "So this is what I suggest. There're six of us. I suggest that each of us generates a reinforced mount for themselves. Tafari has a rhino. Zack gets about on a spider. We have Croc who can carry all of us but not if the group needs to split. A mount like that could become a clan member's personal protection in a fight, so I suggest you choose ones with good combat skills."

"Something fast, powerful and strong enough to carry a rider?" Ola asked. "That's a lion!"

"A bear is stronger than a lion," Jovanna replied with a condescending smirk. "And it's easier to ride, too."

'A grizzly bear?" Eddie suggested.

"Could be. Still, I doubt that our generation choices can be this detailed. In any case, a bear is a good idea," I smiled, thinking about Hummungus. "I like it."

The images in my head assisted me through my search through the catalogue. Very soon, I came across a black bear just like the one I wanted.

Still, my joy quickly turned sour:

Warning! The selected fighting unit does not correspond to the unit branch you chose!
Chosen branch: Dinosaurs
Liquidator, do you want to open the available Dinosaur species?

I heaved a sigh but I wasn't too upset, really. "Never mind. Let it be dinosaurs."

After another half-hour of heated discussion, we became the proud owners of six Utahraptors with +2 to Charisma each. My clan members who'd streamed out of the shelter to take a look at our new stallions, froze in shock.

"I'm not riding this," Leti shook her head. "No way!"

Eddie laughed. "Come on, Leti, look, it's so cute!" he said, trying to climb into the saddle.

The level-6 Utahraptor — a fifteen-foot, thousand-pound version of a Velociraptor covered in feathers — hissed, then emitted a guttural roar right in Eddie's face. He recoiled but stumbled and ended up on his ass.

"You're too quick off the mark. Let me distribute access first," I said, searching through the clan control interface and pinning the dinos' icons to their respective riders. 'That's it. Now you can control them. Try it."

After much cussing and falling out of saddles, Ola was finally the first to master his mount, closely followed by Manu. Together, they started playing chase around the shelter. The others soon followed suit, including Leti who seemed to have gotten a taste for it.

I spent thirty more fighting unit points on creating a Spinosaurus whose arrival completed our base's transformation into a Jurassic Park. The only difference being, our lizards weren't so eager to fight each other or hunt down those tasty crunchy humans.

While Rex, Tank and Croc were studying our reinforcements, more curious about the Spinosaurus than the Utahraptors, we too surveyed our new addition:

Spinosaurus
Name: Spine
Level 6
Close combat fighter
Phil's fighting unit.
Health points: 15000/15000.
Attack: 4200-6300.
Damage absorbed by armor: 60%.
Maximum travel speed: 20 mph.
Weight: 15 tons
Talents: Meat Grinder, Shredder, Smasher, Crusher

I stared at the amount of the resources saved. According to my plan, we had only a couple of minutes left to wait until it reached the required number.

"Clan, prepare yourselves! There's freebies coming!"

By my estimation, we should have enough to make level 10, all of us. We still had lots of things to sort out before nightfall. We had classes to distribute and practice; we also had to decide on the best tactics against mob packs, elite mobs and other clans.

We approached the dome, a cheerful noisy crowd. Then the sky turned dark.

The whole world froze as a giant global

system message took up my entire field of vision.

The first stage of the Trial has ended! Prepare for the decisive battles!

From this moment on, the surface area of each hexagon will be shrinking by 13% every 24 hours until the end of the Trial.

From this moment on, all neutral units will receive +1 level every 24 hours. All elite units will receive +2 levels and all location bosses, +3 levels every 24 hours until the end of the Trial.

From this moment on, the amount of existence resource points available will be shrinking by 13% every 24 hours until the end of the Trial.

The message lingered before my eyes for a long time while all of us remained motionless, as if the Trial had been paused. It looked like the program was waiting for each of us to take in the information.

When it finally happened and our group sprang back to life, I heard my own voice break the thunderous silence with a torrent of the choicest invective which could be summed up in a single word,

"Bummer!"

* * *

We spent all night repelling wave after wave of doughboys, duxio and two-headed odzi snakes seventy feet long, each wave more powerful than the one before it. Had it not been for the defense module we'd installed...

The previous evening all of us except Ola had voted for upgrading the main base. The African, however, tried to convince us to stop investing resources into the base because that might cause their deficit in the future and lead to a considerable level gap between our and other clans. To a point, I agreed with him, but that was exactly why we needed new modules, in order to strengthen our defense and lower the attack potential of any intruder.

In order to upgrade the base to level 4, I needed level 15. Luckily for us, resources still kept flowing in which allowed me to buy four new levels the moment we'd taken the decision to do so.

Level 15 came with a class upgrade and new level-2 talents:

Liquidator
Class level: 2
Level-2 talents:

Inconspicuousness. Allows the Liquidator to blend into the shadows, stealing up on his opponents and penetrating enemy hexagons.

Dodge. Increases the Liquidator's chances of dodging enemy blows for the duration of 10 sec.

In reality, Inconspicuousness proved to be

almost perfect invisibility which was disabled the moment I switched to combat mode. But Dodge made me virtually invulnerable for as long as it remained activated. At least Ola couldn't hit me with his spear no matter how hard he tried, even though I stood motionless in one spot. It was as if the very fabric of space had distorted, preventing his predatory spear tip from as much as touching me.

I'd invested all the characteristic points into Strength which in combination with the new talents made me a perfect killing machine. I had one hell of explosive damage, inconspicuousness, stun and teleportation behind the enemy's back. Now I could take on anybody one on one: Tafari or even Juma because, considering my achievement bonus, I already had 15 characteristic points more for the same number of levels than they had.

After that, we upgraded the base and built two more modules: one for regeneration and the other for defense. Now we had the highest possible number of modules available at this level.

The only thing we didn't have was the artifact module. We'd decided against building it because it sounded like an unnecessary waste of resources.

Base 1
Level: 4.
Number of modules: 8.
Rate of existence resource generation: 250 pt. per hour.
Total generation of existence resources from all bases: 8180 pt. per hour.
You may not upgrade until you reach level

20.

Cost to upgrade base to level 5: 62500 existence resource pt.

Now the fence had turned into a proper castle wall complete with moat and a ring of laser cannons lining the perimeter topped off with predatory barbed wire. The plasma turrets and the glaive throwers had all been upgraded while the Weakness debuff cast on any potential aggressors had now risen to 15% of all characteristics. Our main base had turned into a veritable Stalingrad for anyone who dared attack it.

The regeneration module could restore our heath instantly the moment we entered the shelter. It might sound simple, but you can't imagine how easy it had made night farming. And if you remembered that the defense module also strengthened the dome while allowing us to position turrets anywhere on the base and place watchtowers all over the hexagon, you knew why our investing into the base's development had been worth it. Even Ola had to admit it when he'd made it back to the dome half-dead with one life point to spare, then received an instant health refill.

By dawn, we'd already got our battle tactics choreographed to perfection. Each of us had already received a class.

That's when we finally came across the local boss.

Our group was busy smoking a new wave of doughboys, which was why we hadn't paid much attention to a humanoid figure about eight foot tall.

But we should have taken a closer look at the boss' stats — maybe then we would have taken him seriously instead of sending Rex to sort him out.

Bloodscar
Location Boss
Level 15
XP: 120,000

When Rex's teeth closed around him, the Bloodscar vanished into thin air, then reappeared upon Rex's shoulders and took a swing with his vibrating sword. Blood gushed everywhere. After another series of blows, the earth shuddered as the dinosaur crashed to the ground.

The healing staff I'd taken from Zack didn't help me one bit as the process of killing had been infinitely faster than that of the healing.

The reason I'd noticed it because I didn't even have to fight the doughboys: the team's staffs and Leti's plasma cutters were plenty. I teleported behind the boss' back and stunned him while giving the order to all the surviving dinos to attack.

Spine was the first to react. He grabbed Bloodscar — who was tiny in comparison — with his jaws and began chewing him up. The Utahraptors started springing up, trying to grab hold of his limbs protruding from Spine's mouth. Tank skidded past at full speed while Croc stood expectantly with his jaws open, waiting for the boss' body to drop directly into his throat.

Nothing of the kind happened.

Spine's mouth exploded from within. Croc

---

snapped his teeth, catching the Spinosaurus' smashed lower jaw. I hurried to pump Spine up with health points, hoping to heal him before he was disincarnated — but it was too late. The location boss paid no heed to any of his attackers until he'd completely destroyed the Spinosaurus and sent him to join Rex in their Dino heaven.

By then, my team — who were busy finishing off the last doughboy — had realized something was going wrong and that they hadn't yet received the order to switch target. Now was the time to do it.

"Clan! Get ready! Focus on the boss!"

Bloodscar chose me as his next victim. The moment he'd vanished in order to reappear next to me, I instinctively activated Dodge, then waited as he showered me with blows. Luckily, none of them landed as yet, so I waited the few seconds until the ability expired, then stunned him.

"Smoke the motherfucker!" Manu screamed, trying to take his head off, only to see his sword stuck in the creature's neck.

The team all joined in simultaneously. Ola, our shaman, got busy casting power curses; Manu, our warrior, bared his sword again, trying to hack the creature to bits while our archer Eddie and our hunter Jovanna were shooting from long range, their weapons the only difference between them because Eddie had a square-shaped fire-spewing gun a bit like those used by the jellyfish in the secret instance.

All in all, our class distribution tactic had proved quite balanced, resulting in a combined damage of thousands of points per second.

Within the first four seconds of the five-second Stun, we'd managed to strip him of almost three quarters of his life, but then Tank ruined everything. He's gotten so fed up with running to and fro that he let out a triumphant roar when he'd finally managed to impale the boss on his horn. Unable to stop due to his momentum, he trundled toward the fence, shaking his head as he ran so that the only damage the boss was now receiving came from Eddie and Jovanna's long-range attacks. Ola's spells couldn't reach him anymore. In the heat of the battle, Ola chased after Tank, hoping to get to the target.

The boss had less than 5% Health left when he'd wriggled around and buried his sword between Tank's eyes, then twisted it in the wound and hit him again.

Tank's legs buckled, his dead body sliding over the base's flooring.

Both Croc and our Utahraptor mounts who were just about to spring onto the boss, were once again left with no target. Bloodscar microported toward me again. We attacked each other in unison.

Damage received: 1740 (vibration from Bloodscar's sword).

Your body has been affected by damaging vibrations!
-50 pt./sec to Health.
Duration: 20 sec
HP: 460/2600.
You've dealt critical damage to Bloodscar!

(1150 pt.)

My field of vision flooded with scarlet. I couldn't tell whether it was blood or the system warning about my critically low health levels. Croc saved my bacon by attacking the boss who was too preoccupied by me to react promptly.

The multi-ton pressure from Croc's jaws squeezed the remaining health points out of the boss. I didn't see it though: with three bounds, I'd already found myself in the safety of the dome, regenerating.

Having restored, I returned to the battlefield. My team was excitedly exchanging their experiences. The second stage of the Trial had just shown us what we were up against. Enemies were becoming stronger, resources fewer, and the territories shrinking.

This way, in less than twenty-four hours we might have to face Tafari and Juma.

* * *

"So let's keep on farming," I summed up during our morning clan briefing. "We'll keep moving north and try to seize all the territories from the edge of the Trial grounds to Tafari's lands."

"And what's with that Zack guy?" Leti asked. "Why isn't he in the clan?"

"He doesn't want to. He wants to try and survive on his own."

She sniffed. "That's just stupid! He won't

survive!"

"I think he's playing for time," Eddie joined in. "I wonder if he's trying to get an achievement?"

"What kind of achievement? 'Survive without a clan and make the Top Ten'?" Jovanna said with a sarcastic grin. "There must be something else in it. I can bet anything you want that his plan is simple. He simply wants to join the winners. He can follow our progress in real time and track our ranking positions. So I wouldn't be surprised if he were already on his way to Juma even as we speak."

"To get to Juma, he first needs to cross dozens of Tafari's hexagons," I said. "He won't be up to it."

"Are you sure? We don't even know what class he is or what other surprises he might have on his ability list!"

If anything, anger made Jovanna even more beautiful, endowing her with rosy cheeks and a fiery gaze.

"I promised I'd give him twenty-four hours and it hasn't yet expired," I said. "I suggest we go and pay him a visit after midday, all of us. Let's go! Has everybody got a backpack?"

I waited for them to reply and gave a satisfied nod. We stuffed the extradimensional trunk with a few dozen Superb test subject uniforms which absorbed 60% of incoming damage, plus all the extra artifacts, including the powerful energy shield dropped by Bloodscar. In all honesty, we should have given it to Manu but it wasn't compatible with his two-handed sword and in any case, Manu could pull it out of the bag at a moment's notice.

We then used the research module to invest the rest of the available existence resources into damage.

"Let's get moving!"

All our dinos were now shuffling around by the dome, including our freshly-generated casualties. I just hoped they were still the same good old Rex, Tank and Spine.

We teleported to the outermost northern base. It took us only a few minutes on the Utahraptors' backs to get to the edge of the hexagon and dive into the gelatinous haze: me first, followed by Jovanna and all the others.

Crossing the haze felt like an eternity. Finally, I received a new message:

Warning! You're about to enter a special-purpose hexagon.

Special effects:

Maximum duration of stay: 60 minutes.

Exceeding 60 minutes will activate a permanent debuff, making the intruder lose 1 level per minute.

Oh wow. What if this was another trade hexagon?

I looked around but couldn't see anyone from my team, apart from Jovanna.

She raised a quizzical eyebrow. "Is it a virtual shop?"

"Exactly. Only I don't know yet what it has to offer us this time."

We stood surrounded by the familiar alleys

lined with the statues of champions. No sign of mobs anywhere.

"Where are all the others?" I asked Jovanna.

She didn't reply. Her eyes opened wide, as did mine.

No, there were no perks to be gained here this time.

On the eighth day of the Trial, the special-purpose hexagon is announced a punitive zone!

Special condition: no more than two trial subjects per each copy of the punitive hexagon. Only one of them is allowed to leave it.

A countdown timer appeared:

59:59... 59:58... 59:57...

While I was desperately trying to decide what to do next, Jovanna peeled off her bag and helmet, removed her bow, the pauldrons, the greaves and the elbow guards, took off her jacket and said with a smile,

"How lucky is that? We have a whole hour for ourselves!"

"Jovanna, don't you understand? You'll have to kill me!"

"Of course I understand. Which is why I want to simply enjoy it with you. Because you'll have to kill *me*," she peeled off her sweater and started unlacing her boots.

"Don't be stupid," I said. "You know very well you can't question a clan leader's orders. We have no time to waste. Just make it quick. And don't forget to collect my gea-"

She removed her pants. Now all she had on was her underwear. She pressed her finger to my lips, then shut me up with a kiss.

Sweet as her lips were, I forced myself away. "Jo, please!"

"It's Ms. Jovanna Savich, Phil. If you make it, I want you to find me in Belgrade — or at the tournament in Dubai. Remember my number..."

She dictated me her cell number and demanded I repeat it.

My heart forced me to continue arguing, trying to convince her of the sheer folly of her idea, even though my mind had already realized and accepted the terrible truth of it all.

Having said that.... I needed to check it first...

With a crackling of static, I was thrown back, away from the gelatinous haze.

Liquidator, this is your first warning!
You cannot leave the punitive hexagon until you exterminate the hunter Jovanna!
Each of your subsequent attempts to leave the hexagon will strip you of 1 level!
Put more fire under the feet of your enemy Jovanna, Liquidator!

Jovanna threw her head back and looked quizzically at me.

I shook my head. "It won't let me leave. I might need to kill myself."

"But what if your death destroys all the bases

we've gained? The dinos will disappear! What's gonna happen with the other guys? If you get knocked out, our clan will lose everything. All of us — each and every one! — will lose: me, Ola, Manu, Even Eddie and Leti... We're gonna lose everything we've achieved on earth with our interfaces! I'm not even mentioning Nick and Ilindi's plan..."

"Bullshit! We haven't lost yet! If push comes to shove, you can always join Tafari's clan..."

"Did you hear what he does with girls? Wake up, Phil! The Trial is nearly over! No one's gonna accept us because they think they're gonna win, anyway! And you're gonna die a final death..."

"I don't care! Even if I die temporarily, we're still gonna lose the dinos and all the bases! At this point, an extra life is no use to me, don't you understand?"

"You'll find a way out, I'm sure," she knelt in front of me and began undoing my pants belt.

I stepped back, unwilling to give in, even under these conditions.

"And just in case I forget you..." she said. "I fell for you the moment I saw you, so you have my permission to get to know me IRL. Don't worry, I won't play hard to get. There's no one waiting for me there."

"Jovanna!"

"Shut up."

"Dammit, Jo..." I threw my head back, unable to suppress a groan.

* * *

In the end, I did try. I ordered my girl to kill me. All she did she pressed her body against mine as the timer completed the disincarnation countdown. Her refusal to obey my orders dissolved her body into a cloud of glittering dust in my hands as she died the final death, vanishing into thin air.

I don't think I'd ever felt so low. Not when Yanna had left me; not even when I'd split up with Vicky.

Although I'd only known Jovanna for less than a week, losing her had formed a hole in my soul the size of the Grand Canyon. Whether it was love, or infatuation, of even simple camaraderie — what difference did it make? The only thing that mattered was the amount of battles we'd fought shoulder to shoulder, trusting each other with our lives. Had she not been so generous during our first meeting, I might have become the first player to be eliminated from the Trial.

And even though she hadn't really shown her true feelings over those few days, everything she must have felt for me had now condensed into her ultimate tenderness and the few passionate words of love she'd shared with me during this brief hour.

A few seconds before the end of the countdown, I left the special-purpose hexagon in the same place where I'd entered it.

My team was already there, all present and correct. They were smiling but my face had turned to stone. All I wanted to do was rip both Tafari and

Juma apart in order to end this fucking circus.

"Phil!" Ola breathed a sigh of relief. "We were worried you might sacrifice yourself to Jovanna."

"I didn't for one moment doubt she'd make the right choice," Manu said.

"You seem to forget this was her last life."

Their smiles faded as they averted their stares. I had to speak first.

"How did you do?"

"I killed Manu," Ola said.

"I killed Eddie," Leti said. "He still had another life and I'm on my last one."

"Eddie?" I asked.

"It's okay, boss. We didn't waste time. We made it quick," Eddie gave me a wink, nodding at the blushing Leti. "I resurrected nearby and hurried to get back here."

"Me too," Manu grinned. "Ola isn't my type, though. That's probably why he impaled me on his spear first, then cast a bunch of curses on me. It wasn't the best death, even if I say so myself."

"So what's the outcome?" I asked. "You still have one life each, don't you?"

Eddie shrugged. "Sounds like it. But Leti, Ola and I can still farm more spirit crystals. And Ola now has more of them than any of us."

"Ah, before I forget," I rummaged through my backpack in search of Nagash's pauldrons. "Ola, put these on."

While he was clasping the pauldrons on, the others sighed, mourning Jovanna.

Manu gave me a sympathetic slap on the shoulder. "The girl had the hots for you."

"I already gathered that. I'm gonna find her IRL."

"That's the right attitude!" the ex-drug baron exclaimed. "As my grandmother used to say — and she was a very wise woman, I assure you — absence for love is like fanning a flame: it'll extinguish a weak love and strengthen a strong one. Forget your grief, amigo!"

"You see, *amigo*," I replied, "I'm not even sure she'll remember me at all. And there's also a high probability of me not remembering her, either. So my grief, as you so eloquently called it, is in fact a grief for something that might not even transpire."

Leti wiped away a betraying tear and walked over to me. She gave me a hug, pressing me to her chest, then gave me a tender peck just by my ear.

"All this is very touching but what are we gonna do now?" Ola shook his spear in anger. "Should we attack that wretched executioner, may he be cursed by all the spirits of Nigeria?"

"What do you suggest, a guerrilla war?" Manu asked. "We're not yet ready to face an open confrontation."

"Why not? I think we are," I opened the rankings and checked the levels of the surviving Trial participants. "Judging by the table, Tafari has only one group of five fighters leveled up to 15. They might be his personal bodyguards. All the other fighters, both his and Juma's are only level 10. By the end of the day, all of you will be level 15. And don't forget our dinosaur-"

An alarm sounded, stopping me in mid-sentence.

Test subject! An enemy has infiltrated your territory! Base 26 is under threat of capture!

The edges of my field of vision flashed crimson. A chill ran down my spine. I could smell the all-pervasive stench of a big fire burning as the alarm had affected all of my senses.

"Shit!" Ediie shouted.

The others couldn't have agreed more.

"Back to the base, quick!" I commanded, leaping onto my Raptor's back. "Mount up!"

A few heartbeats later, the alarm sounded again, followed by an avalanche of alerts,

Test subject! An enemy has infiltrated your territory! Base 19 is under threat of capture!

Test subject! An enemy has infiltrated your territory! Base 22 is under threat of capture!

Test subject! An enemy has infiltrated your territory! Base 25 is under threat of capture!

When we reached the base, I didn't know what to do anymore. Thirteen of our hexagons were being attacked simultaneously. With all the best of intentions, we just couldn't be everywhere at once.

Chapter
Twenty-Two

For the Future's Sake

Congressman Sam Albert:
We knew that we had to monitor our
enemies. We've also come to realize that
we need to monitor the people who are
monitoring them...
Carla Dean:
Well who's gonna monitor the monitors of
the monitors?

Enemy of the State

AFTER PANCHENKO'S DISAPPEARANCE, THE AGENTS
took me to a scruffy Korean restaurant. The shock
of losing all hope of ever lifting the curse had hit me
so badly I couldn't even hear what Alex was saying.
He kept telling me that time was an issue and the
people who were waiting for us were losing their
patience.

I didn't argue. I just climbed into the car and
stared indifferently out the window.

As we drove, my resolve grew. I had to do as much as possible in the time I had left, and this meeting was going to become the cornerstone of my plans. Also, you never know, they might help me find Panchenko, why not?

My hopes thus boosted, by the end of the trip I was already fidgeting in my seat in impatience, constantly checking whether Panchenko had reappeared on the map.

I also kept checking Haqqani's whereabouts. Judging by my interface, they hadn't arrested him yet. The terrorist was still in Saudi Arabia albeit in a different part of the country. He seemed to be perfectly alive and as yet in good health, judging by his pulse rate.

He had to be my first target. Once the Americans had him — provided everything went well — I might be able to offer more to them, thus launching my global plan.

Alex stayed in the car while Laura took me inside the Korean restaurant and led me to a table on the second floor. There, two men were already waiting for us: one Norman Doherty, a slender young man in a shirt with rolled-up sleeves, and a Hector Sanchez, a portly Hispanic gentleman about forty years of age wearing a pair of frameless glasses.

Surprisingly, both gave me their real names. Their social status levels were quite impressive, too: both were 10-plus. Strangely enough, Doherty's was much higher than Sanchez' despite him being the younger of the two.

"If you excuse my indiscretion, Phil," Doherty flashed me a guilty smile. "Do you mind me asking?"

Laura was doing the translating, which gave me a bit of leeway to think over my answers. "A bit" being the operative word because she did it very professionally, inserting her translations into the natural pauses in our conversation.

"Absolutely," I replied, chewing on a slice of spicy marinated beef which Doherty was cooking on a small hot plate mounted on the restaurant table. All of a sudden, I was terribly hungry. "Fire away."

He turned a slice of pork over, then produced a pair of scissors and began slicing it. Once he was finished, he finally asked,

"How is it possible that you managed to pinpoint Haqqani's location so accurately from your location in a small Russian town? We checked it out and it was correct to the nearest couple of feet. You have no links to your country's secret services. You've never left Russia at all. You have no contacts whatsoever who might have divulged this information. Do you have any reasonable explanation for all this?"

"Not a reasonable one, no," I raised a conciliatory hand, almost dropping the slice of meat I was holding with chopsticks. "You might not believe me, but I have occasional visions."

Sanchez sat up. "How long ago did they start?"

"Not too long ago. In May, I think."

I chose to be perfectly honest, not knowing exactly how much they'd already found out about me. Major Igorevsky might have mentioned me in a conversation, you never know.

"I was watching a local TV channel when they

announced that a young girl had gone missing. Sorry..."

I popped another slice of meat into my mouth and got busy chewing while inconspicuously checking their stats. Their Interest in me was going through the roof.

"And? What happened?" Doherty asked cajolingly. "Did you sense something?"

"I saw a mental image of the girl, then I knew straight away where she was. It wasn't just her location on the map but even the actual address of the house she was being kept in. It was as if I'd been there myself."

"So what did you do?"

"I called the number given in the announcement. That was crazy, I agree. I wasn't really sure whether I knew it or if it was just a figment of my imagination. I just couldn't tell."

"I see," Doherty said. "So did they find the girl?"

"That's what amazes me the most. Yes, they did find her."

"Incredible," Doherty exchanged looks with Sanchez who nodded.

"Did it happen again?" Doherty asked his next question.

"I was on the Internet and I just came across this site, Rewards for Justice. I was looking through it when I saw Haqqani and the same thing happened. I clearly saw the village in Saudi Arabia and the house where he lived. And more importantly, when I opened Google Maps, I knew immediately which village and which house it was.

That's how I got its address and coordinates, so I just submitted them using the form on the site."

"What prompted you to do so?" Sanchez butted in.

"I just thought that sending this information over to you — not to you personally but to the people who run that site — might be the only way of checking if I was right. At that moment, I thought that if there was a thousandth of a chance of me having this ability, it might be worth it. Terrorists shouldn't walk around with impunity. Did you arrest him?"

"He got away, the bastard!" Doherty slammed his fist on the table, losing — or pretending he was losing — his self-control.

"In this case, why am I here?"

"Maybe you could try it again?" he asked, hopeful. "Only if you want to..."

In the dimmed light, Sanchez' face had taken on an almost-demonic expression. He raised his hand, stopping his partner, then brought his finger up to his ear and listened to his earpiece.

I used the pause to finish my makeshift "sandwich": a juicy slice of meat with marinated garlic wrapped in a crispy salad leaf.

"On behalf of the Government of the United States of America, I'm authorized to ask you to cooperate with us," Sanchez finally said.

"Why do you think I can be of any help to you?"

"Because you're not the first one. A whole number of US citizens have had similar visions within this last year, which continue to occur. These visions can take on different forms, but the principle is the same: all these people suddenly experienced a range of abilities which can't be rationally explained. Some of them could tell the chemical composition of any substance with incredible accuracy, including alloys and liquid solutions. Others were able to tell anyone's name, age and the names of their children just by looking at the person. There was a science teacher from Houston, a puny little guy who'd never carried anything heavier than his briefcase, who took up powerlifting. Within three months, he became state champion. But you know the funny thing about it?"

With great difficulty, I managed to retain my composure. One would think that linking these facts together would be quite difficult, but still they'd managed it.

I stared at Doherty's flabbergasted face. He seemed to be hearing it for the first time, too. He was the one interested in catching the terrorist, first and foremost. Sanchez' goals were much more far-reaching.

I waited for Laura to finish translating. "No, what is it?"

"All of them seemed to lose their abilities all of a sudden once we started working with them. It seemed to happen in waves. We worked with four such "special cases" as we called them, and they all lost their abilities at the same time on the same day."

Aha. It looked like none of them had passed the Trial.

"The same month, new special cases began to

appear," Sanchez continued. "We couldn't find any logical connection between them. They all came from different states and different backgrounds; there was no consistency in their age, race, gender or religion. Just a random selection of people. One of them was a street bum who inexplicably became a millionaire. Unfortunately, we found out about him too late. By the time we'd contacted him, he was homeless again."

"I've no idea what any of this has to do with me," I said, literally sensing my Deception skill rising. "I have no special abilities whatsoever. There just have to be some real psychics among all the would-be impostors who claim they can do this sort of thing."

"Oh no. We're not talking psychics here. What we're talking about are people with an augmented-reality interface from the future. People like you, Mr. Panfilov."

The chopsticks with which I was about to grab some *kimchi*[19] froze in mid-air. "I don't understand."

"Chill out, man," Sanchez raised his hands in a conciliatory gesture. "You probably didn't notice, but you do tend to focus on things above other people's heads. Alex was the first to notice it in Moscow airport, which confirmed our suspicions. Is this how you access information and such?"

"Wait a sec," ignoring the question, I tried to get to my feet. No one was trying to stop me.

"Please sit down," Sanchez said. "Did I

---

[19] Kimchi: Korean dish of fermented vegetables

already mention that you're not the first person we've come into contact with? We don't repeat our mistakes."

"What's that supposed to mean?"

"Our analysts have studied you very well already, so let me be honest with you: we're not going to force you into anything. For some reason, special cases don't perform well under pressure. As for your psychological profile, you absolutely reject any form of coercion but you can do much more whenever you're convinced you're doing a good deed. Or a great job. That's the name of your company, isn't it?"

He waited for me to nod, then continued to smugly reassure me,

"Phil, you're free to go any time you want. The special services guys posted around the building will let you through. If you really want to, you can even leave the country. But first... first I'd like you to listen to our cooperation proposal."

My Lie Detection enveloped me in warmth. He wasn't lying. I relaxed a little. If all the cards were on the table, it made it a lot easier. They may think they had me over a barrel, but I knew it wasn't so. If push came to shove, I could always activate Stealth and Vanish.

"I have no intention of corroborating your theories," I said. "Just tell me how you envision our cooperation."

"We have very little time, Mr. Panfilov. If your interface was installed in May, we have virtually no time left at all. Four months is the limit after which all special cases lose their abilities."

"And you know why?"

"No," Sanchez replied in all honesty. "None of the special cases can remember what happened to them. They can't recollect having any abilities or an augmented-reality interface. You have any theories in this respect?"

"I might, but we'll talk about it later. Haqqani aside, what exactly do you want from me?"

"Your ability to locate people is of great interest to us. What would you like in return? American citizenship? Money? Something else?"

"You're dead right there," I said. "I need something else. The way things are now, I can lose my search ability at any moment. What's more," I paused, wondering how I was going to explain the curse to them. In the end, I decided to simply present them with the facts without naming any exact dates to make sure they didn't do anything stupid. "I have very little left to live."

Sanchez frowned, listening to the translation. "How little?'

"Less than you think. But... That's if you don't help me to locate a certain person. Even if you do find him, it doesn't guarantee my, er, recovery, which is why, apart from that, I'd like to create a fund to which you'd transfer the reward money for every terrorist you catch."

"First things first. What's the nature of your, er, problem? Because if it's some health condition, our doctors are the bes-"

"I don't think so. There's nothing medicine can do. There's only one person who could help me but ironically, he's the only person I can't find. You shouldn't be surprised. He's also a special case like myself. And somehow he's got this ability to hide himself from me."

"What do you know about him?"

"Very little. His name is Konstantin Panchenko. He arrived in the USA three days ago — possibly, under an assumed name. There're no pictures of him available online. There might be some left in HR archives," I took a napkin and jotted down the names of the companies Panchenko used to work for and pushed it across the table to Sanchez. "This morning, he was staying in Bellagio but he might have already checked out. You can check their camera footage if you wish," I gave them Panchenko's description.

Sanchez dictated the information into his microphone and nodded. "We'll find him. And as for reward money... how many people do you think you could find in the time you have left?"

"I can find anyone you're looking for. All the criminals, drug barons, serial killers — and terrorists, of course."

"How many — five? Ten? A hundred?"

"Definitely over a hundred," I replied, doing a mental estimation of my Spirit reserves and their restoration times.

"Please don't take offense," Sanchez rose from the table. "We're talking a lot of money. A decision like this can only be made by President. And for that reason... Would you mind providing us with a little demonstration?"

"Yes, please. Find Haqqani for us," Doherty blurted out, rising from his seat. "Where's that scumbag?"

Laura hurried to translate but I didn't need it. I heaved a sigh and took a leap of faith.

Even if they locked me up and vivisected me like a lab rat, even if I never saw sunlight again, at least I'd die happy knowing I'd rid the world of a couple hundred murderers, rapists and those bastards who blew up women, children and old people.

Also, there was a positive side to all this. I'd been thinking about it since last night — and now that vague hunch had finally taken the shape of a finished idea.

The fact that these agents knew everything about the interface users, including all the events that had happened in the time of their activity, could only mean one thing. Both Khphor and all the others had been lying. True, if you failed the Trial you lost your interface. You wouldn't even remember your ever having it. But everything you'd done remained intact. They didn't rewind time back to the day of your receiving the interface. Which meant that even if Phil 2 failed the Trial on Pibellau, my physical life might go on.

I rose and said in my halting English, staring Sanchez in the eye,

"I'm not gonna charge you for him. Consider it a goodwill gesture. Currently, Jabar Aziz Haqqani is smoking on the balcony of his hotel room in the Mövenpick Hotel in Jedda, Saudi Arabia."

The next moment, their deceptive cool faded away, replaced by a flurry of activity. Doherty dashed out of the room without so much as a by-your-leave. Waving his hands in excitement, Sanchez began blurting something into the microphone attached to his shirt collar.

All of a sudden, the room was seething with men in black.

I sat down and started eating the slightly burned meat, not knowing where my next meal might be coming from.

Then I received 35,000 XP for performing a socially meaningful action. Which had brought me to level 23.

My body spasmed with ecstasy. Failing to conceal my state, I collapsed to the floor, chair and all, hitting the back of my head nice and hard in the process.

The last thing I heard was Sanchez' voice booming,

"Get a doctor!"

* * *

Alex and Laura, my indefatigable escorts, brought me to a large sunlit hotel lobby bustling with activity. Waiters rushed past, serving drinks to the guests lounging in the lobby bar. A long line of people snaked toward the reception.

Laura took my passport and left. By the time Alex and I got ourselves seated on the couches, she was already back with my room key.

"Ninth floor," she said, handing it to me.

"Let's go," Alex said. "I suggest you go to your room now, get yourself cleaned up and go to bed. We have a busy day tomorrow. See you at breakfast at seven a.m."

I cast a longing look at the pool behind a stained-glass window and all the happy people around it.

"You have plenty of time for this," Alex reassured me. "Business before pleasure, as we say."

They took me to my room. I locked the door, then gave the place a rather amateurish check for any surveillance devices. Predictably, I found nothing — which didn't mean, of course, that they'd left me unsupervised.

I peeled off the backpack and headed for the shower to wash away the road dust. I had a shave and brushed my teeth; even the back of my head didn't hurt anymore.

I changed into some fresh clothes, then remembered my Great Job Agency and decided to give Veronica a call.

"How was your flight?" her high voice reverberated in the phone. "Tell me!"

"Nothing to tell, really. I've just arrived in the hotel. How's recruiting going?"

Veronica told me that they were already busy working with Valiadis' companies. Seeing as they didn't have enough people, they hurried to hire new ones from the list I'd left them. Before leaving for the airport, I'd taken a quick stock of the workload associated with J-Mart and its affiliates. Together with Kesha and Veronica, I did an estimate of the kinds of workers we'd need, then hand-picked them with the help of my interface filters. The main thing

I wanted was for the work to continue even without me and my unconventional skills. It stands to reason that the team's Synergy reading was the decisive factor which left me feeling good about the future of Great Job regardless of whether I was dead, alive, or stripped of my interface.

Having finished talking to Veronica, I noticed a little icon flashing an exclamation mark. I focused on it.

Martha materialized next to me.

"What is it, Marth?"

"I've got a message from the other Phil. He's asking you to contact your supervisor ASAP. He needs some advice, quote:

Ilindi, should I go for it or are there other options available?

"Now what does that mean?"

"That's all I received. Without knowing the context, we can't jump to conclusions."

"Got it. I'll get to it ASAP."

To save on my Spirit reserves, I unsummoned Martha, then contacted Valiadis. My phone call found him somewhere in Europe.

"It's five a.m. here, Phil, so it had better be important."

"I'm sorry, sir. I need to find Ilindi. The other Phil on Pibellau needs her advice."

"She's right here. Don't hang up."

My brain exploded with jealousy. Are you serious, Phil?

I listened to him scramble out of bed and

shuffle away somewhere. I heard the sound of a key turning in the door, followed by more shuffling along something soft — a carpet? A knock on a door. Phew.

I heard stifled voices. The phone rustled.

"Phil, speak up," Ilindi's clear voice said.

I communicated her the message. Then she must have covered the microphone with her hand as she conferred with Valiadis as I couldn't hear a thing. Finally, they stopped.

When Ilindi spoke, her voice was soft and tired — unsure even.

"Let me be honest with you. It looks like the "socially meaningful" like yourself have failed the Trial. Most of the Trial field has been seized by the bad guys. So my answer is yes, he should go for it. Let him risk it all."

"I'll tell him. Is it so bad?"

"The next wave of Trial participants will be the last," she sounded noncommittal but I knew she was seething inside. "Valiadis is our only man among the winners. And it doesn't look as if this number is going to change. The union of humans and Rhoa wasn't meant to happen. The probability of our races failing the Diagnostics is close to a 100%."

"I don't know what to say."

"You don't have to say anything, Phil. I was very happy to meet you. Still, it has all been for nothing. I failed to prepare you properly. That's all. Good-bye."

The beeping of the phone sounded like the final countdown. Once I failed the Trial on Pibellau, for me it would be over, even if I managed to somehow find Panchenko and force him to lift the curse. So I really had to spend these last few hours — or days maybe — like they were-

Like they were what? My last ones?

Exactly.

* * *

I met the pale rosy dawn swimming in the hotel pool. When I'd left the room, I'd discovered Alex Tomasik waiting by the door, later joined by Laura.

On my way back upstairs to my room, Alex gave me thumbs-up and mouthed,

"We got him!"

"Great," I said, unsurprised. The XP I'd received was a sure sign they were going to catch Haqqani. I'd already invested some of the available characteristic points, bringing both Charisma and Luck to 20. I'd also managed to raise Agility twice in the course of the last night, even though it meant I'd had to wake up, devour all the snacks and packets of nuts found in the room, and restart the process.

When I saw Sanchez the next morning, he confirmed that the President had given us the go-ahead. Our work scheme was as follows: I was supposed to provide them with the target's coordinates which they then checked and either arrested or eliminated the target, then transferred the bounty money to my account, the exact amount depending on the target's category on the list.

Considering the worldwide scope of my future charity plans ensuring a better future for all humanity, Kira would need a lot of money. Really a lot. Which was why, having finished talking to Sanchez, I headed straight for a financial advisor's office. The backpack I had on me now contained four wads of ten thousand dollars each: the "pocket money" Sanchez had issued me together with the targets file.

"This is for you," he'd said, handing me the plastic bag with the money. "In a place like Vegas, you'll need it."

I didn't play hard to get. Financial advisors' services didn't come cheap.

The man in front of me didn't resemble our dear Mr. Katz in the slightest. With his unblinking stare, the burly shoulders of a retired footballer and a narrow forehead above the heavy eyebrows, he was the opposite of a stereotypical bookkeeper. His name was Gary Grant. According to my interface, he was the best person for my purposes.

Judging by his office, he wasn't doing too well. His business suit was neat and pressed, but you could tell it was bought at least ten years ago. He didn't seem to have too many clients, either, which probably explained why he'd readily agreed to come to his office this Sunday morning.

"I understand," he nodded energetically and blinked for what seemed to be the first time during our meeting. "What you need is to open a private equity fund with a sole founding member. The problem is, you can't do it in the USA in the given time frame. We could, I suppose, open an offshore fund somewhere in the British Virgin Islands or in Panama. There's also Bermuda and Mauritius.

But…"

"Excuse me," I raised my hand, trying to stop him, but he pretended he didn't see it.

"I could make out a full list of all available options and conditions in the course of the day. But you need to know that in today's climate, you might not pass the licensing process. In any case, our choice will be highly limited. I wouldn't be surprised if they rejected your application already at the review stage. All the paperwork has to be faultless: cover letters as well as referrals from influential citizens or companies domiciliated in the country of your choice. The contract…"

"My sister will be the fund's founding member. I'll put you in contact with her and leave it to you two. All I need now is the bank account details where to send the monies to. And as far as the licensing is concerned, how would you like to become the company's manager? I have my reasons to trust you. And as for the choice of the right location, I'll leave that to you."

He paused, looking at me, then nodded. "Very well. What sums are we talking about?"

I gave him an approximation.

He whistled softly. "A manager's fee is usually 1% of the fund's annual net assets."

"Sounds good. Get the paperwork ready."

I had no reason to mistrust my interface — and according to its readings, Gary was a trustworthy guy whose Synergy with Kira was going through the roof.

I rummaged through my backpack and produced three wads of dollars. "Will this be enough to get this show on the road?"

"Plenty. I could use the rest to-"

"Just keep it. Thanks, Gary," I proffered my hand. "I should buy a new suit if I were you. Your life has just changed."

He gave me a long look and shook my hand, then spoke without letting it go,

"The president of a Panama bank happens to be a uni classmate of mine. I'm gonna talk to him about some client with very special needs. You sure you spelled out the number correctly? There's only one letter difference between a million and a billion."

"A ten-digit number, Gary. I mean it."

"I got you. I'll see what I can do."

Today, I was going to clear Sanchez' entire category-A list: the names of the people who constituted the biggest threat to the United States. The list was paid at $25,000,000 a name. There were also categories B, C and D, listing lower-ranking terrorists and criminals as well as major fraudsters wanted by Interpol. There, the prices were progressively lower.

In any case, I wasn't going to wait. I intended to use the Universal Infospace to collect all the data on the names from the A List, then do my best to locate as many names as I could from all the other lists. I'd put them all into a chart and upload it to a cloud, then provide Sanchez with access to it once the time was right.

Alex Tomasik was waiting for me in the financial advisor's reception. He hadn't stopped trailing me for one second. On seeing me, he rose and nodded at the elevators. Together we walked out of the building.

Alex was in a sorry state. His eyes had turned red. He was yawning his head off.

"Do you ever sleep, man?" I asked.

"I slept for ten minutes as I waited for you," he replied with a poker face.

'Is the CIA so low on staff?"

"There's nothing wrong with our staff. It's just that this op is classified."

"You mean, I'm classified?"

With a lopsided grin, he entered the elevator packed with people. I decided to give him a run for his money and stayed outside, watching him elbow his way back past all the passengers. Only then did I step in. The doors slid close behind me.

As we rode down, we didn't say a word. Alex kept pinning me with his glare, daring me to a staring contest while I studied the wall over his head.

As soon as we left the elevator, he started chewing my ears, explaining to me the dangers of such behavior.

"As you Russians say, rumors make the world go round. We're not the only people looking for special cases like you. You know what I mean?"

"Sure. It won't happen again."

"Then off to the car you go!"

The same minibus took us to the hotel. We rode in silence: Alex sleeping, Laura chewing gum and staring at her iPad, the driver driving. And I... I was waiting to hear from Kira.

Once back in the hotel, Alex and I walked right into Sanchez. He gave us a barely perceptible nod, rose from the couch and took another elevator to my floor, pretending he had nothing to do with us. He joined us when we were already in my hotel room.

"Do you have the bank account details?" he asked me.

"Not yet. My fund manager Gary Grant will contact you within the next few days and will give you the account number."

"So what are we supposed to do with your payments until then?"

I suppressed a smile. "Are you so sure you'll get what you're paying for? Are you happy with my little demonstration?"

"Some people tend to think it's some sort of trick, or a coincidence, or even a prearranged plot. Which is why your next targets will have nothing in common."

"Very well. In that case..." I paused, thinking.

It didn't look as if I had much choice. I didn't want to wait any longer.

"You can transfer the payments to my sister's account," I said. "I'm gonna give you the details in a moment."

"Accepted. As for your request to locate your 'old friend', we're still looking. Only yesterday he was indeed staying at Bellagio but he didn't return to his room in the evening. Don't worry, we'll find him. I have to ask you once again to refrain from leaving the hotel on your own. Alex or Laura should accompany you at all times," he spoke dryly and to the point. "What about our next targets?"

"I was waiting for you in order to resume the

search."

"Why? I thought you'd already done it! Our people are waiting..."

"Exactly. Your people are waiting. Unfortunately, there're people everywhere on the globe and they have a very bad tendency to be constantly on the move. Three hours ago, your Fazlullah was lurking in one particular location in the mountains — but now he's in a totally different canyon. Here, mark his coordinates down."

"Start dictating, man!"

The new targets were three in total, one of them the leader of a Pakistani terrorist group responsible for one of the bloodiest terrorist acts in recent history. The Peshawar school massacre had taken lives of 148 people, most of them children.

Instead of jotting the coordinates down, Sanchez repeated them after me. With every number I uttered, I could see the giant secret-service machine kicking into motion, meting out retribution to the monsters who'd lost the right to be called human. Those who blow up little children have no place on this earth.

Having finished dictating the numbers, Sanchez opened the mini bar and produced a few cans of beer. I slumped into a soft chair — just in time as another wave of euphoria flooded over me, awarding me a new level. I was still generously rewarded per each criminal located, even though the amount of XP had dropped to one-third of what it used to be.

I used the pause to invest both characteristic points into Intellect, with a focus of English

Language Skills (one of creative abilities offering +5 levels to the chosen skill)

My head exploded with pain. My vision darkened. The world blinked twice.

To my amazement, I realized I could understand everything that was happening on TV. My English skills seemed to be better than Tomasik's now. I actually seemed to know English better now than my native Russian.

Or at least that's what the interface was trying to tell me:

English Language Skills: (15)
Russian Language Skills: (7)

Tomasik had just walked out the door, only to return with Laura in tow.

"Isn't it a bit early?" she asked, nodding at the bottles.

"We'll soon find out," Sanchez replied. "Let's hear from Doherty first. In the meantime, let's have a drink."

He opened a can and offered it to me. I shook my head, rose, opened the fridge and took out a Pepsi. Seeing as I wasn't drinking, I might just as well celebrate with a soft drink. Today, the world was going to rid itself of three bastards — I knew it because my interface had kicked in the moment Sanchez stopped dictating their coordinates into his microphone.

We had to wait another hour.

"Yes! Yes! Yes to all three!" Sanchez yelled, throwing his hands triumphantly in the air, which was so unlike him.

Alex and Laura joined in. We all raised our hands, toasting with beer.

Once the merriment had subsided, Sanchez walked over to me and said matter-of-factly,

"All targets successfully eliminated. We've just sent seventy-five million to your sister's account."

He slapped my shoulder. Me, I was busy thinking how I was going to explain it to Kira. This wasn't what she'd expected when I'd asked her permission to use her account to "transfer a bit of money for me, do you mind?".

That wasn't even counting the money which was about to drop into her fund's account.

Chapter Twenty-Three

When Something Looks a Little Too Good

Funny how a little 'Holy shit! Somebody's gonna die!' lights a fire under everybody's ass!

Negan, *The Walking Dead*

THE WORST THING PEOPLE CAN DO IN ALL THOSE horror movies and YA thrillers is split up. I mean, there's a serial killer with a chainsaw prowling about — but no, instead of sticking together, the young heroes simply have to part company.

Which was exactly why I decided not to split my group. It takes an hour to seize a hexagon, and I doubted very much that Tafari had enough men to be able to dispatch a combat group of five every time that happened.

"Remember the plan? Let's do it! Are you ready?"

Everybody nodded. Leti nervously licked her lips.

Moved by instinct, I slapped her shoulder. "It's gonna be okay. Let's do it!"

We ported to Base 26, the popping of our teleports reminiscent of gunfire as the arrival of our many-ton dinosaurs displaced the air in powerful circular gusts, like giant boulders thrown into the water.

This hexagon was the first on our list. Still, no one came out to oppose us. For a several long heartbeats, we froze back to back, our eyes searching for enemy but found none. The base was empty.

"Ola, the shelter!"

He nodded.

In less than a minute, he was already back, shaking his head. "There's no one inside!"

"So it's either he hasn't made it here yet or... Fall in!"

Moving in combat formation, we checked every hexagon reported to be attacked but were met with the same silence everywhere. Although we'd already stopped receiving new attack alerts, their logic was becoming quite clear: all the fake attacks had been reported along the division line separating our lands from Tafari's.

Test subject! An enemy has infiltrated your territory! Base 14 is under threat of capture!

"Phil!" Ola shouted.

"It's all right, keep your hair on. All they do, they skirt the bases and keep on walking."

More alerts followed, confirming my words. The enemy fighters had crossed the hexagons bordering theirs without actually capturing them, and now continued to delve deeper into our territory.

That's when I regretted I'd scrimped resources on scouts.

It only took me a few seconds to second-guess all of Tafari's potential next moves. "Let's get to the main base and dig our heels in there. There's only one way they can reach it from both north and east, and that's via hexagon 7 where the canyon is narrow enough for them to cross it. That way even if we lose some of the hexagons, we'll still have enough time to make full use of the resources we've already farmed. That'll allow us to level up, install more turrets and upgrade both armor and damage."

"Sounds good, boss," Eddie said.

Ola nodded. "I agree. There're only five of us plus a dozen dinosaurs. They have at least twenty fighters and a whole lot of fighting units. They'll squash us by their sheer numbers."

"Our main base is level 4! That'll cut their stats down to size, the motherfuckers," Manu added.

"That's not to mention regeneration. That fancy module had better start paying for itself!"

Once back to Base 1, we dissolved into a flurry of activity.

As the best hands-on combat specialist among us, Manu got busy positioning additional plasma turrets and glaive throwers.

Leti who had the highest Speed amongst us jumped on a Utahraptor and rode toward the hexagon's northern edge to set up a couple of watchtowers which would stream images to the command center. It was unlikely he'd attack us from either the south, west or east: our southern and western borders were limited by the Trial field's edges while the only person who could possibly appear from the east was Zack. Whose deadline had already expired, by the way.

I didn't care. He wasn't my biggest problem at the moment.

Should I send Leti to see him? Probably not. Zack might prove dangerous, and sending someone to back her up would weaken our force... which was exactly what I was trying to avoid.

Eddie, Ola and I engrossed ourselves in calculations. Wincing, we cut our own hands with daggers and used the blood to draw complex equations on the shelter floor, trying to determine the best resource ratio to invest into our defenses and firepower. And we had to count quickly.

We had to level up every clan member to 15. That went without saying. It would allow everyone to receive new talents and invest their characteristic points into stamina, not strength. If we wanted to live, we had to max out our survivability. In the heat of the fight, these fractions of a percent could mean the difference between making it to the healing safety of the dome — and disincarnation.

Leveling up the turrets and glaive throwers wasn't that expensive — but it could play a vital role in decimating the ranks of Tafari's fighting units.

I then invested everything I still had over into the research module, improving our gear and raising damage, both our and the dinos'.

The wall of the dome parted momentarily, letting in Manu.

"Those wretched dinosaurs!" he grumbled. "Because of them, I had to plant most of the turrets along the fence. I tried to set some on the base but that was a total waste. They managed to rip them all out while I was busy on the other side of the dome. I don't know who it was, but I have my ideas. It was probably Croc. He does have a problem controlling his tail."

Ola smiled. "Could be Spine. He's new. He's not the sharpest knife in the drawer quite yet."

"Or Rex," Eddie drawled pensively. "He can tear a house down with his tail."

"Does it really matter? Even if it was Tank, so what? What are you gonna do, punish him? As if it's gonna do us any good," I exclaimed a bit louder than I should have.

The other guys exchanged puzzled stares, then exploded with laughter. The tension began to subside.

"Sorry, Phil," Manu finally said.

"Right, guys, now focus. Get buying new levels and studying your talents. Try to work out the situations in which best to use them. Leti will be back in a minute. We'll level her up and then we're as good as-"

My last words were drowned out by a new alert,

Test subject! An enemy has infiltrated your territory! Base 6 is under threat of capture!

Manu fidgeted, uncomfortable with the sight of my dropped jaw and Ola's saucer eyes. "Why, what's wrong?"

"This is the hexagon next to this one," I said. "The one between us and Zack's. I think he's been attacked and now he's running here. I'm gonna meet him. You stay here and wait for Leti. Tell her to level up to 15 and get working on your talents!"

I ran out of the dome, called my Utahraptor, leapt onto his back and raced east.

Depending on how fast Zack's spider could move, the guy should make it to the border in ten minutes max, provided he was moving in the right direction and wasn't going to stray away to any of our other hexagons.

It turned out longer than I'd thought. I was just wondering whether I should return to the base when I made out a human outline looming out of the fog of war.

I squinted at it — but all around it, more and more people stepped out of the mist.

No, this wasn't Zack at all.

I strained my eyes, peering at an enormous army — by the Trial's standards — which was several times larger than even Nagash's horde. There were foot soldiers in full gear, spiked many-legged monster pets and several riders in the rearguard.

I needed to hurry back to the base, but I forced myself to stand still, waiting for the system to reveal their names. All of them wore helmets, preventing me from seeing the faces of those who were coming to us sword in hand.

The moment the system had kicked in, I turned my Raptor around and raced back to the base, paving my way with curses. I'd only seen two of the names — but that was enough to realize I'd been well and truly had.

Juma, human
Level: 26

Zack, human
Level: 15

Jovanna had been right saying that Zack would want to join the #1 in the rankings. The fact that he'd made it to Juma's lands wasn't that incredible, after all: he must have either teleported or even used Inconspicuousness like Carter and myself. But in that case, who was trying to attack us from the north?

Could it be Tafari?

* * *

Juma's army arrived after about an hour, after having unhurriedly captured all three of our hexagons bordering on our main base.

They stopped about 150 feet away from the fence. A rider emerged from their mass, waving a makeshift white flag fashioned out of a T-shirt tied to a stick.

Well, well, well. Now where would I have seen his name before?

Ken, human
Level: 10

As the last "socially meaningful" subject on Ilindi's list approached us, I took at his "stallion". The guy rode a chimera just like the one in the ancient myths, only more realistic, if you know what I mean. It had smooth bare skin, a powerful long scaly tail, its tip studded with bony spikes, and a horselike head covered in chitin plates.

"Yuk!" Leti shuddered.

"Piece of cake for our Rex," Manu said. He seemed to have a soft spot for our alpha dino.

The rider dismounted and removed his helmet. He appeared to be about twenty years old, with a distinctly Asian face and a beaming smile.

"Holy shit!" the guy enthused in Russian. "Are these real dinosaurs? No way! They're freakin' awesome!"

"Hi Ken," I greeted Juma's negotiator.

"I can't believe it!" he exclaimed, peering at us. "Hi guys! Phil, Ola, Manu, Eddie! Hey look, here's Leti too! I've been dreaming about you bunch every night, like! Did you find Carter and Jovanna?"

My friends nodded back, studying him warily.

"We did," I said. "The only person we didn't find was you."

"What a shame. You couldn't, anyway. I got sent to the easternmost hexagon. That's where I met

Juma, so I've been following him basically all this time."

"Shame indeed," I replied for all of us. "You might still join us, don't you think?"

"Sorry, man. I've already sworn my allegiance to Juma. And besides... the guy is so rich you can't even imagine. Know what I mean? He's a member of a ruling Royal dynasty! I have a deal with him. All of us have. We'll follow him to hell and back. We're like mercenaries serving a stinking rich clan leader. He's gonna pay us really well once we're back IRL."

"I see. So you've come to offer us join your clan?"

"Of course. Juma doesn't want to lose his men fighting you. But he might, if you reject his offer, and then he'll pulverize you. So basically, you have fifteen minutes to make up your minds."

"Wait up, isn't Juma afraid of Tafari?" Manu butted in. "While you and your bunch are lounging around here, don't you think he might try and attack Juma's own lands?"

"I can answer this. You have no hope in hell because we've struck a temporary truce with Tafari which will last until sunrise. It just so happened that the carving of the west was the main condition of the truce. Tafari is moving here from the north even as we speak."

"What, that psychopath? How did you manage to come to an agreement with him?" Ola asked. "I didn't know he was capable of listening to other people!"

"Yeah right! He may be a psychopath but he's not crazy enough to attack your dinos on his own!

This way at least they share the risks, so he's happy. By the way, what do you think of these beauties? Much better than what we used to have. We looked everywhere but our roaches were the biggest ones we could find," Ken pointed in the direction of their fighting units. "No idea where he found them but they're something else! They spit some sort of acid which eats right through your eyes. Know what I mean? So keep your helmets on!"

"Thanks for the tip. As for how we got our dinos, it's not a secret at all. Just a unique talent I received with an achievement."

"I see. Okay, then. Shame I had to meet you like this," he heaved a sigh and gave us a particularly compassionate look, then put his helmet back on. "What should I tell Juma? What's your answer?"

Test subject! An enemy has infiltrated your territory! Base 1 is under threat of capture!

"There's Tafari, the motherfucker!" Ola exclaimed. He seemed to nurture some particular dislike for the Nigerian, hatred even.

"What's this, an intrusion?" Ken asked. 'Yeah, that's Tafari. Sorry Phil, but you just can't win this. But if you surrender and join our clan, we'll sure win the Trial."

"We'll think about it."

"Excellent. I'll be off, then. Once you make up your mind, Phil, give us a shout and we'll send you an invitation to join. All the others will join automatically. I've seen it work lots of times," he leapt on his chimera.

"Ken, wait!" I called him. "I thought I saw Zack there with you. How come he's on your side?"

"Zack, heh! Had it not been for him, Juma would have never believed Tafari. It was Zack who confirmed that you had dinosaurs. And by joining our clan, he opened us a portal right into the heart of your lands."

"But how did he get to you? That's a good thirty miles across Tafari's lands!"

"He has this ability to set up a portal to any hexagon of his choice. It has an enormous cooldown but at least it works. This morning he came to us and asked to join the clan. And just as he did it, Tafari's messenger arrived. So we discussed everything and set off straight away. These things don't take long here, you know that."

As he rode back to rejoin his army, we watched a flurry of scared whistlers escape the army's path.

Tafari's clan was almost as big as Juma's. The black man leading his troops was almost as big as Shaquille O'Neal. He was riding a rhinoceros, huge and black but still quite realistic. It had little chance against our Tank, a bit like an army Hummer against a proper tank.

Which was small consolation though. While we might have taken on one of the armies, we just couldn't fight both.

I had a couple of ideas, but both were too risky.

I paused, trying to word a query, then enunciated clearly in my mind:

Martha, I need Ilindi to advise me about the risk I'd like to take. Please send her my query:

>>>>Ilindi, should I go for it or are there other options available?>>>>

I repeated the mental request several times, enunciating every word without parting my lips.

This was crazy. Then again, it might work.

"Leti, report," I said to the Italian girl who was back from her mission of taking stock of the enemy.

"About three hundred roaches and nine chimeras," she said. "Twenty-six humans, all levels 10+. That's Juma. I couldn't finish counting Tafari's men. He might have fewer men and units but not by much."

"What should we do, boss?" Eddie asked. "Their offer makes sense."

"I think," Manu said pensively, "that this is Juma's cunning plan. If we join, all our hexagons will automatically become his. In which case his truce with Tafari would become pointless. So they'll try to sort out their differences right here and now."

"We need to accept Juma's offer," Leti said. "Our dinosaurs won't help us much. It didn't take Bloodscar long to kill both Rex and Tank, remember? Because he's an elite mob, a night prowler. Our lizards might command respect but they can be beaten. None of them can sustain a volley of plasma charges."

"And we don't even know what other talents Juma and Tafari have," Eddie agreed hotly. "What if they can cast mass paralysis? They might freeze us solid."

"Exactly," Ola said, apparently taking the side of those who'd rather surrender. "If even I have a mass curse already, they probably have something similar too. Phil! Look, they're waving the white flag to us! We need to accept!"

As if in confirmation of his words, I received an invitation to join Juma's clan.

And immediately afterward, a blue globe of a system message materialized in my view, unfolding to reveal Ilindi's brief message:

Just go for it!

Well, she must have known the lay of the land better than I did. I had to go for it.

Biding for time, I paused before rejecting Juma's message. I needed the others to see it the way I saw it.

"Listen, guys. Have you ever heard of Kutuzov?"

"Who's that? A Russian president?"

"Wasn't he a friend of Lenin?"

"I know! He was a Soviet soccer player from the 1970s!"

They showered me with suggestions, one funnier than the next.

"Kutuzov was one of Russia's greatest generals," I finally said. "He commanded the Russian army during the Napoleonic wars. He surrendered Moscow to Napoleon because he knew it would help him to win the war in the long run."

Leti rolled her eyes. "And? What's that got to

do with it?"

"Do you know what happens to allies in a truce once they defeat the common enemy? Or if the common enemy is out of their reach?"

Manu beamed. "They break the truce. Happens all the time in Columbia."

"Exactly. We keep forgetting this is a game of sorts. A simulation. The stakes might be high for us, but the game still plays by the rules. It took their two armies several hours to get here. It's less than four hours left until nightfall. Once it gets dark, night monsters will be on a prowl. And their truce expires at dawn. Am I right or not?"

"Dammit, boss!" Eddie beamed. "We can escape, can't we? We just teleport out!"

"Of course. They don't have the time to search all of our hexagons looking for us. They might even turn against each other!"

"But our modules? All the upgrades... it's all here," Leti said, undecided.

"We'll upgrade them again. We can actually leave our dinos to guard the base, just to thin out the enemy ranks a bit."

I peered at the two armies moving toward us. Although they weren't in a hurry, I knew that if we didn't make ourselves scarce right now, in ten seconds' time we might have to face the enemy.

"See you later-" Ola's voice was momentarily drowned out by the popping of the teleport, "...alligator!"

"I'd love to see their faces!" Manu slammed his fist into the palm of his hand and laughed as happily as only a pardoned death-row prisoner can.

* * *

By the time both suns had set, we'd only lost six hexagons. At first, Tafari and Juma had been busy fighting Rex, Tank, Croc, Spine and one of the Utahraptors — all of whom finally met a heroic death. Then the two had to stop and spend some quality time thinking how best to share out their spoils. By then, night had fallen. I had the impression that they didn't dare split their forces to invade any more hexagons, which was why they'd only claimed the ones they'd managed to capture before sunset.

In the meantime, we were sitting it out in our outermost hexagon located on the very edge of the Trial field. There, we promptly upgraded the base and the fighting unit module to level 3. By then, Rex and friends had already respawned and were back with us.

We prepared to spend the night battling it out with elite nocturnal predators, so that in the morning we could level up right to the hilt and embark on a guerrilla war, greatly assisted by the new ability I'd received at level 20: Shroud of Shadow. This would allow us to stealth up as a group and infiltrate enemy hexagons without raising the alarm.

Naturally, both Tafari and Juma would react to any such infiltration — but I very much doubted that they would put their whole army on alert. Most likely, they would only send in combat groups of five which we could easily handle because we'd all be level 20 by morning, if not higher.

Here, the choice of nocturnal elite didn't differ from all the other hexagons. They came in waves which were more frequent as well as thicker and more powerful — so by midnight we'd almost decided to invest into the base some of the resources we'd farmed, just to get the dome regeneration option. In the end though, our common sense had prevailed. We'd better save those 20,000 points for a rainy day.

"Did you see how big he was?" Ola grunted while waiting for his lost arm to regenerate.

"You should invest in another level," I said. "There might be a new wave coming at any moment."

"Too late, boss," Eddie shouted, running towards our flanks. "Incoming!"

"Ola, keep to the rear!" I ordered, climbing to my feet. 'Stop playing the hero with your spear! Are you a shaman or just a pretty face? Your job is to cast DoTs and curses and heal the dinos! You got your staff with you?"

"Where do you think it is, Phil? One-handed it ain't easy..."

His voice was drowned out by a loud popping behind our backs. I swung round.

A huge, glittering-green portal flashed open, disgorging hordes of roaches.

Juma.

"Everybody back! Under the dome!" I shouted. Even straining my voice, nobody heard me except Ola.

The African got busy casting curses on the portal. I tried to highlight and select my clan members, hoping to teleport us out of here, but we were too spread out.

I grabbed Ola's good arm and dragged him toward the others when a voice resounded from behind,

"Freeze!"

A wave of freezing cold descended upon us. I stood stock still, unable to move.

Ola dropped to the ground next to me, also frozen to the bone.

A countdown timer appeared in the corner of my eye, ticking off the seconds of the immobilization debuff.

5... 4... 3...

A halberd sank into Ola's body, cleaving him in two.

Ola's eyes glazed over. His body dematerialized as he left the Trial for good, leaving behind only a few possessions and his spirit crystal which I couldn't even see.

I readied myself for the end of the countdown, planning to immediately stealth up, order Rex to stun the enemy with his roaring, then escape with whoever were still alive.

2...

A warrior charged at Eddie's back, stunning him, then beheaded him with a wide powerful swipe.

1...

Bang! Before I could stealth up, I received a stunning blow to the back of my head, then dropped to the ground as someone cast another immobilization debuff on me.

A new timer. New countdown. Five more seconds of helplessness.

"Greg, keep him stunned!" a guttural voice commanded.

"Yes, sir!"

Although I'd lost all control of both my body and interface, I could still see Rex and Spine collapse under the combined weight of roaches gnawing through their bodies. Studded with arrows and plasma charges, Croc swung in place, trying to grab hold of one of the agile chimeras carrying Juma's warriors. My Utahraptors died one after another, crying out in agony.

I could see Manu behind the fence brandish his sword at the attacking horde. He was even gaining some ground, until an enemy swordsman stepped out of the crowd, equally strong but with a full health bar while Manu's was already at less than 50%.

Next to them, I glimpsed Juma. It was the first time I could see him from such a close distance. He watched the battle calmly with his arms crossed.

Finally, my Stun had expired. Not waiting to get another one from Greg, I rolled aside and activated Treacherous Shadow, microporting behind Juma's back. All his warriors were tied up fighting both Manu and new waves of doughboys that kept coming.

I had to kill him. This was my only chance to

set things right. I stunned him, then assaulted him with an explosive combo, turning his back into mincemeat. I'd already stripped him of 75% health when my stun expired and Juma turned back to me, surrounded by an impenetrable energy cocoon.

"Fifteen seconds of absolute invulnerability, Phil," he said with a soft chuckle. "Being a top player has its good sides."

He crouched and swung his thin long sword through the air, slicing through my legs.

Despite my maxed-out gear, he'd managed to crit me. As I fell, I couldn't feel my legs anymore — what I did feel was the familiar pain just under my knees, agonizing beyond all endurance. I'd love to scream — but not now, not in front of my enemy, so I just crawled away, trying to overcome the several feet to the base from where I could teleport out...

Manu's icon went gray. A new system message informed me of losing yet another clan member.

I activated a new level, leapt to my instantly restored feet — only to be frozen again.

You are now dead, test subject.
Lives remaining: 1.
Time left until resurrection: 3... 2... 1....

I had to resurrect right there and then because by now, there were no neutral hexagons left.

Warning! You have one last life left!
If you lose it, you'll be stripped off of all

your achievements and taken back to the day when you'd been selected as the Trial participant. Your memory of the accompanying events will be wiped clean and the interface will be uninstalled.

Warning! You've lost all of your hexagons!
Time left until full disincarnation: 1 Pibellau day

Warning! Your clan has been disbanded!
Your vassals (Leti) are free again!

I suppressed a scream of pain in my already-healed legs. Luckily, as I stealthed up the moment I respawned, no one seemed to have noticed my arrival.

I stole back to the place where I'd died. Unbelievably, all my gear was still lying there. Juma's clan was too busy finishing off a new wave of doughboys to pick up the loot straight away. That was normal: we'd done it ourselves too many times before.

I picked up my staff, then checked whatever my clan members had left, stuffing everything into the backpack I'd kept while respawning. Not that it made me any happier: the loss of my friends still smarted, plus the fact that I'd lost all chances of winning.

I had only one option left now. I had to attack Juma when he least expected it. If I killed him, I'd get all of his hexagons.

And then we'd see.

By then, Juma's clan had finished off a new wave of doughboys, a couple of duxio and an odzi snake. They gathered by the dome, cheering, as Juma gave a triumphant speech.

I could understand them. They had as good as won. Tafari couldn't survive the combined power of the 2/3 of the Trial field's resources.

Leti stood next to Juma, smiling. The crowd guffawed as their leader slapped her backside, then asked her something. Leti nodded. Juma barked a stream of orders, then pulled the girl toward him and led her under the dome.

I heard the rustling of footsteps next to me.

"Get out of here," a voice said in Russian. "I'm not the only one who can see you. There's another guy who might notice you, and you're lucky he's too far away."

I turned round. It was Ken.

"This place is very well balanced," he mouthed. "For every cunning stunt there's a stunning......"

"Why didn't you raise the alarm?"

"Suppose I just don't want to be a rat. I know you're gonna forget everything, but I won't. We're gonna win and I'll get my money out of Juma. I don't want to spend the rest of my happy life thinking I betrayed someone who had the same values. What's your social status level?"

"It was 17 just before my abduction."

"Respect! I only just made it to 9."

"Ken," I whispered, "Talking about Juma's invulnerability, do you know its cooldown time?"

I was still obsessed by the idea of attacking

him again. Depending on Ken's reply, I had to decide whether it was worth sitting it out here waiting for Juma to reappear.

"What's up, Ken?" someone bellowed. "Is it a new wave?"

I turned round. It was the swordsman who'd battled Manu.

"Nobody, Patrick," Ken replied. "Listen, I keep looking at these stars but I can't seem to recognize a single one. Here, look — one, two, three..."

Counting to fifteen, Ken put his arm around Patrick's shoulder and pointed up at the heavens as he spoke, "Fifteen stars, all so close to each other! What do you think the distance between them is? Is it light hours or light minutes? I have a funny feeling it's minutes, Patrick..."

"What are you talking about, Kenny boy? You can't measure distances in minutes — or hours even!"

"Can't I, really? Never mind. See if I care! Come on, let's go now. You're not on watch tonight, are you? Who are you gonna spend the time with? Christina or Scheherazade?"

Ken led the swordsman away, telling him his vision of Christina's "virtues".

Fifteen minutes. Which meant that I wouldn't be able to kill Juma tonight. I had very little time left until my disincarnation. All I had left to do was to try and farm some more existence resources.

Otherwise I wouldn't live to see the hour out.

Chapter

Twenty-four

Revealing the Concealed

All the young people out into the world should have their own goals, and use their abilities to their fullest to contribute to society.

Teru Mikami, *Death Note*

IT WASN'T THE INTERFACE ALARM THAT WOKE ME UP but a vague feeling of uneasiness. Before I'd even opened my eyes, I recognized the distinct smell of a hospital.

I could hear rustling and yawning next to me. Had Alex and Laura come uninvited to see me while I slept?

I opened my eyes and saw a flaking white ceiling. This definitely didn't look like a five-star Vegas hotel.

Also, I was dying for a smoke.

"What the..." I said out loud, then dissolved in a bout of coughing.

"Oh look, User's back with us!" Ensign grinned from his cot next to mine while picking his nose.

User? Did he mean me? Where did I know him from?

"Not again," Ensign said, looking concerned. "Been dreaming again, User?"

"Dreaming about what? Where am I?" the cot groaned its protest as I sprang from it. "What the fuck's going on?"

"Oh," he drawled through his nose. "So you have been dreaming. You'd better sit yourself back down. Dr. Gauss will be very upset. He thought you were making good progress. And now this! What was it about this time?"

"Has User had a new escapade?" Krasko's voice said. I seemed to know him too from somewhere. "Listen User, how are things going with what's her name now? Ensign, do you remember?"

"Which one?" the old man perked up. "He's got a whole harem of them there! He has Yanna, and Vicky, and Veronica, and also Stacy... Is that all of them?"

While he was mumbling something about my company, mentioning Alik and Mr. Katz, I tried to figure out why they were calling me User. User... user... aha!

I peered at their strange but eerily familiar faces which floated in and out of focus. I wasn't wearing my glasses.

Mechanically I reached out for my bedside

table, picked up my glasses and put them on. The faces came back into focus. Much better.

Now, let's take a look. Who did we have here? Ensign, Krasko and Nick. I was almost home: in the months that I'd been here I'd gotten very used to the place.

That had been one hell of a nightmare. I must have been completely off my trolley, confusing reality with dreams. Luckily, there was no curse, no Trial, just a good old local hospital.

"Here we go again," I heaved a sigh and reached for the cigarettes. The pack was empty. "Have they brought the smokes around already?"

The old man called Ensign shrugged guiltily. "You were sleeping. But I can spare one."

"Thanks."

Ensign offered me a cigarette. He was funny, really: a youthful gray-haired old man with a cavalry mustache. How did he manage to look after us all here?

"Excuse me," I addressed him, "could you please remind me why you're calling me User?"

"That's because you are!" Krasko guffawed. "You keep telling us you have some alien interface in your head. You're a user, so you say."

"Ah, yes, yes, of course..." I cradled my head in my hands, trying to untangle a complex flurry of thoughts. How sure was I I really knew these people?

"So have you won your boxing tournament?" Ensign asked. "You didn't finish the story the last time."

"A tournament?" I strained my memory, but those boxing events seemed vague and distant.

"But... but that's exactly how it ended."

"Also, you didn't tell us what's gonna happen to your company," Krasko added, scratching the back of his head. "Did you make it?"

"Ah, yes, of course, of course. I won the tournament, then took them all on as partners. I hired Alik as a maintenance manager, Veronica as PR, Kesha Dimidko as commercial director..."

"We know, we know," Krasko grumbled. "Now why did you have to take on Gleb? That's something I don't understand. And you shouldn't have left that redhead — Veronica, right? — to Alik. You should have screwed her yourself. Never mind. Tell us what happened next. Don't leave anything out. Come on, tell us."

"Let's go have a smoke and I'll tell you all about it."

For a couple of cigarettes spared by Krasko, I told them all about the last developments in my dream — or was it my parallel life?

They listened attentively, with the exception of Stinky Nick who waltzed around alone to a music only he could hear. I could only imagine what I might have seen had I really had an augmented-reality interface.

Nicholas "Stinky" Vostrikov
Age: 46

I tried to envision those words hovering above his head. It didn't really work.

Those dreams. Just think there used to be a time when I really believed I'd been fitted out with an alien interface. I was so grateful to Professor Gauss who'd sorted my head out. I'd hate to disappoint him.

"So it all ended in America. But it looks like I'm going to lose my interface, anyway. Either that, or the curse will finish me off. Then I woke up here with you. Have I been sleeping long?"

"Nap time has just finished," Krasko replied. "Will you be going to tea?"

"Sure," I rose from my haunches but staggered and very nearly fell over.

My head was spinning. Trying to keep my balance, I waved my hands and collapsed on top of Ensign. My breathing seized up. Everything went dark.

Then I woke up again, still tasting the bitter taste of the cigarettes.

I pulled my head away from a sticky wet pillow, then realized with relief I was where I was supposed to be.

This was Cesar's Palace in Las Vegas.

My vision was perfectly clear. I didn't need glasses.

The dream, so real only a moment ago, faded into nothing, erasing the faces of my ward buddies from my memory. The interface flooded my mental view with alerts reporting my elevated heart rate.

Then my standard morning greeting came into view,

Good morning, Phil!
Today is Monday August 27 2018. The outdoor temperature is 27 C (81 F).

You wanted to wake up at 6.30. It's now 6.24 a.m, which is the best awakening time based upon your sleep cycle.

The state of your health: Good.

Warning! Last night you had a nightmare caused by extreme nervous pressure. We recommend you take it easy today, remove the source of stress and limit the amount of intellectual work in order to allow your nervous system to restore.

Based on your activity levels, we'd recommend you start your day with a breakfast containing no more than 600 calories from proteins and complex carbohydrates.

Here are the tasks you set for today...

I threw the sheets back, rose and began working out. I needed to get my blood going and my body toned up because this promised to be a hard day, one of less than two I had left. Panchenko hadn't been found and with him, my hopes of lifting the curse were fading.

I was trying to be positive and look for something good in the situation. Like, I'd finally had a good night's sleep even though I'd had to wake up again in order to level up Agility.

My latest Optimization had finally run its course, too. I'd completely forgotten how to take pictures — and in return, my Learning Skills had gone through the roof. Now I could learn 23 times faster than a regular person.

Once that done, I was about to go out for breakfast to meet Alex and Laura. You never know, they might have something on Panchenko. My map still didn't show any sign of him.

Just as I was about to go out, my phone rang. I stared at the screen, momentarily transported a few months back, to a time when life had been much more simple.

"Hi, Sveta," I said, unable to hide my surprise.

"Hi, Phil!" said the cheerful voice of the fourteen-year-old Sveta Messerschmitt, the owner of Richie the German Shepherd. "It's a bit late to call but I have real good news for you!"

"Out with it, then."

"Richie's become a daddy! We were promised a puppy. Which means that very soon you'll be able to pick him up!"

"Yes," I shouted into the phone in excitement as my feet started dancing a jig. "Outta sight!"

She laughed too, sharing my joy.

That made me think about my first interface days. I remembered finding Richie and taking him away from the fake "Gypsies". I'd spent the last of my money taking him to the vet and buying him dog food. Those days breathed such warmth, simplicity and clarity that I was now dying to get the puppy in the naïve belief that with it, I could acquire peace.

"Thank you, Sveta."

"You're welcome! I'll give you a call when we have the puppy. Would you prefer a boy or a girl?"

"I'd rather have a boy. I hope he takes after his father."

"Good. What are you gonna call him?"

"I don't know yet," lost in thought, I said the

first thing that came into my head. "I might call him Carter. Or Ola."

* * *

I heard a tactful knocking on the door followed by some coughing and a soft female voice,

"Phil? Are you awake?"

I hurried to wrap a bathrobe around myself and opened the door.

"Good morning," Laura said, looking wide awake for a change. She was holding two paper coffee cups.

"Hi," I said. "Where's Alex?"

"He and Sanchez left for Langley last night. They seem to have run into problems. They should be back tomorrow."

"Anything on Panchenko?"

"Nothing," she shook her head sadly. "I'm the one minding you today. Can I come in?"

"Of course," I stepped aside, letting her in, then shut the door.

Laura walked in, picked up the remote and switched the TV on. A news footage came on: the flickering of images which were so recognizable Middle-East.

"Have you been watching the news?" she asked. "It's absolute havoc over there. They all suspect each other of being the grass."

"As long as you guys don't let the grass grow under your feet, otherwise I'm as good as dead. I'll go take a shower."

Laura's expression turned pensive. *"You*

guys? Okay."

Squeezing my eyes shut from the freezing shower jets, I tried to rethink the entire situation. When I'd initially agreed to cooperate with the Americans, I'd actually imagined it all to be rather straightforward, a bit like with Major Igorevsky. Like, I'd give them the coordinates, then they find their targets, leaving their source undisclosed.

Now I'd begun to realize that this scenario was involving a whole lot of people — way more than a lone Russian police investigator from the sticks had at his beck and call. Let's count: Hector Sanchez, Alex Tomasik, Laura Flores, Norman Doherty plus the mysterious Angela Howard, the supposed US Embassy worker who I was yet to meet, — that made five already. Our plan must have involved any number of operatives, undercover and otherwise — which meant that I'd gotten on the radars of far too many people.

Not that I cared. The twenty-four hours remaining until the activation of the curse weren't going to change anything. As it was, the fund was getting off the ground and new money transfers kept pouring into its temporary bank account.

When I returned to the room, Laura was munching on her sandwich, looking all focused, while scrolling through the list of new targets on her iPad.

"I've ordered some breakfast," she said. "I agree, it's probably better you keep a low profile for a while."

"Are you my only chaperone or are there others around? I have no doubt you're full of surprises and could probably smoke quite a few attackers single-handed, but-"

"But you're right," she interrupted me. "By the way, you didn't tell us yesterday how long you were planning to stay in Vegas. We really should be on the move," she spoke in a level, emotionless voice, staring into her iPad.

"Can't see why not. How about New York? I can't wait to see Fifth Avenue and the Avengers Mansion," I said, my voice oozing sarcasm. "Laura, *please!* I need to find that man!"

She shrugged. I slumped into a chair next to her and attacked my breakfast: sausages, bacon and eggs, some toast and a couple of hash browns, delicious and most importantly, high in calories. I needed all the energy I could get as the system, in its current active mode, guzzled its way through both Spirit reserves and the calories I received with food. I had lots of searches to perform today: many more than on the night I'd been trying to locate missing persons for the Russian search and rescue groups.

The reason I had to do it because Intuition was tolling a warning bell within me.

I had an eerie feeling that some kind of countdown had been activated. The Trial was to be over within the next twenty-four hours — or less even, — in which case I was most likely to lose my interface.

Laura patiently waited for me to finish breakfast. "Are you ready?" she finally asked, offering me the iPad.

"Just a moment. I'll just finish my coffee."

By then, the coffee had already gone cold, but I still needed it to get my metabolism going. Also, I admittedly liked properly made coffee like this.

I took the iPad from her and began reading through all the information. Their analysts had done a good job profiling me as they seemed to push all the right buttons. Each of their case reports put a special emphasis on the number of casualties, precising their details and family ties: children who'd lost their mothers, parents who'd lost their children... The intel like this added nothing to the actual search — if anything, it was wasting my time — but to me, details like these were especially important.

For a few heartbeats, the pressure of the world's grief pinned me to the chair. Flattened under the incoming flood of data, I couldn't even breathe, trying to get a grip, until my glazed-over stare paused on a yet another case.

"The targets are listed in order of importance," Laura said softly. "The first three names are of especial value."

"How many names are there in total? On this list?" I asked, pointing at the iPad.

"A hundred and seventy-two. These are categories A and B. All the other names are in another file which lists all the lower categories."

"I'm going to find them all for you. Are you ready? I'll be giving you thirty each hour. I just can't do it any faster."

Laura gulped. "I need to talk to my superiors," she sprang from her seat. "I'll be back as soon as I can. Don't leave the room!"

I nodded while trying to work out how best to leave the hotel inconspicuously. She may have been thinking I was studying the cases — but in fact, I'd already located almost all of the first ten targets. Almost, because two of them were already dead and resting in peace: one on the bottom of the Hudson Bay, the other somewhere in Chechnya.

Then I received an unexpected but very welcome surprise: a new level of my very first system skill!

Congratulations! You've received a new system skill level!
Skill name: Insight
Current level: 4
XP received: 1000
Allows you to see the essence of inanimate material objects;
Limits the number of KIDD points necessary to locate both living and inanimate objects on the map to 1 pt.;
Allows you to determine the cause and extent of physical damage to any living thing and diagnose medical conditions;
Reveals that which is concealed;
Allows you to see the motives and causal links behind the actions of any living organisms;
Helps you determine the structure and internal workings of any social group as well as its connections with all the others.

The list didn't end there: it went on to describe more of a similar sort of stuff greatly broadening my capacity. But that wasn't the main thing.

The main thing was, I could see Panchenko on the map again. And he was but a stone's throw away.

* * *

When I saw him at the poker table, I immediately realized why the CIA couldn't find him. He looked different now, taller and stronger, his hair blond, his facial features more defined, noble even. You could have called him handsome, I suppose, had it not been for the crooked smile curving his lips. All this looked like an attempt to artificially boost Charisma.

Also, he'd activated a level-3 Mysterious Shroud buff which prevented people from remembering his face, and cameras from getting a clear picture of him. It was probably due to this ability that he'd caught me unawares the night when my alert had failed to go off.

But with my new Insight level, even his ability couldn't conceal him from me anymore.

He seemed to be so cocksure of his buff's charms that he hadn't even left Vegas, apparently preferring to wait it out here for my curse to go off while having fun and making some serious money in this gambling capital.

To say he was surprised to see me would be an understatement. His eyes very nearly popped out of his head with shock. Still, he recovered pretty quickly, scanned my personal data and grinned with satisfaction at seeing his curse still ticking away.

This was a private poker room with only one table which seated several respectable men and an elderly lady in a mink coat, trying too hard to look younger than she was.

They bet big here: I had to buy one million dollars' worth of chips just to get in.

In order to raise this million, I'd spent a few brief minutes playing roulette in the main room with the ten grand I still had left. A Level-4 Insight makes it easy, you see. Every time the ball left the dealer's fingers, I already knew which number it would rest on. The ability would analyze everything in a flash: the wheel's spinning speed and its surface defects, the balls trajectory and lots of other things, including humidity and the dealer's heart rate. Then it simply highlighted the number which was about to win.

The risks were huge, sure, but much to my surprise, the system hadn't punished me this time. It seemed to realize my motives for gambling and my reason for winning.

Panchenko had a stack of chips the size of Mount Everest piled up before him. He was a chancer; at his level 10+ Poker skill, he seemed to be so sure of himself that he was staking all of his cash, meaning everything that he'd already won in Vegas where he'd arrived with whatever little he'd taken off me. I knew for a fact that this was the only money he had.

All of his hired bodyguards were waiting for him outside, unable to enter the VIP room. This was big fun for very big people.

"Hello," I said, taking a seat at the table. "I'm

Phil."

The other players gave me their names. I glanced over their stats, uninterested. I wasn't going to fleece them. I was playing against Panchenko alone tonight.

Panchenko looked perfectly cool, showing no intention of fleeing the room. He even rubbed his hands, apparently having read my Poker skill level which was half that of his.

"We've got a novice!" he exclaimed. "I suggest we raise the stakes! How about a hundred thousand?"

Nobody objected.

I wasn't in a hurry to strip him of his interface. Even when he shook my proffered hand, I didn't do it, afraid that he wouldn't be able to lift the curse then.

The dealer dealt the cards. I passed. These days I didn't even need to cheat by looking at their cards, as I already knew how the hand would end. Panchenko and I were on the same keel, taking turns winning. Other players might win an occasional pot — but as both of us refrained from raising the stakes whenever our hands weren't that special, their winnings didn't amount to much.

After a couple of hours, we were the only ones left at the table. I was having a lucky streak: Panchenko kept throwing his hands in, losing blinds which had already grown to $200,000. By now, he was openly nervous as our bankrolls were roughly the same.

"Listen, man," I told him while the dealer was dealing the next hand. "What do you know about the

Trial?"

"What do I need to know about it?"

"Very soon they'll summon you. You'll have to compete with other interface users. I've no idea what you all will have to do. They too have a Boss, as you call him."

"Okay. I believe you. No point asking you who's gonna summon me where. I can see you're not lying."

"The thing is, there'll be lots of contestants there. But only one of them will win. All the others will lose their interfaces."

His face didn't twitch. He looked at the hand he'd been dealt and pushed it toward the dealer. "Pass."

"If you remove the curse, I'm gonna lose everything I have to you," I activated all of my abilities to make it sound as convincing as I could. "It's almost six million here. They're yours."

"I don't give a shit about your millions, you cretin," he said lightheartedly. "With my abilities, I can make hundreds of millions overnight. Easy. And you're gonna die. No good straining your stupid little brain trying to appease me. In order to take your stupid Trial, one has to live long enough. Which I will."

The sheer coolness of his manner didn't impress me. He wasn't lying, neither was he trying to haggle with me. I could see he wasn't going to lift the curse, and my Lie Detection told me as much.

In which case I simply had to do what I had to do.

We were dealt another hand. I could see that

all odds were stacked up in Panchenko's favor. Still, he didn't know one little thing. Our dealer — who'd been working all night through and was so exhausted he could barely stand on his feet — was about to make a mistake opening the flop, which in turn would completely change the entire scenario.

"In this case, let's finish all this here and now," I suggested, moving my heap of chips toward the center of the table. "I can't take my money with me. All-in."

"Good idea," he hurried to agree before I could change my mind.

"Sorry," I said, then proffered my hand to him, preparing to activate the uninstallation of his interface.

Mechanically he shook it.

He turned pale.

Just then the dealer finished collecting our chips and opened the flop, which wasn't at all what Panchenko had expected.

But that wasn't the reason he'd turned pale because he couldn't see it yet.

Reality blinked several times. Time slowed down. I very nearly fainted but managed to survive a new bout of ecstasy without exposing myself. I only swayed a little in my seat, brushing against a fellow player, who'd stayed in his place to watch us play.

"Sorry," I managed.

Global quest alert: Stop Evil. Quest completed!
You've successfully uninstalled

Konstantin Panchenko's interface, neutralizing him.
  +50% to Satisfaction
  +3 to your social status level
  +3 to all main characteristics
  +3 available main characteristic points
  +30 pt. to your global Reputation with every member of the human race.

Level 27.

On top of that, the system had also shown me a warning, saying that although all of my characteristics had risen, Strength, Agility and Perception would in fact grow gradually.

I glanced at my profile and heaved a disappointed sigh. The curse was still there even though I'd hoped it might disappear the moment Panchenko lost his interface and with it, his quest against me.

"You!" a lifeless voice said in Russian. "How did you do it?"

I looked up. Panchenko's mad eyes seemed to look right through me. "Do what?"

"You took my Boss away! Just when I'd almost made it! I was about to become an *Eroul*," he whispered furiously, wiping tears away from his eyes. "How did you do it? You're useless! The Boss can't have possibly chosen you over me!"

"Your Boss doesn't exist, you idiot. That was just some neural software. A hundred years from now, everybody will have things like that. They'll be like cell phones."

He got up from the table and went for me. I

got up too. He pointed at me, then poked me in the chest, pushing me back. He was hysterical, and alcohol probably had little to do with it, even though he'd drunk quite a bit.

"Bullshit! What do you know about the Great Almighty? He's on his way! His time is coming, and I was about to become his..."

"Get over it. You've made your choice. If you don't get your finger out of my chest, you're gonna regret it."

By then, everyone was looking at us. The security were showing signs of concern. We had to get out of here.

"So what you're gonna do to me? I may have lost my Boss but I still have my money and my influence!"

"I don't think so," I said cheerfully, looking back at the table.

Panchenko swung round and saw that I'd just won.

The quest I'd just closed had raised my reputation with everyone on planet Earth to Amicality, with the exception of those who'd already had bad reputation with me. Now I was witnessing this at work first-hand, observing the reactions of those around me. Everybody seemed to rejoice in my victory. Even the dealer couldn't conceal a smile.

With a loud howl, Panchenko began trashing everything around until security took him away.

He had nothing left. No money, no interface.

Chapter Twenty-Five

Don't Forget to Look at the Stars Before You Die

I have noticed even people who claim everything is predestined, and that we can do nothing to change it, look before they cross the road.

Stephen Hawking

IT WAS RAINING ON PIBELLAU: A POURING ACID RAIN. My gear was still holding out but every drop that touched it produced a hissing cloud of mist that enveloped me, giving my presence away. It was a good job there was nobody around, apart from monsters which followed the rules of mechanics rather than logic.

I kept sinking knee-deep into the mud, getting stuck, as I waded through it with little hope left. I was feeling empty inside. The schism in my heart which had formed after Jovanna's disincarnation had now grown to the size of the Mariana Trench. Had I still had my real-life interface on me, it probably would have shown the extreme stages of apathy and indifference.

I had ten minutes left until my own disincarnation. Due to the lack of resources, I still had zero existence points. Just to please, I hadn't come across a single ordinary mob, as if all of them had become elite upon nightfall. If I didn't farm the obligatory 21 resource points — the cost of supporting a level 21-body for an hour — within the next few minutes, I was as good as dead.

Protected by Inconspicuousness, I managed to avoid all oncoming mobs, leaving what used to be my clan's main hexagon. With every passing minute, the futility of further struggle was becoming ever more obvious. Even if I got the required resource points and managed to keep myself going, I wouldn't be able to seize a single hexagon empty-handed. The moment an alarm went off, I'd have to face either Juma's of Tafari's cavalry who would make quick work of me.

In a moment of weakness, I even looked forward to a quick end, wishing I could get home soon and switch on some brainless but addictive series on TV. Oh to get back to my couch, my warm comforter and a nice big mug of strong sweet tea...

Something enormous was breaking through the trees about a hundred and fifty feet away from me. It was probably a duxio: a giant black beetle with a scorpion's tail, the most frequent visitor to our base. I could make out the sheen of his hard black flank and his long steely tail.

Duxio
Elite
Level 24
Life points: 36000

The situation was like this: either I killed him, looted his resources and started to think what to do next, or I simply failed the Trial in a most ignominious way.

I was holding the dagger and the power fist I'd won on my very first day by defeating the Kreken.

Acid Dagger of Obfuscation
Cunning melee weapon. Its biochemical core produces an active jelly whose concentration in the victim's blood can lead to madness.

It is powered by existence resources (3% of your points for each damage dealt).

Damage: 180-360.

+1% to your chance of making an instant kill with each blow.

Furious Power Fist
The best weapon for close combat.

Powered by existence resources (1% of your points for each damage dealt).

Damage: 240-480.

+50% to critical damage.

I looked at the duxio's outline receding into the darkness, then at the dagger in my hands. Quickly I whipped the backpack off my shoulders and upended it, sending it a mental command to empty itself.

All the weapons my clan had amassed splattered into the sticky red mud. I nervously rummaged through whatever I had available, throwing all the irrelevant stuff back, including the power fist.

Time was at a premium. I hurried to wade my way through the 220 lbs. of trash until I found what I'd been looking for: the life steal dagger. It would allow me to heal myself in the course of combat, because I couldn't level up without gaining some resources first. Luckily for me, it was already loaded with existence points, otherwise it would have been useless.

The moment I picked it up, its handle entwined my wrist and forearm. I felt a bout of sharp pain as the countless tentacles pierced my skin, attaching themselves to my nerve endings and blood vessels.

A healing wave of anger swallowed me, making me furious with my enemies, with the Senior Races, with all the observers and Khphor himself — but mostly with myself. My friend had just brought me back to my senses!

Wicked Dagger of Absorption
Treacherous melee weapon. Each attack

restores 25% of the owner's health from the damage dealt.

It is powered by existence resources (5% of your points for each damage dealt).

Damage: 180-360.

Which meant that thanks to my Strength boost, my every blow could now deal over 1,000 pt. of damage and almost 3,000 pt. of critical damage.

I closed my backpack, threw it on my back and hurried to catch up with the beetle which by now had almost disappeared from sight.

My lips stretched in a smile in anticipation of a battle to come. Here I was, a Phil who refused to give up; the one who was about to destroy all his enemies with the help of his two best friends: his two trusty fangs.

I held Fang One with my right hand: the Dagger of Absorption, capable of endowing me with enough power to last through any battle.

I clutched Fang Two in my left hand: the Dagger of Obfuscation. Piercing the body of my enemy, it injected it with bioactive slime which added 1% to my chances of killing them with my next blow. Which meant that if I withstood long enough, then sooner or later, according to the theory of relativity, I could kill any enemy of flesh and blood in just over fifty hits — less than a minute.

Sensing a movement behind him, the beetle stopped dead in his tracks and thrashed his heavily articulated tail on the ground. I leapt over it, very nearly grazing myself on its long spikes, then rolled over the ground and buried both daggers into his shell, heaving myself up on each one in turn, scrambling up on my arms and legs until I finally climbed onto his almost flat back.

You've dealt damage to the duxio: 1330
Damage absorbed by armor: 50% Actual damage: 665.

Verifying the probability of making an instant kill (0%)...
Verification failed.
+1% to your chance of making an instant kill with each blow (1%).

You've dealt damage to the duxio: 1087
Damage absorbed by armor: 50% Actual damage: 543.
Health points: 136

With a crunching sound, his chitinous armor collapsed under a hail of my blows. I wielded my daggers like the swing needle of a sewing machine, each blow producing fountains of lymphatic fluid.

As the wound widened, the beetle's health bar kept shrinking. I could hardly see anything because my helmet was covered in pieces of the insect's blood and tissue. I couldn't afford to stop and wipe it away because doing so might mean losing the momentum I needed to deal a couple of decisive blows.

As I exhaled, the tip of his tail stung me in the back, transpiercing me and halving my life.

I couldn't breathe. One of my lungs had been

punctured. A bleed DoT and several spine fractures were ebbing my life away. I was swept from his back and smashed against the ground.

I didn't give a shit. As I flew to the ground, I'd managed to puncture him several times through the venom-oozing thick stinger which protruded from my chest.

The last one of these blows finished the monster off. I didn't wait for his body to disappear. In one clean sweep, I lopped off his stinger and disengaged myself from his tail.

He dropped a great big crystal which had dissolved into 680 existence points. I pocketed them, then threw my arms wide and dropped onto my back in the dirt, grinning gleefully as I celebrated my victory over the hideous creature and studied the logs of the fight.

You've dealt damage to the duxio: 1191.

Damage absorbed by armor: 50% Actual damage: 595.

Verifying the probability of making an instant kill (24%)...

Verification complete!

The duxio is dead.

I now had plenty of resources which would last me a long time, or at least until I was disincarnated due to the absence of an available hexagon.

I activated Inconspicuousness and started to plan my next course of action. There were 43 people left in the rankings, out of whom only three actually owned any hexagons. They were Juma who way outstripped the other two: Tafari and some level-6 guy called Björn.

If you added up all of the hexagons they owned between themselves, it didn't correspond with the total number of hexagons in the Trial. Somewhere there was one over, which didn't appear to belong to anyone. Its owner must have died the final death, killed by rampaging monsters.

And I knew exactly where it was.

* * *

Dawn had broken long ago. All the nocturnal monsters were gone, replaced by many packs of daytime ones. Having said that, they were just as predatory albeit smaller and marginally weaker.

Warning! You're about to enter a hexagon captured by another test subject.
Owner: Juma. Level 29
Base level: 1

This was only one of the numerous alerts I'd created by penetrating enemy hexagons — which were normally Juma's with the exception of a few owned by Tafari. Which reminded me of the little boy who'd cried wolf. This time I wasn't trying to go around the base but headed straight for the center of the hexagon, accepting the preplanned risks.

The base was empty. I jumped over the fence and entered the shelter. It was deserted and devoid of any equipment apart from the command center.

Nothing had been done here in the two days that had elapsed since we'd abandoned it, so I wasn't surprised that Juma hadn't bothered to invest into upgrading it.

To capture an enemy hexagon, you must report in person to the command center of the captured territory and remain there for the duration of 1 hour, Pibellau time (13 hours = 1 day) before you can activate the command center.

I spent the one-hour requirement waiting for teleports to start popping. No one had turned up. It might be that the standoff between Juma and Tafari had entered its final phase. Then again, it might be that they'd already received a dozen false alarms, heh! What a bunch of losers!

One way or another, the base would be mine!

I walked over to the white stone and laid my hand on it, the one that was free of my first friend — Fang One.

Do you want to capture the command center?

Cost: 300 existence resource points

Yes!

I initiated the seizure process, then activated Inconspicuousness, prepared to defend my rightful property tooth and claw.

You've captured a hexagon!

**Your command center has been activated.
Name of command center: Base 1.
Owner: Phil, level 21 human.**

The disincarnation timer had disappeared. I even managed to build a level-one fighting unit module and generate a Utahraptor by the time the alarm had gone off again. This time, it was me who'd received the warning. The loss of the hexagon hadn't gone unnoticed as those idiots had finally put two and two together.

Test subject! An enemy has infiltrated your territory! Base 1 is under threat of capture!

Predictably, a group of five fighters turned up in the hexagon. They were Juma's men who'd arrived from the neighboring base.

Too late. I'd already done what I wanted.

All the same, I topped it off by initiating the generation of a new Tyrannosaurus, then lay low, lurking in some prickly undergrowth next to the base under the cover of Inconspicuousness.

If Rex managed to reappear, it would be a nice surprise for the aggressors. And I wouldn't be long in coming.

I didn't get the chance to see Rex though because of the group of warriors who stormed the base. Their leader was level 20, the others, 15. It seemed as if Juma's clan had now resources to burn.

I suppressed my desire to engage them in combat as an irrational departure from my plan. For that reason, I didn't see what happened next because I had already taken flight on my Utahraptor's back. My group Inconspicuousness worked fine for both of us, allowing us to escape unnoticed.

In any case, I'd already received more than I'd bargained for. I'd won a mount and some extra time. Judging by the fact that Rex's interface icon had never reappeared, his generation must have been aborted the moment those losers had seized the base.

* * *

I spent the rest of the day struggling through one enemy hexagon after the other, heading further to the north west where, according to my calculations, was the last uncaptured base. Both the east and the center of the map had long been seized by Juma and Tafari while the west had been claimed by us. The only remaining dark spot was a small patch in the top left corner of the Trial field, hemmed in by a chain of cliffs.

The fact that the surface area of the hexagons shrank every day played right into my hands. In order to cross a hexagon now, I had to run almost a mile less.

That night, I repeated my false alarm trick, seizing another one of Juma's hexagons, only to flee again, this time from two groups of five warriors. To make matters worse, Ken was in one of them so this time they did notice me, but they were on foot so I easily left them behind.

Still, the risk had been worth it as the disincarnation timer had been reset again.

Two hexagons later, I emerged from Inconspicuousness in order to farm some resources. I killed a few more elite mobs: a two-headed odzi snake followed by a kraider: what looked like a kitchen stool with a human body and crab's pinchers for hands, plus a couple of duxio. As one of the effects caused by the fact that the Trial had entered its final phase, these were stronger than those that had attacked the base at night. Had it not been for my friends Fangs One and Two, their attacks would have meant the end of me. Thanks to the theory of relativity, an "instant kill" now took me about twenty blows with Fang Two.

I had enough resources to level up but I was saving them in case I needed instant regeneration in battle.

By dawn, I'd almost reached my objective: the cracked rocky plateau which was overgrown with occasional reddish-brown patches of shrubbery and twisted purple grass.

The plateau offered a breathtaking view of the Trial field dissected by a plethora of motley hexagonal shapes. From here, you could clearly see their edges flicker, distorting what was behind them like streams of hot air rising from overheated tarmac.

A little further to the north I could make out a rocky outcrop. It didn't take me long to get there. But once I'd scrambled up, I could see that in order to get over to the other side, I'd have to cross a wide chasm. Unfortunately, it was the same width everywhere. I walked along the whole outcrop looking for a place where it might narrow until I was confronted by an impenetrable wall of mist which marked the western boundary of the Trial field.

Taking a better look, I noticed a rock that was jutting out on the other side of the chasm. If I took a running jump of a couple of steps, I might just make it.

I shoved both Fangs back into my backpack to make sure they didn't get in the way. In doing so, I'd had to really struggle to peel off the grip of Fang One still entwined around my forearm: the wretched thing just didn't want to listen, so I had to explain to it that this was only a temporary measure. I did it mentally, of course.

Finally, the dagger agreed with my reasoning and slipped from my hand.

Due to lack of space, I had to take off diagonally across the narrow rocky plateau. I took a desperate leap and flew head first, grabbing on to the protruding ledge opposite. Only when I climbed it, I dared to glance down but couldn't see the bottom. Even if I'd survived the fall, I wouldn't have lasted very long, due to all the vampire leeches, the sarasur cockroaches and steely centipedes with spiky bodies who'd be more than happy to take me apart in a matter of minutes.

I heaved my body up and climbed out of the chasm. The flickering veil that marked the next hexagon's boundary was only a few feet away from me.

I stepped through it. Judging by the absence of system alerts, the hexagon was indeed vacant: the one I'd been looking for.

Here, the rocky outcrop gave way to a rainforest abundant with color: tree trunks were ten to twenty feet wide, overgrown with orange, purple and blue.

It was absolutely teeming with wildlife. I equipped my two Fangs and activated Inconspicuousness to make sure I didn't have to waste time on any aggressive mobs.

I forced my way through the undergrowth, heading toward the hexagon's center. Soon I reached a small clearing covered with strange-looking plants. At its center stood a guy: short, stocky and fair-haired, dressed in civilian clothes: blue jeans, a T-shirt and a pair of sneakers.

Björn, human
Level: 7

I was just about to activate both Stun and Treacherous Shadow when I decided to find out more about him first. You never know, he might be one of Juma's or Tafari's men.

"Demetrious[20]?" the guy uttered, his voice ringing with anxiety.

"Hi," I touched my helmet, disabling the visor. It raised, revealing my face.

"Who are you?" he asked in fear.

"Don't worry, I won't harm you," I lied, trying to win this loser's confidence. "You've just respawned, haven't you? What life are you on,

_____

[20] Demetrious is Björn's virtual assistant in *Level Up: The Knockout*, same as Phil's Martha

worm?"

He shrugged without taking his eyes off my daggers. There was definitely something wrong about him.

"Are you Björn?" I paused, waiting for him to answer, then reworded the question. "Is your name Björn, worm?"

"Björn? How did you know? Actually, Mike's the name. Mike Hagen. And I'm definitely not a worm."

"You are the worst kind of worm, Mike Hagen! A useless loser who'd managed to cling onto his pathetic life, while those much worthier than you have already met their final deaths!"

Blinking, he shook his head. A glint of understanding flickered in his gaze. "Who are you?" he repeated. "I can see your name is Phil, level 21. Are you gonna kill me?"

"I don't know yet. If you don't get in the way, I might just capture this hexagon. Then I'll think what to do with you."

Not that I needed him. He was a liability, but his Charisma points might come in handy.

I eased him away from the stone and lay my hand on it, activating the command center. The three waves of energy rippled through the air as they formed the base and the shelter, the last one pushing Björn out from under the safety of the dome.

Excellent. This place could keep me safe for the time being, or at least until one of the two leaders had been eliminated.

I exited the dome. Björn stood behind the

fence, apparently hesitant to re-enter the base.

"Come here, you... Björn, or Mike, whatever."

"Why? Are you gonna kill me?" he leapt over the fence and walked over to me.

"I don't know yet. Where did you turn up from? Are you always so casual? Where's your hexagon?"

"I lost it! Lost everything! Some crazy doughboy did me in!"

"When did it happen? Was it last night?"

"Exactly! *Bilyat!*"

"What did you say?"

"*Bilyat!*" he repeated the Russian cuss word, distorting it beyond recognition, then burst out laughing.

"Where did get that word from, you idiot?"

"You're Russian, aren't you?" he asked confidently. "Back IRL, I'm sharing a jail cell with a Russian guy. His name is Roman. He taught me how to say it."

"What life are you on, worm?"

"It's my last one," he shrugged. "Bullshit. The quicker I get myself killed, the sooner I'll get back to jail. They're probably missing me already."

"Relax. Back on Earth, nothing much has changed."

"I don't think so. I've been stuck here for a week already. More, even. They're probably thinking I escaped," a dark shadow crossed his face. He really seemed to feel out of place here.

"You have any idea how you got here and what you're doing?"

"Sort of. Frankly, at first I thought I was

dreaming. I'd just had a good thrashing in the ring before it happened."

"In the ring? Where, in jail?"

"Yeah," he nodded. "Our director holds illegal fights at nighttime in the furniture workshop. We call it the 'wooden ring'. The director promises to release the champion before his time is up."

"And?"

"And I just got my lights punched out. When I came around, I wasn't even surprised to find myself in a really weird place. There were some strange people hanging round."

As he went on to describe them, I recognized Khphor, Ilindi and Valiadis complete in shining armor.

He went on to tell me how he'd passed the pre-Trial and ended up here. It took him a long time to work out what was required of him. He kept re-reading the messages, trying to make sense of them. The guy wasn't the sharpest knife in the drawer, that's for sure.

"Then another guy came on a black rhino's back. He was very tall, seven foot at least, and he just chopped my head off without saying a word."

"You mean Tafari?"

"*Safari?* I suppose so... judging by the rhino..." he chuckled. "Then I found myself in a different place. It took me almost an hour to work out what was required of me. I didn't know that I could have died again if I hadn't farmed some existence resources. Luckily, there was this creature that looked a bit like a doughboy with tentacles and I managed to kill it in the end. It dropped an existence crystal. After that, I got the hang of it and began farming resources. I finally had enough to make level 3 and activate the command center. And just as I walked over to the stone, I saw there was already another guy hanging around there. His name was Zack."

"No way!" I said, remembering that Zack had indeed told me about meeting a guy called Mike. "What about him?"

"He saw me and tried to pull the wool over my eyes, asking me who I was and what I was doing there. And once I'd lowered my guard, he attacked me from behind."

"Zack attacked you? That useless piece of shit? That's novel!"

Mike frowned. "Ah, so you know him?"

"I do. You're a nice pair of losers, you two!"

"Listen, you think I don't understand?" he exclaimed. "Sure, your level is three times mine, you've got some cool blades and an awesome suit — you're just like goddamn Darth Vader, only your helmet's different — but! I'm not a loser! Nor a worm! Back on Earth, I used to knock out guys whose levels were several times mine! Don't you call me that again!"

"If you say so... worm."

"Heh! Okay, you're tough. I don't give a shit anymore. How do you know that scumbag Zack? What can you tell me about him?"

"Nothing good, I'm afraid," I said, gnashing my teeth at the thought of the treacherous bastard. The fact that this useless guy had already crossed swords with my enemy gave him a couple of good points in my book. "When I see him, I"ll cut him to shreds."

"I see. He wasn't much of a fighter though. When he got the shit kicked out of him, he just ran off on whatever little health he had left. I didn't chase after him. I just captured the hexagon, and then I discovered I'd been awarded an achievement."

"What kind of achievement?"

"Heh!" he chuckled, cleared his throat, then went on, "Apparently, I was last in the pre-Trials, so they gave me -30% to development rate. To compensate for it, they also gave me an extra life and a temporary talent called Hermit. It was triggered automatically the moment I'd captured the hexagon, denying all the other trial participants access to my base."

As it turned out, Mike had spent most of the Trial in his little hole, not daring to leave the hexagon because doing so would have disabled Hermit.

"So basically, last night I got really bored. This was all turning into some sort of Groundhog Day. I spent all my nights under the dome and during the day, I just smoked mobs. I was so bored I built a couple of modules and got myself a few dogs," he smiled. "They were so nice."

"What happened to them?"

"They were the first ones to die. I decided to go for a bit of a walk, just to see what was going on, and I just walked into somebody else's hexagon."

"Whose was it, Juma's? Or Tafari's?"

"Juma's. I got to his base without any hassle, and that's where they pounced on me. I tried to reason with them but they didn't want to know. In the blink of an eye, they'd killed all the dogs and sent me back to my resurrection point. I came round by the white stone. I had no resources left to activate it. I spent almost an hour hiding from mobs and then I decided to take on a doughboy which didn't appear to be too dangerous. Big mistake. I'd never hurt so much in my life! When I died, I spent a long time in a pitch-black void. The pain was mind-blowing. Then I turned up here. I only opened my eyes, and there you were, standing next to me."

This could have been the observers' doing. They must have decided against having Mike resurrect at night, giving him the opportunity to save his last life. That also explained his initial reaction to me: you had to have a very strong spirit to preserve your sanity after several hours in the great void.

"You might be useful to me, Björn," I said. "I'm sending you the invitation to join my clan."

✳ ✳ ✳

There was no point in wasting resources on that nonentity, especially considering his penalties, so I just gave him a set of gear from my extradimensional stocks, plus the Power Fist seeing as he was a boxer anyway, and the Lightning Rod to deal some long-range damage without having to approach the hexagon's high-level mobs.

Meanwhile, I kept a constant eye on the rankings, watching for any developments in Juma and Tafari's standoff. It looked like Juma hadn't yet plucked up enough courage to deal a decisive blow — either that, or Tafari had been trying to avoid throwing all his forces into a direct confrontation. A few participants from both sides had died the final death and been disincarnated and knocked out.

This played right into my hands. My plan seemed to be taking shape. I had to keep on leveling until one of the leaders eliminated the other, then try to steal up on the survivor and kill him, whoever it was. My chances were negligible but I was going to take them even if the odds were one in a thousand.

During light hours, Mike and I kept smoking packs of daytime mobs, then spent the night farming the elite ones trying to proceed very cautiously.

By morning, I had enough resources to buy level 25 and with it, a new class talent.

Liquidator
Class level: 4
Level 4 talent
Liquidator's Marker: allows you to place a marker on any active test subject in order to track their position on the map.
Cooldown: 24 hrs.

I then invested all my characteristic points into Luck. There wasn't much point in building up damage, seeing as I put all my faith into Fang Two's ability to kill instantly. Leveling up Stamina was equally pointless. As for Agility, I didn't need it at all anymore because I wasn't using any long-range weapons. Should I invest in Charisma? Also pointless, as I already had plenty. Neither Intellect nor Perception gave me any advantage in combat. But Luck... my entire strategy was based on that particular stat.

I decided to check my new talent out on Zack. I had a very big bone to pick with him.

As I activated the new ability, I saw a full list of all the current Trial participants. I scrolled it down, then focused on the name I'd been looking for:

Target selected:
Zack, human.
Level 20
Liquidator's Marker has been set.
Put more fire under your enemies' feet, Liquidator!

The message was replaced by a 3D arrow pointing in the right direction. The number underneath it read,

19 miles

"Hey Mikey, how about we pay our friend Zack a visit?"

Mike grinned. "Why not?"

In the time that he'd been with me, I'd learned a lot about him. And the more he'd told me about himself — about his miserable childhood in a slum district and about all the bullying he'd suffered due to his small stature, even about his ability to cry from the slightest of insults, up to the day he'd received his interface — the more respect his life story commanded. I didn't regard him as a useless loser anymore.

In his case, his version of the interface was some take on video fighting games. Predictably, it had no social status levels: Mike received his XP for victories in the ring. But unlike Nagash, he was no scumbag.

The social-status version of the interface didn't automatically turn people into starry-eyed wimps — one look at Zack or Leti was proof enough. However, that meant that the opposite was also true: the standard version of the interface developed by the Senior Races didn't automatically turn men into sociopathic monsters. A lot depended on the person's identity — the very essence of their existence, if you wish.

"How are we gonna find him?" Mike asked, all businesslike, then added a Russian swear word for a good measure.

"My new talent will help us," I said. "Mount up! Rex, you stay and guard the base!"

The new Rex breathed heavily just like the old one as he watched us leave the base on the Utahraptors' backs. It had taken Mike a long time to overcome his fear of Rex; he often said that his Uncle Peter had taught him a lot of things, one of which was never to needlessly hang around big galoots. In Mike's eyes, Rex was bigger and more galooty than all the big galoots he'd known in the past, so it had taken him a whole day of hunting as a team to get used to my Tyrannosaurus.

The chasm which restricted access to our hexagon was no barrier for our Raptors who could easily accelerate to 25 miles per hour and leap up to 30 feet, so our only problem was to hold on to them as tight as we could.

It took us several hours to get to Zack's hexagon, ignoring all the mobs on our way and leaving behind a trail of activated alarms for Juma and Tafari to worry about. We used Inconspicuousness to skirt around all the bases and disabled my talent every time we approached any hexagons' boundaries.

As we approached Zack, I began to realize that strangely enough, he was still cloistered in the same hexagon where he'd spent the last few days according to our agreement. Could Juma really have permitted him to stay unchallenged on his base? What, with his ability to permeate the entire field with his teleports?

Having said that...

I had no doubt that Zack felt perfectly safe. Tafari couldn't get to him without having to cross a good dozen hexagons — and even if an alarm went off, he could either run off or sit it out and wait for help to arrive.

Which meant I had to watch out and activate Shroud of Shadow before moving any further.

Warning! You're about to enter a hexagon captured by another test subject.
Owner: Juma. Level 30
Base level: 3
Special effects:

-10% to all characteristics

"This is our guy," I told Mike. "He's less than half a mile away. Which means he's not at the base but out farming. We're gonna steal up on him now, so please don't rush into anything. First we need to find out whether he's alone and what other forces he might have at hand. Ideally, we shouldn't let him escape. The base is level 3 which means he has at least a few plasma turrets and also the ability to teleport out."

"Got it," Mike said. "Is that all? Let's go already! Time to kick some butt!"

"I'll do all the kicking. You're only level 7, so don't you even think about it. Keep on firing from a distance."

"Why did I have to come with you at all?" he moaned.

"To provide some entertainment on the way. That's your main objective. Let's do it!"

When Zack was less than three hundred feet away from us, we left our Raptors to graze by a big tree and continued on foot.

I was the first to see him. I raised my hand, motioning Mike to stop.

I watched Zack stalk toward us, looking for mobs to hunt. He was now level 20 courtesy of Juma. Judging by his ranking, his class was really rare: Master of the Elements. He didn't seem to have his spiders with him though — so Juma must have taken his Charisma points for himself.

That's when Mike screwed up big time.

"Hi, Zack!" he left the Inconspicuousness

zone and headed for our enemy. "It looks like we haven't resolved our differences last time."

I growled in fury. What an asshole! I slapped the top of my helmet without leaving Inconspicuousness.

Because of this dimwit, I'd have to play it by ear. I could always miniport behind Zack's back in order to stun him.

"You?" Zack sounded surprised. Still, he promptly recovered from the initial shock, taking in Mike's low level. "With great pleasure!"

He raised his hands in the air and clapped them once.

A trail of frost reached out for Mike, freezing his feet, then climbing up, immobilizing his entire body. Although his health remained intact, the Freeze debuff timer began ticking, beginning a 10-second countdown. Impressive.

With a nasty little laugh, Zack waved his hands, then clapped them again, shouting something about fire.

At that moment, I materialized behind his back and stunned him. Thinking about my fallen comrades, I performed a record-quick combo.

Had this been on Earth, he would have already been dead. But here, the game mechanics had played right into his hands.

Mike's body went up in flames. His face distorted with pain.

That was his own fault!

Zack was still immobilized when yet another blow from a combo performed by Fang Two had finished him off.

The player who'd failed to live up to Ilindi's expectations was disincarnated and kicked out of the Trial. His name on the rankings list went inactive, stripping Juma's clan of an important strategic advantage by denying them the ability to teleport to any hexagon they wanted. If they wanted to get to my base, they had their work cut out for them now.

"Come on, level up!" I shouted to Mike. "You have enough resources to heal yourself!"

"I don't think so," he wheezed with a smile on his face. "I've had enough of this shit."

I watched as the Burning DoT stripped him of the last few percent of his life.

His charred face made me shudder. The flesh and bones of his skull had been lain bare, black eye sockets gaping in the bloodied mess.

"Good luck, Phil... See you around..."

"Why, Mikey? Why did you have to do this? That was irrational."

"Dunno... Two against one... without warning.... I didn't wanna stab him in the back..."

I second-guessed his last words because his body had already disappeared, leaving his weapons behind.

No, I wasn't sorry for that weird loser with his old-fashioned ideas of honor. I was even happy I hadn't wasted my resources on him. Still, I knew that once I'd removed the dagger which demanded me to be rational on my way to victory, I'd mourn yet another loss of a fellow fighter.

I swiped away a golden message balloon that had appeared in the air. I'd have to look at it later. I picked up the loot dropped by Zack and Mike and decided to return to the base. The next morning, I would select Juma as Liquidator's next target.

When I finally got to the base, the suns were already setting.

Time to give it your all, test subject!

The global boss Deel'Agha is about to be released into the Trial field!

Kill him in order to receive a well-deserved award:

300,000 existence points;

the legendary Suppressor artifact;

a summoning whistle;

and an extra life for each of your clan members!

Who dares, wins! Put more fire under your enemies' feet, test subject!

Chapter

Twenty-Six

A Chance to Learn Something New

Break the bones and the body will heal.
Break the spirit and the body will die...

Diablo

I ASKED THE CASINO'S MANAGEMENT TO TRANSFER all my winnings — several millions — to a number of charity funds. I didn't need them, but neither did I want to risk exposing Kira in this particular case.

When I'd returned to my room, Laura was in panic. In order to leave the room, I'd used Stealth and Vanish which was my second heroic ability. At the time, it had seemed a good idea: all I wanted was neutralize Panchenko. Still, my mysterious disappearance for several hours had very nearly driven the previously-calm girl to a nervous breakdown. She hadn't reported my escape yet, hoping against hope that I might be back.

"You could have warned me!" she yelled at me. "That way I could have gone with you or at least given you some cover!"

"Stop your noise now. We can carry on with the search now, only let's have dinner first. I'm absolutely starving."

I spent the rest of the day working, ticking off names on the list. Only then did I finally flake out, but not before I'd distributed all the available points equally between Intellect and Perception. I still hoped I might make it to level 30 which came with Tier-3 heroic abilities.

Tier 3
Ability name: Foresight
Ability type: Active, Heroic
Allows you to transport yourself to a new reality model for the duration of 15 seconds, then return to the skill activation starting point.

Tier 3
Ability name: Berserker
Ability type: Active, Heroic
A combat skill which triples all your main characteristics for the duration of 15 seconds.

Tier 3
Ability name: Persuasion
Ability type: Active, Heroic
The skill endows the user with a 100% power of persuasion, allowing him or her to win over all human beings whose social status level is lower than his or her own. The possibility of

winning over those human beings whose social status level is equal or surpasses that of the user wanes accordingly.

Warning! Any attempt to use the skill for anti-social purposes will result in it being permanently blocked.

Tier 3
Ability name: Invulnerability
Ability type: Active, Heroic
The skill creates a temporary nano film which envelops the user's entire body, making him impervious to any attacks or other aggressive acts. The skill can self-activate without the user's knowledge whenever there's an external threat to his or her life or wellbeing.
Duration: 15 sec

Each of these abilities was indeed heroic, allowing me to attain great heights. Still, I put my faith in Invulnerability. You never know, it might just work against Eroul's Curse (as I'd nicknamed Panchenko's spell). Then again, could it really be considered an "external threat"?

In any case, it's not as if I didn't have much to do: I had three more social status levels to make and all the relevant characteristics to level up until midday which was the curse's deadline. Which didn't sound too realistic.

But the human heart always hopes for the best. For a miracle, even.

Thus wishfully thinking, I went for what might become the last breakfast of my life. Then I surpassed myself in locating criminals one after another at record speed, trying not to look at the curse countdown.

"Take this," Laura, who'd left the room momentarily and was now back, handed me a large Coke. "You said you needed more sugar, didn't you? Here's a shedload."

"Thanks. Will you just put it down next to me, okay? You're distracting me," I said without taking my eyes off the map and the notes on the iPad.

She nodded and set the Coke on the coffee table. "I just need one more second of your time, Phil. I need to leave for half an hour. I have a-"

"Okay," I interrupted her, wrinkling my forehead at a sudden pang of intuition which I couldn't quite place. "I'll be in my room."

I was in a hurry, so immersed in my work I didn't even notice her leave. My eyes were fixed on my interface, my hands clutching the iPad containing the files, a laptop on my knees as I corresponded back and fro with Gary Grant.

By now, the searching process had become much easier. One glance at a person's name and picture was enough to trigger Insight which would spin the globe until it showed the right place on the map. I would then enter its coordinates into the right file on the iPad and press Send, which would deliver the data automatically at the CIA.

I patiently copied the coordinates of all the criminals, murderers, and terrorists. Laura hadn't come back yet but my interface kept me company, showering me with XP.

Almost simultaneously I received several new

social status levels:

Congratulations! You've received a new level!
Your current social status level: 30

Congratulations! You've received a new system skill level!
Skill name: Heroism
Current level: 3
Now you can activate the Tier-3 heroic abilities: Foresight, Berserker, Persuasion and Invulnerability, provided their requirements are met.
XP received: 1000

I distributed every single point, but I couldn't decide on the new Heroic ability to choose. My characteristics weren't yet enough to get Invulnerability and as for all the others, I just couldn't decide what to choose.

My Intuition was screaming that I shouldn't choose anything yet, so in the end I obeyed and returned to the task at hand.

The last open name on the system map was a certain Khair Al-Umari guilty of killing and seriously injuring six thousand people. As I focused on his marker, a thought crossed my mind: wouldn't it be nice to see what kind of person he really was. What if everything they had listed in the files was fictitious?

My interface promptly reacted to my request,

offering a long description of everything this person had done in his whole life from the moment of his birth. The text scrolled so quickly it resembled the raindrops flying off the windscreen or a fast-moving car. Apparently, the program had taken my request too literally.

Do you want to activate a data filter?

It wouldn't do any harm. The program offered me a choice of several categories pertaining to the life of Al-Umari: all of its key temporal branches as well as all the actions and events that had affected his social status level.

The filter made my life so much easier, compressing the entire life of this not-the-run-of-the-mill person in a dozen brief lines:

Born in Egypt into the family of a university professor, Khair Al-Umari graduated as a surgeon from the medical faculty of Cairo University, soon becoming one of the leaders of an extremist group in his home country. He was subsequently arrested on suspicion of planning an assassination attempt but escaped to Afghanistan where he helped coordinate the 9/11 attacks...

Once I'd finished reading and knew more about this person, I tried to figure out his motives. The program showed me his connections with Al-Qaeda as well as the Egyptian Islamic Jihad and ISIL.

Focusing on these connections gave me

access to more blocks of text, describing the story of his initial involvement and all the wheres, whys and hows this had incurred.

What a shame my interface couldn't upload information straight to my brain.

Then his connections began branching, entwining the whole world and reaching out beyond the ocean. His family ties were marked green, as well as his partners, financial sources and networks of sleeper cells. All hostile people and organizations opposing him were marked red.

The network kept branching out further, revealing more new names and faces of seemingly innocuous people. "Seemingly" being the operative word.

My throat dried up. I reached for the Coke left by Laura, mechanically checking its chemical composition. Water, carbon dioxide, sugar, coloring, orthophosphoric acid — those were all self-explanatory, listed on every bottle with the familiar red label. But I could also see all the other ones which must have made up the proverbial secret ingredient: the essential oils of orange, lemon and coriander; pentobarbital...

Wait up there. The last ingredient absolutely didn't belong in a bottle of soda.

These days, I had no need for Google: my direct access to the universal infospace immediately offered me the substance's full description. *A derivative of barbituric acid which exerted an inhibitory effect on the central nervous system, causing a soporific effect.*

There! But why?

I took another glance at the spider's gossamer web of threads branching off Al-Umari's marker. One of them, a green one, led directly to a person called Laura Flores: the dowdy bespectacled wallflower whose motives I was yet to figure out.

I opened the girl's profile and activated the filter.

Someone knocked timidly on the door. "Room service!"

I could smell a rat. My pulse quickened. Slowly I rose and took a few steps toward the door. Obeying a signal from my Intuition, I activated Foresight.

The world froze momentarily, blinking a couple times, then went back to normal.

I headed for the door. They knocked again, three light taps with a crooked finger.

"Who is it?" I asked as I unlocked the door.

The door swung open, hitting me hard in the forehead. I dropped to the floor. A human form loomed over me. A syringe needle sank into my neck.

The last thing I saw was a muffled whisper and the rustling of a trolley being pushed in.

Warning! An abnormally high number of instances of aggression detected, targeting a user whose social status level is several times higher than that of his attackers!

In view of this, the environmental safety index can be reassessed and lowered to Code Orange. That in turn will release 3 new available main characteristic points.

The earlier restriction specifying that the

user could only unblock one heroic ability per every 10 social status levels gained can be lowered accordingly to one heroic ability per every 5 social status levels gained by the user.

Accept / Decline

Oh, finally. *Accept.*

The next moment I was standing back by my chair, iPad in hand. My maxed-out Intellect didn't allow me to wallow in hesitation: I grasped the situation instantly, opening my profile and unblocking two of my Tier-2 abilities:

Tier 2
Ability name: Regeneration
Ability type: Active, Heroic
Removes all negative effects from the user, such as Disease, Curse, Poisoning, Bleeding or Exposure to Radiation. Accelerates Recovery and improves Confidence, Self-Control, Satisfaction, Vigor, Mood and Willpower.

Tier 2
Ability name: Sprint
Ability type: Active, Heroic
Ability class: Combat
Accelerates the user 100% by modifying his or her Metabolism and Perception for the duration of 5 seconds.

I activated Regeneration.

How could I have possibly missed the key

word in its description? How? Apparently, I'd been too busy thinking of other things.

A warm healing wave spread over my body. My Vitality (read: Health) was now at 100%. I'd never been so healthy in my life!

My Confidence, Self-Control, Vigor, Satisfaction, Willpower and Mood were all at 100%, too. Every new coming wave smoothed out the scars, erasing all the recent scratches and grazes I'd earned in the days of my intense training. Every single bruise and mosquito bite was gone. My blocked nose — the first sign of an impending cold — breathed freely now.

The process lagged slightly before the arrival of the last and most powerful wave.

My fully restored Spirit began to dwindle — but in the end, the ability did live up to its promise. Both the curse icon and the deadly countdown timer disappeared.

Once again I heard knocking on the door: three light taps with a crooked finger. I picked up the iPad and dove behind the bed.

I heard a click as someone opened the door from the outside with a magnetic card which definitely wasn't mine.

"Room service," a strange woman's voice said.

My increased Perception allowed me to catch the almost noiseless sound of footsteps over the carpeted floor. The footsteps of several people.

"Where is he?" someone asked.

"He has to be here somewhere," the fake "chambermaid" replied. "He probably passed out. She put some sedative in his drink."

Just then, my phone on the desk started to ring and vibrate.

"He's here somewhere!" the woman announced, stopping at the center of the room. "Find him!"

Not waiting for them to discover me, I activated Stealth and Vanish.

So Laura had sold me down the river. Seeing as I had nothing good to expect from my visitors, I activated Sprint.

Time slowed down. All of me — including the bathrobe and the iPad in my hands — became invisible.

The invisibility timer froze on the 3 sec mark. I stood up, taking in several fit guys wearing balaclavas with narrow eye slits. Although I couldn't see their faces, their stats spoke volumes, revealing the gossamer threads of their connections with Khair Al-Umari. These guys had come here to seriously hurt me.

I darted off, threading my way gingerly past their aggressive motionless shapes and past the fake "chambermaid" Miranda who was craning her neck in an attempt to spot me. I grabbed my baseball cap, slid through the still-closing door, dashed past another one of the three minders in the corridor and even managed to make it to the elevator on whatever precious little was left of my invisibility allowance.

Unfortunately, as I entered the elevator, I became visible again — but no one was chasing after me; in fact, no one had noticed me riding downstairs,

Once in the elevator, I checked the three

intruders' Motivations which revealed their terrorist connections, then created new markers for each of them. Another group member was waiting outside in a cab, with two more waiting for me in the hotel's stairwell and the hotel lobby. Which meant they weren't going to kill me.

My interface confirmed my deductions. Apparently, they'd been planning to kidnap me and deliver me to the port of Altamira, Mexico.

I slammed the baseball cap deep onto my eyes and dove into the first cab I saw.

The driver looked up questioningly at me. "Where to?"

"T-Mobile Arena, please," I gave him the only address I knew in this city.

I checked my pockets and heaved a disappointed sigh. I had nothing on me: no money, no passport, no cell phone. What was I supposed to do?

My mind was racing. Apparently, neither Sanchez nor Alex Tomasik had anything to do with what had just happened — but even so, how was I supposed to contact them? The only link I could use without risking to reveal myself to the terrorists was Angela Howard. I could email her, I suppose.

What a shame I'd had to leave my phone and the laptop in my hotel room. Somehow I didn't think those guys would overlook them. It was a good job I never saved any passwords and logins: I kept all the necessary stuff in my head.

Right... where *could* I go? Where could I lie low for a while? Sanchez was due back after lunchtime: I had little doubts he'd start searching for me straight away.

I checked the iPad. It had no Internet connection which meant I'd have to find a nice quiet place with a Wi-Fi and preferably a bit of money to last me a while. I didn't want to escape from the cabbie without paying him — or worse even, apply violence to him.

"Sorry, I've changed my mind," I said, then gave him the address of Mike Hagen, the fellow interface user.

Chapter
Twenty-Seven

what's so wrong with fairy tales?

I didn't deserve to walk away. There are no happy endings.

Max Payne 2: The Fall of Max Payne

IT WAS NIGHT ON PIBELLAU. THE ELEVENTH NIGHT OF my Trial. I'd love to have known how much time had elapsed back on Earth. Although technically the Pibellau day only lasted thirteen hours, subjectively it felt longer. Not much but still.

The starlight cast fancy shadows at Rex's head looming above. By the time I'd come back, he'd already made his way through several packs of low-level mobs which had tried to get to the base, so it had taken me some time to pick up all the existence crystals.

The global boss Deel'Agha announced his arrival with a blood-curdling roar which echoed with vibration within your very bones, It might be the fact that the boss was only three hexagons away from me, judging by his marker on the map, or it could be some special sound enhancing technique. Or it could just be a soundtrack accompanying a new system message.

In any case, the effect was spine-chilling. My heart missed a beat; the hairs of my arms bristled. Instinctively I bared my fangs. The Trial organizers were applying pressure to the participants at all possible levels, mental included. I hadn't even seen the boss yet, but my heart was already in my mouth.

I tried to put myself in my enemies' shoes in order to second-guess any eventual developments. The arrival of the boss was bad news for Juma who, on top of trying to use his resources to methodically squeeze his opponent off the field, was now obliged to consider this new variable.

Because if Tafari's clan managed to eliminate Deel'Agha, that would change the whole power balance. Just think of all the extra lives, an absolute wealth of resources, a legendary artifact whose properties were admittedly vague but whose name spoke of itself: Suppressor. And a summoning whistle: the very fact that it was spelt with little letters implied it was supposed to be something quite ordinary — but who or what was it supposed to summon? Was it supposed to bring a clan's entire force to one particular location? Or did it summon some unknown almighty beings? Or even Deel'Agha himself?

Any way you looked at it, whoever beat the global boss was sure to win the Trial.

In any case, chances were that both clans would arise at dawn and set off in search of Deel'Agha. Doubtful that either of them would dare challenge him at night when there were so many elite mobs on the prowl.

Which just might become my lucky break.

"Rex," I called.

The Tyrannosaurus turned his head and emitted a noisy gasp.

"So, my trusty friend, are you ready? Should we give our enemies a run for their money?"

Rex parted his putrid jaws. *"Whoo!"*

Although you could interpret it any way you want, somehow I thought he was fully in agreement with me.

"Well, in that case, let's try and do it. Be quiet, okay? I'll cast Inconspicuousness on us both."

I decided to set off with the first sunrays, hoping Rex would manage to cross the chasm without dropping in it — or getting stuck halfway down it — and that my Inconspicuousness would be enough to conceal us from Deel'Agha's eyes.

In the meantime, I fully intended to spend the entire night farming. With my leveling bonus, nearly every elite mob I killed would garner me enough resources (give or take a few, depending on each particular mob) to buy a new level. At this stage of the Trial, they offered way more health points — but were also much more dangerous damage-wise. For the rest, they didn't differ much from the old ones: same strategy, same tricks. To tell you the truth, even our video game monsters back on Earth were much more complex tactics-wise.

But first I have to tell you something very interesting. As soon as that funny idiot, Mike "Björn" Hagen, had died the final death, I saw a little golden balloon hanging in the field of my vision. I'd seen two very similar ones when I'd killed Kreken, so I knew it had to be an achievement message.

I have to admit I hadn't been in a hurry to open it. First, I had to leave Zack's hexagon pronto, and later, I decided to wait until I made a safe home run and returned to the base. Which made sense.

Now I popped the balloon, hoping for another freebie from the observers.

Achievement unlocked: The Last Loner
You're the last trial participant in this wave who continues to contest for victory without support from his vassals while not being somebody else's vassal.
Reward: The Rock of Time

Before I could even begin to celebrate, the last line disappeared, replaced by some new text which thwarted my expectations.

Decision aborted! The observers' choice overrun!

By the decision of the Senior Supervisor (Trial Wave 4), the reward has been modified.
New reward:
+1 Life
+1 talent point to invest into a class talent of your choice

This was nothing that could possibly work as the proverbial red nuclear button. Having said that, this unexpected gift did open new avenues of my potential action.

I opened my profile to make sure I had it. Oh yes.

Now I could try and risk it without having to wait until morning. That is, I'd have to risk it, anyway — but now I could do so twice. I really had to try and kill the global boss single-handedly first thing, just to humor the observers and justify their expectations. That's why they'd offered me this bonus to begin with, hadn't they?

Phil, human.
Level: 25.
Class: Liquidator. Level: 4
Health points: 3200/3200.
Damage without weapon: 35-39.
Chance of critical hit: 54.5%.
Bonus: 14% off the cost of character development.
Achievements: Altruist, First Giant Slayer, First Daredevil, First to Die, The Last Loner.

Main characteristics:
Strength: 37
Agility: 11
Intellect: 20
Stamina: 32
Perception: 21
Charisma: 20
Luck: 23

Character stats
Lives: 2.
Captured hexagons: 1.
Ranking: 3/169.
Existence resources: 1259/25000.
Liquidator
Level 1 talents:
Treacherous Shadow. Allows a liquidator to vanish, then immediately reappear behind their opponent's back. Active range: 150 feet.
Stun. Allows a liquidator to paralyze their target for the duration of 5 seconds.

Level 2 talents:
Inconspicuousness. Allows the liquidator to blend into the shadows, stealing up on his opponents and penetrating enemy hexagons.
Dodge. Increases the liquidator's chances of dodging enemy blows for the duration of 10 sec.

Level 3 talent:
Shroud of Shadow. Allows the liquidator and his group to stealth up and infiltrate enemy hexagons without raising the alarm.

Level 4 talent:
Liquidator's Marker: allows you to place a marker on any active test subject in order to track their position on the map.
Talent points available: 1

I studied my talents to see how best to invest

my bonus talent point. As I did so, the program generated pop-up prompts and repeated their contents as a voice in my head.

A level-2 Treacherous Shadow would increase its range to 350 feet, basically doubling it. Not a bad thing when you needed to catch someone or attack them just at the right moment — but it was pretty irrelevant in my situation.

My Stun would be able to paralyze any opponent for 10 seconds instead of the usual 5. That was excellent. A 10-sec paralysis meant twice as many dagger blows. Unfortunately, this particular talent wasn't going to work against the global boss: according to a little side note (which luckily wasn't even in fine print), the probability of successfully stunning Deel'Agha dropped proportionally to the level gap. But in the absence of clan support, it gave me a decent chance to kill someone like Juma.

If I invested the bonus point into Inconspicuousness, it would result in my complete invisibility and prevent anyone at all from disclosing my presence. Even those Juma's guys that Ken had warned me against wouldn't be able to see me.

I made a mental note: this might be an excellent choice.

Investing the point in Dodge wouldn't guarantee my ability to escape every blow, but it doubled its duration. That meant twenty seconds of near-imperviousness, not forgetting that every second or third of my opponent's blows was bound to deal me some damage. Tick.

Investing the bonus point into the Shroud of Shadow would mute any sounds produced by my stealthed-up group. Although admittedly very useful Rex-wise, it was pretty useless in combat, unless I wanted to steal up on one of the two remaining clan leaders and tell Rex to swallow him whole. Not really. The Trial's mechanic wouldn't allow that to happen.

A level-2 Liquidator's Marker, on top of locating the target, would also add a paltry +10% to damage dealt. Only ten percent! But even if it doubled it, it wouldn't be relevant tactics-wise because I was pretty sure that the clan leaders' armor was at least 75% of maximum protection.

Let's take a look...

I checked the manual. Oh wow. With his resources, Juma was bound to have his armor maxed out, which meant -90% to damage dealt.

Which also meant that I had to choose between Stun, Inconspicuousness and Dodge.

This was a choice and a half. To make it, I had to consider all the potential scenarios.

If I wanted to try and kill the global boss myself, hoping for my dagger's chance of making an instant kill, I had to opt for Dodge. But if I aimed to kill one of the two clan leaders, that would require a Stun.

And as for my plan B, it called for the good old Inconspicuousness — something which, if my gaming memory didn't fail me (because the only game erased from my memory did not my entire gaming experience make), was the equivalent of the common-or-garden Stealth which was every rogue's signature ability. Ironically, judging by the choice of my talents, this was exactly what I'd become in the

Trial: a rogue, either as the observers' insider joke or as the result of the Trial system analyzing my mind.

Thus thinking, I hurried to spit a chain of commands at Rex as two duxio had crashed through the fence simultaneously. As his glorious roar paralyzed them, I bared my both daggers and activated Treacherous Shadow, leaping onto the back of one of them.

Brainless nonentities!

* * *

I spent the next several hours in some primeval excitement as I made my way through waves of nocturnal elite mobs until I was faced with a group of nasty acidic doughboys which were immune to physical damage. True, I had my staffs: the electric one, the plasma one and one spewing charges of energy — but chasing those creatures around the dome and shooting back at them wasn't really worthy of a warrior, was it?

Counting the resources I'd had before, what I'd farmed by now was enough to buy me three more levels. I'd been saving them in case I might require urgent regeneration in battle but luckily, I hadn't needed them. Whether it was my boosted Luck or the theory of relativity at work, but Fang Two — the Acid Dagger of Obfuscation — now made an instant kill every 10+ blows. So now, I really should save these resources for my battle with the mega boss who was still busy prowling Juma's and Tafari's respective territories, as large as life and twice as ugly. Which confirmed my theory that neither clan would risk attacking him at nighttime.

"Rex, follow me! Let's do it! Plague, come here!"

Plague was the name I'd given to my Utahraptor mount. The other one — the one which that funny American used to ride — I'd nicknamed Famine. I'd thought it was highly appropriate, in full accordance with the Book of Revelation. War and Death reigned over this Trial, while Mike and I were impersonating the other two Horsemen of the Apocalypse riding Plague and Famine.

Well, everyone is crazy in their own way. Completely alone after the death of my clan members and Mike's stupid demise, not to mention Leti's betrayal, I now had only two friends left: Fang One and Fang Two. And one of these seemed to be changing me every time I picked it up.

Somewhere in the back of my mind I must have known it because the realization of it kept rearing its head, albeit suppressed by the tentacles of the Wicked Dagger of Absorption piercing my skin and penetrating my nerve endings and blood vessels.

The dagger kept severing my mind, disengaging it from everything that was irrelevant — either irrational or *weak* — everything that could either *distract* me or *get in my way*, forcing me to stretch myself to the limit, mentally as well as in battle, no holds barred.

Under the cover of the Shroud of Shadow — which I'd cast to make sure we didn't have to waste time on nocturnal elite monsters — Rex, Plague, Famine and myself left the safety of my hexagon, traversed the chasm and headed toward the global boss.

I heard Deel'Agha long before I could even see him. He was still almost a whole hexagon away when I heard a growing rumble which made the ground shake with a series of tremors. The hexagon appeared dead, completely devoid of both doughboys and duxio, and even the two-headed snakes which came in all shapes and sizes at night.

A sixty-feet wide trench zigzagged across the ground. The earth in it was loose and riddled with deep burrows as if having been dug up by something. Its edges were vitrified as if glazed by fire. A trail of slime lined its sides.

This Deel'Agha had a very peculiar footprint: a cross between a snake and a giant worm.

We walked at some distance from its side to ensure the Raptors didn't break their legs on the uneven pitted surface.

Sensing the approach of his rival in the food chain, the T. Rex accelerated and began running, splintering the trees in his way. Had it been daytime, our path would have already been littered with flat snakes and toothy three-tailed squirrels which had taken shelter in the trees but now there was nothing. It was as if one of the Trial organizers flipped a switch every sunset, ridding the area of the daytime mobs and replacing them with nocturnal ones.

Having reached the edge of the fog of war, I dismounted and stole toward the boss of all bosses.

He'd stopped in an opening behind the forest which could have passed for a prairie had it not been so purple and teeming with life.

The local grass rustled underfoot. "Grass" was a bit of an overstatement, really, as it hunted insects during the day — and God forbid you fell asleep in one such clearing as the grass would clamp its blades onto you and suck you dry never to wake again. It was a good job we didn't need to sleep here — but Ola, I remember, had once lain down for a bit of rest and...

Fang Two vibrated in my hand as if pumping me up with something.

Shut up! That was irrelevant! What was the point thinking about yet another loser, a useless ex-vassal?

By the time I approached the boss, all irrelevant thoughts had disappeared.

Deel'Agha lived up to his weird name. He really *was* weird. His enormous bulk blocked out the view like a twenty-story building lying on its side.

He looked like a colossal slime-oozing worm bristling with spikes the size of a train carriage. His head high in the air, he was busy swallowing a duxio whole.

His monstrous jaws were open wide, revealing an array of teeth spiraling down his throat. Each visceral row of teeth rotated around his jaw, grinding through his prey. His head was lined with a row of giant trunk-like tentacles which worked as mandibles, forcing food down his throat.

I could see fire and molten lava escaping from under his belly, temperatures down there reaching over 2,000 F. I made a mental note: if he collapsed on top of me, it would mean instant death. Very well.

Once again I studied the monster's brief description:

Deel'Agha
The Trial's global boss
Level 78
HP: 2,179,000
Receives a new level per every hour of his existence on the Trial field

With this amount of life, you needed some kind of controlling ability to tackle him — otherwise even Juma's clan might have problems with him, especially considering that Tafari had once again thinned out his vassals' ranks. By the same token, Tafari now had fewer men, too.

All this was academic, though, because Deel'Agha stopped again and with a single blow of his powerful tentacle killed a two-headed snake which was desperately trying to slither out of his way. It didn't make it. Deel'Agha grabbed it by the end of its tail and sucked it into his mouth like spaghetti.

It was time. I dished out orders to the dinos, then waited for Rex to shudder the ground with his thunderous roar, hopefully immobilizing the boss.

It worked! The front part of the worm's long body thudded to the ground, the undigested snake still in his mouth, raising a mushroom cloud of dust and blocking out the starlight.

Darkness enveloped us.

I didn't care. I used Treacherous Shadow to miniport onto the monster's back and went into my hole-punching mode, dealing out rapid successions of blows with both my bladed friends. Far below, my dinos were busy mauling him — but cruelly, the logs showed that our combined damage dealt was minute as his protection absorbed almost all of it.

On top of that, a lot of my blows simply failed to register, unable to pierce his armor. He may have been a worm but a loser he certainly wasn't. This was the king of all worms, the King of Pibellau.

"*Grrrrroahggh!*"

Having recovered from his paralysis, the monster spiraled high in the air, taking me with him all the way up to the stratosphere. I barely managed to grab onto one of his spikes. To fall to one's death from a great height — what could be more stupid or ignominious?

His bulk landed on top of both Rex and the two flimsy Raptors whose icons promptly disappeared from the interface panel.

Momentum forced me to roll from the monster's back, impaling me on a small spike like a fly on a matchstick. My health was quickly slipping into the red. The more I struggled, the lower it sank. I had to level up simply to survive.

Deel'Agha twisted his body in order to pull Rex out from under himself. He grabbed Rex's body with his trunk-like tentacles and dragged it up to his mouth.

In doing so, his raised head had changed its angle. I slid off the spike and dropped to the ground about fifty feet away from him. I hurried to level up in order to restore my health. I really should retreat and rethink my tactics.

The Instant Kill counter had stopped at 4% as only 3 out of over 20 blows had gone through. I must have chosen the wrong place to assault.

I scanned the worm's body, trying to locate a vulnerable spot while he was oblivious of my presence, too busy devouring Rex's body.

Found it.

A narrow strip of white flesh barely two fingers wide separated his red-hot belly from his rock-hard back just under his head. I couldn't get any closer to him over the lake of molten lava spreading in every direction. But I could, I suppose, try to leap and grab at one of the many spikes...

Deel'Agha seemed completely consumed by swallowing Rex whole. It was a good job Tyrannosauri weren't sentient because they would never have dreamt of being devoured without any respect to their size like some petty little rabbit.

I took a better grip of Fang Two and estimated the distance, looking at the spreading pool of lava and the brightening horizon, then took a good running jump.

My calculations had proved correct. I grabbed at a spike and pulled myself up to climb it, risking falling to my death any moment. Once again I activated Stun but it didn't work.

I didn't care. I hit the monster. And again. I must have chosen the right point this time as both of my blows had gone through.

You've dealt damage to Deel'Agha: 2082
Damage absorbed by armor: 90% Actual damage: 208.
Verifying the probability of making an instant kill (4%)...
Verification failed.
+1% to your chance of making an instant kill with each blow (5%).

You've dealt damage to Deel'Agha: 1845
Damage absorbed by armor: 90% Actual damage: 184.
Verifying the probability of making an instant kill (5%)...
Verification failed.
+1% to your chance of making an instant kill with each blow (6%).

I failed to hit him again as the damage I'd just dealt had made me priority target.

The monster shot out his tentacles all along his body, brushing me off the spike. As I flew through the air, I activated Dodge and Treacherous Shadow, miniporting to the mob's back. I failed to stealth up though because Inconspicuousness refused to activate. All I could do was run along his spine, avoiding the spikes, in order to get back down to his vulnerable spot.

A sharp stench of burning filled my throat and nostrils. I blinked, closing a new and very inopportune system message:

Test subject! An enemy has infiltrated your territory! Base 1 is under threat of capture!

Bad timing. If someone was already plundering their way through my hexagon, this was probably the worst possible moment to die.

The moment I thought about it, the worm's body began to vibrate, throwing me off balance. I couldn't run anymore. His back erupted in a series of blisters which began to spew mushroom clouds of black smoke. Craters overflowing with lava gaped open in his skin.

As I took my next step, my foot sank into yet another open ulcer boiling with magma. The worm was sweating fire, his spikes closing around me and threatening to burn me alive.

In desperation I attempted to prolong the agony and leveled up again, simply to be able to stash my daggers back into the backpack.

You are now dead, test subject.
Lives remaining: 1.
Time left until resurrection: 3... 2... 1....

* * *

Having suffered through the Great Void with its after-death experience of being burned alive (which was a déjà vu of my first Pibellau death when the Kreken had spat on me), I finally respawned in the shelter.

Although I couldn't see anyone under the

dome, I had little doubt the enemy was a stone throw's away from the base.

I peeled off my split jeans which reminded me of my last day on Earth before the abduction, then opened my backpack and equipped my gear. I grabbed both daggers, cast Inconspicuousness on myself and slid out of the shelter.

Not a moment too soon.

This time the enemy fighters were two, not five.

Why two? They were still about 150 feet away from the dome so in theory, I should make it. I returned to the command center and initiated Rex' generation, investing every Charisma point I had into it.

That was it. I had less than a hundred resources left. If you counted the ones generated by the base, I had enough to last me five hours or so.

So these few hours would decide my fate. At the moment, I simply had to eliminate my unwanted guests. The two burly level-20 guys with nicknames to match — Killsen and Fatality — had already leapt over the fence.

"He's not easy to kill, is he?" Fatality asked.

"He had his own clan," Killsen replied. "They used to control almost all of the west. But they were no match against Juma."

"What did I say? We had to attack them ourselves when we had the chance. All those hexagons would have been ours by now. We'd have ripped Juma apart like a rag doll!"

Killsen shrugged. "His dinos weren't as strong as we thought they were. All talk and no balls. Come on, let's get in."

The dome's veil parted before them, allowing them inside.

Twenty seconds later, they exited, looking focused and alert. My presence must have prevented them from seizing the command center. I stood barely fifteen feet away from them, but they couldn't see me.

"He must be somewhere around, right?"

"Shut up," Killsen hissed. "Why the fuck did they have to send only the two of us? Before, we always used to go in groups of five!"

"You're the group leader. Tafari spoke to you, not to me. How do I know?" Fatality's chuckle was muted by his closed helmet.

Casting nervous looks around, they walked along the dome.

Rex wouldn't arrive for another five minutes. I could have attacked them myself, but what for? The odds were better with Rex.

The two walked in a loose spiral, peering watchfully around themselves. The group leader clutched a battle-axe as he studied every square inch of the base's surface.

Could he see stealthed-up players? Well, tough. This particular talent of mine was well and truly maxed out.

"I don't even understand why we'd want this hexagon at all," Killsen's stifled voice came from behind his helmet.

"Can you see him?"

"No, I can't! And I can see stealthed-up players at a hundred feet."

"What if it's a glitch? Just some bug in the system that won't let us capture the base. Back in the camp, they're probably about to march out against the boss already. We're gonna miss it!"

The group leader didn't reply, wary of a small pack of whistlers who gathered just behind the fence, casting unfriendly glances at the two.

Fatality raised his sword and headed for the mobs.

"Give it a rest!" Killsen snapped. "We'll kill them if they attack us."

"If you say so, boss," Fatality stopped, removed his helmet and scratched his sweaty head. Now I could see he was almost a boy, fair-headed with a pouted childish expression. "You sure we won't be late for the global boss? I'd love to see the battle."

Killsen cast one glance at his partner and emitted a barely audible sigh. "We do have time, Fats. If Juma had challenged the boss already, Tafari would have messaged me."

"Why can't we attack the boss ourselves?"

"Fats, man, are you always so stupid? Our stealthed-up scouts are high in the air watching him even as we speak! We're gonna wait for Juma and his clan to arrive and aggro the monster, then we'll attack them from behind. What's not to understand?"

"It's just sort of... playing dirty, is it?"

"They were the first to break the agreement, remember? Now shut up! Because if you don't..."

Rex walked out from behind the shelter, stretched his neck and announced his arrival with his traditional thunderous roar, drowning out Killsen's last words.

Not waiting for his soundtrack to end, I ordered him to activate Furious Roar and paralyze the enemy.

"Squash 'em!" I pointed at Killsen.

I reached Fatality in two powerful leaps and showered his back with blows which, although failing to kill him, stripped him of 2/3 of his health. In the meantime, Rex had bit Killsen's trampled body in two and parted his jaws in a carnivorous grin.

"He's all yours, Rex," I said, stepping aside and repeating the command.

Fatality tried to scramble back to his feet when Rex's jaws closed around him. His sword dropped from his hand; his helmet rolled aside. A shriek of terror sliced through the air and was cut short, replaced by the snapping of bones.

Half a minute later, nothing reminded of Tafari's fighters anymore. I picked up the loot and checked it. Bad news: although their gear was better than mine, Rex's teeth had stripped it of most of its durability. After a moment's hesitation, I stashed it away into my backpack, as well as the weapons they'd dropped.

It was time I marched out to check on Deel'Agha. I had a funny feeling this was going to be epic. And I fully intended to play my part in the last act of that drama.

Chapter Twenty-Eight

Blowing Up the Bridges

Eddard Stark:
Tell me, Lord Varys, who do you truly serve?
Varys:
Why, the realm, my good lord, how ever could you doubt that? I swear it by my lost manhood. I serve the realm, and the realm needs peace.

Game of Thrones

"THE OTHER NIGHT, I HAD A NIGHTMARE," MIKE KEPT blabbing. "You and I, we were walking through this weird forest together. Then we attacked some guy and somehow he burned me alive."

"Sure," I mumbled.

I really had to concentrate on the important stuff. Only my good manners obliged me to listen and make all the appropriate noises.

"Phil, I was burned alive!" he repeated. "It hurt so much that I woke all the neighbors up with my screaming!"

It looked like we'd somehow met up during the Trial and even struck up an unlikely alliance, of all things. And he wasn't even on Ilindi's list!

I'd love to know whether my other self had managed to find anybody else on it? Who else was there? Zack, Jovanna, Carter, Ken... I just hoped they'd all got together and given the bad guys a run for their money.

I'd already had markers on all the bad guys who were hunting me in this world and set up an alert system which went off every time one of them appeared within a half-mile range.

Once I'd gotten to Mike's place, I asked the cabman to wait while I nipped into his motel room. He was a sorry sight: yesterday's bout had left him with a broken nose and a huge black eye.

I seemed to have woken him up, as well.

"Hi, Mike. Have you got twenty bucks for me? I need to pay the taxi."

For the next half-minute or so, he'd tried to fathom out what was wanted of him, then he shook himself out of his slumber, nodded and fetched me a hundred-dollar note.

I paid the taxi off and ducked back into his room not to leave it again. Pointless trying to cover up my tracks. If anything happened, the alarm system would go off, anyway, allowing me plenty of time to escape. Also, my stealth had already restored.

Surprisingly, Mike hadn't even asked me why I'd come to see him wearing a bathrobe and hotel slippers without a single penny in my pocket. Neither had he asked what it was I wanted. He'd given me a one-size-fits-all pair of shorts and a T-shirt which I was wearing now as I kept working my way through the CIA lists.

"Mike," I said, "as I understand it, what you dream really does happen, only not here but on another planet."

"What do you mean?"

"Don't you remember how you were abducted?"

Apparently, he didn't. But when I tried to describe to him various things he might have seen there, he managed to remember having dreamed of something similar.

I gave him an abridged version of the Senior Races story, complete with the Trial and abductions; I told him that Terrans were about to face the Diagnostics and that he might lose his interface sooner than he thought — today even.

Strangely enough, the thought didn't seem to scare him, to the point where I thought he hadn't quite grasped the entirety of my explanation, so I repeated it.

He shrugged. "See if I give a shit. I won't lose my fighting skills, will I?"

"No, you won't," I lied. "Sorry but I really need to work."

"Okay. I'll go get some food, then. Would you fancy a Chinese takeaway?"

"Only if there's plenty of it."

He grinned. "Right you are. I'll be back soon."

"Mike," I called after him when he was already heading for the door, "Can I use your laptop again?"

"Totally. The password is Crybaby. But," he grinned again, "make sure you keep your antivirus on when you surf all those porn sites!"

Laughing at his own clumsy joke, he went off, leaving me alone in the room.

I had no idea how long I'd be stuck here. I'd already written to Angela Howard asking her to put me in contact with Sanchez. If I didn't hear anything from her, I might have to use Mike as a go-between. His ability to see people's names meant he could go to the hotel and locate either Sanchez or Tomasik, then bring them here to me. Both were still in Langley, due to be back by the evening.

In the meantime, I'd completed the CIA lists and decided to do something entirely different.

Firstly, I needed to write to Kira. The agreement was, I'd write her a message and save it as a draft in her own email box which she would see the moment she checked her mail. I needed to finally offer her a fictitious explanation of all my mysterious "psychic" abilities allowing me to locate missing persons. I also had to somehow explain away all the money that was already accruing in the two bank accounts, both her own and the one belonging to her foundation, and answer all her questions about the foundation before more money started flooding in.

Secondly, I still had to contact the Russian police and send them the coordinates of the highly dangerous criminals wanted in Russia. True, I harbored very little hope of success: by the time they got their act together and double-checked the information, the villains would probably be already lying low in some other place. Still, this was something I had to do while I still had the interface. You never know, they just might arrest some of them.

Thirdly, I had to collect the coordinates of all the yet-undiscovered treasures and mineral deposits while I could still see them on the map. Although I hadn't yet decided what I was going to do with this information, it wouldn't hurt to save and store it online somewhere. If I indeed lost my interface but kept both my memory and achievements intact, that would provide me with a most valuable source of income.

Fourthly... and probably most importantly, I'd already decided on the most promising spheres of scientific research, those which would ensure humanity's prosperity and would allow our civilization to flourish, solving our most pressing issues such as famine, terminal illnesses, bad ecology, space exploration, overpopulation and unemployment. I was planning on creating scientific groups in each of these spheres, financing them out of the funds received for my terrorist-hunting activities and hopefully also from what I'd get for finding treasures and new mineral deposits.

By the time Mike was back, I was busy working on this last item of my plan. He began unloading the bags, placing little cardboard boxes onto the table,

"Sweet-and-sour chicken, pork and pineapple, noodles, brown rice, dim sum..."

After he'd named each and every item in the bags, he sat down, ripped open one of the boxes and began eating, deftly brandishing his chopsticks.

"Mike, I need to ask you a favor. I need your help."

"I'm free until midnight," he said with his mouth full. "What can I do for you?"

I gave him a brief version of my mishaps and explained what I wanted him to do. By now, Sanchez and Tomasik must have already landed in Vegas.

"I got it," he said. "Alex Tomasik and Hector Sanchez. If I see Laura Flores, I need to steer clear of her. If she's with them, I'll take them aside. I know what to do. Let me finish eating and I'll be on my way."

After another half-hour of stuffing his face, Mike was about to set off. Before leaving, he gave me a smartphone with a broken screen,

"This is for keeping in touch. My number is under Crybaby. Call me if you need me. Just in case you get hungry again," he guffawed as he closed the door behind himself.

After a while, the interface alarm went off. I opened the map and saw the markers of all my enemies approaching rapidly. They were barely two miles away now.

I cleaned the browser history, closed the laptop and bounded out of the room.

I sprinted across the empty street and the neighboring parking lot, then hurried toward a restaurant which offered a view of the motel. I found an empty table by the window and sat down, watching the new arrivals.

A waiter appeared out of nowhere.

"A glass of water, please," I said.

Six people in inconspicuous clothes climbed out of the cars and fanned out, moving toward several rooms at once. I watched as they knocked and, ignoring any residents who opened up, barged past them and disappeared inside only to reemerge after a while and head for the room next door.

One of the groups broke down the door into Mike's room but came out after a couple of minutes, empty-handed.

Shit! I'd left the bathrobe there, hadn't I? It had the hotel's logo on it! Surely they would put two and two together?

They had indeed. Both men stopped outside the door, one of them speaking into his radio. I just hoped Mike wouldn't have problems because of this.

I gave him a call.

"Phil? I'm in the hotel. Can't see any of the guys you mentioned yet."

"Did you give them your real name?"

"Actually, I didn't. I used the name of someone I knew from prison. Why?"

"Stay away from the motel for a few days. They found me but I managed to get out in time. Unfortunately, now they know that I was there to see you."

"Shit! All my stuff's in there," he paused. "Never mind. It's all right. I'll stay here for a while. Your spooks might arrive, you never know. Keep me posted."

I hung up and gulped some water down. My throat felt dry. I deleted the last number dialed just in case.

Then I watched out the window as my would-be kidnappers cut their search of the motel short and started combing the area. Two of them headed for the restaurant.

Despite all my abilities, I didn't have a clue what to do. Fiddling with the knife on the table, I pondered over whether I should go on the run again.

But where to? I had neither money nor any ID papers, even though with my new abilities, money was no longer a problem.

Should I just smoke the bastards? This, to me, seemed to be the most attractive idea.

In any case, I had to wait for Sanchez to arrive. Either Mike would find him, or he might get the message from Angela Howard (who really wasn't an Angela Howard at all). The latter was less probable, simply because it was night now in Russia where the embassy worker was supposed to be.

I could now see Sanchez approach the hotel, while Alex...

"Don't move," a voice said in Russian. "I'm sorry about this."

A gun poked my ribs, followed by a slight prick in my stomach,

Waves of heat began spreading over my whole body. My vision swam. I staggered, losing control, but unseen hands prevented me from falling face down on the table. Straining what precious little was left of my strength, I slowly turned round, facing Alex Tomasik.

How the hell?

"It's all right," he said softly, sitting at the

table next to me. "I'm not with the guys who're searching the hotel. Laura has her own game. I have mine."

"Which guys are you with, then?" I managed through numbing lips. "Are you with the CIA?"

"Whatever there was between us before this, yes. I worked for the CIA. But now I represent other people. They have a business proposition to make to you."

"And did you need the gun for that?"

He didn't reply.

"Alex?"

"I didn't know how you'd react. I thought you might think I was one of those," he nodded at the motel building. "I'm telling you I've got nothing to do with them. But I do know about your abilities. All of us do."

"Which abilities?"

"I'll tell you in a moment. Just promise me you won't do anything stupid. It's pointless, really. This place is packed with my people. All the exits are blocked. My men have infrared scanners and paint spray guns. You can't escape. Are you wondering how I worked it out?"

"Cameras?"

"Of course. You're smart enough to understand, are you? Your hotel room is absolutely chock full of cameras. Imagine my surprise when you just disappeared, then came back into view by the elevators. I expected anything but that."

"But Sanchez..." I mumbled, losing control of my speech.

"Oh, he must be absolutely furious. Still, the

people I represent are way beyond him in status. So all those bugs in your clothes are mine."

All I could do was mumble unintelligibly.

"What did you say? It doesn't matter, anyway. We're now gonna take you to a nice classified bunker in the Mojave Desert. We'll conduct a few tests and will try to extract that thing they planted inside you. You understand the importance of it, don't you? It's a gazillion times more important than the lives of some terrorist lowlifes some of whom are even... never mind. The main thing is..."

As he kept blabbering, trying to justify his actions in his own eyes, I concentrated on my next plan of action. With the help of Regeneration, I could restore control of my body and replenish my Spirit reserves. I could use Sprint in order to slow time and wrestle the gun from his hand. And although Stealth and Vanish wouldn't work against infrared sensors, at least it would confuse some of the assailants, giving me time to either shoot them dead or just leg it.

"Enough talking," he finally said. "This is just something for you to consider as we drive."

I activated Regeneration.

Warning! Your Spirit resources are insufficient to activate Regeneration!
Spirit resources required: 50%
Current Spirit: 36%

That was it.

Angry as I was with myself for allowing my Spirit reserves to drop so low, for entering their trap so stupidly, for walking right into their hands — as the restaurant had apparently been the center of their little operation all along — I couldn't even bemoan my own stupidity.

Tomasik snapped several commands. I was being restrained, handcuffed, shackled and bagged. As they carried me out, I could hear the scared voices of passersby.

"Put him in the van, quick!" Tomasik commanded.

They laid me carefully inside and locked the doors.

Darkness enveloped me, holding the promise of the darkness to come. Would I be able to escape from the bunker?

I couldn't think straight, my mind going in circles, offering one crazy escape idea after the next. I needed new levels in order to finally get Berserker and Invulnerability...

Just as we were clearing the city limits, the world around me faded. My heart stopped. I felt myself falling into the Great Void.

Abducted.

Chapter Twenty-Nine

Fix Your Eyes Upon Your Crude Hands

Every man dies, not every man truly lives.

William Wallace, *Braveheart*

TODAY, THE AIR OF PIBELLAU WAS SO CRYSTAL CLEAR it shimmered with light, allowing me to see the fine web of wrinkles on Tafari's face almost 500 feet away from me.

He and his clan were now in the direct proximity of the global boss: "proximity" being the operative word because they kept out of his field of vision and consequently, his aggro zone.

The boss slithered unhurriedly along their ranks in search for any potential prey. His demeanor confirmed the creature's utter absence of intelligence. Whether by higher design or by some anonymous Trial programmer's whim, his behavioral patterns fell into two categories: either to attack and devour, or, in the absence of a victim, to keep going until he came across one.

I hadn't seen him in full-blown combat yet, so I wouldn't be surprised if he had more attack abilities in store than I'd already discovered: sweating lava, hitting the enemy with his spikes and tentacles and devouring his opponent alive. Considering the fact that the creature was quite clumsy and that the length of his tentacles was no more than half his body, Tafari's clan could choose the tactics of attacking him from behind, constantly shifting aside in order to preserve their initial position.

But I'd thought that Tafari was going to wait for Juma? Apparently, the latter had reconsidered challenging Deel'Agha, preferring the bird in hand to two in the bush. In the meantime, the boss' stats kept growing with every hour, which could explain Tafari's desire to take him on while there was still a faint chance of hitting the jackpot.

I counted fourteen clan members, including Tafari himself, and over a hundred fighting units which looked like six-legged turtles with predatory low-browed reptiloid heads packed with wide jawfuls of sharp teeth. They moved around so fast it appeared they couldn't stand still at all: they fussed about, running in circles and scurrying around in figures of eight like cockroaches rushing around in a campus kitchen when you switch the light on at night.

Unlike Tafari's rhino, they were definitely alien, so I had no idea how he'd managed to get around the Trial restriction requiring all the fighting units to be of the same species.

In the meantime, Deel'Agha must have sensed something. He stopped in his tracks and raised his head.

I could hear Tafari barking orders. His men began taking up their positions in twos and threes, fanning out in an arc to make sure they ended up by the monster's tail.

Rex and I decided to take up our positions too. My stealth ability securely covered us both. We kept a safe distance from Tafari, staying just out of his field of vision so that Rex's footsteps didn't give us away. Pointless joining in the battle now, especially at the risk of being unmasked by one of the boss' mass combat abilities.

Suddenly Tafari's entire clan stopped dead. One of his warriors stepped forward and shouted something. A raven-black cloud formed over the boss, showering him with countless shards of ice.

Like a spectacular show of special effects, the monster crunched to a halt. A Freeze debuff icon appeared over his head, complete with a 10-second countdown timer. Immediately all the close-combat warriors sprang into action and began hacking at his rump.

By the time Tafari commanded the retreat, the clan had managed to strip the boss of 7% of his health. Once the Freeze expired, the monster shot his tentacles out at the backs of a couple of tardy warriors who collapsed, crying out in pain. Coiling around them, the tentacles promptly retracted, bringing their quarry to the boss' mouth.

The monster didn't get the chance to devour them, though. A new warrior stepped out to exercise his own control ability — a mental one this time. It worked: the immobilized creature's tentacles hung listlessly, releasing the two warriors.

This time, however, the countdown was only 8 seconds. Was it the Trial's mechanics at work? Was it what we gamers used to call a diminishing return?

Tafari had been lucky so far. He'd already managed to successfully use two control talents against the boss. A third time, he might not be so lucky.

By the end of the eighth second, Tafari had ordered everyone to retreat, leaving only his fighting units at the scene. The "turtles" lined the whole length of the boss' body, reared up and began ripping his skin apart with their two-foot long claws, dealing damage.

In the meantime, the human clan members switched to shooting at the boss from long range while keeping a safe distance from his tentacles. Over time, I started seeing the method in their seemingly chaotic movement: they were constantly on the go, even while shooting, then immediately shrinking back to make sure they didn't get within the range of the boss' combat abilities.

The monster began sweating lava. The turtles' health bars immediately began to shrink. They tried to scramble up his flanks in order to avoid the fiery pools underfoot, not realizing that lava was also pouring down on them from above.

Time and time again the monstrous worm

shot out his tentacles, catching the panicking turtles which were trying to leap off him; he also managed to attack a few of the less cautious clan members, decimating their health bars.

When all further attempts to control the boss failed, Tafari took the matter into his own hands.

"Strength and Inspiration!" he shouted.

Immediately all of his vassals and fighting units were enveloped in a shimmering white haze, their lives promptly restored. Judging by the new buff's icon, all their characteristics had grown by 50%. Some talent Tafari had!

It must have also reset all the ability cooldowns, because the warrior with the Freeze talent now stepped forward again. Three more vassals in possession of control talents approached the boss too, just to make sure nothing went wrong this time.

Another black cloud; more ice shards; but this time, his talent didn't work. Immediately the mentalist joined in the action, also with zero results

The third controller was too late...

The fact that the clan had already stripped the boss of 25% life must have caused a change in his combat tactics. The worm retracted his tentacles, flattened his spikes and arched his body, then began burrowing into the ground with an ever-growing rumble. A few heartbeats later, he was already out of sight deep below. Both the vibrations and the rumbling noise had stopped, Tafari's snapping commands and the groaning of the wounded the only sounds breaking the deadly silence.

Just then I noticed that Tafari had no fighting units left at all, apart from his personal rhino. Not a single surviving turtle was left on the battlefield.

Boom!

Concentric waves began spreading over the ground. I hurried to step as far back as I could, afraid of coming within their range. Each wave stripped Tafari's clan of 10% life while the sixth and final one paralyzed everyone within its radius.

Then several things happened at once. A great number of black dots loomed out of the fog of war on the opposite edge of the battlefield, approaching rapidly. I could already see that those were Juma's men complete with his army of spiky multiped roaches.

Might that mean that Juma decided to use the very plan that Tafari had conceived against him? In any case, it looked like the Trial was entering its final stage.

Juma's vassals moved in an arc, giving the boss a wide berth and consciously heading toward Tafari's frozen warriors. Just then Deel'Agha shot out of the ground and dropped his entire weight onto the nearest group of Tafari's warriors, his mandibles working hard as he swallowed body after motionless body.

You didn't have to be a clairvoyant or Paul the Octopus to predict that Tafari was finished.

Whoever the boss hadn't yet reached — including Tafari himself astride his rhino — were swallowed up by the approaching waves of roaches. Ignoring the monster's frenetic fury, Juma's warriors concentrated on their competition. Every time Tafari's vassals recovered from the paralyzing vibrations created by the boss, they became frozen again.

"Our turn, Rex!" I said as I sent him to attack Juma's clan. "Squash 'em!"

For the casual observer, the Tyrannosaurus must have appeared out of thin air. Once out of range of my Shroud of Shadow, Rex had added even more noise, chaos and turmoil to the proceedings.

The sky rapidly darkened, overcast with thunderclouds. The first drops of rain evaporated before they could reach the boss' back. He froze for a second, as if listening to something, then promptly sealed all the lava craters covering his body. Thunder rumbled overhead.

I moved slowly and cautiously, skirting the battlefield on the other side of the worm where nobody was at the moment.

Some of Juma's roaches had automatically aggroed the boss who was only too happy with this new source of nourishment. Rex trampled three of Juma's vassals who'd chanced to be in his path, gracing Tafari with some extra time.

Having recovered from his paralysis, Tafari dealt effortlessly with two assailants at once. With one swipe of his sword, he smote an attacker's head off complete with helmet, then barked a chain of commands, ordering the handful of his remaining vassals to spread out and telling the only surviving controller to deal with their treacherous enemy.

Acting simultaneously, the controllers from both camps carried out their orders. In the seconds that followed, many of the warriors from both clans were knocked out of action.

Astride their chimeras, Juma and his bodyguards who'd avoided being stunned rushed toward the frozen Tafari and attacked him a mere couple of seconds before the debuff ran out. But even between the six of them, they'd failed to kill him. The moment he regained his mobility, Tafari set his rhino on Ken who was the nearest to him while he himself hacked through the legs of one of Juma's bodyguards. Yet another bodyguard was screaming his head off as Rex was devouring him alive.

Juma jerked his long thin sword into the air and shouted, activating some sort of a clan leader ability. Everyone within a fifteen-feet radius of him now looked as if they'd been dropped into a bowlful of jelly as time seemed to have slowed down. Juma himself, however, was able to move at the same speed. I could clearly see the effect it produced: the shimmering "glass bowl" and the slo-mo outlines of Rex and Tafari within as Juma next to them was taking a swing with his sword.

It was the last thing I saw because I'd finally gotten near the boss who was busy swallowing his next victim, his enormous bulk blocking the view of the battle.

All of a sudden it started raining cats and dogs — a fierce downpour the kind of which you could only witness on Pibellau. Its huge heavy drops soaked everything, extinguishing the fire and lowering the temperature of the lava pools.

The boss' heath bar was by now almost halved. I really didn't know whether Juma would bother to finish him off after his victory over Tafari. Everything around was consumed by thick clouds of mist and vapor.

Bristling with spikes, the monster's suspended flank loomed momentarily into view. Keeping his vulnerable spot in mind, I moved alongside him, leaping over the solidifying lava puddles. I was still protected by Inconspicuousness — but the moment I dealt damage, it would become disabled.

I was awaiting the right moment to rush into action when something absolutely incredible happened. Deel'Agha's entire body spasmed; he began to convulse, squirming and turning on the spot, expanding and contracting. I was thrown a good hundred feet to the side, losing a good 75% of my life. It felt as if I'd been rammed by an overloaded truck. I clenched my teeth, trying not to scream.

I hurried to reactivate Inconspicuousness before they could discover me, then tried to take a better look at my injuries. A broken rib was protruding from my torn gear. Instinctively I retched but nothing came up: my stomach had been empty for at least a couple of weeks.

I had no resources left to buy a new level and regenerate. All I could do was wait until I'd at least partially recovered, otherwise I couldn't even move.

While I was thus incapacitated — and while the two clans were too busy knocking seven shades of shit out of each other, Deel'Agha curled up in a ball and started rolling around, squashing and flattening everything around. When his colossal bulk started rolling in my direction, I realized I didn't have time to get out of his way.

I glanced at Juma who'd activated his impenetrable energy cocoon, then at the retreating Tafari who was still alive and grinning a bloodied grin through a hole in his helmet. Already sensing the air pressure from the monster's bulk rolling toward me, I activated Treacherous Shadow and miniported behind Tafari's back. The tip of Juma's sword was already protruding from it.

My mind registered the latest changes in the rankings. Tafari was dead but not disincarnated yet. He'd lost his clan and all his territories, the names of his vassals turning gray one after the other.

Juma's men continued slaughtering the boss.

By then, Deel'Agha had stopped his breakdancing, his disco moves replaced by a *summoning call*. How else could I describe the insurmountable desire to walk over to him and allow myself to be devoured, uniting with this great and almighty deity?

Deel'Agha kept calling, luring everyone, until all of the hexagon's creatures had gathered by his enormous swaying head. The place was now teeming with flocks of whistlers, whole kirpi families and swarms of krekniks, the ground underfoot an undulating, quivering carpet of sarasurs.

I watched the gruesome scene from the sidelines. No idea what had saved my bacon: whether it was my level-2 Inconspicuousness making me immune to mind control — or whether it was my trusty friend, Fang One, helping me resist the summoning call of that worthless nonentity. Although I'd sensed his primitive plea and his claim to divinity, to me he was but an overgrown worm with bad metabolism and elevated body temperature.

Kill him, a voice inside me whispered. *Kill... him!*

The alien language kept rustling in my head, making my blood boil, but I ignored its miserable plea. I had better things to do. I needed to restore. I was actually enjoying it, watching my enemies — humans and monsters — slaughter each other, swarming in the mud and trying to finish off their victims even as they drew their last breath.

The boss devoured everyone within reach, grabbing them with his tentacles and shoving them down his throat. Just as I watched, one of Juma's warriors shouted an ecstatic praise to the "God of all bosses" while a tentacle was pulling him toward his final death inside the monster's stomach.

Unfortunately, the boss had only managed to swallow four humans, three of which were Juma's clan members. Seeing this, Juma ordered a retreat and another controlling session. Three of those attempts had failed until one of his fighters managed to freeze the monster, allowing Juma's clan to flee to safety.

It was now or never.

I miniported onto Deel'Agha's back, ran along it toward his head, then climbed back down, grabbing at the spikes. Halfway to the ground I hooked to a spike with my crossed legs, hung head down and began stabbing him with my daggers, aiming for a thin strip of white skin between his red-hot belly and his rock-hard shell.

I invested all of my strength into every focused, rhythmical blow, trying to stab deeper every time to add 1% to the chance of instant kill of that miserable worm. Again and again. Focused, unhurried. To the sound of my own heartbeat. Hammering the toxic acid produced by the dagger's biochemical core into the monster's bloodied flesh.

The worm was screaming his head off, bristling his spikes and reopening his lava craters, splattering lava around in his crazed desperation. I forced myself to stay put and keep stabbing, ignoring the fiery droplets burning through my skin.

On my ninth heartbeat, I did what I had to do.

Lady Luck which had been ignoring me throughout the Trial, had finally sided up with me.

You've dealt damage to Deel'Agha: 2389.

Damage absorbed by armor: 90% Actual damage: 239.

Verifying the probability of making an instant kill (14%)...

Verification complete!

The global boss Deel'Agha is dead.

The giant worm shuddered, throwing me off him. His body slackened; his head thumped to the ground, drawing the rest of him down and pinning me with his weight. Stuck between his spikes out of everyone's sight, I struggled for a while, trying to get out.

Then I listened. Everything was quiet.

Silence reigned. The rain had stopped; the

fighters' screams had died away.

A new system announcement resounded through the air, spreading over all hexagons and visible to all Trial participants.

The global boss Deel'Agha has been defeated by Liquidator Phil, a level-28 human!
Phil will receive:
300,000 existence resource points;
legendary artifact: Suppressor;
a summoning whistle;
an additional life to all of his clan members.

The boss' cadaver vanished. I looked around and saw all the raindrops hover motionless in mid-air. Juma's vassals appeared caught in a freeze frame.

My existence resource counter was spinning, adding 300,000 points to the total. Two new glistening gold buttons appeared on my interface panel: Suppressor and Summoning Whistle.

Suppressor
A legendary artifact from the era of an extinct civilization which used to exist on Pibellau. No material form available.
By implanting itself into the user's mind, the artifact generates a mental aura capable of suppressing any of their enemies' class talents.
Range: 39 feet

I grinned as I figured it all out. No, this artifact wasn't going to help me kill everyone. One soldier doesn't make a battle. But why would you need to kill everybody if all you needed to do was to kill just one person?

"Thanks, guys," I addressed the observers as a great load had fallen from my shoulders. This aura had just put me back in the game.

Something began flickering in the corner of my eye. I looked away from the text and noticed three little balloons, two red ones and one gold one, jumping impatiently in front of me, demanding my attention.

I popped the nearest red one. A new system message came up:

The Trial has been paused!

This is a secret bonus for the great hero who defeated Deel'Agha who'd been terrorizing and petrifying the current wave of Trial subjects.

Duration: 1 Pibellau hour, or until it's been canceled, or until the first damage you deal to any enemy.

My lips parted in a smile. Now I could take my time and sort through all the goodies I'd just received. No matter how desperately I wanted to leave my gaming past behind, what could be better than rummaging through the loot you'd received after you'd killed the biggest and nastiest boss in a game?

Hero! Your clan has no vassals yet. Do you want to give a second chance to some of those you lost in your previous lives?

Resurrection available for the following disincarnated test subjects:
Jovanna
Ola
Carter
Manu
Eddie
Björn

Leti wasn't on the list as she was still alive and remained one of Juma's vassals.

My smile grew ever broader as I ticked off all those on the list. New clan members would make my job so much easier!

You've made your choice, Hero. Do you want to pause the Trial for your vassals?
Yes / No

Absolutely!

The frozen figures of my clan members appeared around me, their eyes still closed. They had already resurrected but were still affected by the Pause.

But first I wanted to check the last balloon, its gold color signifying an achievement. What could it be?

I poked it with my finger. The balloon unfolded, forming a system message:

Hero! You've unlocked a new achievement: God Fighter
You're the first and last test subject in this

Trial wave who has managed to subdue the global boss.

+100% to all damage dealt to all other Trial participants.

I glanced at the new Summoning Whistle icon. As I focused on the opalescent button, I had a feeling I already knew what it was about.

Summoning Whistle
A single-use artifact
Summons a copy of the global boss Deel'Agha to the summoner's side.

When should I summon him, if not now? Not straight away, of course, but immediately after the end of the Pause.

I tried to figure out how best to distribute the whopping heap of resources I'd just received and whether I should share them equally between all of us. In the end, I chose what I thought would be a happy medium. It would be wiser to have strong vassals at my disposal capable of preventing Juma from running off. I didn't need cannon fodder.

I went on raising my levels one after another, then spent just over a half of the resources I'd received to buy myself level 70.

I then distributed the 84 characteristic points between Strength and Stamina. I didn't need anything else at the moment. All I wanted was damage — which now had become so huge that I could kill anyone of Juma's vassals with one blow — and more life points to secure myself against any eventualities.

Suppressor was going to protect me against all the controlling effects and prevent Juma from activating Invulnerability, even if its cooldown had already expired.

All this had taken me about half an hour. It certainly wasn't easy to raise myself 42 levels, distribute characteristic points and study five new class talents. There were no new talents available after level 50: all you could do was level up the existing ones.

Now I had to quickly stop the Trial pause for my vassals because I still had to clue them in on our current situation.

I shifted my gaze back to the message offering to stop the pause for my clan members and focused on "Yes".

I heard a collective gasp from my group of unlucky players who'd very nearly sunk into oblivion, followed by their cries of astonishment.

They might have been strange silly nonentities, but at least they were all mine.

Thinking about this made me remove the dagger. Just in case.

As I switched my gaze from one face to another, I felt a lump in my throat. After an unending chain of failures and losses which had almost made me throw in the towel, I'd not just survived but managed to change the course of the Trial which Juma had almost certainly won by then.

I gulped and smiled, spreading my arms to welcome my friends.

Carter was the first to come round. He took

two steps toward me and slapped my face nice and hard.

Damage received: 47 (a slap from Carter)
Do you want to punish your vassal and activate the disincarnation timer?

"You fucking lowlife!" Carter cussed. "Why did you have to kill me?"

It was a good job I'd removed the dagger. I opened my mouth to give a reply when all hell broke loose. My friends all jumped onto me, dressed in nothing but their civilian clothes, and buried me under a heap of their cheering bodies. I barely stayed on my feet.

"Boss! You did it!" Eddie shouted, knocking the wind out of me with all his back-slapping. "Jesus Christ, you're level 70! This is crazy!"

Manu stood aside from the rest, laughing his head off. Then he turned round and noticed the figures of Juma's vassals frozen in the weirdest of poses.

"Holy Mother of Mary!" he shook his head in amazement. "You sonovabitch, Phil! You did it! How did you do it? What happened?"

"Yoo-hoo!" Ola exclaimed as he danced a jig toward me and tried to give me a kiss with his big rubbery lips.

He was promptly pushed aside by Jovanna. She jumped up and clasped me with both her arms and legs, hanging from my neck. Her kisses made me lose concentration for a while.

In the meantime, my friends exchanged their

experiences of their respective disincarnations and consequent resurrections.

Looking over Jovanna's shoulder, I noticed a very surprised Mike looking himself over.

"I've just been burning alive in some woods," he said with a shrug. "And now it's all over. What happened?"

"Who's that, for crissakes? Hey kid, how did you get here?" Manu demanded. "Phil, is he with us?"

"Where's Leti?" Eddie looked around himself. "And the dinos, where are they? Rex, Tank, Croc and Spine?"

"Rex held till the last," I said. "He's just died, now. You should have seen him fight."

"And Leti?"

"Leti? Oh, she's with Juma now."

Eddie's face darkened. Manu laid his hand on his shoulder. "It's quite understandable."

"It is," I said. "Right! We lost Leti but we have Mike Hagen, aka Björn! And Carter, I told you about him, didn't I? Shake hands, everyone, and listen to me..."

Once they'd exchanged handshakes, I hurried to update them on the latest developments starting with Carter's death, to make sure that both he and Jovanna who'd been the next to die knew the lay of the land.

In my turn, I discovered that for all of them, the period between their respective final deaths and consequent resurrections lasted but a few seconds. Their brain activity must have been stopped at the moment of death and reactivated just now.

"How much time left till the end of the pause?" Carter asked, businesslike. The new information didn't seem to have baffled him in the slightest. "Do we have time to study the new talents?"

"Sure. We still have just under thirty minutes left," I said. "I'm gonna distribute the resources now. I have almost 150,000 pt. available. Ola, what do you think? This should be enough for each of you to buy level 25, shouldn't it? Mike is the only exception, I'm afraid. If my calculations are correct, he can only buy level 20."

The African paused, thinking, then nodded. I sent just over 20,000 pt. to each of them, then watched their levels rise.

"I want you to keep some in case you need to level some more," I said. "You never know. We haven't won yet, but victory is almost within reach. All we need to do is sort out Juma," I pointed at his figure frozen in mid-run about 300 feet away from us. "If we kill him, we've as good as won the Trial. At the moment, he owns all hexagons but one. And you know what's gonna happen when he seizes that last one, don't you?"

"The objective of every Trial candidate is to capture all the Pibellau hexagons," Jovanna quoted the rulebook. "If he claims the last one, he's won."

"Exactly. If Juma makes it back to his base and teleports from there, we'll never be able to catch up with him. We just can't reach our hexagon in time to defend it."

"Then we need to stop Juma from escaping, whatever it takes!" Carter growled. "Then we can deal with all the others."

"Sure. That's the only way to do it. But you still haven't noticed the obvious," I smiled. "Think about it."

"What?" the gray-haired guitarist asked, peering hard at me.

Ola flashed a megawatt smile which could eclipse either of Pibellau's suns. With a triumphant yell, Jovanna threw her hands in the air. Eddie and Manu exchanged a high five.

Mike Hagen grumbled, addressing no one in particular,

"If he has all the hexagons but one, and if that one hexagon belongs to us, it means that if we kill Juma..."

"We'll win the Trial, dammit!" Carter thundered, shaking his fists, then dissolved into a stream of cussing.

I waited for them to calm down. I could understand the reasons behind their excitement. When they'd died their final deaths — which for them had happened only a few minutes ago — we'd had zero chances of ever winning this. Carter had died expecting us to be trampled by Nagash's army at any moment. Jovanna had died realizing both Tafari's and Juma's utter superiority over us. Eddie, Ola and Manu had died without any hope at all, caught between the nocturnal monsters and Juma's clan attacking them from behind. And Mike... by the time I'd met him, even Ilindi wouldn't have bet a bent nickel on our victory.

"Is that all we need to do?" Manu asked me.

"It is. But... I'd hate to sound like a

superstitious old woman but there might be more surprises. We are being watched by billions of alien observers, and there's no knowing what they might come up with next. I wouldn't put it past them to grant some kind of bonus to Juma too, if they haven't done so already, just for the sake of a good show."

"Just give us the word," Carter grinned, scratching his belly. "How do you want us to kill that bastard?"

"I'll do the killing. I'll summon Deel'Agha to help me."

"Yes, but-"

"Yes, but your primary objective is not to get yourselves killed," I snapped at him. "I've no idea if you'll be awarded victory if you die again. I don't even know what to make of these rules now. Our clan was supposed to be disbanded after my death. Had I not brought you back..."

Manu nodded. "Come what may. Or as they say in Columbia..."

I laid my hand on his shoulder. "Not now, please. We don't have the time. Everybody, get leveling."

I spent the next ten minutes listening to my friends' surprised and excited voices as they received new talents. Predictably, Mike became a warrior, just like Carter and Manu.

"I've got Slowing Shot!" Jovanna cheered. "If only I had a weapon!"

I slapped my forehead, slid off my backpack and poured its contents onto the ground. "Now you have! Get your weapons and gear, everyone!"

Once again I thanked our foresight. All those dozens of sets of new gear had suddenly come in handy just as we needed them most.

"Listen up, guys. I repeat: your main objective is not to get yourselves killed. Juma's fighters are the same level as you are now, and his bodyguards' levels are higher than yours. If they try to save their leader, don't stick your necks out. The global boss is our main weapon now. He's so huge he can make short work of Rex even. Understand?"

"Aaah," Ola drawled. "What does he look like?"

"Like an earthworm two hundred feet long, with tentacles growing out of its head, an armor-plated back bristling with spikes the size of a bus, and a belly full of molten lava which oozes out of its pores. Sounds good?"

Ola shook his head. "I can't imagine that, no."

"You need to be one hell of a cheater to smoke a monster like this," Mike Hagen spoke for the first time. "But I'm happy it worked out the way it did. It's good you got your friends back, Phil. I really didn't think someone like you could even have friends."

The others switched their gazes from him to me in bewilderment.

"When I met Mike," I explained, "I was under the influence of that mind-altering dagger. Jovanna, you remember it?"

She nodded. "Sure. I had to shoot you in the wrist to make you keep your word and stop you from killing Zack."

Everybody fell silent as they digested this new

information. Then all hell broke loose. Ola was the loudest, spouting a torrent of curses generously peppered with equal doses of French *gros-mots*, old African proverbs and the entire vocabulary of English invective targeting both Zack and Jovanna's unflinching hand on the bowstring.

Jovanna turned crimson and lowered her eyes. "I had no idea how it would turn out."

I gave her a hug and a friendly slap on the back, then laid my hand on the furious Ola's chest, trying to placate him. "She did the right thing."

"She let Phil preserve his honor!" Manu bellowed. "Is there anything more important for a man than to keep his word?"

"No," Eddie and Carter replied in unison even though the question was pretty self-explanatory.

"Can someone please tell me what the hell you're talking about?" Carter demanded.

"Absolutely. Just let us finish these guys off first," I swept both hands over the battlefield.

By the time everybody was done with retrieving their weapons and gear and discussing the tactical details of the battle, we had less than five minutes left till the end of the Pause. My friends positioned themselves around in order to block off any of Juma's potential avenues of retreat. Their task was simple: they had to survive while making sure he didn't escape in the process.

There were thirteen of Juma's clan members left on the field, counting himself, plus two of Tafari's surviving vassals still frozen as they'd tried to escape. I didn't care too much about the latter. I just hoped that Juma's men wouldn't have time to rush to their leader's aid.

I impatiently kissed both daggers in my hands. My blood was seething, the force within me demanding an outlet.

"Well, you useless worms? Are you ready?" I asked my vassals as the timer was ticking off the last seconds of the Pause countdown.

Carter beat his chest with his fist twice. The others replied in a chorus of uncoordinated voices.

"I can't hear you!"

I noticed Jovanna mouth the word "dagger" to the others who nodded their understanding.

"We're ready!" they shouted in unison.

"That's better! Helmets on!"

I studied my vassals. Weapons in hand, with their high levels and top gear, they didn't look quite so useless anymore. Excellent.

"Let's do it!" I shouted in excited anticipation as I slammed my helmet on and activated Summoning Whistle.

The fabric of reality ripped open, releasing a worm the size of a minibus: a facsimile of Deel'Agha which was ten times smaller than the real thing. With a skeptical chuckle (although small, he was still level 80), I set him on Juma.

"Stun!" I shouted in excitement as I mini-ported behind his still-frozen back and started hacking into it.

Ola's words registered somewhere in the periphery of my mind,

"That's not two hundred feet! It's not even twenty!"

Which one of us had killed Juma, remained

uncertain: whether it had been my daggers or the boss who'd snapped him in two with his jaws. Before I could even finish reading through the logs reporting our victory, the world froze again as if someone had pressed Stop instead of Pause this time.

Everything went dark. My heart stopped beating.

When I opened my eyes, gasping convulsively for breath, none of my friends were there. Nor enemies, for that matter. Only the three half-forgotten figures stood before me: the demonic ten-foot-tall Khphor, Ilindi and Valiadis.

I had no weapons in my hands. I was dressed in an enormous pair of Bermuda shorts and a one-size-fits-all T-shirt.

Was it already over?

I let out a short shriek, grasping at my head. It felt as if all my thoughts and memories were being crammed into somebody else's mind, searching for available spare places in the real Phil Panfilov's brain.

Then I became him — the real Phil Panfilov. I remembered everything that had happened to me on Earth during the Trial. Cyril's betrayal, Panchenko's attempt on my life, my trip to the US, my life in Vegas, reconnecting with Mike Hagen, my work for the CIA, Panchenko's comeuppance, the lifting of the curse, ending with my kidnapping and consequent abduction.

I — the real Phil — fast-forwarded through my Pibellau experience: my arrival there, my death from the Kreken's scorching spittle, my first hexagon, my dinos: the Velociraptors and Dilophosauri, followed by my meeting with Carter and my death at his hands. My first achievement and my first ability (Fusion), my meeting Jovanna and her gift of a dagger; completing the instance; capturing a new hexagon; Rex; my victory over Carter; my alliance with Jovanna; Tank; my agreement with Zack; nebulas and anomalies; and finally, my battle with Nagash and the unexpected reappearance of Carter whom I then killed on Nagash's orders. Ola, Croc, the spirited Striker confronting Nagash; meeting Manu, Eddie and Leti; the special-purpose hexagon and the final death of Jovanna — the girl whom I now realized I loved. The enemy's multiple incursions into my hexagons; my Kutuzov-style plan and the subsequent nocturnal backstabbing of Juma's clan; the death of my friends; Leti's betrayal; Ken's aid and my lucky escape; the desperation; the desire to end all this; my new friends, Fang One and Fang Two; meeting Mike; my revenge on Zack; Deel'Agha; another death and the final battle...

All this may have flashed through my mind in a split second but the memory was so strong and vivid that I was already missing my friends and the girl I loved.

Valiadis took off his helmet, a weary smile on his face. He winked at me. Ilindi's expression was stern but mischief sparkled in her eyes.

Khphor stepped forward and proffered me his hand. I held mine out in response. The Vaalphor grabbed it under the elbow the way the ancient Romans used to do.

His grasp on my forearm burned my skin but I suffered in silence. When he finally let go of my arm, I sensed the growing pain where he'd held me.

His mental speech echoed through my head,

"Congratulations, human! In front of all the observers and supervisors I announce you the champion and the winner of the fourth wave of the Trial amongst your race and your contemporaries. You are to keep your interface and all the achievements you've received with its help. Those of your clan members who remained your vassals at Trial's end will keep all of their achievements too, although their interfaces are to be uninstalled and all relevant memories erased."

"My friends, where are they?" I asked out loud.

"Their replicas have been deleted as superfluous," Khphor's voice uttered, unheard by all others. "Their originals have been extracted from your world and their interfaces are currently being uninstalled with a partial memory wipe."

"You did promise to keep their memories!" I said, struggling to remain calm. "Jovanna, Ola, Carter — does that mean that they're going to forget everything about the Trial, me included?"

"We purposefully misled all test subjects. Otherwise, the clan principle wouldn't have worked as we needed it to."

"What about the rest of them?" I asked, thinking about Ken and Striker. "Did you take them back to the day just before their interfaces were installed and just left them there?"

Was it my imagination or had he smirked?

Although I couldn't see Khphor's face behind his helmet, I heard him chuckle: an almost-human chuckle.

"An operation like this would be too energy-intensive. It's much easier just to wipe their memories and restore their bodies to their previous condition."

So Zack had been right, then. But would they allow him to keep his money and his new wife?

"Does that mean that if an interface user has earned a large amount of money or changed their social status, they can keep it?" I asked.

"Enough of your stupid questions, champion. Your preoccupation with other beings' lives and problems is irrational."

Ilindi shook her head ever so slightly, making me realize that everybody must have heard Khphor's last words.

Oh, well. I might have to ask Valiadis about it later.

"Let's finalize the formalities, champion. The Senior Supervisor of the fourth wave of the Trial amongst your race and your contemporaries has chosen your trophy."

Khphor paused. I waited patiently.

He extended his clenched fist to me, then opened it.

A disk made of sky-blue metal hovered over his palm, surrounded by a shimmering energy aura.

"You're being awarded Qa-Tung: a single-use artifact allowing you one chance of perfecting any of your skills to the level yet unattained by anyone of your species in its entire history. Take it."

I accepted the weightless disk which singed my hand with heat, then vanished as my skin absorbed it. For a while, the palm of my hand emitted a faint glow outlining its shape; then it disappeared too, leaving behind a new knowledge that I could activate the artifact at any moment simply by sending a mental command.

"Use it wisely, champion," Khphor said. "Your existence in your world will elapse soon. The next test wave will be the last for your time period."

"And then what?"

"Then you'll be subjected to Selection like all the other champions," Valiadis replied instead.

"Selection? What the hell is that?"

"I've no idea, Phil," Valiadis said. 'We'll have to wait and see, you and I. I'm also curious to find out what other tricks these Chrononauts might have up their sleeves."

"Khphor?"

"The rules of human Selection are determined by the Droh Ragg: the Council of Elders. It goes without saying that they will take into consideration all of your species' defining characteristics as well as all the suggestions offered by your most prominent representatives."

"Wait a sec. Who's gonna go to the future, is it my replica again?"

"No, human," Khphor replied. "Selection involves interacting with the real world. No creature can exist simultaneously in two different points of a particular temporal branch. I can see the question you're about to ask. Here's my answer: Pibellau is an artificial world which functioned in accordance with the rules decided by the Senior Supervisor of the Trial."

"You mean it's virtual reality?"

"Not really. Everything that happens there is realistic reenactment. But the world of Pibellau follows its own laws. Using the imagery of your world, that world is like stage scenery in a theater. The scenery will be different for the next wave."

"So what's gonna happen to me, then?"

"You'll be disincarnated here, then reconstituted in the future with perfect accuracy. Enjoy your last days in your home world. You should be happy you weren't in the last wave. Their winner won't have this luxury."

I turned to Ilindi and Valiadis. "Did you know?"

Valiadis nodded, averting his gaze.

"I wish I joined Juma's clan!" I exclaimed. "Can I refuse?"

"No, you can't," Khphor raised a warning hand, preempting any further questions. "Enough, human. Send him back."

"No, wait!" I shouted, suddenly remembering that *back there* I was being taken to some bunker in the desert by some crooks in a van, bound hand and foot. "Could you send me somewhere else instead?"

He nodded. "This is possible."

I sensed the cold touch of his thoughts exploring my mind.

"I suppose you'd like to go home? Very well. You shall come round back at your own place."

I desperately racked my brain for things I'd forgotten to ask him about when the demonic rustling of alien thoughts reentered my mind,

"You can forget *them*. They'll never bother you again. Do you understand? Then go."

Everything disappeared. Or was it me who did?

Chapter Thirty

NOT FOR FAME ALONE

Roads? Where we're going, we don't need roads.

Dr. Emmett Brown, *Back to the Future*

ONCE BACK HOME AFTER MEETING KHPHOR, I WAS overcome by a thirst and hunger so powerful that they gradually took over my thoughts, pushing all other worries to the background of my mind.

I drank my fill of the oh-so-delicious icy cold water and set off in search for some food.

I was ravenous, the kind of cravings from hell probably familiar to all of us, when you wake up in the dead of the night, your instincts driving you to the fridge, making you search its shelves and then the whole of the kitchen, scooping up everything that's even remotely edible: the cold leftover borsch, a pack of cookies, slices of cheese and ham, a stale bread roll... anything in sight.

I'd already experienced something similar the night I'd leveled up Strength. That time, I'd had food in the house. Now, however, I had nothing at all because I'd cleaned up the fridge before leaving for the US.

According to the clock on the wall, it was just past 4 (a.m., judging by the early-morning dusk outside). Not a single potato in the whole house, otherwise I'd have made myself a hearty plateful of French fries. The smell of their sizzling golden slices enveloped my nostrils, filling my mouth with saliva.

I had to grin and bear, didn't I?

The silence in my apartment made my ears ring, filling my heart with a desperate rush of loneliness. I switched the TV on and began zapping through the channels until I came to a sports channel showing a tennis game.

Something snapped in my head, forcing me to leave it on.

Should I go out and check the area for a 24/7? I rummaged through the shelves looking for some money. Everything I'd had on me, I'd left in Vegas.

Should I call Kira, maybe? Or Alik?

And how was I supposed to call them? The apartment had no landline. I'd lost my smartphone in the US.

Should I just go to bed? Somehow I doubted I'd be able to sleep.

Then I had an idea. I could go and surprise my parents. Mom was sure to have something nice to eat. Oh, shit, they were at their summer cottage, weren't they? By the time I got there, it would be pointless: I might just as well get to the office.

There was a bakery nearby... it opened 7 a.m. Surely the interface's penalty for stealing a loaf of bread (or two) wouldn't be too serious?

The thought of freshly baked bread rolls sent

my stomach in spasms. My mouth watered as I smelled the aroma of hot buns.

My mind protested against the stupid risk of getting a penalty or even being banned for committing a socially detrimental action. My instincts conflicting with my conscience, I was already putting my sneakers on, about to set off on a prowl for some food.

Just as I grabbed hold of the front door handle, someone knocked.

Blood rushed to my head. Unwanted visitors promised nothing good. I readied myself to activate Inconspicuousness and slow down time, then swung the door open.

Big sigh of relief. Ilindi stood on my doorstep smiling, disguised as Stacy.

"Hi! You hungry?"

I nodded and stepped aside. She gave me a peck on the cheek. Her short skirt, white sneakers and a midriff-baring T-shirt looked stunning on her well-tanned body.

"Suppressed by the Trial, a participant's senses of hunger and thirst suffer a tremendous rebound once all the artificial suppressants have been removed," she said, offering me two shopping bags. "There's cheese, ham, bread, some tomatoes and cucumbers, sugar and instant coffee. Sorry I couldn't get anything else."

As I took the bags from her and opened them, a delicious aroma of ham and other foodstuffs filled the room. I felt inside for the ham, pulled it out and sank my teeth into it, rind and all, growling with pleasure.

Stacy gave me a critical look, shook a disapproving head and slipped off a bulky backpack, the kind used by hikers. Now that her hands were free, she threw her arms around me and hugged me tight. "You did it!"

I shrugged, smiling. "I would be a fool to deny it. But that's nothing. I'm absolutely starving."

"Come on, I'll make you some sandwiches, a salad and some coffee."

"It's all right," I made another attempt to sink my teeth into the ham.

She unlocked her embrace. I used the opportunity to take another bite.

"Phil?" she gave me a stern look, raising an eyebrow.

Reluctantly I released my prey and followed her into the kitchenette. Stacy began rustling the shopping bags and rattling the cupboard drawers in search of a knife. She pulled out a few plates and started cooking.

"Tell me about the Trial. How did you do it?"

"Weren't you watching us?"

"Not really. Valiadis and I only had access to the statistics, judging by which every day of the Trial could have become your last. That's why your victory was all the more unexpected," she smiled. "You should have seen Nick screaming and shouting with joy. We really wanted you to win."

"Got it, thanks. In that case, I'll tell you all about it, Stace. Just let me eat first. My stomach thinks my throat's been cut."

Having devoured — for lack of a better word — everything that Ilindi had brought, I felt terribly drowsy. Carefree little birds were chirping through the wide open windows. The city was gradually awakening from its slumber, car doors creaking, janitors swashing their brooms about, motors starting up as my neighbors left the parking lot.

I was listening to the usual hubbub of a big city which to me seemed almost surreal. This must have been the Trial withdrawal. Back there, everything was so strangely different: all those unearthly sounds, colors and smells.

Noticing my lethargy, Stacy used her healing ability on me. My drowsiness disappeared. I perked up no end. My Spirit, Mood and Confidence counters span, soaring to 100%. What an interesting effect. No drugs could compare with this.

Taking about effects...

"I could do it myself, you know," I smiled to her. "I have Regeneration, don't I?"

She nodded impatiently as if I were a little boy boasting his first plasticine model. "I know. You'd better save it. You might still need it."

She must have seen the surprised look on my face because she added,

"I'm sure you must have a lot of unfinished business. You might not have much time to sleep."

I listened to her without actually hearing her. Her proximity and the less than modest attire she'd chosen again were driving me crazy. I struggled to keep my gaze fixed above her seductive cleavage — and even more so, avoiding the sight of her thighs revealed by her hiked-up mini skirt.

"...and you won't be able to come back to this time period."

Banishing any raunchy thoughts, I replayed her last words in my mind until their meaning had sunk in. "But why?"

"Khphor already explained. The Selection requires your physical participation. Whether you pass it or not, you'll have to spend the rest of your life in their time period — in other words, your future."

"What if I pass?"

"You'll take part in the Diagnostics of the Junior Races."

"And if I fail?"

She sighed. "Phil, I really don't know all the details. I suppose, you'll have to stay in the future, anyway. Humanity's descendants have come up with a special program for forced time migrants like you. It offers social adaptation and benefits, as well as all kinds of privileges."

"That's right! My social status level is quite high, isn't it? My virtual assistant did tell me that the higher the social status, the more perks it gives you in the future."

She sighed again. "It's not that simple."

"What do you mean?"

"You're gonna find out," she averted her gaze. "Whichever way it goes, you're not an ordinary human being anymore, and the 22nd-century humans realize it perfectly well. They consider each one of you a potential hero and a champion for humankind. Especially because they've been watching every step of your progress through the Trial."

"Wait a sec. Were they the observers?"

She nodded with a vague, hooded-eye smile. "Them, too. As Trial winners, you're all celebrities there."

She rose to pour me some more coffee. As she did so, she peered at something over my head.

"You've got the Sexual Frustration debuff," she said, shaking her head in concern. "Would you like me to help you remove it?"

"Eh..."

Noticing my hesitation, she giggled, then exploded in a bout of infectious laughter. Embarrassed, I averted my eyes to the TV screen.

My heart clenched. The tennis game was still on — with Jovanna's face filling the screen. She was serving, grim and focused like the first time I'd met her.

I watched her for a long time. I knew perfectly well she wouldn't recognize me even if we met. Still, I decided to follow up on her request and try to meet her again, try to start it anew, despite the precious little time I had left.

Ilindi whispered something. Her invisible touch spread a healing wave over my body. I shuddered, then breathed a sigh of relief as I felt good again. The debuff icon was gone.

I grinned. "Is this what you meant?"

"I could have used an alternative method, but it would have been much more time-consuming," she winked at me. "And time is the luxury we don't have."

"I agree," I replied. I already knew what to do next.

"Actually, Khphor was quite pleased with the

results. He said that you had potential. Said the Trial had done you some good. It was thanks to him that Nick and I managed to do something for you."

She rose and headed for the hallway, then returned with the backpack. She opened it and began unloading my stuff on the table. My passport, my smartphone, the laptop, the wallet...

"Shit! We forgot the agents!"

"Relax," Ilindi said. "The moment you'd won the Trial, Khphor was fiddling with the memories of all those who'd showed an unhealthy curiosity in you. They've lost all interest in you now. Your passport has been properly stamped: legally speaking, you've left the territory of the USA and re-entered that of the Russian Federation so you can safely enjoy your last days here."

"Oh really? Now why would he be so charitable? How did he do it, anyway?" I rose and sifted through my newly-found possessions. I'd never thought I'd be so happy to see my ID papers again. "What's with the generosity?"

"Phil, you have any idea how many resources were invested into the Trial? How many humans received the interface in your wave alone and how many of them made it to the Trial? How many abductions had to be performed? All for some overzealous local secret agents to turn you into a brain-scorched vegetable? Also, you're now a star with all of the observers, not just human ones. The Senior Races love some entertainment too, whatever we might think about them."

She sneezed, wrinkling her little nose in the funniest way. You'd think that with her healing

---

abilities...

"Bless you," I said.

"Thanks. That wretched allergy! I keep reactivating Healing the moment the cooldown expires but your local dust and pollution still manage to affect me. Never mind. Just tell me everything that happened to you during the Trial, and I'll leave you alone. We'll see if we can use your experience to better prepare the final wave candidates."

Back on the TV screen, Jovanna was losing, angry and emotional.

I couldn't wait to get rid of Ilindi and start doing things. I eased myself away from her, sat on a chair, took a swig of coffee and began,

"So I arrived at the Trial field wearing nothing but a pair of ripped jeans and spent some time studying the rules..."

"You can skip that," she interrupted me.

"Sorry, but it's important. Because that's what made me realize I needed resources. So I got down that ravine and came across this Kreken, a local boss, who killed me on the spot..."

* * *

My sister Kira used to laugh at our Mom's infatuation with psychics, clairvoyance, ESP and all that esoteric crap. When she'd heard that her mother had visited some sort of a local soothsayer to find out whether her daughter would ever get married, she freaked out and read our mom the riot act. I was there when it happened, and Kira's disgust of "village superstitions", as she called them, had kept growing ever since.

So I decided not to beat around the bush and confess my abilities to her in all honesty. Seriously. Especially after her furious screaming monologue on the phone.

I'd called her the very next day but barely managed to say hello. She did all the talking while I listened, occasionally taking the phone away from my ear to spare my eardrums.

She didn't ask me any questions about having just become a founding member in my nascent foundation (most likely, she simply hadn't yet seen the kinds of sums Sanchez had wired her). On the contrary: she appeared to be quite content to wait for explanations until I saw her. But even so, her versions of the provenance of the millions arriving in my offshore account were a collection of fantastical fabrications which, funnily enough, weren't too far from the truth.

I had indeed become involved with some bandits (read: extremists). I had indeed gotten involved in some dubious scheme (read: the Trial) and everything that it entailed. There had indeed been a price on my head. Had I told her that on top of that, I'd become mixed up with some aliens who'd signed me up for some time games, she would definitely have called the men in white coats and had me committed.

So basically, we agreed that she'd come and fetch me next weekend and we'd go see our parents at their summer cottage where I'd tell her all about it. She insisted on seeing me straight away, demanding an explanation, but I put my foot down. I needed to spend the coming week in complete isolation in order to hone my plans and make sure I was well prepared.

I only made time for Alik and Veronica's phone calls, trying to offer them some moral — if not physical — support. They were up to their necks in our rapidly expanding business, so much so that I'd had to find the time to visit them in the office once, to work through their enormous list of unemployed and give Kesha a few tips regarding our new staff and potential subcontractors.

In the meantime, Gleb had already gotten himself two assistant designers and called himself no less than art director. Greg and Marina were both heads of disparate new departments — which was Kesha's idea.

Mr. Katz had completely come to life. He looked ten years younger and took the most active part in all our activities. Rose's bookkeeping department kept growing too as the company could barely keep up with the influx of profits and the number of new contracts, especially now that the rumors started by Panchenko had finally stopped. You'd think I'd only been away for a very short while but the changes in our office made your head spin.

Before I left, I took another look at my workers' stats to weigh up all the possibilities and potential Synergy ratios. I strongly discouraged them from hiring two very good experts who might create big problems for us in the future. Kesha and Rose tried to reason with me because both experts were in fact their proteges, but my Commander's Aura helped me to talk them round. Both trusted my opinion, after all.

The first post-Trial week had flown past. I'd had virtually no time for sleep, using Regeneration to restore both myself and my Spirit numbers. I'd managed to finish everything I wanted.

Almost.

There was still the most important thing left — but I didn't doubt for one second that Kira would go along. My interface never made mistakes.

Now we both were at our parents' summer cottage. Dad, Mom and my nephew Cyril went in for a nap after the big lunch which consisted of an assortment of salads, a hearty bowl of borsch and platefuls of meat and cabbage stew. Kira and I stayed outside, lounging in the garden hammocks attached to a large pine tree.

My sister produced a vape pen out of her purse and took a deep drag on it.

"Don't look at me like that," she said, noticing my surprised stare. "With my kind of job, smoking is the lesser evil. At least this way it's not as bad for my lungs."

"I don't mind," I said. "Just didn't expect it, that's all. You've always been my role model, Sis."

"What if I'm fed up with being a role model? You have any idea how hard it is, being the big sister? Mom keeps calling me every day asking me about you. She still thinks I'm responsible for you," she added with a sad smile. "Never mind. Spit it out. What's all this about and when should I expect a visit from Interpol?"

"Do you remember that day last May when Yanna walked out on me?"

"Sure," she nodded, letting out a thick cloud of vapor.

The air smelled of sweet bread rolls — a warm flavor which mingled with the aromas of the last day of summer, creating a very special atmosphere. I took in big lungfuls of it, trying to commit to memory the moment scented with apples, flowers, pine needles and roadside dust.

"Did you notice how I changed after that?"

"You bet," she choked on her cigarette and exploded in a bout of coughing. "So is it because of her?"

"To a degree, yes. She was instrumental in my transformation, sort of. But it started even before that. I'm gonna tell you everything now. I can't discuss the really important things before I know that you believe me. But first, allow me a small demonstration to prove my point. Look at me."

Kira froze. When I disappeared, she dropped her vaper and very nearly fell out of her hammock.

"Fucking shit!" she exclaimed. A neighbor's dog began barking like mad behind the fence. "Phil, you shouldn't joke like that with me. I have a heart problem. Where are you?"

"I'm right in front of you. I'm going to touch you now, so don't be scared," I reached out, my fingers brushing her smooth cheek.

Kira flinched but didn't recoil. She lay her hand on my arm and cussed in amazement.

"Now I'm gonna make myself visible again. Are you ready? Look right in front of you."

I disabled Stealth and Vanish and was unable to suppress laughter looking at her long face and saucer eyes as she rubbed them with her hands. She was a sight! Normally, she never lost her cool... provided she wasn't mad at me.

"What's this for circus tricks, little brother?" she took another tug on her vaper the moment she'd recovered from shock. "What the fuck was that? Did you practice to be a magician? A flippin' conjurer? David fucking Copperfield?"

Whenever she was nervous, she just couldn't stop talking. Still, I had no time to listen to her theories.

"Shut up," I interrupted her. "Keep watching. I'm gonna walk a few steps back and you hurl your vaper at me as hard as you can."

"Eh... why? It costs a lot of money."

"Just because. It's not gonna break, don't worry. On my signal, just throw it at me and make it as hard as you can."

I counted ten steps back and raised my hand. "On the count of three! One... two... three!"

Just as she hurled her hefty Vaper at me, I activated Sprint.

Time slowed down. I could see that she missed, her vaper flying in a different direction. I ran over to it, caught it in flight, then ran back to Kira, laid the vaper on the ground by her feet and returned to my place, then disabled Sprint.

Kira sat there, blinking in amazement. "What was that? You sort of blurred and... and where's that goddamn cigarette?"

"Look down."

When she saw the vaper lying by her feet, her jaw dropped. She picked it up and fumbled with it, studying it as if looking for a catch. Mechanically she took a deep tug on it and fell pensive, tilting her head to one side.

No points for guessing what she was thinking about.

"Any more tricks?" she finally asked.

"Why not? Wanna play questions and answers?"

"You bet! I have lots of questions to ask you!" she sounded pleased. "What about all those millions of dollars on my bank account? Where do they come from? What did you-"

"Wait," I was forced to interrupt her again. "The other way round. I'm gonna ask you questions and you're gonna reply. Then I'll tell you whether you told me the truth. But every now and then, you need to tell a lie. Think you can do it?"

"I don't know. You're the expert in blatant lies in our family. But we could try. Go ahead."

"Would you like to get married?"

"No!"

"You're lying. You'd love to get married. Where are you going on vacation this year?"

"To the Maldives."

"That's right. Are you going alone?"

"No, Cyril's coming with me."

Her words breathed warmth. She'd told me a half-truth: there was somebody else going with them.

"That's almost right. You're going with Cyril and someone else. Is that correct?"

"Well," she drawled, "that's easy to guess."

"What's the guy's name?"

"Andrew," she said.

Her answer sent a cold shiver down my spine. "That's a lie."

"Okay, Michael."

"That's a lie, too."

"Sergei," she blushed and fidgeted, then went pale.

"Another lie."

"I haven't got anyone!"

Her words felt warm but not hot enough. "I think you do, but your relationship is probably isn't as intimate as you'd like it to be. Is that right?"

"That's enough! This is all bullshit, Phily!" she snapped indignantly without actually answering my question. "What else do you want from me?"

The fine thread of an emotional and sexual connection led from Kira to a certain Arvidas, a lower-ranking employee at the same bank. I studied his profile. Not a good match for my sister. The guy was an irresponsible lothario.

"Kira, just trust me. Arvidas isn't the best choice for you. Apart from you, he also has a relationship with an Olga Vilskaya and Natalia Loseva. You know them?"

"What?!" Kira flew off the hammock like a furious harpy, tripped and very nearly fell. She grabbed me by the shoulders. "What are you on about? How would you know about that? If this is a joke, it's a real cruel one, Phil!"

"I'm sorry. I promise I'll explain it to you a bit later on today, but it's not a joke. Let's just finish with this demonstration, okay?"

"I don't want any more of your demonstrations!" she replied tersely, returning to the hammock.

She stared at the sky, not looking at me anymore. Understanding her state, I didn't push her any further. She was tugging on her vaper while I went and lay on the lawn next to her.

Biting a sweet blade of grass, I lay my hands behind my head and stared at the clouds. We spent a good ten minutes like that until she calmed down a bit.

"Didn't you have something else?" she said dryly. "Show me."

"This is the last thing I'm going to show you. After that, I'll have to talk long and hard. Have you got your telephone with you? Good. Give me the name of a good friend of yours that wouldn't mind you disturbing them right now."

"Okay..." she scrolled through the contacts, looking through the names. "Let's see... here. Irina Atanova."

I found her among Kira's connections together with her address. "Your friend Irina Atanova, born in 1986. You met her at a financial workers' conference in Istanbul four years ago. She's not married and has no kids. She works for the Pyramid Financial Group. She has a sister called Marina. At the moment, she's at the Canary's Emporium shopping mall. Give her a call now and ask her where she is."

The moment she'd heard the name of the mall, she was already dialing the number. She spoke at length. This wasn't a brief masculine exchange along the lines of, "Hi, where are you? Cool man, bye!" This was a whole feline-style ceremony with lots of sniffing and circling each other, meowing about all sorts of irrelevant things. They started by discussing a few characters unknown to me, not realizing that I'd immediately looked them up, just for kicks, and dispelled a few flawed bits of gossip the two women were exchanging.

Then finally, Kira moved to the point. Having heard her friend's answer, she hung up.

"She *is* at the Canary's. How did you know?"

"By the way, she's not your friend at all. She can't stand the sight of you."

"I'll keep that in mind," she said, then repeated, emotionless. "How. Did. You. Know."

"Remember the day Yanna dumped me? Good. That's when it all started..."

* * *

I had to delay my trip to see Jovanna. I called Valiadis to find out how much time I had left. According to him, the next wave of the Trial wasn't to begin for at least another two weeks. Which meant I had at least another month — provided the Trial participants hadn't eliminated each other on their very first day in the game.

Kira was the reason I was behind schedule. The things that had seemed so simple and clear to me (indeed, what could be easier when you have the money, the names, a step-by-step project development plan and her experience in finance) had turned out to be not quite so clear for her.

She'd quit her job at the bank, renouncing the severance pay and signing a statement promising not to seek employment with the bank's competition.

That day at my parents' summer cottage, talking everything through had taken much longer than planned. In the evening, we'd left her son Cyril with my parents, bidden our goodbyes and went to my place where we'd sat up all night talking as I'd finished my story, then explained what was required from her and what was the actual purpose of the foundation.

I wouldn't have said that Kira was convinced by all the fantastical details, but at least my earlier demonstration had eased some of her skepticism. She'd refrained from her habitual retorts and sarcasms. The story of my abduction, Khphor, the Senior Races and the Trial made her gasp and clutch at her heart. I even offered to introduce her to Ilindi who was the Rhoan representative on planet Earth, provided Ilindi agreed, but Kira refused to meet the alien point blank.

"I don't think so," she said firmly. "I'm scared."

I approached the last page of my story with a heavy heart, not knowing how to explain to her my upcoming disappearance.

But she, with her powerful analytic mind, had already put two and two together. "So this Selection will take place in the future? In the twenty-second century? How cool is that? And then the

Diagnostics? Does that mean that you'll be able to visit another planet and see it with your own eyes?"

"Yeah, sort of. I've already been on Pibellau," I said with an inner chuckle, amazed at my lack of enthusiasm.

"Phily, you're the luckiest person I know! And your abilities! Do you realize you've made the dream of every male on Earth come true? You can become invisible, dammit!"

In reply to all her enthusing, I couldn't find anything better to do than to shrug and nod. She wanted to add something when a new thought struck her,

"Will you be coming back?" she asked in a soft, scared voice.

I shook my head. She turned her face away. I glimpsed her eyes welling with tears.

"Kira, I can't refuse. Think for yourself: would you have refused something like this? Apart from you, Mom and Dad, there's nothing that keeps me here. I haven't got family here, and as for friends... okay, I've made some now but I'll feel much better knowing you're taking good care of them."

"I understand," she said softly. She turned to me, grabbed my head and kissed me on the forehead.

She drew me toward her and stroked my back for a long time without saying anything. She didn't sob but I felt her tears drench my T-shirt.

Once she'd calmed down, she pulled herself together and got down to business as was her way, forcing all the emotional stuff from her head. I pulled out my notes regarding all the scientific and business projects based on my very first presentation for my future Great Job co-workers. Prospecting, pharmaceuticals, scientific research, investing in revolutionary technologies, augmented-reality projects, a talent scout agency, a sports boarding school...

Having studied it all, Kira asked me a number of clarifying questions, then concluded,

"The sheer scale of the project is impressive, but had it ever occurred to you that I might not be able to pull it off on my own?"

"Not on your own, Kira! Definitely not! Look: Gary Grant will help you to run the foundation. Next. If we take the sports boarding school, for instance, what better person to run it than Alexander Tereschenko from St. Petersburg? And what better place than this empty plot of land over in Rostov? I'd already checked out the city officials' attitude toward a potential sports school. They'll go along with it. Here's a list of the most talented children in various sports, as well as the most suitable candidatures of the coaches depending on the children's age. All you'll have to do is speak to Tereschenko and provide him with financing. The rest he'll do himself. He'll poach the coaches, speak to the children's parents and get busy building."

"You've any idea what figures we're talking? This isn't just a sports school! What about all these science labs, the arts academy and..."

"These are all non-profit projects, Kira, although I'm sure that one day they might start paying for themselves. In ten years' time, your first footballers will graduate and be bought up by some of Europe's biggest clubs. Each kid on the list has the potential to become one of the top one hundred in the world, if not the new Messi. At the very least, they're guaranteed to make the Russian national team."

She heaved a sigh. "This I understand. I'll just bite the bullet and do it. I'm sure I can... maybe."

"I know you can. According to my notes, in the mid-2020s your scientific group will come up with an effective cancer cure without any side effects. Here's a detailed list of things you'll need to do in order to not just monetize it but make it available and affordable to everyone. Here, look: in the 2030s, you'll have an opportunity to develop an Aspirin-like pill which will grant temporary immunity to the majority of now-terminal conditions. Its action is simple: the pill will teach the body a more efficient way of using its own immune system to combat any infections and viruses, destroying them at the moment of actual contamination. And all you need to do in order for this to happen, is get six people together in a lab and provide it with some financing. The probability of their accepting your offer is almost a 100%."

I glanced through the list of talented children until I came to the few names I'd ticked off. "Look. These names are especially important. For instance, in another fifteen years' time, this boy is going to invent a tricorder. Do you know what it is? It's a portable machine which can evaluate a person's physical condition in real time. It can provide an accurate diagnosis without the need for any heavy apparatus and medical tests. Tell me that's not cool!"

"It is," she agreed.

She seemed to mean it. It was as if she'd only just begun to realize the whole scale of my plan.

"You bet. I'd like you to take him and others like him under your wing. I need your foundation to find an excuse to pay for their education or something like that. Before they graduate, you can already engage them in research."

"Children I can do. But all this means more long-term investments. How do you want me to finance all these non-profits?"

"You have almost half a billion at your disposal. Here's a memory stick. On it you'll find all the information you need regarding the buying and selling of stocks: the company names, the right amounts, everything. It's all in code. The password is the combined birthday dates of Dad, Mom, you and myself with no spaces. This is valid until the end of next year. Trying to predict any further might cause mistakes because there're too many unknown variables involved. The forecast's accuracy will start dropping already after the New Year, albeit negligibly, so you'd better use the time left to your full advantage to accrue as much capital as possible."

"Leave this to me," Kira said, taking another tug on her vaper and laughed nervously. "I've been round the block a few times. Let's go for it! Fortune favors the brave!"

"Hey, cool it. What's with the amateur theatrics? I need you to be focused."

I knew that my every word weighed heavy on

her, adding to the load of future responsibility. Still, I knew she could do it.

"Next. Here in this file is the list of all major undiscovered mineral deposits. Do you have any idea how much governments and private companies pay for prospecting and seismic surveying these days? I understand that for you it's all double Dutch..."

"That's where you're wrong. It all makes perfect sense to me because our bank owns one of the country's biggest geophysical companies. And I'm the liaison person with their local branch."

"In that case, there's nothing for me to explain. It's up to you to decide how to use this data worth trillions of dollars."

We continued in the same vein, going through all the other projects in view of the current global situation. We played around with the order of project launches and the initial staff list as well as the future holding company's jurisdiction.

Finally, I moved to what I considered the most important thing — for me at least. "At some point, you will need security staff. And personal bodyguards. You'd better get on with it now before you get bogged down with other things. The more time they spend with you, the more loyal they'll be, especially because they'll associate the venture's success with their own efforts. Here's a list of potential candidates, in this file. All of them will be absolutely loyal, both to you and the firm. Make sure they're happy. Pay them well. Then you won't have any problems with them."

Kira knew better than to argue this. She

wasn't born yesterday, after all. She knew she'd have to deal with attempts to hijack her business, with competitors' sabotage, probably even with attempts on her life. Her enemies might try to apply pressure to her family, too. In the end, we decided that she should keep a very low profile becoming an invisible mastermind. It would be a good idea to send Cyril and our parents out of the country — not now, not straight away, but as soon as the moment was right.

She stayed at my place for the night. I didn't sleep at all, too busy going through several lists or wanted criminals by country, sending the search results anonymously to those most interested in finding them — those who, in the program's opinion, were sure to use the information. Talking about which, I'd already become an expert in online anonymity, bringing the corresponding skill level to 6.

At a continental breakfast next morning, I brought up the subject of going to Belgrade to see Jovanna, but Kira asked me if it could wait another week. Having checked my remaining to-do list against Jovanna's game schedule, I agreed to finish everything I still had to do here. In ten days' time, Jovanna was to participate in a ladies' tennis tournament in Tokyo, and I could go and see her there.

Having received a Japanese visa, I spent the few days left until my flight helping Kira. I made my company share over to her, introduced her to the staff — I still had to explain my future disappearance to them somehow — and spent every spare moment with our parents.

As for Great Job Recruiting Agency, Veronica had become its new director (the second most optimal choice, according to the interface, the first one being myself) with Kira as a founding member. Considering the sheer volume of future projects, she was unlikely to find time for a tiny local business like this one.

Among other good news, Kostya Bekhterev had returned from Germany. His sister Julie had completely recovered. Kostya had perked up. He smiled more often these days, completely engrossed in his work in our company. He'd quickly blended into the team — but he'd quit boxing entirely. According to him, my rapid successes had made him lose all motivation.

I suggested he concentrated on his IT skills instead: he had enough potential to become a top expert in that area.

So basically, things just got going.

*** * ***

The day before my departure for Japan, I remembered something very important. I called Sveta Messerschmitt.

She picked up the phone straight away. "Phil! It's so good you phoned!" she chirped into the microphone. "Your puppy is so cute! Yesterday he climbed into a..."

"Sveta, that's exactly why I'm calling you," I swallowed the lump in my throat. "I'm afraid I..."

"You what? What happened?"

"I'm afraid I can't take the puppy."

"Why?" she sounded very upset. "You wanted him so much!"

"I still do! But my job involves constant traveling," I ad-libbed off the top of my head. "I'm afraid I just can't take good care of him."

"You're right, that's not good," she agreed. "A dog requires training and attention. Better not to have one if one can't afford the time. But it's such a shame! He's so cute!"

"I know, I saw him. He's adorable. Send my love to your dad and please give Richie a pat from me, okay?"

Having said good-bye to her, I spent some time just sitting there, thinking how my life might have panned out and how many wonderful things might have come my way had it not been for the wretched Selection I was facing.

Then I started thinking about everything I had to do.

In actual fact, I'd already managed to do everything that I'd planned, and then some. Kira was spending every waking hour in the Great Job offices, working on her plan of action, making phone calls and arranging meetings all over the globe, trying to work out an optimal route for a protracted business trip. We'd decided to fly out at the same time to make sure we could spend as much time together as we could: she wasn't going to come back to Russia for quite a time, while I might not even come back at all if my next abduction took place while she was abroad.

I'd been lucky that I was at home alone when the sudden torrent of level-ups had flooded over me. No idea what had triggered it but if felt like a sudden downpour. I'd already had a similar albeit much weaker outburst when I'd been sending out the anonymous tips about the criminals I'd located: that time, I'd received several levels one after another.

This time, however, I was transported to such heights of bliss that it took me over an hour to come to.

Congratulations! You've performed a number of socially meaningful actions, triggering a chain of events which will lead to a multiple increase in your civilization's wellbeing, increasing the average Satisfaction index of the Humankind faction by 7.2 times and its Happiness index by 4,2 times. It will usher in a multilevel technological breakthrough which in turn will accelerate the progress of the Humankind faction.

XP received: 360000
Congratulations! You've received new levels!
Current social status level: 45
Characteristic points available: 18
Skill points available: 9

Congratulations! You've received a new system skill level!
Skill name: Heroism
Current level: 4

XP received: 1000

Congratulations! You've received a new system skill level!
Skill name: Insight
Current level: 7
XP received: 3000
Now you can receive an answer to any question by simply posing it.

XP points left until the next social status level: 21350/46000.

At this point, I asked myself a question. And I got the answer.

So I activated Qa-Tung. I now knew exactly what I wanted to become to be the best in the annals of human history.

I also knew why.

The program's reaction was prompt:

Qa-Tung activated

The message was followed by what appeared to be the already-familiar skill notification:

Congratulations! You've received a new skill level!
Skill name: Creative Writing
Current level: 99
XP received: 91000.

These two levels didn't bring me much joy as

their effect was too weak, and I was too excited about other things. Those few extra seconds of pleasure felt almost annoying, like I was wasting my time.

I then invested some characteristic points into where they were needed the most: Charisma as well as some Charisma-related skills. I also brought up the psi-field of both my Commander's and energy auras. To do what I was about to do, I needed the highest possible Leadership and Communication skills, as well as Public Speaking, as each new Charisma level added five levels to each skill.

That done, I worked on all the other requirements, even throwing in the Taming skill for good measure. That allowed me to activate all the remaining Heroic abilities: Taming, Berserker, Persuasion and Invulnerability.

Just for fun, I then tamed a little spider that had conveniently dropped into view. Obeying my request, he began spinning a new web exactly where I'd asked him to.

Smiling, I sat at the desk, opened my laptop, started a new text document and began typing at 1000 strokes per minute.

The book I had in mind wasn't going to be thick if it ever got published (then again, what was I saying? Not *if* — but *when* it got published!) — if anything, it was going to be thinner than *all the others*.

Unlike all those *other* books, mine wasn't going to contain any moss-covered fairy stories, vague prophecies, unintelligible admonitions and hopelessly dated life counsel.

In it, I wanted to compile the answers to every possible question one could ask themselves; the questions that hundreds of generations kept asking themselves ever since man had first looked up at the stars. What is the meaning of life? What is love? How can you love and be loved? What makes one happy? Where do you find truth and justice? What is spirit? What is the Universe? How to live your life "so as to feel no torturing regrets for wasted years"[21]? What is soul? Does it even exist? And what is the perfect ideal? Why? How? What? When?

Smiling, I deleted the paragraph which answered the question about Kennedi's assassination. Not important.

I tried to write so that everybody could find something interesting in it: an inexperienced child as well as a wise old man, the wealthy as well as the poor, a teenage idealist and a fickle young lady, a factory worker and an artist, a gamer and a professor, any and every man and woman on planet Earth.

I was writing without stopping to reread or edit. There was nothing to edit, anyway: the lines about Kennedi's assassination added in a sudden bout of frivolity were the only deletion in the whole manuscript. Kira had already come home and kept

---

[21] An excerpt from a popular Russian quotation: "Man's dearest possession is life. It is given to him but once, and he must live it so as to feel no torturing regrets for wasted years, never know the burning shame of a mean and petty past; so live that, dying, he might say: all my life, all my strength were given to the finest cause in all the world—the fight for the Liberation of Mankind" (Nicholas Ostrovsky, *How the Steel Was Tempered*)

calling me for dinner in vain. I was on a roll and didn't feel like eating at all.

In the last part of my book I wrote about everything one should avoid doing in life. All the bad habits, selfishness, betrayal, greed, hypocrisy, lust, theft, anger, envy, laziness and everything else you wouldn't wish on yourself or your loved ones. In order to get a move on, I wrote it in Sprint mode; I'd also activated Persuasion hoping that that would help.

I'd finished the manuscript by first light, giving myself another Regeneration halfway through the night. Then I spent until midday writing an English-language version of the book, ignoring Kira's constant grilling.

After lunch, I self-published the book everywhere I could, using the pen name Homo Sapiens. I used the same alias to submit the manuscript to all the biggest publishing houses in Russia, USA, Asia and Europe, renouncing all royalties.

And when I'd finally finished, I was overtaken by such a bliss that it made me feel one with everything and everybody. This time my euphoria lasted so long that I only came round late in the evening. I'd been showered with so many social status levels that they now required a three-digit number.

Congratulations! You've received a new achievement: The First Hero of your local segment of the Galaxy (location: planet Earth).
You've achieved the highest social status

level in the history of your race.

Reward: **Time Cheat, a passive Heroic ability**

Preserving the life of society's most valuable member is the highest degree of its social protection. A Heroic ability requiring the combined investment of Spirit from all the sentient beings of the local segment, Time Cheat will reload the world at the exact moment of the user's death.

Additional reward: **The Sower, an active Heroic ability. Allows you to install an** *Augmented Reality! Platform. Home Edition* **interface to all persons of your choice.**

In order to install the interface, you must maintain tactile contact with a potential user for the duration of 3 seconds.

I didn't feel anything. You might think I should have but I didn't. I was so drained that I didn't have enough Spirit to even summon Martha in order to share my successes with her.

Instead, I looked at the clock, then turned round to see a very scared Kira behind me.

"Phil? Are you all right? Everything okay?" she touched my forehead. "I thought you'd never come round. You didn't even breathe but your heart was beating," she whispered. "Your flight is in four hours. I should be going to the airport too. Are you gonna pack? Would you like us to leave together?"

I asked myself another question, received an answer and nodded. "Of course. I have nothing to pack. Let's just go. Can we pop by the office on our way? Please give everyone a call. Alik, Veronica, Kesha, Gleb, Kostya, Greg, Marina... and Mr. Katz and Rose. I'd like to say goodbye."

* * *

There was only half an hour left till midnight. All those whom I'd asked to come to the office to have their interfaces installed had decided to come with me to the airport. Before fitting them, I gave my workers a quick demonstration, leaving, however, the superpowers out. The only thing I actually showed them was my lie detection ability. They already knew how my search skills worked. Having explained to them the principle of the augmented-reality interface, I activated Persuasion and told them that this interface was in fact a gadget from the future where I was now heading never to come back.

"You're something else, bro," Alik managed.

"And you ain't, *bro*?" I mocked him. "Now listen up. Whatever happens, keep your cool. The program will behave differently depending on your personal preferences, but the main principle is the same as mine. As long as you use the interface for the common good, you'll keep leveling up. Veronica, didn't you want to be a bit taller? Now you'll have the opportunity provided you level up Charisma. Just make sure you don't focus on it to the exclusion of all else. You're a company director now, so there're other qualities that are no less important for you. Alik, I would like you to invest every available characteristic point into Intellect. I'm serious. Gleb, you need to concentrate on Self-Discipline. Because if you accidentally stumble into another poker club, you'll be too tempted to cheat the system and will be penalized for it. Here's a list of all your abilities with the biggest potential. You should be concentrating on them first and foremost..."

"I have a heart problem," Mr. Katz interrupted me in a plaintive voice, then immediately cut to the chase. "Will this, as you call it, *interface* in my head, help me to extend my life?"

"Quite so, Mr. Katz. The program will prompt you what you should and shouldn't be doing. Once your social status level is high enough, you'll have special abilities available, including a complete recovery of the user's body. How's that for an incentive to cultivate kindness?"

Katz pursed his lips, about to say something, but reconsidered. "Ah, whatever!" he said with a dismissive shrug. "Go ahead and install it! I want to be the first!"

I knew he would say that. By the same token, absolute knowledge does take spice out of life.

"First or second, it doesn't matter," I said. "I'm programming the system activation for 6 a.m. tomorrow. That'll give you some time to prepare yourselves for what's coming. When you wake up, the interface will already be installed. You might have some problems with your vision at first, but it's normal so you shouldn't worry about it too much..."

My decision to delay the interface installation till next morning had been dictated by my desire to make their adaptation as smooth as possible. This was also part of my absolute knowledge.

Once I'd installed all the interfaces including Kira's, and repeated my instructions to everyone on how to find their way around them, we went downstairs and walked out onto the porch. Everybody started getting into their cars.

Two dark silhouettes — Yagoza and Sprat — were hovering at a distance. Alik walked over to me and whispered, staring guiltily at the ground,

"Phil, could you wait a second? I promised to lend some money to the guys..."

"Let's go together," I said. "I'd like to say goodbye to them too. It's not as if we're strangers."

Realizing who it was approaching them in Alik's company, Yagoza threw his arms wide and cracked a jailbird's crooked smile,

"Howdy, sir! Long time no see!"

"Hi, Igor. Hi, Alexey," I used their real names for the first time.

We exchanged long handshakes and a couple of meaningless phrases. Yagoza kept shifting from one foot to the other, scratching his chin. I knew he felt uncomfortable in my company, especially because he had no intention of paying Alik back. He realized I wouldn't tolerate this, expecting him to pay the money back by hook or by crook.

In any case, it wasn't worth the trouble. Alik would surely survive the loss of a couple thousand rubles[22].

One of us — Kira — impatiently honked the horn of her car. We had to leave. Time to say goodbye.

---

[22] A couple thousand rubles is about $30.

"Okay, guys," I said to Yagoza and Sprat, "I'm already late for my flight. Just one final piece of advice to both of you: you've got to quit smoking and drinking, find a normal job and make sure you do some exercise. May your conscience guide you. Trust me it's more reliable than your gang law. You're better than that. Good luck!"

I bade my farewells to them and headed for Kira's car.

When I looked back, I saw Alik cast a furtive glance around (probably afraid of Veronica seeing him embezzle their family budget), slip Yagoza a few bills, and bid them a hasty goodbye.

As Kira started the car, the idiotic smirk still lingered on my face.

Tomorrow at 6 a.m., Sprat and Yagoza were going to start a new life. Not only had I just fitted their respective heads with alien wetware, I'd also managed to *convince* them in something that so many had failed before me.

It was a good job that my increased Spirit allowed me to use Persuasion more often than just once every 24 hours.

* * *

When I came down to breakfast in the Tokyo hotel where Jovanna Savich was staying, I took a table by the window opening onto the terrace. I melancholically poked at my omelet, finished a piece of cheese on toast, then just sat there drinking coffee and waiting. I knew she'd come here at 7.20 a.m. sharp, just like she'd done for three days already.

I'd been admiring her from a distance because I *knew* that any attempt to approach her was going to fail. She was too focused, too concentrated on the game to afford being distracted by stupid stuff.

I could have activated some of my skills, of course, but I really wanted to attract her attention without all those bells and whistles. And knowing Jovanna, I would only get one chance to make a first impression. This girl spoke as she found: if she rejected me outright, I'd never get another opportunity.

The date of my next abduction was approaching, so I spent all my spare time working on my optimal travel route and arranging all the visas. Regardless of whether I got a second chance with Jovanna or not, I wanted to find my old friends I'd met on Pibellau and have their interfaces reinstalled. I didn't care if they didn't remember me anymore: the Trial had shown their worth.

I'd also added Ken and Striker to the list. You can call it indulgent if you wish.

My book, *The Answers*, had already become a new Internet sensation, its popularity growing with each passing day. Some people were apparently already translating it into Spanish and Chinese which would guarantee it an almost worldwide readership. Millions of new readers kept quoting the book, recommending it or arguing about its entries; one thing they all agreed on was that it was a must read. Some were coming up with a variety of conspiracy theories, trying to second-guess the identity of its author — but they, too, were about to accept the book's message, imbibing it without really bothering about the authorship.

I even knew that some time from now, a lot of people would suggest a new theory of the book's origin, one which would mention God's name. Jokingly and tentatively at first, their voices would soon ring with confidence as each would offer their own God's name to put on the book cover. This version, too, would eventually be mired in arguments and fade into oblivion: simply because the book already had the answer to the question about God. It wasn't some higher being: God was something within each of us.

All the tables in the hotel restaurant were taken, so Jovanna headed for my own.

"Excuse me," she said. "May I sit at your table? Do you mind?"

"Absolutely not. I've almost finished my coffee, anyway," I replied with an ulterior motive.

She set two plates on the table, overflowing with what looked like an athlete's perfect breakfast. A boiled egg, a chicken breast, some vegetables, a bowl of porridge, a muesli and yogurt mix, some hard cheese and a few slices of toast doused in maple syrup.

She sat opposite me, picked up a salad leaf and sent it into her mouth without lifting her head. I admired her long lashes, her chiseled face and the graceful movements of her strong suntanned arms.

"You're a tennis player," I dared speak to her first.

She didn't reply. Her Mood dropped a notch, my Reputation with her losing a few points.

Never mind. Let's do it again. My Foresight suggested the right approach.

She set her breakfast on the table and sat opposite me. Without looking up, she picked up a salad leaf and sent it into her mouth. I finished my coffee, wished her a good day and left the restaurant.

The next morning, she saw me there again and sat opposite me, even though this time these were empty tables available.

I scrolled through my smartphone, apparently ignoring her. The hype around *The Answers* was gaining momentum as celebrities all over the world had picked up on it. A Russian footballer's ex-wife, now a reality show star, had posted a brief review in her Twitter account, garnering tens of thousands of reposts. In the West, the *#bookofanswers* hashtag was trending like mad.

I could sense her gaze. I raised my head and smiled.

Slightly embarrassed, she still didn't lower her eyes. "I'm Jovanna. What's your name?"

* * *

"You have an interesting life," Jovanna said. "Now my head spins from all the flying. Kazakhstan, South Africa, Cameroon, Columbia — and we never stopped anywhere for more than a couple of days at a time. And this is the fourth American city in three days!"

Her head was resting on my chest, her hands stroking my body.

We were in bed in our Las Vegas hotel room, taking a break after our flight and resting after another passionate session.

In the last week, we'd traveled all over the globe. As soon as the Tokyo tennis tournament had wound up, I'd offered Jo — as I now called her again — to join me in my travels. Her coach wasn't happy, but I'd managed to talk him into it. Considering my current level of persuasion, it hadn't been that difficult.

First of all, I went to Kazakhstan to visit Ken. I bumped into him as if accidentally in a packed elevator inside one of the governmental buildings in Astana and fitted him with a delayed-activation interface similar to those of my friends.

From there we dashed over to Johannesburg: an eighteen-hour flight with a stopover in Dubai. I left Jovanna in the hotel and went to see my South African friend.

I found John Carter in a recording studio. Having maxed out my Charisma in order to get past an uncooperative manager, I then spent more than an hour sitting and listening to my friend sing.

Afterward, I introduced myself to him as one of his fans and asked him for an autograph. As you might have guessed, I shook his hand long and hard as we parted.

When I left the studio and walked back out onto the colorful noisy street, I spent a long time struggling with the temptation to see the actual woman who had been Martha's prototype. Jenna Petersen. According to her marker on my interface map, she was in town. With my abilities, I might even get to know her.

Still, I decided against it. The arrival of Jovanna in my life had admittedly changed my idea of female beauty, so there was no point in being impulsive about it.

What's more, it felt as if a load had fallen from my shoulders. The very thought of meeting Jenna felt like I was betraying Jovanna.

We took a 24-hour break in South Africa before embarking on the next flight to Cameroon where I met Ola.

Luckily, he wasn't in his village anymore. He'd already moved to the capital city of Yaoundé where he'd found a job as a math teacher. I caught up with him as he was leaving the school and asked him how to get to the library, then thanked him by shaking his hand.

"He who is covered in cotton shouldn't get near a flame," I said as we parted, leaving him totally befuddled.

"Granddad?" I heard his confused voice behind me.

It took us almost 24 hours to get from the Cameroonian capital to Bogota via Paris and from there, another hour to Medellin. There I walked right into some problems. While Jovanna was waiting for me in the hotel, my search for Manu had brought me to some particularly dangerous criminal area in the city.

I activated Berserker, Sprint and Invulnerability, then had some fun knocking seven shades of shit out of some truly macho types whose Aggression numbers were big enough to make a

Tyrannosaurus blush. The fight had attracted a rather large audience one of which turned out to be an MMA fights promoter. He didn't speak a word of English, and my Spanish wasn't enough to explain to him that I wasn't interested. He snapped out a command into the crowd, summoning a new bunch of local troublemakers which took me another couple of minutes. I daresay that the resulting fight surpassed anything out of Bollywood.

By then, Manu had already left. Cussing, I had to steal somebody's pushbike (I knew whose bike it was but it was stolen already, anyway), after which I just had to pedal like hell against time.

After a dozen blocks, I finally caught up with my Columbian friend as he was leaving the car. I rammed him on purpose. While he was trying to crawl out from under me, cussing in Spanish, I installed the interface.

"Lo siento," I offered an apology in my best Spanish in response to his threatening frown.

As if nothing had happened, I picked up my bike and pedaled off to the hotel to see Jovanna. Later that night, we flew off to Orlando where I visited Eddie, then on to New York to see Striker.

And now, Las Vegas. Mike was the only one left to see. I'd already installed Jovanna's, delaying the activation until I'd split. I had no idea why (actually, I had but I was too ashamed to admit it), but I didn't want her to see my actual feelings to (and my Reputation with) her.

By now, I was pretty sure that even if I didn't have to travel to the future, things wouldn't have worked out for us. As soon as I'd come back home after the Trial, the impassive interface had already shown me our extremely low compatibility levels. That had been the first thing I'd done, tormented by my longing for her (the thirst and hunger had only come later).

So why was I with her now? It wasn't me being selfish. I simply had to do it. In fact, I'd already done it. Jovanna was pregnant with my son.

* * *

Leaving the girl to sleep it off in the hotel room, I went to see Mike Hagen busy pummeling the punch bag in the gym.

"Hi there!" he exclaimed on seeing me. "Are you new here? Fancy a bout of sparring?"

It seemed that apart from losing the interface and all the achievement that came with it, he'd also forgotten me. He must have fallen an accidental victim to Khphor's memory wipe after I'd been rescued from the US.

"No, thanks," I said, smiling at his enthusiasm.

"Oh, come on, don't give me that! You're no chicken shit! What's your name?"

"Phil. But you haven't got a hope in hell against me."

"Ha! You're really funny!" he turned around and shouted to a swarthy Mexican sitting on a bench next to the old Coach Ochoa. "Hey, Gonzalo! Throw me the gloves! I found somebody's ass to kick instead of yours!"

Oh. Why not? Just to get my circulation going

and get some kicks?

I ducked under the ropes, fully intending to have a quick scrap, when my phone rang. I answered it, knowing who it was and what I was about to hear.

"Phil, you've got an hour to get ready. I hope you've managed to finish up all your business," Valiadis said dryly, then hung up.

"Sorry, man, I gotta be somewhere quick. No offence," I gave him my extended fist which he bumped with his glove.

"Ha! Didn't I say you were chickenshit?" he teased, still hoping for a good punchup.

I grabbed his arm, installed the interface and let him go.

"What the hell was that, man?"

"Nothing. Just wanted to look at your tattoos, bro. I'll see you around, Mike Hagen!"

He watched me leave, wondering how the hell I knew him. In the end, he decided that I must have already seen him fight. Thus reassured, he promptly forgot all about me.

His interface would be activated tomorrow.

* * *

Jovanna's son would be called Luka. He would bear his mother's surname. His youngest son — my grandson — would be called Zoran.

For the umpteenth time, I remembered one of my first conversations with my virtual assistant — at the time when Martha had been nothing but a bunch of scripts.

"Who was the founder of the First Martian Company?"

"The company was started by Zoran Savich."

"Is he a human being? What planet is he from?"

"He is originally from Earth, born in the Eurasian Union in 2058."

Jovanna was smiling in her sleep. The timer was counting down the last minute before my abduction into the future.

I'd already written my farewell note. On the bedside table sat the Ring of Veles and the figurine of Netsuke Jurōjin which I'd recovered from a local pawn shop. Jovana would keep them and give them to her son when he grew up.

As an afterthought, I hurried to leave Kira a message, telling her about my future son and asking her to keep an eye on him. A few seconds later, the answer came back:

I swear to God, brother! Wherever you are, Phily, I love you! Look after yourself!

I kissed Jo on the neck, taking in lungfuls of her scent while I still could. I needed to remember it once and for all, never to forget.

Even though I might still have a few flings, I knew that I would never love anyone the way I loved her.

3...

2...

1...

Abduction.

Abducting the user... Success

Uninstalling the interface... Error

Uninstalling the interface... Error

Uninstalling the interface... Error

Error evaluation...

An unauthorized AI detected

Resetting Spirit to 0... Success

Deleting the AI...

Success! The AI has been deleted

Transferring the user's mind to the local segment server... Success

Disincarnating the user's physical body... Success

Analyzing the user's mind...

Unauthorized skills and abilities detected!

Resetting the unauthorized skills and abilities to 0... Success

Resetting the user's main characteristics back to their initial status... Success

THE FINAL TRIAL

Generating a new physical body... Success

Integrating the user's mind into their new body... Success

Teleporting the user's body... Success

Preparing to awaken the user...

Success! The user has been awakened! Code name: Phil Panfilov, human Champion, 4th wave 2018

I opened my eyes.

END OF BOOK THREE

An Afterword from the Author

Dear Reader,

Thank you for joining me and Phil on this long journey. I'd just finished the last sentence of the epilog, and I feel both happy and extremely fatigued.

Why fatigued? Well, it wasn't easy doing all the math, tracking down all the changes in Phil's XP points, characteristics, skills and levels in both worlds — and not only Phil's but all of his clan members. I'm pretty sure my Excel charts are every bit as good as those of Rose!

And why happy? Because finally I've written a complete story.

The first trilogy — the one describing Phil's life in the 21st century — is complete. There's nothing to add to it. If you carefully read the last chapter, you already know what's going to happen with his friends and loved ones. And the most attentive of you must already realize what happened to Phil during his last abduction (hint: this has something to do with the last top-tier heroic ability he'd received).

But the story of Phil's life in the 22nd century is only just beginning. I already know all about the adventures that await him on Earth (or Mars) in the 22nd century. Still, both the story and the worldbuilding still require a lot of work and finetuning. As soon as I'm done with this, I'll start writing.

The work title of the fourth book is Selection (Level Up Book #4). If you'd like to know what's going to happen to Phil next, you should bookmark the series' Facebook group at https://www.facebook.com/dansugralinovslevelup or my publisher's site at https://www.facebook.com/magicdomebooks/

Thank you so much for your high rating of the book, your comments and all your support! They made writing the series so much easier. Three books in a year — I think it's a pretty good result.

When I was finishing *The Final Trial*, I started another series: *Disgardium*. This is a fantasy LitRPG set in the Level Up world, with a teenager from the second half of the 21st century as the main character. By then, our planet's entire population has already been divided up into social status levels, with the most useless ones — noncitizens — forced to earn their living in a virtual reality game. The first book in the series has won an international LitRPG contest among all Russian-speaking authors. It's already been translated and will be released <u>on Amazon</u> on April 22 2019.

Apart from that, I really recommend you read another LItRPG series: *Adam Online*, written by my friend and co-author Max Lagno. The first book of the series, *Absolute Zero*, is already available on Amazon and let me tell you: this particular LitRPG is real science fiction as it should be! Max's novels have won numerous science fiction competitions, and after *The Knockout,* this is his first independent series in our favorite genre. You can preview it <u>here</u>.

That's it for the time being!

But Phil will be back. See you at the Selection!

Want to be the first to know about our latest LitRPG, sci fi and fantasy titles from your favorite authors?

Subscribe to our NEW RELEASES newsletter: http://eepurl.com/b7niIL

Thank you for reading *The Final Trial!*
If you like what you've read, check out other LitRPG novels
published by Magic Dome Books:

Level Up LitRPG series by Dan Sugralinov:
Re-Start
Hero
The Final Trial
Level Up: The Knockout (with Max Lagno)
Level Up. The Knockout: Update (with Max Lagno)

Disgardium LitRPG series by Dan Sugralinov:
Class-A Threat
Apostle of the Sleeping Gods
The Destroying Plague

World 99 LitRPG Series by Dan Sugralinov:
Blood of Fate

Adam Online LitRPG Leries by Max Lagno:
Absolute Zero
City of Freedom

Reality Benders LitRPG series by Michael Atamanov:
Countdown
External Threat
Game Changer
Web of Worlds
A Jump into the Unknown

**The Dark Herbalist LitRPG series
by Michael Atamanov:**
Video Game Plotline Tester
Stay on the Wing
A Trap for the Potentate
Finding a Body

Perimeter Defense LitRPG series by Michael Atamanov:
Sector Eight
Beyond Death
New Contract
A Game with No Rules

Point Apocalypse *(a near-future action thriller)*
by Alex Bobl

Captive of the Shadows *(The Fairy Code Book #1)*
by Kaitlyn Weiss

The Game Master **series by A. Bobl and A. Levitsky:**
The Lag

You're in Game!
(LitRPG Stories from Bestselling Authors)

You're in Game-2!
(More LitRPG stories set in your favorite worlds)

***Moskau* by G. Zotov**
(a dystopian thriller)

***El Diablo* by G.Zotov**
(a supernatural thriller)

More books and series are coming out soon!

In order to have new books of the series translated faster, we need your help and support! Please consider leaving a review or spread the word by recommending *The Final Trial* to your friends and posting the link on social media. The more people buy the book, the sooner we'll be able to make new translations available.

Thank you!

Till next time!